The University and its Disciplines

CADQ

University teaching and learning take place within ever more specialized disciplinary settings, each characterized by its unique traditions, concepts, practices and procedures. It is now widely recognized that support for teaching and learning needs to take this discipline-specificity into account. However, in a world characterized by rapid change, complexity and uncertainty, problems do not present themselves as distinct subjects but increasingly within trans-disciplinary contexts calling for graduate outcomes that go beyond specialized knowledge and skills. This ground-breaking book highlights the important interplay between context-specific and context-transcendent aspects of teaching, learning and assessment. It explores critical questions, such as:

What are the 'ways of thinking and practicing' characteristic of particular disciplines? How can students be supported in becoming participants of particular disciplinary discourse communities?

Can the diversity in teaching, learning and assessment practices that we observe across departments be attributed exclusively to disciplinary structure?

To what extent do the disciplines prepare students for the complexities and uncertainties that characterize their later professional, civic and personal lives?

Written for university teachers, educational developers as well as new and experienced researchers of Higher Education, this highly-anticipated first edition offers innovative perspectives from leading Canadian, US and UK scholars on how academic learning within particular disciplines can help students acquire the skills, abilities and dispositions they need to succeed academically and also post graduation.

Carolin Kreber is Professor of Higher and Community Education and the Director of the Centre for Teaching, Learning and Assessment at the University of Edinburgh.

The University and its Disciplines:

Teaching and Learning Within and Beyond Disciplinary Boundaries

Edited by Carolin Kreber

Routledge
Taylor & Francis Group

NEW YORK AND LONDON

First published 2009
by Routledge
270 Madison Ave, New York NY 10016

Simultaneously published in the UK
by Routledge
2 Park Square, Milton Park, Abingdon, Oxon, OX14 4RN

Routledge is an imprint of the Taylor & Francis Group, an informa business

Transferred to Digital Printing 2010

Typeset in Minion by
Keystroke, 28 High Street, Tettenhall, Wolverhampton

Library of Congress Cataloging in Publication Data
The university and its disciplines : teaching and learning within and beyond disciplinary
boundaries / editor, Carolin Kreber.
p. cm.
Includes bibliographical references.
1. Universities and colleges–Curricula. 2. College teaching. 3. Education, Higher–Aims
and objectives. I. Kreber, Carolin.
LB2361.U55 2008
378.1'99–dc22
2008008802

British Library Cataloguing in Publication Data
A catalogue record for this book is available from the British Library

ISBN 10: 0–415–96520–9 (hbk)
ISBN 10: 0–415–96521–7 (pbk)
ISBN 10: 0–203–89259–3 (ebk)

ISBN 13: 978–0–415–96520–0 (hbk)
ISBN 13: 978–0–415–96521–7 (pbk)
ISBN 13: 978–0–203–89259–6 (ebk)

Contents

Figures and Tables

Figures

Tables

Contributors

Charles Anderson is a Senior Lecturer in the School of Education, University of Edinburgh. Recent research includes working with a colleague, Kate Day, on the history strand of the "Enhancing Teaching-Learning Environments in Undergraduate Courses" project; a study of Masters' degrees and the evaluation of a higher education ICT initiative.

Marcia Baxter Magolda is Distinguished Professor of Educational Leadership at Miami University of Ohio (USA). Her books include *Learning Partnerships* (Stylus Press, 2004), *Making Their Own Way* (Stylus Press, 2001), *Creating Contexts for Learning and Self-Authorship* (Vanderbilt University Press, 1999), and *Knowing and Reasoning in College* (Jossey-Bass, 1992).

Janet Donald is Professor Emerita at McGill University in Montreal, Canada, a Fellow of the Royal Society of Canada, and Distinguished Member of the Canadian Society for the Study of Higher Education. Widely published, her books include *Learning to think: Disciplinary perspectives* (Jossey-Bass, 2002), and *Improving the environment for learning: Academic leaders talk about what works* (Jossey-Bass, 1997).

Lewis Elton is Honorary Professor of Higher Education, University College London and University of Manchester; Distinguished Visiting Scholar, University of Surrey; Fellow of the American Institute of Physics, the Society for Research into Higher Education and the Higher Education Academy; and Honorary Life Member of the Staff and Educational Development Association.

Joëlle Fanghanel is Director (Research & Policy in Higher Education) of the Centre for Educational and Academic Practices City University London. She is Convenor of the London Scholarship of Teaching and Learning International Conference, and Editor of SoTL work. Her research interests include socio-cultural approaches to teaching and learning, HE leadership, change management, and quality enhancement policies.

Vicky Gunn is a Lecturer in both the Learning and Teaching Centre and the Department of Theology and Religious Studies at the University of Glasgow, Scotland. Currently, she coordinates the University's mandatory postgraduate certificate in Academic Practice as well as an Honors course in The Body and Belief. Her research interests span several disciplines from ecclesiastical history to the ethics of interprofessionalism.

Dai Hounsell is Professor of Higher Education at the University of Edinburgh, where he was founding director of the Centre for Teaching, Learning and Assessment. His recent research includes externally funded projects on "Enhancing Teaching-Learning Environments in Undergraduate Courses", "Integrative Assessment", and "Innovative Assessment across the Disciplines".

Alan Jenkins is Emeritus Professor at Oxford Brookes University (UK) where he long worked first as a geographer and then as an academic developer/researcher. He was founding co-editor of the *Journal of Geography in Higher Education* and lately has published widely on teaching/research relations.

Carolin Kreber is Professor of Higher and Community Education and the Director of the Centre for Teaching, Learning and Assessment at the University of Edinburgh. Smaller edited collections include *Revisiting scholarship, Exploring research-based teaching, International policy perspectives on improving learning* and *Internationalizing the curriculum*.

Katarina Mårtensson is an academic developer at Lund University Centre for Educational Development. She has recently been responsible for a national project in Sweden to support professional development for academic developers. Her main research interests and publications include strategic educational development, and significant networks, social perspectives on learning and cultural change in higher education institutions.

Robert G.S. Matthew is Vice Principal (learning and teaching) at the University of the Highlands and Islands in Scotland; before that he was head of the Academic Development Unit at the University of Glasgow. His interests at the present time concern the enhancement of the student learning experience through the development of independent learners particularly in professional disciplines such as dentistry, nursing, medicine and education.

Jan McArthur was a Lecturer in higher education at Napier University Edinburgh from 2003 until 2007. Prior to that she worked as a researcher with the Centre for Teaching, Learning and Assessment at the University of Edinburgh. She is currently undertaking a PhD in Educational Research at Lancaster University.

Velda McCune is a Lecturer in the Centre for Teaching, Learning and Assessment at the University of Edinburgh. Her research interests focus on students' perspectives on their learning experiences in higher education and how these relate to their identities. Recently she has also been investigating how faculty see themselves as teachers and how this influences their teaching.

Andy Northedge is Professor of Learning and Teaching in Higher Education at the UK Open University. He has been closely involved in theory and practice of educational innovation at the OU since its earliest days. His book *The Good Study Guide* is widely used by students and teachers in the UK and elsewhere.

David Pace is a Professor of European History at Indiana University, co-director of the Freshman Learning Project, a fellow in the Carnegie Academy for the Scholarship of Teaching and Learning and the Mack Center for Inquiry on Teaching and Learning, co-author of *Decoding the Disciplines*, and recipient of the American Historical Association's Eugene Asher Distinguished Teaching Award.

Jane Pritchard is a Lecturer in the Academic Development Unit, University of Glasgow, currently on a two-year release to the Higher Education Academy Engineering Subject Centre. Her work here focuses on new lecturers, part time teachers and working with educational development units across the UK HE engineering sector. Her research interests are the role of education in supporting social change and social justice.

Gary Poole is the Director of the Centre for Teaching and Academic Growth and the Institute for the Scholarship of Teaching and Learning at the University of British Columbia. His research interests in higher education include the identification of valid measures of educational impact at the institutional level and understanding students' experiences in community service learning environments and self-directed projects.

Nicola Reimann is a Principal Lecturer at Northumbria University where she leads a Postgraduate Program in Academic Practice for university staff. She was a Research Fellow for the Enhancing Teaching-Learning Environments in Undergraduate Course (ETL) Project with specific responsibility for the Economics strand. Prior to that she taught German in higher education, both in the UK and Germany.

Torgny Roxå is an academic developer at Lund University. His main interest is strategic educational development (i.e., how to change an entire institution in relation to teaching and learning). He has been responsible for several national and university-wide initiatives, and has published on how cultural change relates to the social processes where individual academics form their understanding of teaching and learning.

Paul Trowler is Professor of Higher Education at the Department of Educational Research at Lancaster University, UK. His research is about change processes and the implementation of higher education policy particularly at institutional and departmental level. He has particular interests in the enhancement of teaching and learning in higher education.

Mantz Yorke is currently Visiting Professor in the Department of Educational Research, Lancaster University. He has held senior positions at Liverpool John Moores University and at the Higher Education Quality Council. He has published widely on higher education, his recent work focusing on employability, student success, and assessment.

Foreword

Ronald Barnett

Just how might we think of disciplines within contemporary higher education? Some seem to think that, if they are not yet dead, disciplines are on the wane. Characteristically, the argument runs that disciplines are a result of a combination of historical features that are no longer present.

On the one hand, there is a historical-social story: disciplines developed and become a supremely powerful way of knowing the world especially in the late nineteenth and early twentieth centuries when the academic class had become a kind of oligarchy, in the control it came to exert, both over universities and over the educational processes within those institutions. For disciplines, read academic power and control. On the other hand, there is a more philosophical point of view: disciplines reflected objectivist and realist epistemologies. They sprang from a sense that there is a world that we can know (however abstract) and that it is the task of disciplines to furnish proper understandings of it. Many disciplines might bequeath many perspectives but still, each discipline was a kind of edifice, rock-like providing secure knowledge, accrued through rigorous investigation and debate.

Both of these axioms are sometimes felt to be weakening. Firstly, it is observed that the construction of valid knowledge is no longer the prerogative of the academics; the clerks have lost their monopoly over the determination of Knowledge (with a capital K, as it were). As a result, definitions of knowledge widen with alacrity. Now, the universities are told that knowing how to do things is as important as knowing that such-and-such is the case. And so arises the agenda of 'skills'. Secondly, it is observed that we live in a more pluralist age where many competing definitions of a situation can and should live – if not very happily – alongside each other. As a result, the voice of the student becomes important in its own right. It is not enough to become initiated into a conversation that stands independent of oneself with its own standards. Now, students are expected to make much of the running themselves in their own development.

Against the background of considerations such as these, this book could hardly have been better timed. For me, it asserts the continuing presence of disciplines as disciplines: they are real and they exert real effects on lecturers' approaches to teaching and also on the student experience. But, for me, too, the book goes further than this, and in doing so, it perhaps connects with the critiques of disciplines that we have just rehearsed. For, in delving into 'teaching and learning within and beyond disciplinary boundaries', the book makes vivid the liveliness of disciplines as they are taken up, explored and experienced within the pedagogical relationship.

In these explorations, we are led into layers of learning in higher education. We are invited to consider, for example, the extent to which learning is context-dependent and the extent to which it is, in that sense, context-transcendent. Where it is context-dependent, that dependency may owe to disciplines but, we are also cautioned, it may owe to the culture of a department. One department of modern languages may have a preferred teaching style in favour of conversations and turn-taking, offering spaces for the student voice, while another department of modern languages, on the floor above (or below!), may favour pedagogic interactions that are more dependent on the teacher as a sage, and where voice is much more constrained. We are also drawn into an exploration of context-transcendence. Here, learning may be framed, at least in the university's self-rhetoric, around a language of 'generic skills'. But we are also reminded that the university characteristically connects to the wider world in manifold ways, both through the student's own networks and more broadly still. The voices of society are also to be heard, if *sotto voce*, in the pedagogical relationship.

We have, then, in this book, in its careful explorations of the day-to-day lived character of disciplines at work in curricula and in pedagogies, a folding in of complexity on complexity. This is significant because, to pick up our earlier critiques of disciplines, we glimpse here a sense that disciplines, insofar as they are taken up in the teaching situation, are always in-the-making. They are not fixed edifices, which the student simply has to surmount or knock against – or even fall from. They are rather fluid regions, with intermingling and conflicting currents, in which the student can – to a significant extent – chart her own journey. And here is opened the way for a term that runs strongly in this volume, that of 'self-authorship'. The student is enjoined to make herself in these postmodern times and, it so happens, pedagogically, that is precisely what is happening day in and day out in our universities. The disciplines live on but as lively areas where students can even swim against the current. Even amid disciplines, students can – and should – become their own learning agents.

Preface
Background and Structure of this Book

Carolin Kreber

University teaching and learning take place within ever more specialized disciplinary settings, each characterized by its unique traditions, concepts, practices and procedures. This specialization invites diverse questions, such as: To what extent can recent graduates be assumed to have had similar learning experiences? To what extent does the undergraduate experience prepare students for the complexities and uncertainties that characterize their later professional, civic and personal lives? What 'ways of thinking and practicing' are characteristic of particular disciplines? Is what students learn in one subject or discipline useful for their learning in other contexts? How can students be supported in becoming participants of particular disciplinary discourse communities? Moreover, can the diversity in teaching, learning and assessment practices that can be observed across departments be attributed exclusively to disciplinary structure or do other factors come into play?

Background to This Volume

In June 2005 the Centre for Teaching, Learning and Assessment at the University of Edinburgh held a two-day international Colloquium on the theme of "*Teaching and Learning within and beyond Disciplinary Boundaries*", where the above issues were examined. One goal of the Colloquium was to explore, through recent research in both North America and the UK, what is distinctive about teaching and learning in particular disciplines. However, there is now a growing awareness that in a world characterized by rapid change, complexity and uncertainty, problems do not present themselves as distinct subjects but increasingly within trans-disciplinary contexts, thereby calling for graduate outcomes that go beyond specialized knowledge and skills. Moreover, notions such as 'employability' and 'Personal Development Planning' feature prominently in higher education policy documents in the UK and elsewhere, and many countries now perceive a need for higher education to play a profound role in contributing to a socially responsible (in the sense of critically aware rather than just compliant) citizenry. For these reasons it was an equally important goal to situate discussions of academic learning within the disciplines within the wider perspective of complex graduate outcomes. A key question raised by the aforementioned considerations is whether the teaching of specialized skills and knowledge in particular contexts can be balanced with the teaching of more 'generic' ones, without compromising the integrity of academic programs on offer.

The Colloquium featured five invited presentations by educational researchers from the UK, Canada and the United States, each introducing a unique lens or perspective. The Colloquium succeeded in promoting dialogue, not only between UK and North American researchers but also between educational researchers and faculty from a wide range of academic disciplines, on how the research presented might inform university teaching and learning. To take these discussions further, it was agreed to publish the five presentations as a book together with some reactive chapters. This volume presents the outcome of this project.

Purpose of This Volume

This book is concerned with the role of the academic disciplines in influencing teaching and learning and how academic learning within particular disciplines might contribute to the larger or overarching goals of higher education. It is not, in essence, a book about 'teaching tips', but it is very much intended to assist university teachers in better understanding how academic learning within particular disciplinary settings can help students acquire the skills, abilities and dispositions they need to succeed academically and also in their professional, civic and personal lives. It offers five different lenses or perspectives through which to explore the issue.

Audience

The book is targeted at a diverse audience. As all the reactive chapters are contributed by academics directly involved in providing support for teaching, it highlights the practical application of the research perspectives presented. The book is therefore useful for new and experienced academics with teaching responsibilities (indeed, it offers very appropriate reading material to be included in courses on teaching and learning in higher education). Furthermore, educational developers seeking to balance generic educational development initiatives with more discipline-specific opportunities will also find this book helpful. Lastly, researchers and postgraduate students in the field of adult and higher education will find this text attractive, given the different research perspectives it offers.

Structure and Outline of Subsequent Chapters

Each of the five research perspectives is discussed in a separate part of this book. Each is accompanied by two 'reactive chapters' which, as well as offering interpretation and further observations also highlight the practical implications of the research. All authors draw on at least two other chapters in the book thereby emphasizing the conceptual linkages across the various contributions.

The structure of the book is also a response to a frequently expressed observation that much educational theory is overly jargon-ridden and not really connected, or even relevant, to the experience of higher education teachers and leaders. Having a theoretical text commented on and interpreted through the eyes of at least two other people might be helpful in bridging this disconnect. Of course it needs to be acknowledged here that the respondents are not unaffected by the particular discipline they studied and most strongly identify with, which is made most explicit perhaps in the chapters by Matthew and Pritchard, Pace, and Gunn. Because with edited volumes it cannot be assumed that readers will take a look at all the chapters but rather go about their reading more selectively, the authors of reactive chapters were asked to briefly summarize the main ideas of the chapter they were responding to. The resulting degree of repetition across the contributions within each part of the book is intentional, therefore. While some readers will prefer to engage with the research-based chapter prior to turning to the reactive ones, others might find it more helpful the other way around.

Part I provides the general introduction and framework for this volume. In *Chapter 1* I focus on the book's main theme, specifically the continuous interplay between the context-specific and 'context-transcendent' aspects of teaching and learning. I set this discussion against two major challenges posed by the contemporary higher education environment: Increased diversity in the student population, on the one hand, and on the other, the need for higher education institutions to help students achieve complex graduate outcomes that would prepare them adequately for their future professional, civic and personal lives. I distinguish two different approaches to teaching towards these overarching goals of higher education: those that are merely *adjunct* to regular academic study and those that are *integral* to it. Finally, drawing a distinction between subjects and disciplines, my intent is to explore what is involved in teaching a 'subject' in such a way that students not only learn lots about a 'subject' but know *how* they learned it and *why* what they learned *matters* to their understanding of and interaction with the world around them.

Chapter 2 explores the evolution of the academic disciplines within the modern research university and provides a brief overview of what we have come to understand about the disciplines through past and recent research. I discuss some problems with typologies such as Biglan's 'hard versus soft' and 'pure versus applied' classification, thereby paving the way for the issues addressed later in this book. I conclude that university teaching and learning could be enriched by opening up our disciplinary 'silos' to more frequent cross-disciplinary encounters, highlighting, in particular, the promise of the scholarship of teaching and learning in effectively promoting these exchanges. While the focus of the opening chapter is on the context-specific and context-transcendent aspects of *learning*, in the second chapter the focus shifts to teaching.

Part II of the book focuses on disciplines and their epistemological structure. *Chapter 3* is the actual *opening address* that was delivered by Janet Donald at the Edinburgh Colloquium. Donald reports on her findings from an extensive twenty-five year empirical research program into learning and teaching across academic disciplines, focusing on English, law and engineering. She discusses the nature of the concepts taught in each discipline, the thinking processes required to learn them, the validation processes involved, the dominant attributes of pedagogy observed in each, the ideologies underlying them and the challenges for teaching in these subject areas. She concludes that each discipline has its own *signature pedagogy*; she also describes what the three have in common with regards to the thinking processes they call for. The observation that there are certain thinking processes that cut across disciplines is shared also by Hounsell and Anderson in Chapter 6. Despite these commonalities, Donald concludes that "the sociological and intellectual parameters of the disciplines set the scene for the pedagogies used and for student learning" (p. 37). Trowler, in Chapter 15, offers an insightful critique of the notion that disciplinary structures *alone* direct teaching, learning and assessment practices but he certainly would agree with Donald that they do play a role.

Towards the end of her chapter Donald comments that "One of the most evident yet disquieting findings from these studies across disciplines is that students in one program of study are experiencing a totally different education from students in another" (p. 46). This is a significant observation in light of the issues explored in this book. As we are delving more deeply into the pedagogical implications of promoting learning within and beyond disciplinary boundaries, it is critical that, next to exploring the unique contributions individual disciplines can make, we also locate this discussion within the broader and more fundamental question of what constitute the wider purposes and goals of an undergraduate education. This question is taken up most explicitly by Baxter Magolda in Chapter 12 (and the two accompanying chapters), but is addressed also by many of the other contributors.

In *Chapter 4*, Gary Poole considers the pros and cons of disciplines and the departments they spawn as contexts for teaching and learning and the extent to which disciplinary distinctiveness is desirable. He also revisits the notion of "signature pedagogies" exploring specifically the purpose these serve in the socialization process in the professions. In *Chapter 5*, Bob Matthew and Jane Pritchard critique some of the assumptions underlying the "hard" versus "soft" classification of academic disciplines as well as the role of "signature pedagogies", with a particular focus on engineering education. They ask whether the disciplines and their signature pedagogies enhance the students' learning experiences or rather cement disciplinary boundaries and acceptable "ways of thinking and practicing" (WTP, see Chapter 6). They also explore the extent to which the notion of 'graduateness' is a subject-specific versus generic construct and consider some of the current practices within engineering education drawing on examples from different departments in different countries.

Part III explores the notion of *"Ways of Thinking and Practicing"* (WTP) in particular disciplines. In *Chapter 6*, Dai Hounsell and Charles Anderson report findings from a large research project on undergraduate students' and faculty's perceptions of learning in biological sciences as well as history courses. The concept of *Ways of Thinking and Practicing* (WTP) serves to advance insight into what students actually learn when studying on specific courses in these disciplines and offers the opportunity to identify aspects of what students learn that may transcend disciplinary boundaries (see also Donald). WTP are not exclusively of a cognitive nature (i.e., they are not only about *how to think* within the discipline) but have also intuitive, performative and perhaps even ethical qualities. Some aspects of WTP may be preverbal or tacit and hence only teachable by allowing students the opportunity to carry out the tasks characteristic of the discipline. Students thereby develop a feel, for example, for the conventions governing scholarly communication and for how data are generated and evaluated, and hence for how knowledge itself is constructed. Through extensive interviews with faculty and students, Hounsell and Anderson show that WTP characteristic of history and biological sciences guided the 'pedagogy in use' as well as student learning in both disciplines. Moreover, they illustrate that what students learn in particular disciplines, at least to some extent, transcends disciplinary boundaries. Equally importantly, Hounsell and Anderson remark that the "interaction of institution-level and module-level factors had a strong bearing on what teaching strategies and activities made sense within a given context" (p. 78). This observation is echoed by Paul Trowler, in Chapter 15, who persuasively argues that context plays a decisive role in the particular teaching efforts employed by individuals, departments or institutions and that, for this reason, concepts such as WTP should be considered only one of several influences on pedagogical approaches.

In *Chapter 7*, Nicola Reimann examines the use of WTP in academic development workshops. Faculty benefited from the opportunity to make their own WTP explicit, and interdisciplinary exchanges contributed to their understanding of (trans-) disciplinarity. WTP as participation in a disciplinary community generated student-centered, socio-cultural conceptions of teaching and learning. In *Chapter 8*, David Pace places Hounsell and Anderson's analysis of WTP in history classes in the context of the recent literature on learning history produced by educational researchers in the United States and describes efforts to apply the "decoding the disciplines" approach to this field of investigation.

Part IV explores teaching from a socio-cultural perspective. In *Chapter 9*, Andy Northedge and Jan McArthur argue that critical to understanding the role of teachers within the context of higher learning is their membership of a disciplinary community. The authors view learning in higher education not as a purely cognitive process but as a multi-faceted one of students becoming engrossed in the ways of thinking and knowing of a particular discourse community. As students strive towards becoming members of that community, the main challenge for them is to make meaning within unfamiliar discourses. The outcomes of learning can be observed as students develop the capacity to engage more effectively with the discourses of the discipline according to the discipline's accepted standards and practices.

A critical concept they introduce is that of *a state of intersubjectivity*, which describes the activity of mutual meaning making between two or more people. The pedagogical practices required to generate a state of intersubjectivity between students and teacher share important features with those

Baxter Magolda describes as being effective in promoting learning partnerships (see Chapter 12). Hounsell and Anderson's observation that what is significant with regards to what students learn is "the wider expertise students are acquiring as scientists in the making" (Chapter 6, p. 75) resonates well with Northedge and McArthur's view that learning in higher education involves students developing their capacity to participate effectively in the discourse of significant knowledge communities. While Donald's research is concerned for the most part with identifying the thinking skills students require in order to grasp the concepts characteristic of a particular discipline, Hounsell and Anderson, Northedge and McArthur, as well as Baxter Magolda, while recognizing the importance of thinking skills, apply a broader lens that brings into view some of the contextual and social factors influencing learning as well as the importance of a learning climate that is conducive to students' experimenting with the practices of the discipline.

In *Chapter 10*, Jan McArthur builds on the chapter she authored with Northedge by focusing on how students can be supported to maintain and develop their own voices while participating in disciplinary discourses. She considers the importance of faculty sharing both their disciplinary authority with students and the voices through which they express their belief in the importance of their discipline. The chapter rests upon an understanding of disciplines as rich, creative and flexible spaces in which diverse voices take part in common meaning making. In *Chapter 11*, Lewis Elton offers some observations on academic writing as an essential aspect of "acts of shared meaning making" (p. 131). Raising some of the challenges posed by tacit knowledge and the limits of language in making it explicit, he suggests that to make tacit knowledge explicit requires a combination of words and actions. Hence, he proposes that enquiry-based learning might be a vehicle for unlocking students' writing skills and allow for a unification of students' academic practice and writing about that practice.

Part 5 looks at the notion of learning partnerships in disciplinary learning. In *Chapter 12*, Marcia Baxter Magolda reports on her longitudinal study conducted over twenty years starting with a group of 100 undergraduate students and following them well into their adult years to better understand the various factors influencing their learning and development. Through her research, Baxter Magolda was able to gain crucial insights into how, and in response to what kinds of experiences, the ways in which individuals make meaning change and how this process could be fostered in the university classroom through disciplinary learning.

Baxter Magolda's chapter is firmly situated within the larger or overarching goals of higher education and she takes a serious look at the developmental capacities that these require. Among them is the need to move from authority dependence to what she calls "self-authorship", the capacity to internally define one's beliefs, but also one's identity and social relations. Her chapter, therefore, is rooted in a whole-person view of learning where cognitive academic learning is not separated from the actual person. The goal of the chapter is to show how the disciplines can make a contribution in assisting students in being able "to translate their disciplinary learning into supercomplex and transdisciplinary contexts" (p. 152).

Baxter Magolda introduces the *Learning Partnership Model* which calls for a re-conceptualization of the nature of the teacher–student relationship in higher education. It suggests that students are supported in their learning and development when they are validated in their capacity to know, encouraged to bring their own self into the learning and invited to engage in mutual knowledge construction. Hence, teachers or course teams who understand themselves exclusively as knowledge experts whose main responsibility is to dazzle students through brilliantly delivered excursions into what "is known" about a particular subject, may not adequately support student learning. Many readers will agree that it is equally important that students learn how knowledge is constructed and evaluated. In addition, some of us will argue that it is also critical that academic teachers understand their role even more broadly than that, not *exclusively* as assisting students in learning a particular subject, as in helping them to "think like historians, or physicists, or lawyers", etc. (although there can be no doubt that teaching the discipline has to be their main role; an argument will develop more fully in Chapter 1). Baxter Magolda describes how faculty might help students develop self-authorship, and thereby contribute towards the larger or overarching goals of higher education through their discipline, without compromising the academic integrity of the courses they teach.

There are similarities in the pedagogical practices recommended by Northedge and McArthur (Chapter 9) and the suggestions offered by Baxter Magolda. The major difference between the two perspectives is that the former do not make the same claims with regards to the role of higher education in promoting students' general development and confine their purpose to exploring the role of the teacher in enabling students to effectively participate in disciplinary discourse.

In *Chapter 13*, Alan Jenkins endorses the key ideas of Baxter Magolda's chapter with its view that a key role of faculty is to support student long-term intellectual growth. He argues that discipline- and department-based approaches to course design are practical ways to realize this vision. Such curricula should explore and emphasize the different epistemologies/perspectives *within* discipline-based courses. In some institutions, requirements for cross-departmental or cross-disciplinary synoptic courses, or central careers-based Personal Development Programs, may offer ways to support all students to understand the complexities of knowledge and chart their development post university. In *Chapter 14*, Vicky Gunn, focusing on teaching within the humanities, explores to what extent the traditional structures of higher education hinder using the self-authorship foundation and the Learning Partnership Model. A further issue considered is whether faculty are willing to reframe their role as authorities in order to enable learners to become authorities.

Part VI explores the interactions of disciplines with local cultures or *Teaching and Learning Regimes* (TLR). In *Chapter 15*, Paul Trowler explains that TLR constitute a subset of academic culture specific to teaching and learning practices. Trowler is not foremost concerned with how to teach, nor does his main interest lie in what students need to learn; instead, his chief purpose is to explore the factors at work in shaping TLR in particular contexts or departments. The aim of his chapter is to contribute to a deeper understanding of the nature of disciplinary differences and their effects on teaching and learning. Trowler argues that although epistemological differences between disciplines do exist, it is an over-generalization to conclude that epistemological structure *determines* teaching and learning efforts.

An important concept in Trowler's analysis is the notion of "agency", that is the idea that the "regularities imposed by social structure are always provisional" (p. 181) and that individuals, and by extension departments and institutions, have scope to chart their own course on teaching and learning practices. This insight is most significant in promoting understanding of why certain practices work well in some contexts but not in others.

In *Chapter 16*, Joëlle Fanghanel examines the extent to which the notion of TLR can be applied to higher education contexts that readers are familiar with, and outlines domains in which this theoretical framework can usefully inform practices from the perspective of academics, managers and faculty developers. She finally identifies ways of furthering understandings of boundaries in TLR. In *Chapter 17*, Torgny Roxå and Katarina Mårtensson explore how the concept of TLR could contribute to teachers' understanding of their own teaching and learning context. They explore ways of transforming informal "significant networks" that academics consult in their role as teachers, into something that could serve a developmental function within a department or discipline. The scholarship of teaching and learning is discussed as a way of assisting teachers in influencing their personal space of action and the local culture (or the ruling TLR).

Part VII comprises two chapters that present more general observations. In *Chapter 18*, Mantz Yorke explores the importance of "the self" and of higher-order learning in the development of employability and citizenship, proposes an assessment methodology that aligns with expectations for employability and citizenship, and outlines some implications for teaching and learning. In *Chapter 19*, Velda McCune offers some concluding remarks on the themes addressed in this book, highlighting in particular the challenges the proposed ideas pose for higher education teachers.

Carolin Kreber,
Edinburgh, Scotland

Acknowledgments

I am deeply indebted to all the contributors to this book who worked very hard on making it a useful resource. The frequent cross-referencing throughout the volume attests to the collaborative spirit in which the idea for this book was first conceived and eventually carried through to completion. I would like to thank my colleagues at the Centre for Teaching, Learning and Assessment at the University of Edinburgh, whose insights into higher education pedagogy I constantly benefited from while this book was taking shape. Special thanks also to Kim Addison who, as usual, proved to be of invaluable help in the organization of the Higher Education Colloquium in 2005 that served as the foundation for this volume (and made sure that this manuscript got shipped on time!). My Routledge editor, Sarah Burrows, made this project possible and I much appreciate the encouragement and support I received from her. Finally, I am grateful to Shelley Sikora for her honest feedback and suggestions (and for reminding me that there are essential things in life other than the study of higher education). For additional acknowledgements, I refer readers to individual chapters.

I
Introduction

Setting the context

1

Supporting Student Learning in the Context of Diversity, Complexity and Uncertainty

Carolin Kreber

University of Edinburgh

> Perhaps the classroom should be neither teacher-centered nor student-centered but subject-centered.
>
> (Palmer, 1998, p. 116)

> Teaching from the microcosm, we exercise responsibility towards both the subject and our students . . . We honor both the discipline and our students by teaching them how to think like historians or biologists or literary critics. . . .
>
> (Palmer, 1998, p. 123)

Introduction

One might reasonably expect a book with the subtitle "*Teaching and Learning Within and Beyond Disciplinary Boundaries*" to begin with some substantive comments about the nature of 'academic disciplines': how they are defined, how they have evolved over time, what is known about their similarities and differences, and whether the latter might explain particular tendencies in the teaching and assessment practices that can be observed in departments. These questions, however, are the subject of Chapter 2. In this opening chapter I draw attention to the central theme running through this book, that is, the continuous interplay between the contextual aspects of teaching and learning and those which might be described as '*context-transcendent*'.

The chapter begins with an overview of contemporary higher education concentrating on issues of diversity within the student population and the need to prepare undergraduates not only for further specialized study but the, so-called, 'real world', one widely perceived to be both complex and uncertain (Barnett, 2000; Donald, in Chapter 3). Although this discussion could appear in any book on higher education teaching, it is especially pertinent to the focus of this volume. The reason we are concerned with disciplines, and the learning *within* as well as *beyond* them, is precisely that we perceive a need to prepare our students for the complexities and unpredictability characterizing their future professional, civic and personal lives. As I will propose below, it is by introducing students to the ways of thinking, the concepts, procedures and practices characteristic of our various disciplinary communities that this might be achieved. And surely, we are better equipped to succeed if we know who our students are.

I then describe different ways of preparing students for these challenges, contrasting approaches that are seen as an adjunct to regular academic study from those that are integral to it. I also offer some observations on the difference between 'subjects' as '*what is looked at*' versus 'subjects' as '*what is looked through or with*' (i.e., 'disciplines'), suggesting that this distinction can usefully inform our decision-making around how to prepare students for future learning in diverse contexts. In the final section, drawing on the evocative notions of "teaching from the microcosm" (Palmer, 1998) and "learning partnerships" (Baxter Magolda, Chapter 12 in this volume), my intent is to expose and describe what actually happens in situations when teachers succeed in fully connecting their students with their subject. Success is defined by students not only learning lots *about* a subject, but knowing *how* they learned it and *why* what they learned *matters* to their understanding of and interaction with the world around them. As students acquire certain bodies of knowledge, procedures, conceptual tools, practices and even values within the particular contexts of our various subjects, their learning is context-specific but also 'context-transcendent'.

Contemporary Higher Education

Who Are Our Students?

Regardless of whether one visits university classrooms in Canada, the US, Australia or the UK, what is immediately striking is that the move from a system of an elite to one of mass higher education has led not only to much larger but also much more diverse classes. It is surely not surprising then that today's undergraduates have been shown to differ in terms of their educational aspirations and attitudes towards university study (e.g., Dey, Astin, & Korn, 1991; James, 2002; Levine & Cureton, 1998). Most students aspire to enter the labor market upon graduation, far fewer seek to continue with post-graduate studies and a smaller number still consider stepping into their teachers' footsteps to become professors themselves.

Although much more needs to be done by way of removing barriers to higher education for certain sections of society, particularly in 'elite' institutions, many of today's students are the first of their family to enter university and may lack the cultural capital that is positively associated with success at university. Aronowitz (2000) suggested that an increasing number of students now admitted into our programs are insufficiently prepared for the demands of university life or lack the basic study skills and confidence needed to succeed. Many institutions therefore recognize that making university study possible for students from disadvantaged social groups is not limited to providing access but involves a commitment to providing the needed additional support once these students have arrived.

It is important to realize, however, that it is not only wider access students who need support in their learning. All students would probably benefit from a clear explanation of expectations at the beginning of the course and the provision of prompt and constructive feedback on assignments, to mention just two examples of 'support'. These examples reflect a view of 'learning support' that is not focused on the idea of a centralized service (that those who appear to struggle most can be referred to) but is integral to teaching itself. Linking support for learning with teaching means that faculty, student advisors and course organizers/coordinators play a key role in helping students develop as learners. However, as student enrolment continues to increase, the question of how to provide adequate support for effective learning for all students is an issue in urgent need of attention.

As a group, students are also much more culturally diverse than in the past. Some students, therefore, may find that aspects of the course content and/or the pedagogical processes employed challenge their religious and/or cultural beliefs. Being aware of cultural diversity may help teachers understand why some students might have trouble connecting with the course and as a result be more motivated to respond sensitively. Numerous guidebooks have been developed that offer advice on how to make courses more culturally sensitive and inclusive in terms of both content and process as well as on how to embrace cultural diversity on campus more widely. Many universities make these guidelines available on their websites. The University of Washington (2004), for example, has developed a website that is easy to use and highlights many inclusive teaching strategies.

An increase in immigrants, exchange programs and students studying on visas means that more and more of them study in a foreign language. Taking the UK as an example, in 2006 there were almost 320,000 international students attending UK universities (making up about 13% of the entire student population), of whom about one third were from countries belonging to the European Union (EU). Most non-EU or overseas students came from China, followed by India, the United States, Malaysia and Hong Kong (HESA, 2006). It has been predicted that over the next two decades there will be a drastic increase of international students *worldwide* due to factors such as growing interest in studying abroad, expected household wealth, increased demand for higher education, and lack of capacity for some countries in meeting this demand (Boehm, Davis, Meares, & Pearce, 2002).

Clearly, language difficulties that international students, but also immigrants, may experience can easily impede understanding in lectures, inhibit participation in tutorials and may cause problems in comprehending course requirements. Language difficulties may also, at least initially, make it more difficult for these students to connect with their peers and become integrated in campus life. Another point to consider is the intimate connection between language and culture. Although local students tend to report positively on teachers using examples based on popular culture to explain certain points (as by making reference to famous TV series or radio talk shows), such practices may not support the learning of students less familiar with popular culture. Likewise, in fields such as social policy, political science and education it is not unusual that the laws, policies and practices of the 'home' country (i.e., the country where higher education is offered) dominate the curriculum. International students, however, will have little or no prior experience of these, making their learning presumably much harder.

International post-graduate students, perhaps more so than undergraduates, may also challenge some of our assumptions about how certain subjects or disciplines are to be taught, learned and assessed. Although we will see later that links have been identified between certain aspects of teaching and the disciplines' fundamental epistemological structure, there is an alternative view that considers the teaching practices that can be observed in departments to be just as much influenced by local cultures (see Trowler in Chapter 15 of this volume).

Many students entering higher education are mature learners with family and work responsibilities and a growing number are pursuing their degrees part-time. In fact, within the North American context Donald (1997) observed that "fewer students in postsecondary programs actually define themselves as students" (p. 85), which, by extension, means that they are less engaged in university life. As faculty we need to keep in mind that for these students what happens during class-time may be even more important than for full-time students who have greater opportunity to seek out advice from peers and professors informally. However, it is important to realize that even among our full-time students many are 'commuter students', who experience considerable constraints on their engagement with their studies.

Students' lifestyles and values also reflect diversity. Some students identify with mainstream culture and, hence, can readily connect with teachers and course aspects that portray mainstream culture as 'how things are'; others will connect with these teachers and course aspects less well because they are not reflective of their world (one may think, for instance, of certain employment trajectories that are portrayed as examples of 'success' or how a family and partner are 'defined' when ordinary life is talked about in courses or personal conversation with students). True, these latter aspects of diversity do not influence the ways in which students learn a foreign language, observe cells under the microscope, or think about the factors leading up to major world events. However, these aspects of diversity influence how students connect with the wider learning environment and community in which they study: whether they perceive it as affirming, reflective of the world as they know it and relevant or, instead, as somewhat alienating, unconnected from the world as they know it and irrelevant.

Students also differ in their epistemological development, that is, their understanding of the nature, certainty and limits of knowledge. Some seem to almost immediately grasp the notion that knowledge in the subjects they are studying is uncertain, constructed and contested, while others might graduate without having reached this understanding (see Baxter Magolda, 1992 and Chapter 12 in this volume). Students' epistemological development is linked to the expectations they hold of their teachers and the extent to which they are prepared to consider their peers as valuable resources for learning. Knowing that students in one class are not a homogeneous group in terms of their epistemological development also helps us to understand why they may show quite varied reactions to our attempts to have them take greater responsibility for their learning.

Furthermore, students' learning style (Kolb, 1981), that is the preferences they develop for certain learning tasks, can be seen to directly influence how they might engage with a particular subject or discipline. Kolb identified relationships between the discipline's cognitive structure (defined by the two axes of "soft versus hard", and "pure versus applied", see Chapter 2) and students' learning preferences. In essence, Kolb concluded that the cognitive structure of the discipline brings about a certain learning style. For example, a hard and applied discipline, like mechanical engineering, would bring about a learning style that excels in tasks requiring application of existing theory, a style Kolb called *convergent*. A soft and pure discipline, like English literature, would bring about a style that excels in tasks requiring openness to experience, looking at problems from various angles, and generating ideas, a style Kolb called *divergent*. It is, of course, equally possible that students with a certain learning style tend to choose certain subjects, and that their learning style then gets further reinforced by that choice. This would mean that a student who is used to pursuing learning tasks typical of one discipline could have difficulty with the tasks typical of another, due to the learning style that has been reinforced up to this point.

Clearly, there are numerous dimensions of diversity and all present certain challenges to teachers. Yet, readers may reach this point concluding that only the last two dimensions really matter to supporting student learning within and beyond disciplinary boundaries, and that others, though perhaps adding breadth to the discussion, are of little relevance. However, teaching is principally about *connecting* and *communicating* with people about our subjects. Surely we are more likely to succeed in entering into community with our students, and connecting our students with our subjects (Palmer, 1998), if we are aware of and welcoming of all aspects of diversity. In other words, while teaching must be "subject-centered" (Palmer, 1998, p. 116), it cannot avoid also being student-centered if it is to truly engage with students' lives and worldviews. Moreover, many of us hope higher education will instil in students a positive attitude towards diversity and more liberal socio-political views. While exposure to specific courses, for example, on multiculturalism, may be positively related to such desirable attitudes (see below), it stands to reason that such learning is further supported if faculty, and others with teaching responsibilities, respond positively to different dimensions of diversity and employ inclusive practices. Recognizing and valuing diversity offers the opportunity to enhance the learning experience of all students.

Employability, Civic Responsibility and Lifelong Learning as General Graduate Outcomes

In the twenty-first century, the process of 'globalization' has exercised an undeniable influence also on higher education. National governments call on universities to provide the educated labor ('knowledge workers') needed to ensure the country's competitiveness in the global market. As a consequence, many countries have identified the 'employability' (Knight & Yorke, 2003) of students as an important graduate outcome within the new knowledge economy (e.g. DfES, 2003; Teichler, 1999; UNESCO, 1998). The issue of preparing students for 'employability' is contested in higher education circles largely because people interpret its meaning in different ways.

A common tendency is to equate it with preparing students for specific jobs. Not surprisingly, many academics do not consider this to be part of their role. Another frequently encountered interpretation centers on the view that the entire 'employability scheme' reflects an attempt to fit students into predetermined roles in society, by meeting certain standardized goals, without engaging students in challenging or questioning dominant agendas. Clearly, many academics see this as violating core academic values and aims, chiefly among them the critical interrogation of the status quo and a key role as 'society's critical friend'.

Readers may find it more helpful to think of 'employability' in terms of general skills, abilities and personal qualities. Taking this perspective, Knight and Yorke (2003) identified several essential aspects of employability, including among others: self-management, critical analysis, creativity, ethical sensitivity, and the capacity to act morally, solve problems, resolve conflict, make decisions, negotiate, work in teams, and to work cross-culturally.

Next to employability, the need for responsible citizenship increasingly enters the debate when general graduate outcomes are discussed (e.g. Baxter Magolda & Terenzini, 1999; Colby, Ehrlich, Beaumont, & Stephens, 2003; Nussbaum, 1997). The need for civic responsibility arises from an understanding that modern societies are organized in complex ways and demand decisions on controversial problems calling for ethical judgments and intercultural understanding. The need for graduate outcomes associated with lifelong learning (e.g. Knapper & Cropley, 2001) has long been recognized within the academy. The demand for lifelong learning is informed by the observation that the knowledge, skills and attitudes required to participate effectively at work and in wider society are rapidly changing. Surely, the debates within particular disciplines on what these terms mean will probably be varied. The concept of lifelong learning is probably the least contested of the three outcomes given that it is a personal value for most people choosing academic careers and, by extension, the one most easily interpreted within faculty's own disciplinary context. However, the concept of 'employability', although rather unproblematic in professional fields such as law, engineering or medicine, might be highly contested, for reasons already mentioned, in fields such as physics, history or English. Likewise, preparing students for civic responsibility may take on quite different interpretations in law than in English, where the critical interrogation of how dominant agendas, rules and regulations have come about and can be resisted *might be* more common (this is not to suggest that this Frankfurt School type of thinking cannot be found in law). In physics and medicine, matters of social responsibility may be linked more tightly to research ethics.

Overall, most faculty agree that students need to develop not only subject-specific knowledge as a result of their university education but also skills, abilities and dispositions that help them make informed decisions, self-manage their affairs – including their learning – and act in socially responsible ways at work as well as in wider society. The issue to be raised, therefore, is not that there is much disagreement about these larger goals of higher education; instead, the issue to highlight is that it is often not clear for faculty where in a student's program of study they consider the responsibility for these outcomes to be located. Moreover, the question of 'location' may also invite different responses depending on whether one teaches in the humanities, sciences, or professions. Some faculty will consider much of this present discussion a non-issue and contend that these general outcomes are taught "by default" given their subject area; others will argue that there is just not enough time in the academic year to teach these "extra things".

Promoting Student Learning towards Civic Responsibility, Employability and Lifelong Learning

Common Approaches

It is not unusual for institutions, particularly in North America, to require all students to take particular courses that are intended to prepare them for the complexities they will encounter in later life. With regards to educating students for effective citizenship, Martha Nussbaum (1997), for example, recommends that all students take courses on ethics and multiculturalism, taught by faculty from the philosophy department. This suggestion finds empirical support in a North American study by Henderson-King and Kaleta (2000) showing that, although it has long been argued that the North American liberal arts undergraduate degree, as such, is associated with a sense of increased humanitarianism, civic responsibility and the development of more liberal socio-political attitudes (e.g., Astin, 1977; Chickering, 1970; Pascarella & Terenzini, 1991), it is only *particular courses* that show such desirable effects.

Courses that explicitly teach students *how to learn* and other 'generic skills' are also common. So-called 'sandwich courses' provide students with the opportunity to pick up work-related skills in conjunction with academic study. In North America, students often have the opportunity to participate in "community-based education" or "service learning" (Rhoads & Howard, 1998), which is seen to promote both civic and work-related skills relevant to the real world. 'Service learning' (not to be confused with 'service *teaching*' in the UK, which refers to teaching of introductory or overview courses) combines the specific tasks to be completed within a particular community or organization with "structured opportunities that link the task to self-reflection, self-discovery, and the acquisition and comprehension of values, skills, and knowledge content" (National Service Learning Clearinghouse [NSLC], 2007).

As the above approaches illustrate, some courses focus on exposure to particular content areas (e.g., a course on ethics) while others emphasize skills development (e.g., learning how to learn). However, Nussbaum's suggestion that courses on ethics and multiculturalism be taught by faculty from the philosophy department implies that students would be introduced not only to content knowledge as it pertains to ethics and multiculturalism but also to the ways of thinking characteristic of philosophy. Indeed, most academics in philosophy would probably find it hard to imagine teaching philosophy without also teaching how to think philosophically. A similar case may be made for other humanities subjects, such as English literature. In Chapter 2 we will see that the medieval university curriculum considered the study of dialectic (part of the *trivium*) as a prerequisite for the study of the *quadrivium* (the four mathematically based disciplines). Dialectic (or logic), was concerned with how to structure an argument and detect inconsistencies or flaws in a line of reasoning. Nussbaum's suggestion that all students should be expected to take a philosophy course is to be understood along these same lines.

Nussbaum proposes that it is through the study of ethics and multiculturalism, with the guidance of philosophers, that students learn how to think critically about their role as global citizens. Not everyone agrees with this view, some dismissing it on the grounds that it further contributes to a hierarchy within the academy in terms of the value attributed to different disciplines. While much could be said about the 'value' attributed to science and technology as evidenced in the amount of research funding allocated to these fields as compared to the humanities, this chapter is not the place to enter into this debate (note that a similar point is taken up by Matthew and Pritchard in Chapter

5). I will add though that Nussbaum's proposal is one that should be considered carefully, even if in this book the focus is on how any of the academic disciplines can contribute to complex graduate outcomes.

The above approaches reflect not only an emphasis on either content or process (or, of course, both); they also reflect a particular stance with respect to whether preparing undergraduate students for the complexities associated with their later civic, professional and personal lives is seen as integral or adjunct to their regular course of study (or their 'major'). To be more specific, underlying all of these approaches seems to be a view that, firstly, it is prudent to leave larger questions of educational purpose to program coordinators and/or philosophers and secondly, faculty responsible for teaching regular courses (e.g., in physics, history, biology, accounting, law, etc.) should focus on helping students acquire mastery of that particular discipline and not concern themselves too much with these 'other goals'.

As I will discuss below, it is precisely by introducing students to the ways of thinking, the concepts, procedures and practices characteristic of our various disciplinary communities that we can help prepare them for the complex challenges they are likely to encounter in their post-college work and personal lives. However, I am not so sure that as we teach our individual courses it is always on our 'radar' that the overall purpose of our collective teaching efforts is to prepare students for successful future learning in increasingly diverse, complex and uncertain contexts. And this, I suggest, might have implications for *how* we teach our subjects.

A notion that usefully informs this present discussion is that of "generic graduate attributes," a term widely used in Australia, beginning to be used in the UK, but at present only rarely used in the US. In a sense generic graduate attributes are linked to what, at different times, have been called transferable skills, generic skills, general skills, or basic skills; then again, as I will illustrate below, for some the term (as does 'employability') encompasses quite a bit more than just 'skills'.

The "Generic Graduate Attributes" Approach

Barrie (2006) identified several qualitatively distinct interpretations of generic graduate attributes, which differ in terms of the relationship they assume between generic outcomes of higher education and discipline-specific knowledge. At the one end of the spectrum, generic graduate attributes are understood to be basic prerequisite skills that students should already possess before they enter university. At the opposite end of the spectrum attributes are understood as complex abilities that infuse learning and knowledge and are learned through the way students engage with their university studies.

The University of Sydney agreed on three overarching generic graduate attributes that are meant to offer guidance to the education students can expect to receive: *scholarship, lifelong learning* and *global citizenship*. These three overarching attributes encompass five clusters of more specific ones: personal and intellectual autonomy; research and inquiry; ethical, social and professional understanding; communication, and information literacy. Importantly, all programs are designed around these generic attributes but the latter are then interpreted differently in different disciplinary domains.

Modeled after the Australian experience, the Quality Assurance Agency (QAA) in Scotland also identified a set of generic attributes that are to be interpreted within particular disciplinary contexts. The website (QAA, 2006) states that as a result of their undergraduate experience, students should develop:

- a critical understanding
- a sense of being informed by current developments in the subject
- an awareness of the provisional nature of knowledge, how knowledge is created, advanced and renewed, and the excitement of changing knowledge

- the ability to identify and analyze problems and issues and to formulate, evaluate and apply evidence-based solutions and arguments
- an ability to apply a systematic and critical assessment of complex problems and issues
- an ability to deploy techniques of analysis and enquiry
- familiarity with advanced techniques and skills
- originality and creativity in formulating, evaluating and applying evidence-based solutions and arguments
- an understanding of the need for a high level of ethical, social, cultural, environmental and wider professional conduct.

While not identical, this list is compatible with the dispositions, abilities and skills Knight and Yorke (2003) had developed within the context of "employability." The authors had suggested in their report that these were critical not only for being successful in the work setting but also for contributing effectively in other social environments.

It is easy to see how the Australian and Scottish attributes relate to the larger educational goals discussed earlier: civic responsibility, lifelong learning and employability. Translating these overarching educational goals into attributes, that is into complex abilities, dispositions and skills sets, conveys more readily how they can be promoted through approaches that are *integral* rather than *adjunct to* the study of regular courses. As the examples from Scotland and Australia illustrate, attributes become interpreted through particular disciplines.

It has been suggested that one way of promoting such complex graduate attributes is by strengthening teaching–research linkages (Brew, 2006; Healey, 2005). One promising way of enhancing teaching and research synergies at undergraduate level would involve making explicit to students not only what is known about a particular subject but how it has become known and what 'knowing a subject' means. This, in turn, implies helping students appreciate that knowledge in the subject itself is socially constructed and contested. Below I offer some observations about the difference between subjects and disciplines, suggesting that distinguishing between the two might be a useful way of moving this discussion forward.

The Distinction Between Subjects as 'What is Looked At' and Subjects as 'What is Looked Through and With'

Dorothy Sayers (1948), perhaps better known for her detective novels than for her thoughts on the purposes of education, once wrote a captivating essay provocatively entitled "The lost tools of learning". In her introduction, Sayers engages her readers with the following question:

> Do you often come across people for whom, all their lives, a 'subject' remains a 'subject', divided by watertight bulkheads from all other 'subjects', so that they experience very great difficulty in making an immediate mental connection between, let us say, algebra and detective fiction, sewage disposal and the price of salmon – or more generally, between such spheres of knowledge as philosophy and economics, or chemistry and art?
>
> (Sayers, 1948 in Burleigh, 1973, p. 235)

At the heart of Sayers' critique is her perception that formal education fails to acknowledge the need for a constant interplay between the context-specific and 'context-transcendent' aspects of learning. She asks: "Is not the great defect of our education today ... that although we often succeed in teaching our pupils a 'subject', we fail lamentably on the whole in teaching them how to think" (p. 238).

Sixty years have passed since Sayers's essay was first published, yet her remarks resonate with us as we continue to grapple with the question of whether our universities prepare students adequately for a "supercomplex" world (Barnett, 2000); a world that, at the very least, requires them to be able to continue learning after graduation, cope with uncertainty, and relate constructively to others in increasingly complex and diverse socio-cultural and political contexts.

Sayers' comments also hint at the possibility of a "unity of knowledge," the idea that the knowledge we acquire through the study of different fields allows us to develop a more integrated and hence enlightened understanding of the fundamental questions mankind is concerned with. While many of us feel that this unity got lost forever when university study became increasingly specialized (see Chapter 2), others feel that the very notion that such unity once existed is an illusion.

Inspired by Sayers' comments, I add below a few further remarks about the meaning of 'subjects' with the goal of laying the foundation for some of the arguments made in later chapters.

Surely, the term 'subject' can mean very different things. One might think of a 'subject', for example, as a 'topic' in a conversation, but this meaning is not really relevant here. More relevant meanings of 'subject' include: a) a theme or focal topic in a task, activity or project of limited duration; b) a curricular field of study delimited by a certain body of knowledge; c) a 'discipline', in a sense of not just a body of knowledge but a set of conceptual and methodological tools employed in creating and critiquing this knowledge. One might also, although this is less common, think of a 'subject' as d) a complex problem or real-life issue that could be studied from more than one conceptual and methodological perspective (this might include version a but could go beyond that). Sayers conceives of a subject in the senses of versions a and b; hence, in her essay she can easily distinguish between 'subjects' and 'disciplines'. For many readers, however, such a distinction would prove problematic for the reasons just mentioned. Many of us, including the contributors to this volume, tend to think of subjects as both a coherent body of knowledge in a particular field (version b) *and* as disciplines (version c), and often also as a theme (version a). However, being explicit about what we mean when we use the term 'subjects' is important because our underlying conception has implications for what we think is involved in teaching our subjects. To simplify the above definitions, we might say that, on the one hand, 'subjects' can refer to a *body of knowledge* or *knowledge product* that *we look at* (versions a and b) and, on the other hand, to a *disciplinary lens* that *we look with* and *through* (version c).

Let us assume, for the purpose of illustration, that the '*subject we look at*' is History, perhaps with a focus on Elizabethan England, for example. I may learn this 'subject' (versions a and b) principally through extensive reading, listening, visiting museums and memorizing what has happened during this period. Using these approaches, I certainly shall learn *a great deal* about what other people know and, hence, write or say about this epoch. However, I may not learn how these others came to know what they know, nor will I necessarily have developed any sense of informed judgment about the validity upon which my own claims to knowledge in this subject are based. Of course, I might approach my learning entirely differently.

I might look *at* this same 'subject' (versions a and b) *through* the ways of thinking and practicing that are characteristic of history, at least at a given point in time (version c). The 'subject' I'm studying, then, refers not only to '*what is looked at*' but also to '*what is looked through or with*'. My learning now is probably not only more focused but also much more systematic. If, in addition, the ways of thinking, the procedures and the practices employed are made *explicit* to me – to the extent that this is possible – I may more easily acquire the ability to apply the same thinking skills and practices to another 'subject' ('*what we look at*') in history.

As part of my studies, I probably do not only take courses in history but also, for example, a psychology course, a science course, a philosophy course, and so forth (although it should be noted that the undergraduate learning experience in the UK and Australia is much more specialized than in the US). If in each of these courses the particular disciplinary approaches that inform it ('*what we look through or with*') are made transparent to me (which, in some cases, will involve not just that

I am being *told* but that I am afforded opportunities to *observe* or *do*), it may become possible for me to eventually apply different lenses to the same 'subject' ('*what we look at*').

To stay with the subject of 'Elizabethan England' ('*what we look at*'), this could be studied also through the conceptual and methodological tools employed in English literature, art, politics, music or business, to mention but a few possibilities ('*what we look through or with*'). Importantly then, learning about the conceptual and methodological tools associated with particular subjects – or disciplines – ('*what we look through or with*') may allow me to apply what I have learned through the study of one 'subject' ('*what we look at*') to my learning of another ('*what we look at*'), thereby, over time, attaining a much deeper and richer understanding of the 'subjects' I'm studying (i.e., both *what we look at* and *what we look through or with*).

By learning the ways of thinking, the procedures and practices that are characteristic of particular subjects or disciplines (*what we look through or with*) in the context of a specific course or subject (*what we look at*), what I learn is at the same time context-specific and context-transcendent. Although I acquired the knowledge, practices, procedures and ways of thinking within the particular context of a certain topic or course, I will be able to employ these beyond the context in which I learned them. If, by contrast, my studies afforded only opportunity *to look at subjects* rather than *look through or with* them, my learning would be only context-specific, and, possibly, throughout my life "a 'subject' [would] remain[s] a 'subject', divided by watertight bulkheads from all other 'subjects'" (Sayers, 1948 in Burleigh, 1973, p. 235). The term 'context-transcendent' then has two meanings. Firstly, it refers to my learning having relevance beyond the specific subject content taught within a given course. To stay with the previous example, what I learned through the study of Elizabethan England will be helpful to me as I go on to study the Napoleonic wars. But secondly, it refers also to my learning having relevance beyond those topics typically explored through the particular disciplinary lens I was exposed to; that is, my learning is context-transcendent because I might apply the practices, procedures and ways of thinking learned within the particular context of one discipline or subject (e.g., history) to problems or issues not typically considered part of that discipline (e.g., intercultural relations).

A recent study I carried out with colleagues from the Centre of Teaching, Learning and Assessment at the University of Edinburgh explored the kinds of thinking processes faculty believed a particular undergraduate course they were teaching required of students. Below I feature three examples of responses we received to this question, respectively from a professor of English, law, and physics. The quotes are excerpts from interviews that were transcribed verbatim. They are particularly interesting in relation to the question of what aspects of learning are discipline-specific versus beyond the boundaries of a particular discipline. The first example is from a fourth year English course, where students were introduced to theoretical frameworks for text interpretation.

> Everything we talk about emerges from a text. So the sort of thinking processes would be those sorts of hermeneutic or analytical skills. What is this text doing? Sort of the engagement with the precision, the detail of the text itself. But I suppose the other skill would be the ability to extrapolate from the ideas of a particular text. Thinking about contemporary culture. So analysis and extrapolation and the sorts of skills of sensible debate.

The second example is from a law professor teaching a second year taxation course.

> It is assimilating information. It is sorting out the relevant from the irrelevant. It is the thinking through things in a logical process. The processes that your brain goes through in a legal problem – when you are talking about private law as opposed to some sort of philosophical course or something – are always the same. You need to know the law. You need to be able to look at a bunch of facts and sort out the relevant and the irrelevant and work out which bits of the law are relevant to that bit of the facts.

The third example is from a physics professor teaching a third year optics course.

> It is the classic physics. It's the analytical problem solving. It's setting up a problem, applying mathematics to a problem. Being able to look at a mathematical equation and not just see the symbols but see the underlying physics to it. I think all the physics is the same. Much of physics is this ability to be able to do the manipulation. And also when you have done the manipulation to know what you've just done, which is actually the really, really hard bit.

All three faculty members stress that the skills their specific course requires of students are characteristic of their particular discipline. Note word choices such as "Everything we talk about emerges from a text. So . . . hermeneutic or analytical skills," "The processes that your brain goes through in a legal problem are always the same," "It is the classic physics . . . all physics is the same". At the same time, all three emphasize critical thinking in the sense of using analytical skills.

Ramsden (1992) observes that faculty strongly endorse critical thinking and problem-solving as chief goals of higher education. Yet, he writes that these "gain their meaning through the specific subject content in which they are expressed" (p. 22). This means that the skills associated with critical thinking are learned in particular contexts, just as the above interview excerpts suggest. It is a *particular* English course, law course and physics course where analytical skills come to bear. Then again, as was argued earlier, some of the intellectual skills associated with critical thinking that students acquire through engagement with a particular subject (here English, law and physics) can also inform their academic learning in other subjects (see in particular Chapter 3 by Donald and Chapter 6 by Hounsell and Anderson in this volume).

Baxter Magolda (in Chapter 12) argues that "graduates must be able to translate their disciplinary learning into supercomplex, transdisciplinary contexts" (p. 152). In other words, students need to be able to apply their learning to 'subjects' in the real world (see version d of 'subject' introduced earlier). Being able to do this hinges on them having developed an awareness of *how they have come to know things* about any of the subjects they have studied at university. This also implies that they acquired a critical understanding of how disciplines are different and similar in how they approach particular problems. This is crucially important given that the real-life 'subjects' that students will need to confront after they graduate are complex – one might think of issues such as climate change, intercultural conflict resolution or health – calling for more than a single disciplinary lens but multiple lenses to inform them.

Similarly, Rowland (2006) argues for students being involved in learning that is characterized by dialogue across disciplinary boundaries, where they develop the capacity to challenge the ideological positions and assumptions (or here, 'ways of thinking and practicing') that underlie the different disciplinary perspectives they encounter.

Disciplines, or 'subjects' in the sense of '*what we think through*', are about distinct ways in which knowledge is created, interpreted, critiqued and applied. It is in this sense that they are the "tools of learning" (Sayers, 1948 in Burleigh, 1973, p. 239) that, at least in principle, can be applied to any subject (in a sense of '*what we look at*'). As already noted, making explicit the approaches characteristic of particular disciplinary communities, in many cases, will involve more than *telling*. For the purpose of illustration, let us, for a moment, revisit the quotes from the three professors featured earlier. The thinking processes they described as being critical for their students to master included "analysis and extrapolation and the sorts of skills of sensible debate", "knowing how to sort out the relevant from the irrelevant", "applying mathematics to a problem and knowing what you have done". It is doubtful that students would pick up these skills simply by being told – perhaps more to the point, what would you *tell* them? What does sorting out the relevant from the irrelevant mean, if I do not know what constitutes irrelevant material? What if I apply an algorithm accurately but do not know what I have done? What if I have no sense of the skills of a sensible debate? For students to acquire these complex skills and abilities, they need to be afforded opportunities to observe experienced others perform these tasks as well as of engaging in these tasks together with these experienced others. In the final section of this chapter I discuss what the latter implies for the practice of teaching.

Good Teaching as Connecting Students with our Subject

In his book *The courage to teach* Parker Palmer (1998) introduces the evocative notion of "teaching from the microcosm". By this he means that every academic discipline, be it philosophy, physics, nursing, accounting or music, can be taught by diving deeply into *particularity*, where the discipline's core ideas, concepts and ways of functioning can be practiced. This is achieved not by trying to tell students everything that is known about a given subject, but by bringing students into "the circle of practice in this field, into its version of the community of truth" (p. 122). The circle of practice is the disciplinary community with its particular ways of functioning. It is also a community of truth, as it applies its particular validation procedures to the issues explored.

Earlier I suggested that although there is little disagreement among members of the academy on what ought to be the goals of higher education, the latter are not necessarily always on our 'radar' while we teach our subjects, and that this might have implications for *how* we teach. Palmer describes what teaching looks like if the overarching purpose is for students to know in the end not only *what* they learned about a given subject but *how* they learned it, and why learning this subject *mattered*. Drawing on some interview data collected as part of a recent study as well as Baxter Magolda's idea of "learning partnership", I intend to capture the essence of what Palmer means when he argues that 'good university teaching' is neither teacher-centered nor student-centered but *subject-centered*.

If we were to take snapshots of all our observations of 'good university teaching' and arranged them side by side, what might strike us is the countless versions of what it is to be a good teacher. Indeed, Palmer (1998) observes that good teachers find a way of teaching that is integral to their own nature. However, the diversity that can be observed among good teachers does not mean that they do not have anything in common. When my colleagues and I explored with faculty from physics, English literature and law what in their view constitute the essential characteristics of 'good teachers', they all identified a love of the subject, deep knowledge of the discipline and caring for students. Their undergraduate students similarly considered these features important. Specifically, they commented that good teachers:

- have a depth of knowledge (physics student, age 28)
- are very knowledgeable and obviously very interested in their own subject (law student, age 34)
- are passionate about their subject (English student, age 22)
- made me feel like an equal (physics student, age 21)
- are prepared to give more time to students (law student, age 19)
- make students feel inclusive (English student, age 38).

However, students, more so than faculty, placed a strong emphasis also on the teacher's ability to engage them with the subject in meaningful ways. According to students, 'good teachers' also do the following:

- offer well-prepared and thought-out explanations (physics student, age 22)
- communicate clearly and effectively – even complex concepts (law student, age 18)
- engage with students (physics student, age 24)
- strongly encourage student participation (physics student, age 21),
- encourage new ideas and student dialogue (English student, age 22)
- try to understand what a novice finds difficult (physics student, age 20)

- show respect for students' ability – instill confidence (law student, age 20)
- encourage a healthy debate (law student, age 20)
- encourage you to think for yourself (law student, age 18)
- make an effort to include interesting and current examples that one can easily relate to (physics student, age 22)
- challenge my perceptions (English student, age 21)
- highlight controversy and encourage you to bring forth your opinions (law student, age 20)
- go beyond exam requirements by drawing connections between how the subject is applied in the real world (physics student, age 22).

The students' descriptions of what good teachers do offer insight into those moments in the classroom when students feel that their learning is supported: they are asked to participate, their thinking is engaged, they are treated as equals, their assumptions are challenged, they are asked to articulate their point of view, they are taken seriously, etc. The students' comments imply that although teachers' passion for their subject and caring for students make a difference to their learning, what seems to be critically important also are the teachers' ways of presenting the subject and connecting students with it. From the students' point of view, it seems that good teachers not only have deep knowledge of the subject they teach but they know how to build bridges between their own sophisticated understanding of the ideas under consideration and the students' present ways of meaning making. Northedge and McArthur (in Chapter 9 in this volume) speak of the importance of university teachers creating a state of *intersubjectivity* (or shared understanding) where students and teacher are involved in an act of mutual meaning-making. Barnett (2007) has something similar in mind when he recently introduced the notion of a *pedagogy for inspiration*. The students' comments also convey a sense of teachers demonstrating "empathic understanding" (Rogers, 1983), that is, the ability to step into the students' shoes and see the world from their perspective.

I already noted that Palmer (1998) argues that good teaching is a matter of teachers being true to themselves; however, he also suggests that it requires teachers to be true to their subject. The latter includes teaching the subject in an enthusiastic and engaged way, but it means more than that. Being true to the subject also means conveying what this subject, at its *core*, is about and *why it matters* to know about it. Good teaching, thus conceived, is characterized by "authenticity" (Kreber, Klampfleitner, McCune, Bayne & Knottenbelt, 2007). On a first level, teaching is authentic because it has the important interest of students at heart. On a second level, it is authentic because teachers convey how the subject *matters* in the real world, and possibly in their own lives. On a third level, it is authentic because learners become involved in "authentic conversations" or dialogue around significant or unresolved issues in relation to the subject and, thereby, in the process of knowledge construction leading them to understand the issues concerned in a new, and I might add, in their own way.

The *Learning Partnership Model* (see Baxter Magolda in Chapter 12) describes how undergraduate students can be supported in moving towards self-authorship, the latter referring not only to intellectual but also personal and interpersonal maturity. Likewise, Barnett (2000, 2007) argued that universities today need to prepare undergraduate students not only for 'knowing' and 'acting' but also, fundamentally, for 'being' in the world. Students need to develop an authentic identity from which to find their bearings within the multitude of often conflicting evidence, interests and demands they encounter in life.

Baxter Magolda (1992) suggests that in order to support students' development towards self-authorship, teaching needs to be characterized by the following three 'principles': students need to be validated in their own ability to know, learning needs to be situated within their own experience, and they need to be involved in mutual knowledge construction. The students' comments featured earlier suggest that good teachers are perceived to be practicing these principles.

As Baxter Magolda shows in Chapter 12, teaching that is based on these principles addresses the dimensions of intellectual, personal and interpersonal development, all critically important for preparing students for civic responsibility, lifelong learning and 'employability'. Specifically, students are supported in developing more complex ways of meaning making as they are offered opportunities to experience that knowledge in the particular subject is socially constructed. When learning is situated within their own experience, the process of knowledge construction is tightly interwoven with their construction of an internal identity. Not only the students' thinking but also their 'being' is engaged in the process. Mutual knowledge construction requires teachers and students to share expertise and authority in the learning process, equally the mark of mature and productive relationships in wider society.

Palmer and Baxter Magolda's ideas complement one another in that both enrich our understanding of the continuous interplay between context-specific and 'context-transcendent' learning. According to Palmer (1998), 'good teaching' is "neither teacher-centered nor student-centered but subject-centered" (p. 116). By 'teaching from the microcosm', good teachers connect students with the essence of the subject in such a way that the students see how the subject is learned and why learning this particular subject *matters* to their understanding of and interaction with the world around them. The subject then becomes important on two levels. On the first level, students learn much about the particular subject itself, acquiring not only content knowledge but also procedural knowledge. By approaching it from a particular disciplinary lens, they learn how to think within that subject, develop an argument, learn the concepts or core ideas that inform it, and the procedures used for dealing with problems that arise within the context of this subject. On the second level, they learn how this way of exploring a subject can be useful to them for their learning of other subjects, and hence, ultimately, for them dealing with "the formidable mass of undigested problems presented by the modern world" (Sayers, 1948, in Burleigh, 1973, p. 261).

Summary

Disciplines provide particular lenses or frameworks through which to explore, understand and act upon the world. They can be conceived of as "tools of learning" (Sayers, 1948, in Burleigh, 1973), each characterized by certain ways of thinking, procedures and practices that are characteristic of its community. If in each of the courses students take as part of their studies the disciplinary lenses employed are made explicit to them, and they are afforded opportunities to practice these, they may come to appreciate more easily how different disciplines are distinct and similar in how they function. Knowledge of how different disciplines function, that is, how they articulate a problem, investigate it and report on the outcomes, and knowledge of the values that guide their thinking and practicing, provides students with a wider repertoire of learning tools, which is clearly an advantage in a complex world.

However, being equipped with multiple "tools of learning" may not be sufficient a preparation for a world that is characterized also, increasingly, by *uncertainty* (Barnett, 2000, 2007). One might suggest that a university that hopes to prepare students adequately for supercomplexity and uncertainty would offer an undergraduate program that affords rich opportunities for students to be exposed to conflicting frames of reference. When dialogue around a particular problem is encouraged not only *within* but, importantly, *across* disciplinary boundaries, students can no longer stay within the comfort zone of one discipline and argue from only this particular discipline's point of view. Instead, the conflicting assumptions and ideologies underlying the 'ways of thinking and practicing' of the different disciplines involved in the dialogue (regarding how the problem is defined, how it is analyzed, what counts as evidence, etc) require students to question existing frames of reference and hence engage in serious critique and negotiation of their underlying assumptions (Rowland, 2006).

To deal with uncertainty students need to construct a secure identity, a way of being in the world, from which to navigate through the myriad of challenges distinctive of modern life. Issues such as intercultural conflict resolution or saving our planet require not only an ability to construct an argument but a capacity to choose from a series of often conflicting alternatives, to defend one's position and yet be prepared to revise it in light of new insights and contradicting evidence. Most fundamentally, they demand a disposition to bear the very fact that certainty, that is the perfect solution, may never be attainable.

My intent in this chapter has been to show how the university's larger goals, such as civic responsibility, lifelong learning and "employability", are consistent with the learning goals of regular academic programs and courses. The notion of "generic graduate attributes" (Barrie, 2006), that are interpreted and developed within the context of particular disciplines or subjects, is particularly useful in understanding this claim. Graduate attributes can be promoted by inviting students into the ways of thinking, the procedures and the practices of our disciplinary communities.

Undoubtedly, the various dimensions of diversity discussed at the beginning of this chapter make student involvement in these processes more difficult and the challenges this entails should not be ignored. Then again, diversity is also a resource for learning. The potential for students to experience profound changes in knowing and being, or transformative learning (Mezirow, 1991), is probably enhanced in environments where multiple rather than uniform perspectives are present.

This book provides insight into the interplay between the contextual and 'context-transcendent' aspects of teaching and learning. This opening chapter (and several of the chapters that follow) seeks to show how faculty can make a contribution towards the general goals of higher education, such as civic responsibility, lifelong learning and employability, through their discipline and, one might add, without compromising the academic integrity of the courses they teach. The subsequent chapter addresses the evolution of disciplines and departments within the modern university and, against this background, explores the contextual and context-transcendent nature of teaching and assessment.

Acknowledgments

Many thanks to Dai Hounsell and Mantz Yorke who kindly agreed to offer comments on an earlier draft of this chapter.

References

Aronowitz, S. (2000). *The knowledge factory: Dismantling the corporate university and creating true higher learning.* Boston, MA: Beacon Press.

Astin, A.W. (1977). *Four critical years: Effects of college on beliefs, attitudes, and knowledge.* San Francisco, CA: Jossey-Bass.

Barnett, R. (2000). Supercomplexity and the curriculum. *Studies in Higher Education,* 25(3), 255–265.

Barnett, R. (2007). *A will to learn.* Maidenhead, UK: Society for Research into Higher Education & Open University Press.

Barrie, S. (2006). Understanding What We Mean by the Generic Attributes of Graduates, *Higher Education,* 51(2), 215–241.

Baxter Magolda, M. B. (1992). *Knowing and Reasoning in College: Gender-related Patterns in Students' Intellectual Development.* San Francisco, CA: Jossey-Bass.

Baxter Magolda, M., & Terenzini, P.T. (1999). Learning and teaching in the 21st Century: Trends and implications for practice. (ERIC Document Reproduction Service No. ED430446) Retrieved November 7, 2007 from ERIC (Educational Resources Information Center database).

Boehm, A., Davis, T., Meares, D., & Pearce, D. (2002). *Global student mobility 2025: Forecasts of the global demand for international higher education.* Canberra: IDP Education Australia.

Brew, A. (2006). *Research and teaching. Beyond the Divide.* New York, NY: Palgrave Macmillan.

Chickering, A. (1970). Civil Liberties and the Experience of College. *The Journal of Higher Education,* 41(8), 599–606.

Colby, A., Ehrlich, T., Beaumont, E., & Stephens, J. (2003). *Educating citizens. Preparing America's undergraduates for lives of moral and civic responsibility.* The Carnegie Foundation for the Advancement of Teaching. San Francisco, CA: Jossey-Bass.

Dey, E.L., Astin, A.W., & Korn, W.S. (1991). The American freshman: Twenty-five year trends, 1966–1990. (ERIC Document Reproduction Service No. ED340325) Retrieved November 7, 2007 from ERIC (Educational Resources Information Center database).

DfES (2003). The future of higher education (White Paper). Norwich, UK. Ref No: 031853, Learning and Skills Development Agency.

Donald, J.G. (1997). *Improving the environment for learning*. San Francisco, CA: Jossey-Bass.

Healey, M. (2005). Linking research and teaching. Exploring disciplinary spaces and the role of inquiry-based learning. In R. Barnett (Ed.), *Reshaping the University: New Relationships between Research, Scholarship and Teaching* (pp. 67–78). Maidenhead, UK: McGraw-Hill/Open University Press.

Henderson-King, D., & Kaleta, A. (2000). Learning about social diversity: The undergraduate experience and intergroup tolerance. *The Journal of Higher Education*, 71(2), 142–164.

HESA (The Higher Education Statistics Agency) (2006). http://www.hesa.ac.uk Accessed November 7, 2007.

James, R. (2002). Students' changing expectations of higher education and the consequences of mismatches with reality. In OECD Report *Responding to students' expectations* (pp. 70–80). Paris, France: Head of OECD Publication Office.

Knapper, C., & Cropley, A. (2001). *Lifelong learning in higher education (3rd ed.)*. London, UK: Kogan Page.

Knight, P., & Yorke, M. (2003). *Assessment, Learning and Employability*. Maidenhead, UK: Society for Research in Higher Education and the Open University Press.

Kolb, D.A. (1981). Learning styles and disciplinary differences. In A. Chickering. (Ed.), *The modern American college* (pp. 232–255). San Francisco, CA: Jossey-Bass.

Kreber, C., Klampfleitner, M., McCune,V., Bayne, S., & Knottenbelt, M. (2007). What do you mean by 'authentic'? A comparative review of the literature on conceptions of authenticity. *Adult Education Quarterly*, 58(1), 22–43.

Levine, A., & Cureton, J.S. (1998). *When hope and fear collide: A portrait of today's college students*. San Francisco, CA: Jossey-Bass.

Mezirow, J. (1991). *Transformative dimensions of adult learning*. San Francisco, CA: Jossey-Bass.

NSLC (2007). National Service Learning Clearinghouse http://www.servicelearning.org/ Accessed November 6, 2007.

Nussbaum, M. (1997). *Cultivating humanity: A classical defense of reform in liberal education*. Cambridge, MA: Harvard University, Cahners Publishing.

Palmer, P. (1998). *The courage to teach. Exploring the inner landscape of a teacher's life*. San Francisco, CA: Jossey-Bass.

Pascarella, E.T., & Terenzini, P. (1991). *How college affects students*. San Francisco, CA: Jossey-Bass.

Quality Assurance Agency (2006). Research-Teaching Linkages: Graduate attributes. http://www.enhancementthemes.ac.uk/themes/ResearchTeaching/attributes.asp/ Accessed November 7, 2007.

Ramsden, P. (1992). *Learning to teach in higher education*. New York, NY: Routledge.

Rhoads, R.A., & Howard, J.P.F. (Eds.) (1998). *Academic Service Learning: A pedagogy of Action and Reflection*. San Francisco, CA: Jossey-Bass.

Rogers, C. (1983). *Freedom to learn for the 80s*. Columbus, OH: Charles E. Merrill Publishing Company.

Rowland, S. (2006). *The enquiring university. Compliance and contestation in higher education*. Maidenhead: Society for Research into Higher Education and Open University Press.

Sayers, D.L. (1948). The lost tools of learning. Reprinted (with original date) in A.H. Burleigh (Ed.), *Education for a free society* (pp. 229–265). Indianapolis, IN: Liberty Press, 1973.

Teichler, U. (1999). Higher education policy and the world of work: Changing conditions and challenges. *Higher Education Policy*, 12, 285–312.

UNESCO (1998). Higher education in the twenty-first century. Vision and action. *Volume I, Final Report*. World Conference on Higher Education. Paris: UNESCO Publishing.

University of Washington (2004). Inclusive Teaching. http://depts.washington.edu/cidrweb/inclusive/ Accessed November 7, 2007.

2

The Modern Research University and its Disciplines

The Interplay between Contextual and Context-transcendent Influences on Teaching

Carolin Kreber

University of Edinburgh

> The 1880s and 1890s saw the emergence of a variety of new disciplines within the university, and an increasing development, both in new and in older disciplines, of "vernaculars"—their own specialized jargons, closely linked to favored bodies of material, kinds of questions asked and methods employed.
>
> (Damrosch, 1995, p. 23)

Introduction

Disciplines pervade academic life. One might think of the learned societies we belong to, the academic journals we read, the conferences we attend, the courses we teach and the colleagues we choose to collaborate or communicate with about our work. Disciplines frequently provide the basis for how academic departments are organized and they tend to manifest themselves in the ways in which departments and offices are adorned; that is in the artifacts and symbols that can be observed there, which are readily understood by other members of the disciplinary community.

Given the profound role that disciplines play in our academic lives, it seems intuitive to deduce that they should exert a strong influence also on teaching, learning and assessment; not only in terms of what we teach and assess but in terms of how we teach it, how students learn it, and how their learning is evaluated. Indeed, Trowler (Chapter 15) argues that faculty feel strongly that their discipline plays a profound role in university pedagogy. Marincovich and Prostko (2005) make a similar point when they remark that most academics "are probably comfortable with the notion that their disciplinary background deeply influences not only what they teach but how they teach" (p. 1).

This strong sense that discipline *matters* to academics is reflected also in calls to combine generic provision of educational development with local or discipline-specific initiatives (e.g., Gibbs, 1996; Jenkins, 1996). It further underlies the disciplinary focus taken by national organizations and private foundations that support teaching and learning. For example, the recently created *Carrick Institute for Teaching and Learning* in Australia, the *Higher Education Academy* in the UK (through its twenty-four subject centers) and the *Carnegie Academy for the Scholarship of Teaching and Learning* (part of the Carnegie Foundation for the Advancement of Teaching) in the United States encourage faculty to explore teaching and learning within their own disciplinary contexts. These initiatives are responses to a growing recognition that the generic approaches characterizing educational development since the 1970s were perhaps too one-sided to adequately address the complexities of teaching and learning across different academic fields.

Today the debate no longer focuses on whether or not disciplinary perspectives need to be taken into account in the provision of support for teaching but on the extent to which a balance needs to be achieved between "generic" and "discipline-specific" educational development opportunities (Grace, Smith, Bradford & Elvidge, 2004; Jenkins 1996). These deliberations, in turn, are reflective of the wider debate around the possible drawbacks of too much specialization in the undergraduate curriculum (e.g., Axelrod, 2002). The latter, in particular, may be best appreciated by looking back to how the university evolved from an institution once perceived to reflect the unity of knowledge to one that is seemingly characterized by ever-growing fragmentation of knowledge.

This chapter offers some observations on the nature of "academic disciplines": how they are defined, how they have evolved over time, and what is known about their similarities and differences. Knowledge of commonalities and differences among academic disciplines are often based on typologies that classify them in terms of their underlying epistemological structure. Focusing on Biglan's (1973a) typology of "pure versus applied" and "hard versus soft" fields, I discuss some problems with typologies of this kind, thereby paving the way for the issues addressed in this book. Towards the end of the chapter I argue that university teaching and learning is enriched by opening up our disciplinary "silos" to more frequent cross-disciplinary encounters, highlighting, in particular, the promise of the scholarship of teaching and learning in effectively promoting these exchanges. While the main theme running through the previous chapter was the continuous interplay between the context-specific and context-transcendent aspects of *learning*, this chapter continues the discussion with a focus on *teaching*. Specifically, I explore to what extent disciplinary structure can be assumed to explain particular tendencies in the teaching and assessment practices that can be observed in departments.

From Unity to Specialization

Disciplines have characterized higher learning since the founding of the first universities in the Middle Ages. Higher education in the medieval world was strongly influenced by the Roman educational heritage and emphasized the seven liberal arts (Axelrod, 2002). This meant that in the early universities there was an expectation that students first needed to demonstrate proficiency in grammar, dialectic and rhetoric (the *trivium*) before they continued with the study of the mathematically based disciplines arithmetic, geometry, music and astronomy (the *quadrivium*).

Grammar in the medieval world meant the study of the structure of languages, which, in essence, referred to learning Latin but also Greek. Dialectic was concerned with how to structure an argument and detect inconsistencies or flaws in a line of reasoning. Rhetoric involved learning how to express oneself elegantly and persuasively through language. It is easy to see how proficiency in the *trivium* would have provided the basic skills, or "tools of learning" (Sayers, 1948 in Burleigh, 1973, p. 239), that facilitated the study of other "disciplines."

Upon successful study of both the *trivium* and *quadrivium* students obtained a Bachelor of *Arts* degree and were free to pursue further learning in the superior faculties of theology, medicine and law.

By the end of the Middle Ages liberal education was firmly rooted in Christian theology but was also still influenced by the Greek tradition. "Philosophy" (moral philosophy, metaphysics, and natural philosophy) was strongly shaped by the power of the church. The university curriculum of the Renaissance continued to be characterized largely by tensions between theological or scholastic-based higher learning and the spirit of critical inquiry associated with the philosophical "humanistic" tradition, and these tensions continued well into the nineteenth century (Axelrod, 2002).

During the Enlightenment, some universities (particularly in Scotland) opened their doors to new philosophical ways of thinking and philosophy developed gradually into a discipline distinct from theology. Natural philosophy, now less dependent on church approval, eventually split into various natural science disciplines. The University of Cambridge, for example, formally recognized chemistry as an academic discipline only in 1702 (Archer and Haley, 2005), although it was practiced there much earlier.

The late nineteenth and early twentieth century witnessed the evolution of the social sciences that became established as academic disciplines (e.g., political sciences, sociology, linguistics, etc.) and many humanities disciplines (e.g., modern literature and cultural studies, creative writing, ethics, etc.) and professional fields (e.g., agriculture, engineering, business, etc.) followed or became more specialized.

Universities prior to the nineteenth century, and in some cases well into the twentieth century, were largely teaching institutions that prepared students for their later professional or vocational roles. The evolution of the modern university with its dual function of teaching and research is often attributed to Wilhelm von Humboldt, a Prussian (German) diplomat and Minister of Education in the first part of the nineteenth century. In 1810, von Humboldt formulated his vision for the new University of Berlin (an institution eventually named after him), suggesting that universities have two main roles: to teach and to pursue science.

Two hundred years later we tend to take this dual function for granted, particularly those of us who work in institutions whose public funding depends on them making visible contributions to the advancement of knowledge. In the early 1800s, however, von Humboldt's vision was revolutionary. The extent to which this was the case can be appreciated only by looking back even further in time.

Since the Thirty Years War (1618–1648), which had shattered large parts of Europe, a more secular and practical orientation had become characteristic of the German *Zeitgeist*, which, in turn, had led to wide-spread contempt for the humanistic and non-utilitarian curricula of earlier universities (Altbach, 1991). In the seventeenth and eighteenth centuries the old universities were then complemented by new institutions, so-called *Berufsakademien*, whose principal function was to train individuals for work-related roles. Von Humboldt was highly critical of the traditional older German universities as well as the newer academies, which he considered to be mere instruments of the state. He had a very different vision of the role a university ought to play in society.

It is vital to point out that for von Humboldt the idea of research, or rather science, was not confined to what we now call the "natural sciences," the latter being divorced from the humanities. Instead *science* (as a weak translation of the German word *Wissenschaft*) meant scientific and academic knowledge in general and was seen to encompass all areas of human learning. He suggested that a university education should strive towards the fulfillment of an ideal of *Bildung*, a lifelong process of learning and development aimed at the cultivation of an individual's intellectual and moral potential.

Importantly, it should do so by teaching university subjects through free *scientific* inquiry (Lilge, 1948). The freedom to teach (*Lehrfreiheit*) and the freedom to learn (*Lernfreiheit*), without state intervention, was, therefore, a critical aspect of von Humboldt's vision. University education should take the form of professors and students engaging in free scientific inquiry, or research, together in the pursuit of new knowledge. Indeed, von Humboldt suggested that "It is further a peculiarity of the institutions of higher learning that they treat higher learning always in terms of not yet completely solved problems, remaining always in a research mode (i.e. being engaged in an unceasing process of inquiry)" (quoted in Elton, 2001, p. 44).

While von Humboldt considered scholarship and scientific specialization important in universities, he argued, at the same time, for an integration of the research results into a general framework of humanistic values. He strongly advocated the view that universities should provide a liberal education as well as specialization, and that both were essential for the development of an enlightened and humane as well as civilized and productive society.

Von Humboldt's views on the purposes of a university are often contrasted with those articulated by John Henry Newman (1801–1890), an English scholar and clergyman who had a considerable influence on higher education in the Anglo-Saxon world. Nonetheless, von Humboldt and Newman (1982) would have agreed that universities should be places that cultivate the intellect and offer opportunities for learning for its own end rather than for career preparation. However, whereas Newman held firmly that teaching and the advancement of knowledge were two distinct functions and made a case for the exclusion of research and the professional schools from the university, von Humboldt perceived the integration of teaching and research as essential to the purposes of a university.

Abraham Flexner, a North American educational reformer and founder of The Institute of Advanced Study at Princeton, visited Germany in the early twentieth century, where the by then well-established German research university system made a profound impression on him. Flexner endorsed von Humboldt's notion of the importance of research being carried out within universities and also sympathized with Newman's view that intellectual inquiry and not practical training was the university's main purpose (Flexner, 1930). Then again, his ideal vision of the university was grounded in the notion of research institutes, to be created within universities, where undergraduate students had no place but where professors and a few select (post)graduate students would engage in highly specialized inquiry. Despite this emphasis on specialized study, he shared with Humboldt the perspective that there needed to be a balance between academic specialization and the idea of unity of all scientific endeavors. It was in this spirit that he saw it as a key characteristic of The Institute of Advanced Study that it promoted intellectual exchange across disciplinary boundaries (Wittrock, 2002).

Since World War II further specialization within academic fields has become typical of universities as traditional fields have split into numerous sub-disciplines and many new disciplines emerged (e.g., accounting, journalism, computer science, film studies, oceanography, etc.). Presumably, this ever-growing specialization is unstoppable. American scholar David Damrosch (1995) argued that this specialization into multiple disciplines and their sub-disciplines created a disciplinary territorialism and parochialism that violates the traditional idea of the university as a broad "community of inquirers" as upheld by von Humboldt and others. He observed that "the present state of advanced specialization is such that one person cannot master more than a small handful of fields even in a single discipline, still less do really meaningful work across more than two or three disciplines" (Damrosch, 1995, p. 15).

Indeed, by the early 1960s the very idea of a *uni*-versity was challenged by Clark Kerr, then Chancellor of the University of California at Berkeley, who introduced the notion of the "*multiversity*." In his now classic text *The Uses of the University*, Kerr (1963) observed that in contrast to earlier periods, the modern research university had to serve multiple purposes and functions and the traditional notion of a university grounded in the ideal of a unity of knowledge could no longer be realized in the contemporary world. Indeed, Kerr is frequently cited as having referred to the research university of the mid-twentieth century as "a series of individual faculty entrepreneurs held together by a common grievance over parking" (p. 15).

The ever-growing specialization of knowledge and resulting fragmentation of academic communities was observed also by Burton Clark (1963), who noted that academics identify much less with the institution they are part of than with their discipline and there is little communication across departments, including those located within the same building. Tony Becher (1989) eventually employed the term "academic tribes" to refer to the creation of academic subcultures based on increasingly specialized domains of knowledge and modes of enquiry. Specifically, Becher argued that disciplinary communities are distinguished by an array of characteristics such as their "traditions, customs and practices, transmitted knowledge, beliefs, morals and rules of conduct, as well as their linguistic and symbolic forms of communication and the meanings they share" (p. 24).

Given that academic disciplines have evolved drastically in terms of numbers and degree of specialization, it is timely to ask what, if anything, do we know about the disciplines now represented within the academy and the similarities and differences between them?

The Nature of 'Disciplines' and What We have Come to Understand about Them

How might one conceive of a "discipline"? Donald (1995) observed that "the method by which knowledge is arrived at in a discipline, the process of knowledge validation, and the truth criteria employed in that process are essential to the definition of a discipline" (p. 6). In a more philosophical discussion, Winchester (1986) illustrated how complex and challenging the task of identifying the key defining features of academic disciplines can be. The first defining feature, he began, is that they are both continuous yet changing through time; yet, the extent to which this is the case varies by discipline. A further defining feature, he continued, is their mutual independence. However, with respect to this second feature, Winchester immediately cautioned that the claim could not really be upheld given the extent to which disciplines also inform one another. For example: mathematics clearly informs physics; both grammar and dialectic inform rhetoric; and all the liberal subjects actually inform law, theology and medicine. Nonetheless, some disciplines, one might think of dance or representational painting, tend to be indeed rather independent of the disciplines just mentioned. Hence, the idea that they are mutually independent doesn't hold up as a defining feature across *all* disciplines.

Winchester went on to suggest that disciplines are based on an organized body of facts and theories which are treated as true. Many disciplines, such as history, mathematics or physics, are characterized by speculation and there is always some control of that speculation. This point is similar to Donald's (1995) finding that disciplines are characterized by certain "truth criteria by which propositions are assessed and the methodology employed to produce the propositions" (p. 6).

Winchester (1986) further proposed that each knowledge-based discipline "has, besides characteristic subject matter, definite methods of control" and "the methods of control for a discipline appear to be connected with the presuppositions of an era or an epoch" (p. 184) that are shared and usually unconscious. The methods of control that are acceptable in one era may change over time. This latter observation is perhaps best illustrated by Hounsell and Anderson in Chapter 6, where the authors acknowledge that the "ways of thinking and practicing" (WTP) in history, for example, change or evolve over time. Disciplines, therefore, are organic entities and defining their commonalities and differences appears to be at best challenging and at worst impossible.

Winchester drew an important distinction between disciplines that are based on knowledge that is primarily "sayable" (for example philosophy) and those based on knowledge that is primarily "showable" (for example classical dance or violin playing). Providing a rationale for why such a distinction should concern us at all, he observed:

> In reviving Wittgenstein's distinction between the sayable and showable in the case of disciplines such as dance, I do not mean to suggest that there is an absolute cleavage here such as he developed in the *Tractatus*. Nor do I think that the realm of the showable is a mystical or transcendent realm. I am thinking rather of the question "*How would you teach it?*" [emphasis added] as being an important one for distinguishing among kinds of disciplines.
>
> (p. 180)

He then suggested that the answer in some disciplines may be to "tell them [the students] all about it and see whether they can carry on the discussion," in others to "tell them some things and show them others," and again in others to "show them how to do it and say nothing" (p. 180). In practice the first and the last scenario would rarely exist and "it is rather the emphasis or dominance of saying over showing or vice versa which tends to make a discipline more like dance or Zen Buddhism than like physics or literary criticism" (p. 180).

Although the conclusion may strike one as somewhat simplistic, it does highlight the possibility that academic disciplines, due to the specific bodies of knowledge and methods of inquiry they represent, invite certain pedagogies. It further raises awareness of the fact that particular disciplines are defined not only by certain forms or bodies of *knowledge* but also certain *practices*. Most importantly perhaps, by drawing attention to the distinction between that which is and that which is not "sayable," Winchester, without stating it explicitly, encourages us to consider the idea that there might be aspects of knowledge that are "not sayable" also within the so-called "knowledge-based" disciplines (such as philosophy, history, etc.). However, as we saw earlier, commenting on the methods of control for a discipline, Winchester did note that they are based on presuppositions that are usually unconscious (which, of course, implies "not sayable").

Becher (1989), in this context, makes reference to the importance of tacit knowledge that students develop as they become socialized into a discipline. The notion of "tacit knowledge" is typically associated with Polanyi (1966) and refers to the phenomenon that "we know more than we can tell." According to Becher the most important aspect of tacit knowledge that students need to acquire over the course of their education is command of the repertoire of scientific discourses, such as being able to distinguish relevant contributions from irrelevant ones and good arguments from not so strong ones. Importantly, the notion of tacit knowledge also extends to the values that are guiding particular disciplines, and as students progress through their programs their task is to internalize these.

The challenges associated with helping students learn the tacit aspects of a discipline will concern us in greater detail later, in particular in the chapters by Hounsell and Anderson (Chapter 6) and Northedge and McArthur (Chapter 9). As Reimann and Pace acknowledge in their chapters (Chapters 7 and 8), it is typically not easy for faculty to make their taken-for-granted assumptions explicit. And yet, as was argued previously, being made aware of how disciplines function, and how they are different from and similar to others, is empowering to students. It is empowering in that it enhances their capacity to tackle new problems independently, and possibly, if introduced to more than one discipline during the course of their studies, from a variety of disciplinary lenses.

Typologies and Their Limitations

The study of academic disciplines, more precisely the differences and commonalities among them and the implications these entail for teaching and learning in university settings, have concerned researchers for some time. In the early 1970s, Anthony Biglan (1973a) carried out a study that investigated faculty's own judgments of the similarities and differences between several academic fields. He classified these perceptions according to three dimensions: "hard versus soft" (or "paradigmatic versus non-paradigmatic"); "applied versus pure"; and "concerned with life systems versus concerned with non-life systems".

In keeping with this framework the natural sciences would qualify as hard and pure, but may be concerned with either life systems or non-life systems. The social sciences would qualify as soft since they do not subscribe to a unifying paradigm or a fixed body of theory that all members in the field agree on, but may be either pure or applied, and concerned with non-life or with life-systems. The humanities would meet the criteria as soft, pure and concerned with non-life systems. Within the professional areas, civil engineering, for example, would be seen as hard, applied, and concerned with non-life systems and education as soft, applied and concerned with life systems.

As Trowler explains in greater detail (Chapter 15), disciplines can be classified in terms of a cognitive and a social dimension. While Biglan's typology focuses on the disciplines' *cognitive dimension*, it was Becher (1989) who called attention to their *social dimension* (i.e., whether they are "convergent" versus "divergent" and "urban" versus "rural"). Together, the cognitive and social dimensions describe the discipline's epistemological structure.

It was, in particular, Biglan's typology of academic disciplines (specifically the distinction between soft/hard and pure/applied fields) that served as a highly influential framework for further studies on disciplinary differences. Numerous studies explored whether the cognitive dimension of the disciplines' epistemological structure might explain certain aspects of teaching and learning, focusing, for example, on learning style (Kolb, 1981), research–teaching linkages (Smeby, 1998), knowledge validation procedures (Donald, 1995), concepts to be taught (Donald, 2002; Hativa, 1995), attitudes towards teaching (Biglan, 1973b), goals of undergraduate education (Smart & Ethington, 1995), teaching practices (Murray & Renaud, 1995; Neumann, 2001; Smeby, 1996) or engagement in reflective practice on teaching (Kreber & Castleden, 2008).

Despite some important insights that these studies have generated there has been growing skepticism in more recent years with respect to the broad generalizations drawn on the basis of the soft–hard and pure–applied framework suggested by Biglan and his followers. This skepticism is rooted in several arguments.

Ignores the Need for Transdisciplinarity

The first reason why such typologies are increasingly questioned is based on the observation that many academic fields now transcend traditional disciplinary boundaries. One might think of interdisciplinary fields such as evolutionary psychology, mathematical physics, urban studies or neural engineering, where the boundaries of "soft versus hard" and "pure versus applied" become blurred. Linked to this is the perception that the nature of knowledge production has been changing into one that is not determined by disciplinary structure ("Mode 1") but is increasingly "transdisciplinary" ("Mode 2") (e.g., Nowotny, Scott & Gibbons, 2001).

"Transdisciplinarity" refers to research that is directed at problems that go beyond, or transcend, the boundaries of particular disciplines. In this "Mode 2" form of knowledge production, knowledge is seen to originate not in disciplinary problems but within the framework of real life application where solutions are required for complex problems, demanding different forms of expertise and skill sets than those typically associated with academic study of a particular discipline. The application of knowledge is as important as its production, and knowledge is interdisciplinary.

The implication for higher education is that unless institutions pay closer attention also to "Mode 2" knowledge production, students may not be adequately prepared for the demands of the modern knowledge society. According to this perspective, identifying the cognitive structure of individual disciplines (i.e., whether they are "pure versus applied" or "soft versus hard") has little to offer by way of guidance for the development of university curricula that are relevant in the twenty-first century.

Ignores the Importance of Faculty's and Students' own Interpretations of their Discipline

The second reason why typologies like Biglan's are questioned is that grouping disciplines *a priori* as either "soft or hard" and "pure or applied" is seen to ignore how faculty or students *themselves* understand their discipline. People's own interpretation of their discipline, so the argument goes, is the really critical variable if the goal is to better understand why people teach and learn the way they do. While this line of reasoning makes sense, it should be noted that the two approaches do not necessarily yield conflicting results. This latter claim is demonstrated by comparing the results of two recent studies.

In the first study, Prosser and colleagues reported relationships between faculty's subjective experience of their subject and their conceptions of teaching (Prosser, Martin, Trigwell, Ramsden & Lueckenhausen, 2005). In the second study, Lindblom-Ylänne and colleagues observed linkages between conceptions of teaching and epistemological structure, this time, however, faculty were grouped based on Biglan's (1973a) categories (Lindblom-Ylänne, Trigwell, Nevgi & Ashwin, 2006). In both studies, conceptions of teaching (or relatedly approaches to teaching) characterized by conceptual change beliefs (i.e., teaching seen as a process that promotes conceptual changes in students' understanding of the subject matter) were found to be stronger with academics in the humanities and social sciences, that is in the so-called "soft disciplines."

Findings are Based on Overgeneralisations

The third reason why typologies are subject to criticism relates to how the findings from studies based on such frameworks have been interpreted. In other words, critics question the meaning and implications of the results.

For example, if certain methods for evaluating student learning have been found to be associated with certain disciplines (e.g., Neumann, 2001), does this necessarily mean that it is the epistemological structure of the discipline that determined these practices or do other factors come into play? Is chemistry taught differently from English literature because the one is hard (and convergent) and the other soft (and divergent), or have these disciplines developed certain teaching and assessment practices due to other, perhaps less well understood reasons, for example, how they choose to define themselves? Moreover, can it be assumed that the same discipline is taught similarly across different departmental contexts and, if so, is this "signature pedagogy" (Shulman, 2004) the result of epistemological structure or of tradition? Most generally, critics ask to what extent contextual factors other than epistemological structure are being considered when findings from these studies are interpreted. I explore this issue a bit further.

In order to better understand why certain teaching and assessment practices evolve, and how and why they are retained, it is important to take into account not only the epistemological structure of the discipline but also the institutional or departmental culture within which these practices are located. The context for teaching is then defined not only by the epistemological structure of the discipline and the conventions of the disciplinary community to which faculty members belong, but also the department with its own conventions and practices (e.g., Becher, 1989; Becher & Trowler, 2001). The extent to which the department is perceived to value good teaching has been shown to be linked to how faculty approach their teaching (Prosser & Trigwell, 1999).

However, although both the disciplinary and departmental context likely exert an influence on the ways in which faculty approach teaching and assessment, individual teachers' "personal theories of teaching" as well as their perceptions of self, surely also play a significant role. "Personal theories of teaching" refer to how we conceptualize teaching and learning (e.g., do we think of teaching as transmission of information and of learning as accumulation of facts, or do we think of teaching as promoting conceptual change and of learning as a transformative process possibly leading to the creation of knowledge?). Perceptions of self refer to our self-concept and the degree of self-efficacy (Bandura, 1995) we experience with regard to our role as teachers. It has been suggested that the ways in which teachers define themselves, that is the identity they construct as teachers, is the result of the dynamic interaction between personal theories of teaching and perceptions of self, both shaped by (or further interacting with) the *social* (here disciplinary) and *occupational context* (here departmental) (Little, 1993; Zeichner, Tabachnik & Denmore, 1987).

One surely would assume that teacher identities are constructed also in interaction with many other factors (e.g., past and present learning experiences, observations of past teachers, and how one is uniquely positioned, within the department but also the wider society, in terms of the intersection of numerous other socio-cultural factors, including race, ethnicity, age, SES, religion, gender, sexuality, etc.). However, the point of this discussion is to show that neither departmental culture nor disciplinary context straightforwardly *determine* teaching and assessment practices; rather the practices that can be observed among individual teachers within departments are likely influenced by many additional factors mediated by both departmental culture and discipline. In his chapter in this volume, Trowler suggests that the teaching and assessment practices that can be observed within departments are rooted in so-called "Teaching and Learning Regimes," the latter referring to a constellation of rules, assumptions, practices and relationships that describe the local culture within the department.

To what extent, one might then ask, is teaching context-specific? The response to this question depends, not least, on what one means by "context." For example, it is far from clear that the epistemological structure of the discipline has quite as strong an influence on teaching and assessment practices as some studies try to make us believe. Moreover, even if context is defined by departmental and disciplinary culture as well as epistemological structure, there are many other mediating factors, such as individual teachers' identities (or subjectivities), that will exert an influence (and, one may argue, reconstitute the context as such). On the other hand, it would be very hard to argue that teaching and assessment practices are not contextualized. These considerations invite serious questions about whether the reluctance that can, at times, be observed among departments to look beyond their own immediate teaching and assessment "silos" is justified and about the potential of opening these up through exchanges of practices across disciplinary and departmental boundaries.

Prevent Innovation by Reinforcing Disciplinary and Departmental Silos

The fourth reason why a growing number of people have become skeptical towards typologies of the Biglan kind is that they tend to set boundaries for what is perceived to be possible. Once disciplines have been defined and described in certain ways, it becomes even more difficult to break away from entrenched practices or traditions and engage in innovations in teaching. This latter point, in particular, is taken up by Matthew and Pritchard in Chapter 5.

Transcending Disciplinary Teaching Silos through Cross-disciplinary Encounters

Huber and Hutchings (2005) observed that faculty today need to be better prepared "to meet the challenges of educating students for personal, professional and civic life in the twenty-first century" (p. x). Specifically, they argued that drastic changes in the learning environments over the past decade (e.g., types of students entering university, content to be taught, advances in technology) not only *invite* pedagogical inquiry but make it a necessity. As a consequence, the authors concluded, "the scholarship of teaching and learning is an imperative today, not a choice" (p. 13).

I already noted that national organizations and private foundations such as the Higher Education Academy in the UK, the Carrick Institute in Australia, and the Carnegie Foundation for the Advancement of Teaching in the US, offer a range of initiatives intended to support teaching and learning with a focus on particular subject areas. The Carnegie Academy for the Scholarship of Teaching and Learning (CASTL) supports faculty from different disciplines in engaging in systematic inquiry into how their own subject is best learned and taught. Exploring how certain subjects are best learned, and thereby identifying the concepts that tend to cause students difficulty, helps participants to construct "pedagogical content knowledge" (Shulman, 1987). Shulman defined the latter as the "blending of content and pedagogy into an understanding of how particular topics, problems or issues are organized, represented, and adapted to the diverse interests and abilities of learners, and presented for instruction" (p. 4). Reflection on pedagogical content knowledge encourages faculty to explore why, within their own departments, teaching is approached in a particular way.

Upon analyzing the *questions* particular disciplines ask about teaching and learning, and the *methodological approaches* they employ in their investigations, Huber and Morreale (2002) identified distinct "disciplinary styles" in the scholarship of teaching and learning. They argued that these styles can be very valuable in answering particular questions about pedagogy; however, they also suggested that our knowledge of university teaching and learning could be usefully extended, and the disciplines themselves enlightened, if these questions and methods, as well as the resulting insights and innovations, were shared and traded across disciplinary boundaries.

Several years earlier, Hutchings and Shulman (1999) had suggested that the scholarship of teaching may not only address questions such as "will this method lead to better learning?", but also those that are aimed at describing, and thereby more fully understanding, teaching and learning phenomena. They proposed that the latter type of question would address problems such as "what does it look like when a student begins to think with a concept rather than simply about it?" (p. 5). While one may think of the first type of question as being *instrumental* in nature inviting hypothetical-analytic approaches establishing cause–effect relationships, the second type qualifies as *communicative* and is based on hermeneutical and interpretive approaches. The scholarship of teaching, then, was seen to invite both instrumental and communicative inquiry, and I had added that it furthermore called for critical or *emancipatory* investigations (Kreber, 2005). However, others have argued that learning about teaching is, in essence, communicative in nature, and only very rarely instrumental, and that this is the case regardless of the nature of the discipline itself (e.g., Cranton, 1998; Cross, 1998). Importantly, as we have seen, instrumental and communicative approaches invite very different kinds of questions to be asked. Communicative learning, however, might pose a significant challenge to colleagues in disciplines where more instrumental ways of inquiry are dominant (Healey, 2000). Brew (2006), for example, recently argued that "engaging in the scholarship of teaching and learning means confronting ideas about the nature of knowledge" (p. 121) and contended that "in the hard sciences reflective practice in relation to teaching is not the norm" (p. 105).

It appears then that there are some tensions between encouraging the disciplines to develop their own styles of pedagogical inquiry (leading to certain innovations and, hence, teaching practices) and observations that these "disciplinary styles" might delimit the focus and scope of the scholarship of teaching and learning.

The goal of the scholarship of teaching and learning is essentially to promote reflective practice on teaching and communicating the resulting insights to others (Kreber & Cranton, 2000). Given drastic changes in the higher education environment (see Chapter 1), Elton (2000) suggested that faculty and institutions striving to improve their practice need to focus less on "doing things better" and more on "doing better things." In other words, reflection that is targeted exclusively at improving traditional teaching and assessment practices, which may no longer be meaningful in a system of mass education—let alone a world that requires students to achieve complex abilities, skills sets and dispositions—is no longer seen as adequate by itself. What becomes increasingly important, therefore, is reflection that focuses on "doing better things," the latter involving *critically* reflecting upon why certain practices continue to characterize our teaching and assessment and considering alternatives (Kreber, 2007). While a concern with "doing things better" invites questions that can be adequately explored through instrumental approaches, a concern with "doing better things" invites questions that call for communicative and emancipatory approaches to inquiry (Kreber, 2005).

An issue that educational developers continue to grapple with is how to facilitate the process of reflection, particularly *critical* reflection, on practice. Commenting on this problem, Kahn (2007) suggested that educational development activities should intentionally encourage dialogue among faculty and target specific reflective processes. Pickering (2006) proposed that critical reflection on teaching practice is best supported when faculty are afforded the opportunity to interact with colleagues from the same or similar disciplines, as it is there that questions of what is "possible and plausible within specific contexts" (p. 332) are best interrogated.

It clearly is the case that learning about teaching, like learning in any other professional field, is "situated" (Eraut, 2000; Wenger, 1998), and this "situatedness" calls for discipline-specific support. However, it is also true that our teaching and assessment practices, to a large extent, are rooted in core assumptions that we hold about how our subjects ought to be taught. These assumptions, although shared among the members of our disciplinary or departmental communities, are not necessarily obvious to us. Instead, they often remain "tacit" (Polanyi, 1966); that is, they float beneath the surface although they guide our behavior and decision-making. The fact that these assumptions are tacit does not make them wrong or unsound; however, their tacit nature makes it harder to subject them to critical reflection on their validity.

Tacit assumptions we hold about teaching, learning and assessment are likely brought to the surface more easily if we engage in communication not only with like-minded colleagues from our own department but also with colleagues from a wide range of other disciplinary cultures. It is when we encounter ways of thinking about teaching and assessment radically different from our own, that we cannot avoid looking at our own practice more critically. When discipline-focused dialogue is enriched through cross-disciplinary exchanges, the environment that is created has both supportive and challenging elements, rendering critical reflection on practice more likely to thrive (Brookfield, 1987).

To be clear, both discipline-specific and generic support for teaching, learning and assessment are needed. Courses on learning to teach in higher education, now offered at many universities, as well as conferences and journals that disseminate the scholarship of teaching and learning from a wide range of disciplines (e.g., The International Society for the Scholarship of Teaching and Learning and its corresponding journal *The International Journal of the Scholarship of Teaching and Learning*), intentionally encourage this dialogue across disciplinary border zones.

Summary

The belief that disciplines determine teaching practices runs deep within the academy. Disciplines have indeed been shown to be related to how academics and departments define themselves, the teaching and assessment practices they employ and how and what students learn. Nevertheless, a deeper understanding is still needed of the distinctive features of teaching, learning and assessment in particular disciplines, how and why these evolve, and to what extent they can be enriched, particularly through cross-disciplinary and cross-departmental exchanges.

The first two chapters set the framework for this volume highlighting the continuous interplay between the context-specific and "context-transcendent" aspects of teaching, learning and assessment. The following chapters revisit this theme, exploring questions such as: What do students in particular disciplines learn? To what extent does the undergraduate experience prepare students for their later professional, civic and personal lives? Is what students learn in one subject or discipline useful for their learning in other contexts? How can students be supported in becoming participants of particular disciplinary communities? To what extent does disciplinary structure determine teaching, learning and assessment?

Acknowledgments

Many thanks to Dai Hounsell who kindly agreed to offer comments on an earlier draft of this chapter.

References

Altbach, P.A. (1991). The academic profession. In P.A. Altbach (Ed.), *International Higher Education: An Encyclopedia* (pp. 23–45). New York, NY: Garland Publishing.

Archer, M.D., & Haley, C.D. (Eds.) (2005). *The 1702 Chair of Chemistry at Cambridge. Transformation and Change.* Cambridge, UK: Cambridge University Press.

Axelrod, P. (2002). *Values in conflict. The university, the marketplace, and the trials of liberal education.* Montreal & Kingston: McGill-Queen's University Press.

Bandura, A. (Ed.) (1995). *Self-efficacy in changing societies.* New York, NY: Cambridge University Press.

Becher, T. (1989). *Academic Tribes and Territories: Intellectual Enquiry and the Cultures of Disciplines.* Milton Keynes: Society for Research into Higher Education and Open University Press.

Becher, T., & Trowler, P. (2001). *Academic Tribes and Territories: intellectual enquiry and the cultures of disciplines (2nd edition).* Buckingham: Open University Press/SRHE.

Biglan, A. (1973a). Characteristics of subject matter in different academic fields. *Journal of Applied Psychology,* 57(3), 195–203.

Biglan, A. (1973b). Relationships between subject matter characteristics and the structure and output of university departments. *Journal of Applied Psychology,* 57 (3), 204–213.

Brew, A. (2006). *Research and teaching. Beyond the Divide.* New York, NY: Palgrave Macmillan.

Brookfield, S. (1987). *Developing critical thinkers.* San Francisco, CA: Jossey-Bass.

Clark, B.R. (1963). Faculty cultures. In T.F. Lunsford (Ed.), *The study of campus culture* (pp. 39–54). Boulder, CO: Western Institute Commission for Higher Education.

Cranton, P. (1998). *No one way: Teaching and learning in higher education.* Toronto, ON: Wall and Emerson.

Cross, P.K. (1998). What do we know about students' learning and how do we know it? Paper presented at the AAHE National Conference on Higher Education, Atlanta, Georgia, March 24, 1998.

Damrosch, D. (1995). *We scholars. Changing the culture of the university.* Cambridge, MA: Harvard University Press.

Donald, J.G. (1995). Disciplinary differences in knowledge validation. In N. Hativa & M. Marincovich (Eds.), *Disciplinary differences in teaching and learning: Implications for practice* (pp. 7–18). New Directions for Teaching and Learning, 64. San Francisco, CA: Jossey-Bass.

Donald, J.G. (2002). *Learning to think.* San Francisco, CA: Jossey-Bass

Elton, L. (2000). Danger of doing the wrong thing righter, in "Evaluate and Improve", Conference proceedings, Open University.

Elton, L. (2001). Research and Teaching: conditions for a positive link. *Teaching in Higher Education,* 6, 43–56.

Eraut, M. (2000). Non-formal learning and tacit knowledge in professional work. *British Journal of Educational Psychology,* 70, 113–136.

Flexner, A. (1930). *Universities. American, English and German.* New York, NY: Oxford University Press.

Gibbs, G. (1996). Supporting educational development within departments. *The International Journal for Academic Development,* 1, 27–37.

Grace, S., Smith, B., Bradford, M., & Elvidge, L. (2004). Maximising the synergy: disciplinary and generic approaches in academic staff development. In L. Elvidge & Associates (Eds.), *Exploring academic development in higher education: issues of engagement* (pp. 97–113). Cambridge: Jill Rogers Associated Limited.

Hativa, N. (1995). What is taught in an undergraduate lecture? Differences between a matched pair of pure and applied disciplines. In N. Hativa & M. Marincovich (Eds.), *Disciplinary differences in teaching and learning: Implications for practice* (pp. 19–30). New Directions for Teaching and Learning, 64. San Francisco, CA: Jossey-Bass.

Healey, M. (2000). Developing the scholarship of teaching in higher education: a discipline-based approach. *Higher Education Research and Development,* 19(2), 169–189.

Huber, M., & Hutchings, P. (2005). *The advancements of learning: Building the teaching commons. The Carnegie Foundation report on the scholarship of teaching and learning.* The Carnegie Foundation for the Advancement of Teaching. San Francisco, CA: Jossey-Bass.

Huber, M., & Morreale, S.P. (Eds.) (2002). *Disciplinary styles in the scholarship of teaching and learning: Exploring common ground.* Washington, DC: American Association for Higher Education and The Carnegie Foundation for the Advancement of Teaching.

Hutchings, P., & Shulman, L. S. (1999). The Scholarship of Teaching: New Elaborations, New Developments. *Change Magazine,* 31(5), 10–15.

Jenkins, A. (1996). Discipline-based educational development. *The International Journal for Academic Development,* 1(1), 50–62.

Kahn, P.E. (2007). Supporting reflective processes—insights from a review of research for practitioners, and for SEDA. *Educational developments. The Magazine of the Staff and Educational Development Association,* 8(2), 15–17.

Kerr, C. (1963). *The Uses of the University.* Cambridge, MA: Harvard University Press.

Knight, P., & Yorke, M. (2003). *Assessment, learning and employability.* Maidenhead; Society for Research in Higher Education and the Open University Press.

Kolb, D.A. (1981). Learning styles and disciplinary differences. In A. Chickering. (Ed.), *The modern American college* (pp. 232–255). San Francisco, CA: Jossey-Bass.

Kreber, C. (2005). Charting a critical course on the scholarship of university teaching Movement. *Studies in Higher Education,* 30(4), 389–407.

Kreber, C. & Castleden, H. (2008) Reflection on teaching and epistemological structure: Reflective and critically reflective processes of academic teachers in pure/soft and pure/hard fields. *Higher Education.* Available online at: http://dx.doi.org/10.1007/s10734-008-9158-9 accessed July 10, 2008.

Kreber, C., & Cranton, P.A. (2000). Exploring the scholarship of teaching. *Journal of Higher Education,* 71(4), 476–495.

Lilge, F. (1948). *The abuse of learning. The failure of the German university.* New York, NY: The Macmillan Company.

Lindblom-Ylänne, S., Trigwell, K., Nevgi, A., & Ashwin, P. (2006). How approaches to teaching are affected by discipline and teaching context. *Studies in Higher Education,* 31 (3), 285–298.

Little, J.W. (1993). Professional community in comprehensive high schools: The two worlds of academic and vocational teachers. In J.W. Little & M.W. McLaughlin (Eds.), *Teachers' work: Individuals, colleagues and contexts* (pp. 137–163). New York, NY: Teachers College Press.

Marincovich, M., & Prostko, J. (2005). Why knowing about disciplinary differences can mean more effective teaching. *Essays on Teaching Excellence. Towards the Best in the Academy,* Vol 16(6). A publication of The Professional and Organizational Development Network in Higher Education. http://www.podnetwork.org/publications&resources/teachingexcellence.htm accessed August 21, 2006.

Murray, H.G., & Renaud, R.D. (1995). Disciplinary differences in classroom teaching behaviors. In N. Hativa & M. Marincovich (Eds.), *Disciplinary differences in teaching and learning: implications for practice* (pp. 31–41). New Directions for Teaching and Learning. San Francisco, CA: Jossey-Bass.

Neumann, R. (2001). Disciplinary differences and university teaching. *Studies in Higher Education,* 26(2), 135–146.

Newman, J.H. (1982). *The idea of a university.* Notre Dame, IN: University of Notre Dame.

Nowotny, H., Scott, P., & Gibbons, M. (2001). *Re-Thinking Science: Knowledge and the Public in an Age of Uncertainty.* London: Polity Press.

Pickering, A.M. (2006). Learning about university teaching: reflections on a research study investigating influences for change. *Teaching in Higher Education,* 11(3), 319–335.

Polanyi, M. (1966). *The Tacit Dimension.* Garden City, NY: Doubleday & Co.

Prosser, M., Martin, E., Trigwell, K., Ramsden, P., & Lueckenhausen, G. (2005). Academics' experiences of understanding of their subject matter and the relationship of this to their experiences of teaching and learning. *Instructional Science,* 33(2), 137–157.

Prosser, M., & Trigwell, K. (1999). *Understanding learning and teaching. The experience in higher education.* Milton Keynes: Society for Research into Higher Education/Open University Press.

Sayers, D. (1948). The lost tools of learning. Reprinted (with original date) in A.H. Burleigh (Ed.), *Education in a free society* (pp. 229–265). Indianapolis, IN: Liberty Press, 1973.

Shulman, L. (1987). Knowledge and teaching: Foundations of the new reform. *Harvard Educational Review,* 57 (1), 1–22.

Shulman, L. (2004). *Signature pedagogies.* Plenary address to the International Society for the Scholarship of Teaching and Learning, The University of Indiana, Bloomington, IN, October.

Smart, J.C., & Ethington, C. (1995). Disciplinary and institutional differences in undergraduate education goals. In N. Hativa & M. Marincovich (Eds.), *Disciplinary differences in teaching and learning: Implications for practice* (pp. 49–58). New Directions for Teaching and Learning, 64. San Francisco, CA: Jossey-Bass.

Smeby, J.C. (1996). Disciplinary differences in university teaching. *Studies in Higher Education,* 21(1), 69–79.

Smeby, J.C. (1998). Knowledge production and knowledge transmission: The interaction between research and teaching at universities. *Teaching in Higher Education,* 3(1), 5–17.

Wenger, E. (1998). *Communities of practice. Learning, meaning and identity.* New York, NY: Cambridge University Press.

Winchester, I. (1986). On disciplines. *Interchange,* 17(2), 178–185.

Wittrock, B. (2002). Institutes for Advanced Study: Ideas, Histories, Rationales. Keynote Speech on the Occasion of the Inauguration of the Helsinki Collegium for Advanced Studies, University of Helsinki, December 2, 2002.

Zeichner, K.M., Tabachnik, B.R., & Denmore, K. (1987). Individual, institutional, and cultural influences on the development of teachers' craft knowledge. In Calderhead (Ed.), *Exploring Teacher Thinking* (pp. 21–59). London, UK: Cassell.

II
Disciplines and Their Epistemological Structure

3

The Commons
Disciplinary and Interdisciplinary Encounters

Janet Gail Donald

McGill University, Canada

The Commons

To attempt to understand teaching and learning within and beyond disciplinary boundaries, we must first comprehend how disciplines function and interact as social systems. In honor of the venue of this colloquium at the University of Edinburgh, and in keeping with an inclusive British tradition, I will situate my discussion in the history and philosophy of this island. The idea of 'the commons' provides context to explore disciplinary regions and interrelations. 'Commons' has three definitions in the *Canadian Oxford Dictionary* (1998): land set aside for public use; the common people as opposed to those in authority; the common people viewed as forming part of a political system. These definitions evoke the sense of occupied terrain that Becher (1989) suggested in *Academic Tribes and Territories*, but also one that is shared communally. An additional connotation, in 'the common people versus authority', is the challenge to traditional practices or legitimacy. The geographical origins of the commons in British history are described in the following manner:

> In Domesday [1086] the villages cluster thickly along the spring-line at the foot of the Downs. It was during this period that the open-field system seems to have developed: the lands of each estate were divided into two or three great open fields which were ploughed in strips by the peasantry, a system which continued right through the Middle Ages and even into the twentieth century.
>
> (Wood, 1986, p. 35)

Wood continues by noting that charters (lease documents) from the villages provide the first clear evidence of the classic intermixture of the common fields where "the open pasture is common, the meadow is common and the ploughland (arable) is common", and where "the lands cannot be described on any side by clear boundary points because to right and left the acres lie in combination one with another". Thus British history suggests a pattern of human organization in which we are located close to a source of water sharing three types of resources – pasture, meadow and ploughland – without clear boundaries. What is the message? Certainly one of interdependence, although we also note charters or lease documents that declare individual rights and contracts.

Two centuries later Common law statutes provide inclusive justice, replacing feudal or local customs (Ferguson & Bruun, 1958). During the rule of Edward I (1272–1307), social organization was extended to guarantee equal treatment as a bulwark or safeguard against feudal and local oppression. Again, history shows the complexity of this organization. In 1297 representatives of the commons (now the middle class of town and country) were needed (a) to consent to non-feudal taxes, (b) to explain local conditions to the court, and (c) in return, to explain acts of government in their towns or shires. These representatives began to consult among themselves, thus paving the way for a separate House of Commons. Law and law making were vested in the Commons.

Another connotation of 'common' adds further substance to the meaning of learning within and beyond disciplinary boundaries. In *How the Scots invented the modern world* (Herman, 2001, pp. 262–263) the philosophy of common sense as described by Thomas Reid in 1751 is stated: all human beings come equipped with an innate rational capacity called common sense, which allows them to make clear and certain judgments about the world, and their dealings with it. Common sense tells us that we can understand and navigate our way through the real world, and the more we know about that world, the better we can act on it, both as individuals and as members of a community. The Scottish philosophers of that era recognized that knowledge is power, and that human progress rests on expanding that power to its utmost and to as many people as possible, so that we can all become truly, morally free.

So the goal of exploring teaching and learning within and beyond disciplinary boundaries can be situated in this eighteenth-century Scottish philosophy, a philosophy that is empirical, pragmatic, and yet moral in the most positive sense of the word. These philosophical criteria of empiricism, pragmatism and morality will guide my discourse.

Interdisciplinary Encounters

Challenging the view of a community built on principles we can readily understand and relate to is the specter of uncertainty, with garish examples in the twenty-first century of terrorist attacks on New York and London. At the 2003 annual conference of the Higher Education Research and Development Association of Australasia (HERDSA) I was asked to address the effects of complexity and uncertainty on the academy (Donald, 2003b). I suggested that uncertainty may pose a greater problem to us as university professors than complexity in the twenty-first century. Inherent in uncertainty is the connotation of 'unboundedness', which may provide freedom of movement, but can also deter learning if we cannot enunciate a starting place, goals, or appropriate procedures. One effect of living with uncertainty is to create our own boundaries, retreating into our disciplines and becoming gatekeepers, thus limiting if not preventing perspective. For example, we do not tend to read what is written in other disciplines or other cultures. I was reminded of the extent to which this occurs when I participated in an international francophone conference on university pedagogy (Donald, 2003a). Speakers referred to Piaget and to other noted continental European pedagogical researchers; none to British or North American researchers, even though the topics were about paradigm shifts and competencies, matters that have been discussed in depth in the English-speaking world.

This is not an isolated incident. Over the past twenty-five years, I have conducted a series of programs of research on teaching and learning across disciplines with more than one hundred participating professors, senior academics chosen to represent their disciplines in universities in Australia, Canada, the United Kingdom and the United States. The general intent was to understand intellectual development across disciplines, and the findings were published in *Learning to think: Disciplinary perspectives* (Donald, 2002). I began with studies of how professors used important or key concepts in sixteen courses across disciplines, followed by studies on how students learned the concepts. I then looked at the intellectual or thinking skills required in different disciplines and how they were taught. This involved interviews with professors followed by ethnographic research in which graduate student researchers attended classes as participant observers and audiotaped the classes while taking notes on their experience. As part of one of the research programs, we examined the kinds of pedagogical research reported in the indexes of the journals of physicists, engineers, psychologists and educators. In each discipline studied, a body of research had been published on teaching without reference to research on teaching from any other field, including higher education. I was not surprised, therefore, when I wanted to publish an article on professors' and students' conceptualizations of the learning task in physics courses (Donald, 1993), that to reach physicists, I had to join the Society for Research in Science Teaching. We could probably all recall incidents of attempting to communicate with someone from another discipline, and finding that we were using different terms to talk about similar phenomena, or the same terms to talk about rather different occurrences, or that there was a slight twist in meaning beyond immediate grasp.

And yet as a graduate student in the 1960s, when I attended a multidisciplinary seminar on Communication, where geneticists, English professors, Canadian Broadcasting Company (CBC) producers and educators discussed the new communications possibilities, I found the learning experience particularly rewarding because of the challenge of multiple perspectives. At McGill University, our graduate course in pedagogy and our teaching workshops for instructors are organized so that people from different disciplines work with each other to discover each other's language and educational proclivities. But we do not appear to readily bridge the frontier existing between our disciplinary areas. Despite this situation, as educators we are obliged to pose the question, "If complexity and uncertainty are problematic for us within our university environments, to what extent can we be responsible for preparing the next generation to deal with them?" The solution may lie in making examples of ourselves, and so I will now look at three examples from different areas of endeavor to see if some light can be shed on the role of a discipline.

Teaching and Learning within the Disciplines

From the disciplines studied in my research in the physical and social sciences and humanities, I have chosen three, each with a long tradition as a discipline, and each serving as a model to other related disciplines. Each received anthropological attention from Becher (1989) as a tribe or territory, thus potentially enriching our dialogue. The sociological and intellectual parameters of the disciplines set the scene for the pedagogies used and for student learning, hence each description begins with a brief analysis of these variables. Sociological parameters include relative power or status within an institution, economic status, degree of social convergence or divergence, and adherence to core academic values (Donald, 2002). Central among the intellectual parameters are degree of structure – how paradigmatic or unrestricted is the discipline, methods of inquiry, and criteria and processes used to determine validity or authenticity. Guided by the philosophical tenets of empiricism, pragmatism and morality, I will begin by examining how each discipline organizes itself, and what message it delivers to students. My focus in *Learning to think: Disciplinary perspectives* (Donald, 2002) was what kind of thinking processes students were expected to develop, thus the nature of concepts in the discipline and the development of thinking processes merit consideration. I also want to consider the attributes of the pedagogy displayed in each domain and the challenge of instruction. The descriptive quotations of the three disciplines are excerpted from *Learning to think*.

Becoming an Engineer

I gave the chapter on engineering in Learning to think the title "Hard thinking: Applying structured knowledge to unstructured problems". Uncertainty is a defining characteristic of the arena in which engineers perform: they deal with unbounded problems, with too little or too much information, and must set the limits of their problem space. Engineering programs although housed in universities must respond to the sociological context of the profession. The industrial-corporate world is a controlling factor in engineering education. For example, because of the global demand for increased technological expertise, salaries in industry for engineers are higher than for graduates from doctoral programs, which leads to continuing shortages of faculty. Research funding in engineering was slower to develop than that for the pure sciences, but the development of funding has supported the trend in schools of engineering to become more theoretical, while students complain that their under-graduate education is oriented toward postgraduate degrees rather than the workplace (Donald & Denison, 1996). Engineering professors have an image of practicality and pragmatism, but present a diverse pattern to some extent dependent upon their area of specialization – mechanical, chemical, electrical, civil, and computer. As Becher (1989) noted, they think of themselves as hardworking, stable introverts; creativity and inventiveness outpace communication skills. They tend, however, to be entrepreneurial and cosmopolitan.

What does this sociological context mean for the intellectual context? The knowledge and skills needed in engineering reflect both a high degree of theoretical structure and the procedures and strategies for applying them. The resulting curriculum problem is to find the time to fit all that must be learned within a limited period. Pressure to expand the length of the program is continual, to recruit students with sufficient background in science and mathematics, to ensure exposure to the humanities and social sciences, and to provide instruction in ethics and communication skills. Cooperative learning programs provide professional training earlier in students' undergraduate education, but may extend time in the program by several years. Through accreditation processes for programs and/or graduating students, the profession exerts a degree of authority over program and curriculum.

Most memorable in my studies of learning to think in engineering was the student experience of becoming professionals. From the audiotapes of our ethnographic study of learning in engineering, we hear a professor telling students to use Grandma's language and not lawyers' language to simplify an explanation and illustrate a better understanding, that doing problems is: "not to please me, it is the vehicle to practice. If you want to get fit, you go to the gym and you lift weights. The act of doing it is the learning." The professor continually differentiates between engineers and those in other disciplines, "Physicists do the liturgy; engineers do the useful stuff like feed people." In their interviews the professors note the vicissitudes of an engineer's life, and what their students will face in the professional world. Learning to be an engineer includes estimating risk and taking responsibility for their decisions.

The learning task in engineering is heavier than that of most science or arts students. Entering engineering students are expected to have succeeded in previous mathematics and physical science courses; grades in calculus, both in first and second year, are most strongly related to success in engineering coursework (Pike, 1991). Relative to arts and science students, they are more self-reliant, willing to take responsibility, act on practical logical evidence and keep to the point. They prefer to work and make decisions with other people and depend on social approval; they are conventional and go along with the group. They prefer learning kinesthetically (actively) more and auditorily less than arts students, but nevertheless attend lectures as their main source of schooling, although they have more hands-on experiences in labs than arts students (Zhang & Richarde, 1999). In summary, expectations are that engineering students will have mathematical and physical science skills, will be able to act on logical evidence, and will be able to work with others.

The Nature of Concepts in Engineering

Language is used within a system or at the service of intellectual processes. Most basic, as vocabulary, is the mathematical and physical science terminology demanded of students in the program.

Engineering professors expect students to integrate their knowledge into systems or into the problem-solving process. Understanding occurs as a result of joining concepts to actions; in the terminology of information theory, retrieval from memory depends upon how well knowledge is encoded in schemas. As students progress in their program, there appears to be a consolidation of concepts rather than an increase in knowledge; learning is viewed as a pyramid in which basic knowledge is synthesized and applied in different ways at the top.

Students view the learning process as confusing when assignments involve procedures to be followed or they do not understand a particular design technique. Specifically, students requested more examples and greater explanation of ideas behind the concepts, but also bewailed the amount of work required.

> "I have to understand the problem first before solving. For my math course, I don't really have to understand the problem first. You have to know the basics before doing anything."

> "There's a lot of work. You have to get used to it. It's overwhelming. You have to adjust."

The Development of Thinking Processes

In engineering, problem-solving and design are the terms most frequently used to describe the thinking processes needed and developed. What stood out most clearly in the interviews with professors was their emphasis on students' needing to change their approach – that students had been misled by the criterion of efficiency. As one professor noted,

> "Whenever there is a way to go through school without thinking, unfortunately that way is taken more often than not by most students. . . . There is a small set of basic ideas that you have to memorize, but just through using them repeatedly you will memorize them. . . . But the real value in engineering is being able to think and apply these fundamentals to new problems you have not seen before. . . . This is really hard, because a) the students do not want to, b) they are not experienced and c) their life experience up until now has told them: 'Don't think, it's inefficient and you might not get the same marks, you may make mistakes'."

The Challenge of Instruction

The engineering professors who contributed their insights to understanding learning in their field emphasized the need for problem-solving skills but were equally concerned with design and quality issues. This led one expert to suggest that most engineering skills require a great deal of calendar time to master, hence a skill that was started in one course will be acquired over a period of years. The unit of learning is not a course but a program plus postgraduate study or experience. Major challenges for engineering instructors are to improve students' problem-solving ability and their design skills, but then to be able to apply these skills in the industrial and larger economic milieu.

Instructional methods in engineering courses are for the most part lecture; in a study of 35,000 faculty across disciplines in the United States, 78% of engineering faculty indicated that they used extensive lecturing in all or most of the classes they taught, higher than the overall average of 54% (Milem & Astin, 1994). Almost half (45%) responded that they also used class discussion in all or most classes, compared with an overall average of 70%. Group projects were used by 16%, matching the overall average, but a higher percentage than in other physical sciences, which averaged 5%. Engineering professors reported using cooperative learning (14%), more than other sciences, but lower than the overall average of 27%. Thus active learning methods were recognized, but not used as much as might be expected given the problem-solving and design tasks of engineering students.

What are optimal ways of cultivating thinking processes in engineering programs? One comprehensive approach is to coach students to understand the nature of problems in workshops or tutorials by having them draw a cognitive map or diagram on the specific topic or problem, write the rules for executing a particular procedure, articulate the relationship between problems, or design an inverted problem themselves. 'Teaching students how to fish' is the analogy used in the McMaster University workshops, which may cover such diverse topics as self-assessment, stress management, and creativity (Woods et al., 1997). In design projects students learn group dynamic skills, since they must also learn to rely on others. Cooperation is promoted by giving a single grade to the group, and student teams evaluate each other. Courses on systems engineering, value analysis, or technology assessment help students gain an understanding of the ecological context of engineering. Throughout their training, students are being inducted into a profession that values hard thinking in order to solve unstructured problems.

The picture that emerges from this examination of learning to be an engineer is not easily summarized. Students are expected to be good problem solvers with uncertain or incomplete data; they must learn to be designers, taking into account risk and efficiency. Is there in engineering a 'signature pedagogy', that is, an idiosyncratic organization, set of artifacts, assumptions and practices particular to learning and teaching in the discipline (Shulman, 2004)? The classrooms I visited, whether in Canada, the United States, the United Kingdom or Australia, were large lecture halls, many shared with other undergraduate programs. It is in the design laboratories, for example, the structural testing labs, that we see a way of learning specific to engineering. Cooperative programs are part of the engineering signature compared to other science programs. Artifacts include surveyors' tripods, specifically designed labs and computer facilities. What assumptions underlie this set of professional programs? The language is 'like Grandma's' – that is, straightforward or grounded, but the thinking processes are distinguished in many ways from those of physicists or lawyers, as are the tasks. 'Does it work?' is the validation query, a question distinctive to this discipline. Engineering students recognize early that their education is different from that of their friends in arts and science – they have longer hours, no time to muse, specific tasks that must be accomplished, and a sense of urgency running through their lives. Their programs invoke and display the criteria of empiricism and pragmatism. Morality could be noted in the requirement for recognizing risks and adhering to codes or standards, and in being able to work with others.

Thinking like a Lawyer

"Precedent and reason: Case versus logic" was the title of the chapter on learning to think in law, because some law professors focus on the interpretation of legal doctrine while others see themselves as solvers of puzzles. The learning context is highly influenced by the legal profession; an abstract technical vocabulary and the need to work within a framework of statute and precedent requires that students be both verbally proficient and aggressive. One professor noted at the end of our conversation that law schools are unruly places, where received wisdom and controversy vie for attention. Legal education was established in the medieval university as one of three advanced faculties, with theology and medicine. As Kreber discusses in the previous chapter, completion of the trivium (grammar, rhetoric, logic) and the quadrivium (arithmetic, music, geometry, astronomy) was considered necessary to acquire a broad base of knowledge before undertaking the study of judicial procedure. In the university, the path from profession to scholarly discipline has been erratic and problematic.

The difficult path may be due in large part to a series of paradoxes or antinomies that run through the discipline. The first antinomy revolves around the status of law as a scholarly or intellectual discipline. Law is studied both as a general education for leadership and administration, and as a necessary qualification for professional status recognizing juristic competence (Lewis, 1992). According to one scholar, the cultural divide between theoretical law school and instrumental or results-oriented bar has limited convergence and therefore coherence in the field (Janda, personal communication, 2000). Becher (1989) noted that the predominant notion others in the university have of academic lawyers is that they are not really academic. Compared to other disciplines, legal scholars tend to be functional and utilitarian in their use of knowledge, concerning themselves with protocol and procedure (Toma, 1997). Since it is the legal profession that produces knowledge in the form of statutes, and interprets precedent, the profession dominates the academy rather than the reverse.

The second paradox or antinomy is the place assigned to values in law. Although frequently portrayed in the media as the amoral agent of a client's ends, as society's hired gun, this portrayal runs counter to the idea that everyone has a right to be defended (Somerville, personal communication, 2000), or that social problems are the basis of law, as one of Becher's (1989) legal respondents claimed. In the teaching of law the tradition, similar to the sciences, is that the discipline is value free, but reformists see a critical function within legal studies, as a force for social change. We could expect legal scholars, as social scientists, to engage in this kind of normative work, to concern themselves about what something should be, beyond what something might be. Toma (1997) divides law professors into (a) mainstream *legal realists* who focus upon understanding the social factors that influence legal principles, (b) *critical scholars* who argue that reality is shaped over time by social values and that their role is to change the law and its practice, and (c) *interpretive scholars* who employ hermeneutical methodologies. For example, in a study of a statute on civil rights, realist scholars might explore the data underlying the decision of the legislature and would analyze how the law applies. Critical scholars would focus on social forces that afforded certain groups in society influence in its passage, while interpretive scholars might deconstruct the text itself. Legal realism, however, dominates law school classrooms.

The third, most specific antinomy is the insularity of the discipline in relation to the university. Students may have a wide range of disciplinary backgrounds, and other disciplines may have potential mutual impact with law, but a technical and unfamiliar terminology supports insularity and Becher's characterization of law professors as arcane. One dean of a law faculty in the United States has suggested that the insularity of law schools may lead to their being cut off from their host universities, being left to their own financial devices, especially in graduate research universities (Weidner, 1997). The law profession competes successfully with other disciplines in the university for the attention of legal scholars, rendering interdisciplinarity more difficult.

The Nature of Concepts in Law

To think like a lawyer requires a high degree of analytical ability. In the study we did of concepts in the course on Tort, which investigates wrongful acts and the responsibility for them, *Common law methodology*, the superordinate concept, encompassing all others in the course, was defined by the professor as:

"a system of analysis by which litigation is determined and which entails the observance of precedent in that determination. The court may find that previously decided cases, though similar, are distinguishable on the basis of their facts, controlling legislation, or public policy."

Concepts are highly abstract but tightly structured and logically related, and students in the law course on tort made greater gains in their concept knowledge than students in any of the other fifteen courses. We therefore pursued a second level of analysis in which we examined propositions in the course, and found that the three professors teaching Tort tended to agree on the importance of concrete but not abstract propositions in the course text. The students in the course agreed on familiar and specific propositions. From these findings we can deduce that abstract concepts will not be as readily agreed upon within the discipline and that they therefore will not be as easily taught or learned. The tendency is to teach law at a highly abstract, philosophical level. This is a very specific example of limited disciplinary convergence and its effects on learning.

The Development of Thinking Processes

An immense vocabulary of abstract, nuanced terms, precedents, statutes and other principles guide the process of thinking. Because in common law legal analysis is based on the rule of precedent, the facts in a case must be seen to be similar to or different from those in prior cited cases in order to make an argument. In *functional analysis*, lawyers seek to understand the meaning or scope of a rule or category according to its purpose (Bryden, 1984). Students therefore need to know the relevant doctrines or policies that apply to the case. For example, when creating a contract to supply goods exclusively, one needs to know if there are statutes that define whether such a contract would be enforceable or not, and whether the statutes apply in a given instance. The methodology of a legal expert consists of looking at the facts, looking at the issues, looking at the results and analyzing the reasons, and critiquing these both distinctively and constructively. Lawyers must determine what was held and why to produce an argument.

The Challenge of Instruction

The principal challenge for instruction is to organize a program that meets both scholarly and professional requirements; a pluralistic approach is needed. Although it is an aphorism that the casebook method teaches students how to argue about the law, some have suggested that students appear to learn to argue without thinking about the law: the techniques of rhetoric outpace logic (Watson, 1996). Optimal teaching methods such as macro-analysis, where students analyze a multi-faceted problem as it might appear in a lawyer's office, are increasingly used – early apprenticeship or simulation is effective in encouraging careful thought. Specific legal analysis skills can be taught by computer or by simulations. Underlying these challenges is the need for students to examine the social context in which they will be working and to determine the role of values in their personal and professional lives, as these will act as guiding principles in their thinking as lawyers. Understanding one's own assumptions leads in turn to better negotiation skills and positive lawyer–client relationships, increasingly critical in the twenty-first century.

To what extent do the principles of empiricism, pragmatism, and morality guide this course of study? To an empirical social scientist it is unnerving to realize that in law empirical evidence is considered 'circumstantial' – that is, requiring inference from known facts hard to explain otherwise, and hence incidental and limited in value – compared to that of a witness, particularly when we recognize the limits of human memory. The settling of disputes or grievances is by definition pragmatic, but pragmatism is often seen to vie with morality in this discipline as legal realists joust with critical scholars. This conundrum may place law at the center of the issues of pragmatism and morality. Certainly students question the underlying principles and the usual outcomes of legal procedures. At my university we have a joint law and social work program that studies these issues. Has law a signature pedagogy? Vested in cases, argument, statute and precedent, law is a pedagogy of uncertainty, of tension and negotiation, of multiple interpretations, and of risk.

Thinking in the Humanities

Criticism and creativity, imagination, aesthetics, synoptics – the integration of a culture – are uppermost criteria in the humanities. Compared to engineering and law, the parameters in the humanities are extensive and expansive. The great stories by which humankind lives (Sperna Weiland, 1992) require a multiplicity of approaches to reach understanding. Compared to the antinomies or paradoxes of law, the humanities are defined by much larger rifts or dialectics – initially challenging and breaking away in the Renaissance from theology to use the Greek and Roman classics to interpret western civilization. Logos – reason, speech or word – is the controlling principle; the study of the classics was thought of as a humanizing force in society. The earliest model of inquiry – hermeneutics – was inherited from the interpretation of biblical text, thus the sacred and secular are examined using the same method. In the model discipline chosen to describe inquiry in the humanities, English literature, the sacred and the secular, and the aesthetic and the practical vie for attention.

As in law, *rhetoric*, the art of effective or persuasive speaking or writing, was an early focus of student learning in literary studies, but this focus on rhetoric had to contend first with the conception of literature as entertainment, then with the practical demand for written communication. In the nineteenth century, scholarship and composition were divided, so that scholarship was vested in the study of language itself (text) and its history (context). The discipline has swung on a pendulum between text and context ever since (Vendler, 1988, personal communication, 2000). The next rift occurred between literary theory and humanism with Matthew Arnold voicing the humanities criterion that literature is a coherent criticism of life, and the field coverage principle that led to curricular compartmentalization into different historical periods. Because of the sensitivity of the humanities to society and the 'model' role that English literature plays for other disciplines within the humanities, English professors in particular may find themselves in the position of lightning rods, signaling the inherent conflicts between university and society. Controversy is part of the fabric. Students have to juggle perplexity and contention with feeling and imagination. As the participant observer (graduate student researcher) in one of the English literature courses noted at the end of his report in his advice to students taking the course:

> There are many skills students need for this course. The first is a good memory. It is important to remember who wrote what, as well as the subject matter of each work. The second is an ability to read critically, noticing patterns of images and recurring ideas or themes. It is also important to be able to synthesize material, to see how each work connects with other works, and also how they connect to the main themes or ideas of the course.

The Nature of Concepts in English Literature

Taking meaning from text is the essential skill in the close reading that students are required to do. *Text* is more inclusive than the term *concept* used relatively easily in other disciplines: *text* encompasses a logical structure or schema, the organization of concepts showing their relationships, and further adds to it the effect on the receiver of the communication. The unit of analysis in English literature, then, is larger and more complex than a concept. The openness of text structure – the fact that texts do not contain all the elements needed for their comprehension – means that the reader must infer and integrate separate textual elements into a general meaning. The background knowledge needed to interpret particular linguistic events is often specific: knowledge of particular social situations and participants involved (the context of events) and small-scale social facts or customs, for example, marriage or burial customs (Short & Candlin, 1989). The reader must simultaneously make inferences where the text leaves out references to the empirical world, while integrating internal relationships that are not explicit.

In the study of how students learn concepts, we chose an English course entitled *An introduction to Shakespeare*. The main goals of the course were: "to make students approach dramatic text and the ways of dealing with such texts, and the use of performance as a learning technique".

Most essential for students to learn was to be active in a group situation, as well as interpretation of plot, action, theme and characters in order to perform the material. The key concepts in the course described the different aspects of drama, from *performance* to *gestures* to *stage business*. Compared with the other courses studied, there appeared to be less cohesion among the key concepts. Consistent with the visible performance aspect in this course, nine of the thirteen key concepts had concrete definitions. In the course outline, students are given a list of pointers on their presentation. The first is that there is just one focal point, and they must determine what they want the audience to watch and why. In their concept map at the end of the course, students most frequently linked *performance* and *audience*, showing the attention paid by them to the course goal and its manner of validation.

The Development of Thinking Processes

If text is the stimulus, loaded with structures to be perceived and interpreted, what thinking processes does one need to develop in order to make sense of it? *Literary criticism* asks what makes one text better than another. As we might expect, the development of critical analysis has taken a dialectic route, with new forms resulting from the insufficiencies of previous ones. For the analysis in *Learning to think*, I created a table (pp. 248–249) of the development of literary criticism, the forms it has taken and their proponents, and the evaluative criteria used in each approach (see Table 3.1).

The major criteria used in the different forms of textual analysis have shifted from the global – the application of ideas on how to live – to the particular – the organizing principle that unifies a work's elements and identifies its uniqueness. Different approaches espouse different ways of expressing this organization: through context, archetypes, codes and patterns of oppositions, paradox, hidden aspects of text, the interpretive community or strategy, the consequences of values in text for the community, the interaction of text and culture, a shared story, and cultural metaphors as for gender or economic bondage. These organizing principles are neither discrete nor contradictory; each would appear to add to our understanding of the text. Pluralism recommends the use of the best fit of approach to task. Thus literary criticism appears to deal as much with the representation of knowledge as its evaluation.

As an approach to thinking processes, a commitment to close reading may be the nearest thing to a shared principle in contemporary criticism (Rabinowitz, 1992). One of the English professors described the thinking process in the following manner:

> The student must know what the content of the text is; that is understanding at one level. But to really understand a text, one must start to see relationships; one must see what would be abstracted or generalized as the artistic form of this particular work. What characters are like other characters; in what ways are they alike or different; is there enough likeness to establish a connection; once the connection is established, in what significant ways are they differentiated?

The process of inquiry extends from *identifying the context* in which text is placed, to *judging the validity* of an interpretation. Argument requires description, selection, representation, inference, synthesis and verification. The difficulty is that one cannot call upon an objective reality, as in the sciences, to support one's argument. One is bound by text, yet must render it explicable by inference. The methods of inquiry most frequently used to describe the process in English literature are hermeneutics – the construction of textual meaning through a dialectic between understanding and explanation, and critical thinking – a reasoned or questioning approach in which one examines assumptions and seeks evidence.

The Challenge of Instruction

The challenges in helping students to learn English literature lie in the breadth of the discipline, in the multiplicity of approaches to understanding it, and in the intricacy of the process of inquiry.

Table 3.1 Forms of critical analysis and their major proponents

Moral and philosophical criticism	Evaluation of a work's ideas and values by determining their truth, usefulness, clarity, consistency, complexity. (Dominant 1500–1900) [Plato, Tolstoy, Matthew Arnold]
Historical criticism	Traditional approach to analyzing literature by synthesizing factual data from various sources using rules of scholarly evidence – logic and objectivity – to offer interpretations of literary works. (1500s – Renaissance on) [Richard Altick, R. H. Miller]
Formalism	Form of the text as an aesthetic object; analysis of meter, genre, plot, point of view, language, particularly irony and ambiguity, symbols, sounds, imagery but not history or intent. (New Critics 1930–1960) [Cleanth Brooks, T. S. Eliot?]
Mythic and archetypal criticism	Use of sacred stories and universal symbols (scapegoat, earth mother, the quest, redemption) to explain text. (1870s, to peak in 1950s) [Northrop Frye, C.S. Lewis]
Psychoanalytic criticism	Uses particular symbols such as the unconscious and identity as explanatory principles. (1900–) [Jacques Lacan]
Structuralism	The codes, structures or pattern of a text – signs and semiotics. (Most influential in the 1960s and 70s.) [Ferdinand de Saussure, Claude Lévi-Strauss, Roman Jakobsen, Roland Barthes]
Reader response criticism	Focus on intellectual expectations and responses of the reader; a reaction to the New Critics' denial of reader interpretation. Asks what constitutes a valid reading. [Roland Barthes, Stanley Fish]
Deconstruction, Postmodernism	Reveal the limits or hidden aspects of individual texts by pointing out incongruities; expose the joints and gaps in a text. (1970s–) [Jacques Derrida, Michel Foucault]
Pluralism	Welcomes the multiplicity of literary theories as they multiply the roles of critics; compares and interrogates literary theories; proceeds from the ethical obligation to understand and respond to each other. [R. S. Crane, Richard McKeon, Stephen Pepper]
Rhetorical criticism	Examines the influence of text as a political instrument; based on rhetoric as a cooperative discussion in a community; questioning makes values available for reassessment and revision. [Kenneth Burke]
New historicism	Cultural materialism or poetics reads literature as a force within its culture, its social energy. [Stephan Greenblatt, Raymond Williams]
Ethnocriticism	Postcolonial movement in which those categorized as the 'Other' attempt to reclaim their voice, heritage, and move beyond victimage. [Edward Hall, Edward Said]
Feminist criticism	By examining text for gender roles, seeks to end the subordination and oppression of women. [Mary Wollstonecraft, Virginia Woolf, Simone de Beauvoir, Betty Friedan, Kate Millett]
Marxist criticism	Based on the principle espoused by Marx that social existence, particularly economic, determines consciousness; text is a consumer commodity that operates according to a set of economic rules. [George Lukacs, Louis Althusser]

Forms of literary criticism, if they cannot delimit the learning process, can provide potentially useful approaches to pedagogy. For example, formalism, focused on decoding structures of signification, provides an approach for seeking the organizing principle that unifies a work's elements, and ambiguity or paradox in the text – the central tendency and variance around it. The processes espoused in deconstruction are aimed at exposing the mechanisms by which texts generate meaning.

One pedagogical issue raised in the field that did not arise in others is an unwillingness to accept the student as a legitimate voice. Tompkins (1996) has argued that the educational process infantilizes students, taking away their initiative, and teaching them to be sophisticated rule followers. Although student voice or, in less radical language, relevance of the curriculum may be an issue in other disciplines, it was raised only in the context of English literature. Another critical issue arises from the amplitude of the discipline: What is legitimate text, primary or canon? Although historical categorization in allocated survey courses, and potential expansion of the curriculum do not resolve the issue of legitimate text, they are pragmatic and feasible responses. Another suggestion is to create an intellectual community in which students live the language of literary criticism by working within a theme such as the politics of representation, leading students to connect different aspects of the subject matter. Close reading, following the steps of an argument, and modeling different forms of literary criticism help students to better understand authorial intent and audience reception. Students need to be helped to find patterns and to search for evidence in order to draw conclusions and to formulate their own questions.

What place do empiricism, pragmatism, and morality have in the study of English literature? Morality has been a central issue since the days of Matthew Arnold. Empiricism and pragmatism could be described as non-issues, although the understanding of context requires close attention to a worldview, if not with an over-riding deference to objectivity. A signature pedagogy is found in great works, close reading, and the diverse forms of literary criticism.

A Return to Interdisciplinary Encounters

Now the most difficult question – what do these disciplines have to say to each other? What do they have in common? Where, how and why do they differ? Is there a signature pedagogy that makes a difference in the lives of students? One of the most evident yet disquieting findings from these studies across disciplines is that students in one program of study are experiencing a totally different education from students in another. Signature pedagogies imply idiosyncratic organizations, artifacts and practices, but our findings suggest that the differences lie not merely in distinctive identifiers but in much larger worldviews (or *Weltanschauung*). The immediate implication of this is that teaching and learning may be highly specific to the discipline or program: a 'university education' is a non-empirical phenomenon. It is only when we scrutinize our own programs of study that we can see what students are expected to learn and how they might learn to think. An engineering student learns to problem solve and to design, using mathematics and the physical sciences as the basic building blocks. Empiricism and pragmatism are uppermost. The law student is faced with a series of antinomies or paradoxes, and must balance pragmatism and morality. The student of English literature must create and yet must pay attention to an enormous history – that is perhaps the greatest conundrum for the humanities student. All have a specific and abstract language to be learned. All have rules, but the rules are different.

If the building blocks and rules differ, what do the disciplines have in common? I would argue that similarities exist across disciplines in the thinking processes developed. For example, to become expert in any of the three areas discussed in this chapter, there are common thinking processes although the phenomena dealt with vary. The first and probably the foremost thinking process is to *identify the context*. The engineer must see what information is necessary to problem solve or design, then represent it, getting into the ballpark. The law student must learn to establish how close the context of the current case is to previous similar cases, and how different, and whether the similarities and differences work in favor or against the client being represented. For the English literature student, the context may be a particular period of history or a particular culture, but it may also be the mind frame and dilemma of a character.

In each area, the expert must *recognize organizing principles*. To do this in engineering, students are taught how to draw diagrams. In one professor's words, students will not be able to solve the problem unless they can isolate the system and show what forces are acting on it. In law, representation consists at a basic level in identifying existing laws and methods; at a creative level, one would identify potential laws and methods. In English literature, one example of an organizing principle is that Act IV of a Shakespearean tragedy is almost always less intense than Act III and V. In Act III the tragic mistake is usually made, the consequences are borne out in Act V, with a quiet moment between them.

The ability to *change perspective* is a third thinking process the disciplines have in common. In engineering, one professor talked of how he structured a course to design something to make the campus more convenient for blind students. Students are blindfolded to find out what the problems are – not in navigating, it turns out, but with keeping their socks matched. In law, the ability to change perspective is essential in the construction of a range of possible decision outcomes or to see new possibilities. In English literature, a professor talked of moving from temporal and personal provincialism to see that there are alternative visions of experience. There are thus common thinking processes, but they are expressed in different ways.

How do the signature pedagogies compare? Each discipline has its own organization, artifacts, assumptions and practices particular to learning and teaching. In engineering, these consist of design laboratories, surveyors' tripods, computer facilities, and an overriding sense of urgency. The validation question is, 'Does it work?' In law, principles and practices rest on the case method, argument, statute and precedent, negotiation, and the potential of multiple interpretations. The validation question is, 'Does it fit?' In English literature the signature pedagogy is found in the rifts or dialectics, in close reading and in literary criticism. The validation question is, paradoxically, given the framework of contention in the discipline, 'Do you agree?'

Consistent with the hypothesis of encompassing *Weltanschauung* or worldviews that characterize and delimit disciplines, we have discovered only limited agreement with the commonsense guiding philosophy of empiricism, pragmatism, and morality. In engineering, we see emphasis placed on empiricism and pragmatism, with morality important when it comes to risk and responsibility for what is produced. In law, the importance of scientific empiricism can be questioned when we observe the secondary value placed on 'circumstantial evidence', but certainly evidence in its many forms is important in a law court. Pragmatism appears to vie with morality, giving rise to paradoxes or antinomies in law. In English literature, limited or constrained empiricism is noted in the strategies of close reading and the search for historical context, but would not be held widely as a guiding principle. Pragmatism would be less popular still. Morality was the cornerstone or touchstone of early literary criticism, but is less honored today, although in the form of the great stories by which humankind lives, it has some power. We are brought back to the philosophy of common sense, which now shows itself to be a cautionary tale:

> Common sense tells us that we can understand and navigate our way through the real world, and the more we know about that world, the better we can act on it, both as individuals and as members of a community.

The disciplines tell us that we have to tread carefully, because although there are commonalities in the way we think, the philosophies under which disciplines operate are distinct and require different navigation patterns. The implications for us as instructors can be viewed as challenges. We need to create an environment that will alert students to the important thinking processes needed in each discipline and then sustain their endeavor. Institutional policies are needed to establish a supportive learning context. Students need to become aware of their role and responsibilities as learners. Faculty must of necessity play a major role in formulating an explanation of the context and process of scholarly inquiry, how it governs their lives, and how students have the opportunity to engage in this process.

Rather than envisaging boundaries between disciplines, we could promote the concept that disciplines provide homes within the larger learning community because they determine the domain of knowledge, the theoretical or conceptual structures and the mode of inquiry that guide learning. Disciplines provide examples of systematic scholarly inquiry, and therefore serve as scaffolding for students in the process of exploring different ways of constructing meaning. The trend of students to pursue a series of degrees in different areas of study demonstrates their recognition of the need to acquire different structures and modes of thinking. To determine the scope of a discipline and its commonalities with other disciplines, more detailed investigation within courses of study may be needed. For example, what questions does the discipline ask and how are these questions related to those asked in other fields? How does the expert in the discipline function? What effects does the discipline have on other disciplines and in the larger community? What are the unknowns? Interdisciplinary encounters could begin here with the commons becoming the community.

References

Barber, K. (Ed.) (1998). *The Canadian Oxford Dictionary.* Don Mills: Oxford University Press.

Becher, R. A. (1989). *Academic tribes and territories.* Milton Keynes: Open University Press.

Bryden, D. P. (1984). What do law students learn? A pilot study. *Journal of Legal Education,* 34, 479–506.

Donald, J. G. (1993). Professors' and students' conceptualizations of the learning task in physics courses. *Journal of Research on Science Teaching,* 30, 905–918.

Donald, J. G. (2002). *Learning to think: Disciplinary perspectives.* San Francisco: Jossey-Bass.

Donald, J. G. (2003a). Pédagogie universitaire: Principes et conditions, in *L'engagement en pédagogie universitaire : quatre parcours, quatre visions de la « professionnalisation » de l'enseignement,* Au 20ᵉ Congrès de l'Association internationale de pédagogie universitaire (AIPU), Sherbrooke QC, May 2003.

Donald, J. G. (2003b). *Learning for an unknown future: complexity, uncertainty, challenge.* Opening plenary address to the annual conference of the Higher Education Research and Development Society of Australasia, Christchurch NZ, July 2003.

Donald, J. G., & Denison, D. B. (1996). Evaluating undergraduate education: The use of broad indicators. *Assessment and Evaluation in Higher Education,* 21 (1), 23–39.

Ferguson, W. & Bruun, G. (1958). *A survey of European civilization.* Boston: Houghton Mifflin.

Herman, A. (2001). *How the Scots invented the modern world.* New York: Random House.

Lewis, P. S. C. (1992). Legal education. In B. R. Clark & G. R. Neave (Eds.), *The Encyclopedia of Higher Education* (pp. 1132–1146). Oxford: Pergamon Press.

Milem, J. F., & Astin, H. S. (1994). *Scientists as teachers: A look at their culture, their roles, and their pedagogy.* Paper presented at the annual meeting of the American Educational Research Association, New Orleans LA, April 1994.

Pike, G. (1991). The effects of background, coursework, and involvement on students' grades and satisfaction. *Research in Higher Education,* 32 (1), 15–30.

Rabinowitz, P. J. (1992). Against close reading. In M.-R. Kecht (Ed.), *Pedagogy is politics: literary theory and critical teaching* (pp. 230–243). Urbana: University of Illinois Press.

Short, M., & Candlin, C. (1989). Teaching study skills for English literature. In M. Short (Ed.), *Reading, analysing and teaching literature* (pp. 178–203). London and New York: Longman Group.

Shulman, L. (2004). *Signature pedagogies.* Plenary address to the International Society for the Scholarship of Teaching and Learning, The University of Indiana, Bloomington, IN, October 2004.

Sperna Weiland, J. (1992). Humanities. In B. R. Clark & G. R. Neave (Eds.), *The Encyclopedia of Higher Education* (pp. 1981–1989). Oxford: Pergamon Press.

Toma, J. D. (1997). Alternative inquiry paradigms, faculty cultures, and the definition of academic lives. *Journal of Higher Education,* 68 (6), 679–705.

Tompkins, J. (1996). *A life in school: What the teacher learned.* Reading, MA: Addison-Wesley.

Vendler, H. (1988). What we have loved. In J. Engell & D. Perkins (Eds.), *Teaching literature: What is needed now* (pp. 13–25). Cambridge, MA: Harvard University Press.

Watson, A. (1996). Introduction to law for second-year law students? *Journal of Legal Education,* 46 (3), 430–444.

Weidner, D. J. (1997). The crises of legal education: A wake-up call for faculty. *Journal of Legal Education*, 47 (1), 92–103.

Wood, M. (1986). *Domesday: A search for the roots of England*. London: BBC Publications.

Woods, D. R., Hrymak, A. N., Marshall, R. R., Wood, P. E., Crowe, C. C., Hoffman, T. W., Wright, J. D., Taylor, P. A., Woodhouse, K. A., & Bouchard, C. G. K. (1997). Developing problem solving skills: The McMaster problem solving program. *Journal of Engineering Education*, 86 (2), 75–91.

Zhang, Z., & Richarde, R. S. (1999). *Learning-thinking Style Inventory: LISREL and multivariate analyses*. Paper presented at the annual meeting of the American Educational Research Association, Chicago, IL, March 1999.

4

Academic Disciplines
Homes or Barricades?

Gary Poole

University of British Columbia, Canada

Introduction

In the previous chapter, "The Commons: Disciplinary and Interdisciplinary Encounters," Janet Donald suggests that, to use disciplinarity in a constructive way, we should see disciplines as "homes within the larger learning community" (p. 48, this volume). The compelling aspect of this metaphor is that it invites us to leave our homes to join others in the broader community, thus enjoying the benefits of our discipline without being locked up in it. At the same time, it is this very notion of "home" that makes disciplines, and the academic departments they spawn, problematic places, restricting our "world views," to use Donald's language, creating we/they mentalities within university structures, and making it more difficult for us to solve problems or engage in discourse that would benefit from multi-disciplinary perspectives. Thus, the notion of "home," a term often invoked in the contexts of disciplines and departments, has its pros and cons.

Faculty members refer to their department as their "academic home." Home is a secure place. Within a university, it is through departments that resources are garnered and protected. While there are surely interdependencies among departments and disciplines, we rely on our "academic homes" to advocate for our share of "water and land," to return to the feudal images Donald presents. In this chapter, I will attempt to delve more deeply into the costs and benefits of organizing our intellectual lives in terms of disciplines and departments—the securities and limitation they yield. These costs and benefits will be weighed, primarily, within the context of teaching and learning in higher education.

For university faculty members, academic justice starts within the department and is shaped by the rules of the discipline. Witness the nature of paper authorship in medicine compared to history. Papers published in medical journals often feature author lists that faculty members in a history department might view as a "cast of thousands." Also, the meaning of being the last-named author differs from one discipline to the next, and thus the justice associated with credit and career advancement will differ accordingly. So, when we venture outside our "homes," perhaps to publish with a colleague in another discipline, we are not surprised to learn that considerable negotiation is required, as was the case when Donald moved into the world of physics. We will see that this negotiation applies more broadly than just to publishing. Leaving one discipline to teach or learn in another will also require considerable negotiation regarding the legitimacy of pedagogy, curriculum, cognition, student behavior, and discourse.

The security that comes from knowing the rules as well as the genre reinforces discipline-based thinking and helps maintain these rules as principal sources of a faculty member's identity. Not surprisingly, then, disciplinary affiliations trump institutional affiliations, sometimes to the chagrin of university administrators when they refer to mission statements and institutional pride as motivators for constructive change only to find that all this means less to faculty members than does their own reputation in the eyes of discipline-based colleagues across institutions.

Paradoxically, disciplines appear to help us make sense of our academic worlds while at the same time limiting our ability to do so. It is important, therefore, to take a closer look at the costs and benefits of the kinds of discipline-based thinking and pedagogy that Donald outlines in her chapter.

Learning to Think like a . . .

Donald frames learning outcomes within the disciplines in terms of "learning to think" in particular ways. This approach helps us distinguish among the disciplines, and it invites us to explore the pros and cons of discipline-specific thinking. What are the advantages of "thinking like an engineer?" Such discipline-specific thinking allows for the maintenance of a genre in which to write term papers and journal articles, learn particular modes of analysis, and develop dialogue that becomes familiar and comfortable—like home.

This comfort is very important for those working in a modern academic world that, Donald reminds us, features both complexity and uncertainty. While there is considerable overlap between the challenges posed by complexity and uncertainty, at the risk of oversimplification, I would suggest that complexity taxes us cognitively; whereas, uncertainty taxes us emotionally. Perhaps this is why Donald asserts that uncertainty is a greater threat to academics than is complexity. We are trained to deal with complexity. Indeed, most disciplines thrive on the application of intellect to reduce or at least explain complexity. Uncertainty is another matter. Our students expect complexity in their university course work. Generally, however, they abhor uncertainty. It is one thing to tell a class that a concept is difficult. It is something else again to tell them that there are a number of concepts that could be employed in a given context and we are unsure as to which is the best one. Our disciplines reduce the number of competing concepts and bring some degree of comfort to us and to our students. Note Hounsell and Anderson's description of first-year biology laboratory experiences (Chapter 6 in this volume). Instructors go to considerable effort to get students to accept that there might be more than one possible outcome to an experiment and this is more exciting than it is frustrating. The message is clear: this is what it means to do science. This message is not lost on the students.

Uncertainty is reduced considerably by homogeneity of thought processes within a discipline. Also, there is much less "starting from scratch" within the discourse of the discipline when people share a way of thinking. For teachers, this provides something important to teach in the way of processes and language. The disadvantage is that the discipline discourages diverse thinking patterns, epistemologies, or approaches to problems. The discipline stays insular and homogeneous.

This point was driven home for me when I was part of a multi-disciplinary group preparing a grant application to support the scholarship of teaching and learning across our campus. One of the first obstacles we encountered in this work was the fundamentally different ways each discipline construed the nature of research. This was captured well by an exasperated art educator who said of her colleagues in the physical sciences, "Why are they so hung up on cause and effect?!" Those colleagues would not call a focus on cause and effect a "hang up." Rather, cause–effect relationships are at the heart of their discovery process. Other approaches to scholarship are deemed unscientific.

In terms of curriculum, it would be hard to imagine a science course in which one of the topics was "The folly of cause–effect thinking." Rather, students and teachers alike share the assumption that cause–effect thinking is fundamental. Within a discipline, there are also fundamental assumptions about the size and scope of the causes that are the target of research and elements of the curriculum. Ask a cardiologist what causes a heart attack. Then ask a psychologist and a sociologist the same question. With each discipline, you will find that the causes get progressively more macroscopic in nature. In our teaching, these differences in scope can become real challenges. Anyone who has tried to teach medical sociology to medical students will have encountered these challenges. While the medical students are spending the bulk of their time being socialized (ironically) into a biomedical, reductionist profession and set of disciplines, the medical sociologist tries to convince the students that clean drinking water will do more to affect health than anything the students will do when they are physicians. Of course, some students will understand this. Typically, these will be the students who already have a degree in a discipline focused on macroscopic causes, as is sometimes the case in North America where medical students enter with at least one academic degree already completed.

As another example, consider a course entitled, "The sociology of advertising," offered by the Sociology Department in a Faculty of Arts. Now consider that the course was also presented as an elective to students in the business school. I have seen this result in an extraordinarily challenging teaching assignment—half of the class was there to expose the "evils of advertising" and the other half were marketing majors who considered advertising to be essential to a healthy economy and so they expected to learn how to advertise more effectively. There is the potential for such a course to be very exciting, provided the different points of view are well expressed and respected. Realizing this potential is no easy matter, however. In the context of this chapter, we can see the challenges stemming, in part, from a collision of disciplinary perspectives and values. If you are a faculty member in the humanities or business, how would you approach the teaching of this course?

In programs requiring the understanding of a broad range of perspectives, disciplines can collide in the classroom. For sociology majors entering a professional school like medicine, this might be the first time they realize they don't "think like physicians." The thinking patterns they learned in other disciplines might not have been articulated in any of their learning. In fact, I would argue that few disciplines do a good job of articulating learning objectives aimed at shaping thought and language, certainly at the undergraduate level. Donald's ability to clearly articulate what it means to think like an engineer, for example, would make for great reading in the discipline of engineering. This isn't to say that ways of thinking aren't developed in students within a discipline; rather, this development is more often the result of implicit, not explicit, strategies.

How uniform is the thinking within a discipline? My experience working with departments on curriculum revision has taught me that some disciplines do a more thorough job than others of achieving consensus regarding the nature of thought in that discipline. Also, this work has revealed times when the *perception* of consensus was greater than the actual consensus.

To sound very much like a psychologist for a moment (I am, after all, a product of my discipline too), we underestimate the amount of *within-group variance* when talking about discipline-based thinking. As educators, we also might see ourselves as forces meant to reduce within-group variance in our students. At the same time, if our disciplines are to be truly distinctive and, thus, comforting, we must also believe there is a considerable amount of *between-group variance*. There is a good deal of psychological research dating back to the 1960s (e.g., Tajfel & Wilkes, 1963; Tajfel, Flament, Billig, & Bundy, 1971) to indicate that social identity requires a certain amount of accentuation, if not exaggeration, of within-group similarity and between-group difference.

When it comes to thinking patterns, therefore, we may well exaggerate the divides between disciplines in order to maintain our discipline-based social identity and, thus, the protective benefits of those disciplines. For example, Donald has observed that law students must learn to use precedent. In cognitive terms, this involves searching memory, or records, for relevant cases. This search, in turn, requires an ability to identify similarities among cases in order to locate viable comparitors, and an ability to generalize from the precedent to the current. Surely, these cognitive processes are not unique to law. Medical students and residents learn to develop and use "case memory," often asking themselves, "Where have I seen something like this before?" The same must be true for a range of disciplines. Witness the graduate student in English literature, quoted by Donald, stating that an important skill involves "noticing patterns of images and recurring ideas or themes" (Donald, this volume, p. 43).

Ask your colleagues, "What does it mean to think like someone in your discipline?" The ensuing discussion might reveal a couple of things relevant to this book. First, there are some ways of thinking that are so ingrained as to be unquestioned and understood at what I have heard called "the knee-jerk level." For example, in my discipline, psychology, there is a strong underlying assumption that behavior can be quantified. Psychologists accept that this quantification might be difficult, but rarely impossible. To "think like a psychologist," therefore, often means asking, "How can this be measured?" Consistent with this thinking, almost all psychology programs require students majoring in the field to take at least one course in quantitative methods.

Following this line of thinking, we shouldn't be surprised to find student surveys of teaching in Psychology departments containing a series of statements and Likert-type scales. Having "grown up" with this type of survey and its underlying assumption, I was taken aback when a colleague in the English department suggested that it was nonsense to believe something as complex as the human condition could be reduced to numbers. Needless to say, the student survey of teaching in that department looked very different from that used in psychology.

Real discrepancies within and between disciplines, as revealed in these discussions, should be seen as an opportunity, not a problem. The view here should be that divergent views regarding the nature of thinking within a discipline should be encouraged because these views enrich the discipline. Similarly, as educators, we need to strike a balance between curricula that socialize students into a way of thinking and curricula that welcome new forms of discourse and thought. Inevitably, students will talk about concepts "in their own way." We must decide if these ways constitute flaws that need to be "educated out" or fresh perspectives that need to be "brought in."

Darwinians argue that a species cannot evolve without within-species variation, even though it is within-species similarities that define the species in the first place. The same principle holds true for variation in thinking processes within a discipline. As Donald points out, disciplines can serve to limit perspective and, thus, limit the ability of a discipline to evolve. This becomes particularly evident in the scholarship of teaching and learning (SoTL). Many faculty members are unfamiliar with the literature in this area because it typically exists outside their discipline. We could go so far as to say it is outside many faculty members' comfort zones—their "homes." The edges of these zones are defined by the kinds of boundaries referred to by Donald, and I am not surprised to read of the challenges she encountered when trying to engage disciplines such as physics in the language and methodology of SoTL research.

All the same, I applaud Donald and others for persevering through these challenges. I agree entirely with Kreber's comment in Chapter 2 that it is through such cross-disciplinary encounters that we can overcome the "silo effect" of disciplinary and departmental structures.

In summary, then, what should we conclude about the costs and benefits of "thinking like a . . .?" Certainly, both costs and benefits exist. Without some clearly defined patterns of thought, there is no discipline—uncertainty reigns and we are homeless. In terms of curriculum, we would be left to teach little more than a disjointed collection of facts and concepts. Some cynics might say this is just what we are currently doing, as we rarely address with our undergraduates the nature of thought and discourse within our discipline. A very encouraging counterexample is presented in Hounsell and Anderson's description of teaching in the biological sciences (see Chapter 6). The research they present provides evidence that final-year students can articulate the discipline-based processes that are being espoused by those teaching the courses.

On the other hand, blind adherence to one form of thinking flies in the face of what it means to be an academic and places untenable limits on our ability to solve problems, make new discoveries and appreciate fresh insights. How many times have we been grading student work, be it a term paper, an answer on an exam, or some other more innovative form of assessment, and been torn between the belief that the work is naïve or misguided and the possibility that we have a truly innovative thinker on our hands who might have a great deal to offer? This conundrum illustrates the costs and benefits of discipline-based thinking.

Signature Pedagogies as Sources of Identity and Constraint

In February of 2005, Lee Shulman, President of the Carnegie Foundation for the Advancement of Teaching, provided an excellent exposition of the notion of "signature pedagogies" when he addressed the Math Science Partnerships Workshop in Irvine, California (Shulman, 2005). It is important to note at the outset that Carnegie's work in the area of signature pedagogies has been drawn from the Foundation's research on professional schools; specifically, law, medicine, engineering and the clergy. This is an important point because professions are not the same as disciplines. Professions contain disciplines. Thus, to develop a signature pedagogy within a profession means, in part, to create pedagogies across disciplines. The forces at work to create a professional identity must be powerful, therefore. Accreditation processes, active professional organizations, and rings on the pinkie finger all work to form this identity. Professions don't just create boundaries, they create boundaries with uniformed guards.

We have already explored Donald's point that disciplines are defined, in part, by their thinking patterns. The professions are defined by thought *and* action. Indeed, Shulman states that an important purpose of signature pedagogies is that they help students connect thought and action in ways that are accepted within the profession. This does not mean that disciplines cannot have signature pedagogies. They do. However, the overarching purposes of those discipline-based pedagogies are less likely to include some of the things Shulman identifies from the Carnegie work.

For example, using language that is reminiscent of Pratt's Teaching Perspectives (Pratt, 1998), Shulman refers to purposes of signature pedagogies in terms of "apprenticeships"—cognitive, practical, and moral. He also talks about "educating for character" (Shulman, 2005, p. 3), consistent with Donald's use of the morality dimension in her analysis of the disciplines. In sum, signature pedagogies in the professions are strong forces of socialization.

Other purposes for signature pedagogies include the assurance of pedagogical continuity across courses, years, and even institutions. A faculty member who taught third-year medical students at Vanderbilt would not face a major adjustment in a move to do the same teaching at Stanford, at least not in terms of pedagogy. There would still be cases and teams and rounds. Shulman also asserts that signature pedagogies enhance students' accountability because most of these pedagogies require that students' thinking become visible (or audible). In none of the pedagogies identified in the Carnegie research did students have "places to hide."

Even with this continuity, Shulman observes that signature pedagogies can change over time. Bedside teaching changes when medical advancements result in patients spending less time in bed. Still, these pedagogies ensure that "the rules of the game are clear" (Shulman, 2005, p. 6).

By definition, signature pedagogies are distinct to the profession. It is interesting to note, however, that Shulman acknowledges such pedagogies might work well in more than one profession. For example, the case method as practised in law teaching might be very useful in medical education. However, the Carnegie research found that it is not common for a signature pedagogy to migrate from one profession to another. In this, we begin to see one of the disadvantages of pedagogies that both stem from a profession or discipline and come to be defining. The constructive sharing of pedagogies is restricted. There are exceptions, of course. A good one would be the use of problem-based learning (PBL) in medical schools and its subsequent adoption by business schools and others.

Shulman argues that signature pedagogies persist because they work. I wouldn't disagree, but I would add that they survive also because they exist in an insular world that reduces the likelihood that better methods will be introduced. If new methods are introduced, the road can be rocky. The adoption of something like PBL in medical schools has not occurred without challenges. People working in medical education can tell stories of faculty members who chose to leave a program rather than adopt PBL.

Donald points out that signature pedagogies literally shape architecture. Those involved with the Carnegie research would say that a U-shaped theatre design is much more common in American law schools than it is anywhere else. These spaces are designed to allow the instructor maximal eye contact with the class to call upon specific students to provide interpretations and answers. (I have heard this called "sniper pedagogy.") The spatial design facilitates the pedagogy. Similarly, our medical school at the University of British Columbia has "PBL rooms," which seat ten people at most and have white boards on all walls. These rooms could be used for other small-group learning experiences, but the walls don't retract to allow for something bigger. This isn't necessarily a bad thing, but it is a limiting thing.

Shulman tells us that signature pedagogies help professions educate for character. They are intended to facilitate the development of professional*ism*. Many professional schools refer to professionalism in their mission statements, but it can be difficult to define clearly. If signature pedagogies are viewed generally as good things, and I think they are, it may well be due to their potential to help students achieve the sometimes-elusive goals associated with professionalism and, thus, help a school achieve a vital objective.

The term "professionalism" is used in reference to everything from in-class behavior to interactions with the general public. Essential attributes have been identified within each profession. In medicine, these attributes include putting patients' interests above one's own, upholding high ethical and moral standards, being responsive to the needs of society, and evincing values such as empathy, integrity, and altruism (American Board of Internal Medicine, 1995). In engineering, professionalism is viewed in terms of acting responsibly and gaining public trust (Online Ethics Center for Engineering, 2006). Responsible action includes showing due regard for the environment and the sustainability of the resources used.

It is interesting to juxtapose these various attributes of professionalism with Marcia Baxter Magolda's categories of learning outcomes: cognitive maturity, integrated identity and mature relationships (see Chapter 12). Baxter Magolda ties these categories nicely to considerations of citizenship and ethics, which relate well to the attributes of professionalism identified in medicine, engineering, and other professions. Baxter Magolda argues that a sense of self-authorship must be attained if these outcomes are to be realized. With this in mind, it is worth looking at the ways in which an important precursor to self-authorship, self-assessment, is emphasized in different professions.

In engineering, educational research has looked at the extent to which students' self-assessments correlate with scores on other forms of assessment, such as exams and projects. The goal here is to determine the "accuracy" of self-assessment (see, for example, Greene & Jalkio, 2004). In medicine, self-assessment is viewed, not just as another source of data for assigning grades, but as a valued skill in itself. Thus, the *process* of self-assessment becomes as important as the outcomes. Epstein (2007) states that physicians must be able to engage in moment-to-moment monitoring of their ability "in order to meet patients' changing needs, to recognize the limits of his or her own competence, and to manage unexpected situations" (p. 392).

Compare these outcomes of what Epstein calls "mindful practice" (1999) to Baxter Magolda's notion of self-authorship—the capacity to internally define one's beliefs, identity and social relations. This comparison provides insights into the ways fundamental learning processes take shape within disciplines and professions. In medicine, students learn about their identity, in part, in terms of their limits and competencies. Given the prominence of these characteristics in medical education, it might be reasonable to expect that these characteristics of identity would be equally prominent in other professions.

Some believe that it is getting harder rather than easier to teach professionalism (Sullivan, 1999). Certainly, discussions of professionalism have become more pressing in the eight years I have spent in our medical school. The classroom, real or virtual, may provide starting points for the teaching of professionalism, or discipline-based ethics, but such venues, no matter how well designed, have their limitations. Students must see how professionalism is manifest in practice and so the pedagogy of the profession must afford such opportunities. Again, these opportunities differ depending upon the profession or discipline providing them. Clinical experience is fundamental to medical education, and co-operative, or work-based education to engineering. These experiences differ in ways that go beyond their locations, duration, or other details. Community service learning, for example, has been analyzed in terms of its underlying political ideologies and goals of educational transformation (Butin, 2006). This might help explain why these learning opportunities can look quite different when comparing such contexts as business schools and schools of social work. For example, I have heard some students criticize community service learning options as being inherently "left wing." For people in the so-called helping professions or humanities, this critique is reminiscent of physical scientists being criticized for being obsessed with cause and effect. Each might ask, "Where's the problem?"

My Discipline, My Home, My Walls

I see the world through the eyes of a psychologist. When consulting with people about their teaching, I listen for causal attributions—the ways they explain what is happening and not happening in their classes. I try to be mindful of our tendency to underestimate the power of context and overestimate the role of personality or character when making sense of the world around us. I teach these ideas as though they are foundational. In addition, I do think that certain aspects of human behavior and thinking can be quantified. However, I have been fortunate enough to work with other social scientists who have taught me that there is great value in asking open-ended questions and searching for themes in people's responses. Had I stayed strictly within my discipline when I was just starting to do psychological research in hospital settings, it would have taken much longer for me to learn this. Thus, my students learn about "illness narratives" along with the quantitative interpretation of things like the subscales of the Post-Traumatic Growth Inventory (Tedeschi & Calhoun, 1996).

Matthew and Pritchard (in the following chapter) state that the tradition of dividing a university into disciplines is so ingrained that "We cannot think of it being any other way" (p. 58, this volume). While this may well be an accurate observation, I would implore us to try and think of other ways. Doing this within a well-established university—disbanding departments and implementing some other structure—might be too daunting a task to realistically consider. However, if we were designing a university "from scratch," could we think of a better organizational scheme?

We faced this very question at UBC when asked to help the government of Kuwait design a new institution that brought together technology and business as its main "disciplines." An important stated objective for the institution was to graduate students who could combine engineering knowledge and business savvy. In our planning, we discussed the possibility that discipline-based departments would hold the institution back in its attempt to achieve this objective. In these discussions, much was made of the notion of disciplinary "silos" (see Kreber in Chapter 2). As an alternative, we designed a structure that used major issues and problems as its organizational nodes. These ended up looking like multi-disciplinary institutes focused on such things as water conservation and computer-aided communication. These weren't research institutes, they were teaching institutes, as it were. (Of course, there were also research components as well.) At the same time, the engineers on the planning committee were very mindful of expectations related to program accreditation, a strong force for disciplinarity. Such discipline-based forces kept bringing us back to traditional structures, curricula, and course offerings. It remains to be seen just what this institution will look like.

Our educational development centre at UBC recently invited people to take part in a discussion under the heading "Building a University from the Ground Up: Some Assembly Required." I would highly recommend this topic to those of you who organize educational development events on your campus. The discussion was lively and creative. Participants were able to think of the university being some other way without worrying about the threat of homelessness.

References

American Board of Internal Medicine (1995). *Project Professionalism*. Accessed April 28, 2008. <http://www.abim.org/pdf/publications/professionalism.pdf>

Butin, D.W. (2006). Disciplining service learning: Institutionalization and the case for community studies. *International Journal of Teaching and Learning in Higher Education*, 18(1), 57–64.

Epstein, R.M. (1999). Mindful practice. *Journal of the American Medical Association*, 282, 833–839.

Epstein, R.M. (2007). Assessment in medical education. *The New England Journal of Medicine*, 356(4), 387–396.

Greene, C.S., & Jalkio, J.A. (2004). *Evaluation of the accuracy and effectiveness of portfolio based student self-assessment*. Presentation to the Annual Conference of the American Society for Engineering Education, June, 2004. Salt Lake City, UT.

Online Ethics Center: Background Concepts for Teaching Engineering Ethics Online Ethics Center for Engineering (2006). 6/11/2006. National Academy of Engineering. Accessed January 1, 2008. <www.onlineethics.org/CMS/edu/instruct guides/concepts.aspx>

Pratt, D. (1998). *Five perspectives on teaching in adult and higher education*. Malabar, FL: Krieger.

Shulman, L. (2005). *The signature pedagogies of the professions of law, medicine, engineering and the clergy: Potential lessons for the education of teachers*. Presentation to the Math Science Partnerships (MSP) Workshop, February 6, 2005. Irvine, California.

Sullivan, W.M. (1999). What is left of professionalism after managed care? *Hastings Center Report*, 29(7), 7–13.

Tajfel, H., Flament, C., Billig, M.G., & Bundy, R.P. (1971). Social categorization and intergroup behaviour. *European Journal of Psychology*, 1, 149–178.

Tajfel, H., & Wilkes, A.L. (1963). Classification and quantitative judgment. *British Journal of Psychology*, 54, 101–114.

Tedeschi, R.G., & Calhoun, L.G. (1996). The Posttraumatic Growth Inventory: Measuring the positive legacy of trauma. *Journal of Trauma and Stress*, 9(3), 455–471.

5

Hard and Soft – A Useful Way of Thinking about Disciplines?
Reflections from Engineering Education on Disciplinary Identities

Robert G.S. Matthew and Jane Pritchard

University of Glasgow

Introduction

It would be hard for us to imagine a university today that was not organized by disciplines and some arrangement of schools, faculties and departments. The division of knowledge and underlying epistemologies into defined disciplinary regimes is seemingly part and parcel of the post-industrial western university. We cannot think of it being any other way. How would we possibly manage the numbers of students we have and the *need* to have individuals with specialized knowledge? These may well be real questions, but the role of university education within society (not just for those participating in it) also needs to be continually examined.

What are the generic qualities, be it knowledge, skills and attitudes, of a university graduate and what are those that are reflective of a particular degree program? How does identifying the features that distinguish the discipline (i.e. the 'signature pedagogies', see Donald, Chapter 3, or the 'ways of thinking and practicing', see Hounsell and Anderson, Chapter 6) contribute to enhancing the student learning experience? By focusing on disciplinary practices we compartmentalize the institution and put boxes around knowledge domains rather than creating a common space for enquiry. After all, surely the focus of the university is to foster and support a culture of enquiry and preparing students for life beyond the disciplines.

A Challenge?

Within the disciplinary distinction we often hear reference to the 'hard' and 'soft' disciplines. This description comes originally from Kuhn (1962) who studied the characteristics of the physical sciences and this was extended to thirty-six academic areas by Biglan (1973). In classifying disciplines as 'hard' Biglan meant disciplines that "are characterized by the existence of paradigms that specify appropriate problems for study and the appropriate methods to be used" (p. 195).

For Biglan 'soft' disciplines were those that are non-paradigmatic. We need to be clear that we propose that the 'hard' subjects, as defined by Biglan, are often perceived to be difficult subjects for study, usually, although not exclusively, because of a strong mathematical content to the curriculum.

This is a misinterpretation of the use of 'hard' and 'soft' as a means of describing disciplines in this context and is perhaps the result of an unfortunate choice of words. Perhaps 'inflexible' and 'flexible' may have been more appropriate descriptors of disciplines although these are still problematic.

We wish to challenge the use of descriptors such as 'hard' and 'soft' disciplines in this chapter and assert that they are not always used as Biglan had originally defined them. We consider the terminology of 'hard' and 'soft' to be reflective of the individuals' perceptions of their own disciplinary preferences and strengths rather than an accurate descriptor of the nature of knowing and understanding within a discipline. For example, there is a widespread notion that engineering is somehow a 'difficult' subject because it is one that involves the study of mathematics. This is an idea that we wish to reject, although we accept that some people find mathematics difficult or, as Meyer and Land (2006) would describe it, full of troublesome knowledge. Likewise, we would assert that some people find language learning, for example, to be equally full of troublesome knowledge.

We would much prefer that we do away with these classifiers and just accept that for different people different subjects may present a degree of difficulty! That disciplines may have a paradigm that they use does not mean that they are fixed as disciplines, indeed the opposite is true. 'Hard' disciplines have to continue to review the paradigms underpinning them to ensure that they stay relevant and up to date in an everchanging world. They are flexible disciplines rather than 'hard' ones!

However, let us be clear that we are both engineers (a civil engineer and a materials scientist/engineer) and we accept that our original discipline may have left us with a certain way of thinking and being (i.e. you can take the person out of engineering but not the engineer out of the person); thus our view of engineering and the paradigm(s) that may underpin it may be colored by our disciplinary background. It seems to us that the labeling of a discipline as 'hard' (be it used in the original Biglan definition or as an indicator of inflexibility) is almost to set in stone how you should teach and learn it. If you believe that a discipline is hard, then you are stating categorically that there exist some appropriate problems for study and fundamental methods for problem solving. The issue for us is that the world does not stand still. What was taught in engineering courses in the 1970s is now almost unrecognizable from what is taught today and the same may be said of a number of degree programs. The types of problems tackled today just could not be tackled then as the methods we now use were unknown at that time. Within engineering there is debate about analytical approaches. Thinking of the discipline as 'hard' limits the thinking about what is taught and is likely to produce engineers who are limited in their vision and thinking.

What are We Trying to Do in a University Education?

It might be useful to firstly consider what the purpose of higher education is as we may not all agree. Baxter Magolda (see Chapter 12) offers a detailed analysis of the espoused outcomes of higher education in both the US and UK. She puts it succinctly as ". . . a transformation from authority dependence to self-authorship, or the capacity to internally define one's beliefs, identity and social relations" (p. 143).

In the UK this idea of what makes a graduate is often referred to as 'graduateness' (Higher Education Quality Council, [HEQC] 1995). HEQC defined these qualities of 'graduateness' as

> those attributes that one might expect to have acquired through the particular experience of higher education study as well as ancillary qualities that would be expected of graduates, but which had not previously been regarded as the responsibility of higher education to teach.
>
> (p. 5)

The document went on to describe what some of these attributes might actually be and included 'responsibility' and 'ethical understanding' in the list.

Barrie (2007) takes the concept of 'graduateness' a little further and discusses 'generic graduate attributes' (see also Kreber in Chapter 1). He developed a hierarchy of attributes with the most complex or integrated conception being:

> Generic attributes are understood to be interwoven aptitudes and abilities such as academic inquiry and intellectual curiosity, the ability to accommodate diversity and alternative perspectives, the ability to create and defend ideas, and the ability to use communication as a vehicle for learning.
>
> (p. 456)

We would like to explore this idea of 'graduateness' a little further. What constitutes 'graduateness' is shaped and influenced by many, including the individual, the university, society at large, and the professions (where appropriate). We have to accept that for some disciplines within a university there are professional standards to be met, for example in medicine, dentistry, veterinary medicine, engineering, nursing, or education. In the UK this means that university provision is subject to accreditation by a professional body. For example, degrees in civil engineering are accredited by the Institution of Civil Engineers and lead to exemption from some professional examinations.

An engineering education has to be 'fit for purpose' in that it should produce graduate engineers who are 'fit to practice' as graduate engineers, in an ethical manner. Students do not become, in the eyes of the profession (i.e. their peers), engineers until they attain 'Chartered Engineer (CEng)' status, normally some three years after graduation from university after a period in practice.

Given the strong influence of the Engineering Council, there is a considerable tension in universities about how to keep a balance between 'education' and 'training' in undergraduate engineering provision. The distinction between education and training is not a semantic argument; it is a real one, and one that has created considerable debate. For example, the advent of computer-based methods of analysis of structures has led to a marked decrease in manual methods being taught. Instead many students use computer packages (often 'industry standard') to analyze structures. This is clearly useful *training* in the use of a software package and many such graduates are in demand by industry as they can 'hit the ground running' when they enter professional practice. However, when these students come across a situation or problem for which the software is inappropriate (and they may not even know it is inappropriate) there is a real risk of them engineering an inappropriate (and sometimes unsafe) solution. What is missing, then, is the *education* in what and how the software is actually doing the analysis. This has led to a number of embarrassing 'disasters' in practice.

This balance between education and training is also apparent in the legal profession. As Donald (Chapter 3) writes: "the principal challenge for instruction is to organize a program that meets both scholarly and professional requirements" (p. 42). In the humanities, responding to professional requirements is not a curriculum consideration and therefore the curriculum is not subject to the same tensions between education and training.

A recent UK news report informed that the Taxpayers Alliance identified 401 university courses as non-courses and coined them 'Mickey-Mouse' degrees. The response from Universities UK has been that society needs to think more broadly about higher education and recognize that these 'non-traditional' courses respond to employers' needs (BBC News, 2007). This raises the questions of how we, as teachers in the university, feel about the array of degree programs that are on offer. If we find ourselves perhaps mocking some of these degree programs, for example any derision of the 'surfing degree', then maybe we need to think seriously about what it is exactly that we find unsuitable about them and what it is that makes it difficult for us to think of them as appropriate for degree-level study. Maybe we are starting to identify what we think a university education is about.

Alternatively, we need to identify what it is about the degrees we typically find acceptable that would make these new degrees more suitable. This whole debate needs to be seen, in the UK, within a context of government imperatives on the employability skills of graduates, enhancing graduate attributes, and personal development planning. Thus, it is particularly timely to consider what subjects we consider being appropriate for university degree courses. This will also include further exploration of the training versus education debate, i.e. how much of a degree should be about training students for the world of work and how much about educating them in the subject matter. This is a real tension for many in higher education at the present time and does lend itself to a simple solution. Usefulness is not necessarily a sign of a lesser degree or a less scholarly degree, is it? Surely as we highlighted earlier with the quote from Baxter Magolda (Chapter 12), the main purpose of all university degrees is that they should foster a sense of inquiry and enable graduates to be adaptable not just to multiple career routes but also with regards to different futures for society.

Using Donald's three philosophical lenses of *pragmatism, empiricism* and *morality* let us look at the moral argument. For engineering and law educators the issue is how to achieve a balance between the requirement to train people to enter the profession and be 'fit to practice' but at the same time educate them so that they can respond to the future needs of the profession and life outside the discipline. We admit we have not heard humanities educators discuss the notion of 'fit to practice' so we assume that it is not a concern; however, supporting students' professional development planning and identification of transferable skills is a key issue for *all* disciplines in the modern university.

The employability agenda in UK higher education (Knight & Yorke, 2004) does not identify particular disciplines but looks at graduate attributes across the spectrum of degree programs. Although the 'fit to practice' notion, so familiar to the professions, may not be of quite the same 'tone' as in other disciplines, there tends to be an increasing 'job-readiness' associated with *all* degrees, which impacts on what it is students should be able to do by the end of their degree. For those outside the academy, assurance of the competencies of engineers is provided through the accreditation of degree programs by professional bodies, in the UK under a framework produced by the Engineering Council (Engineering Council, 2004), and in the US through the ABET Inc. accreditation process (ABET Inc. 2007). This has facilitated the international movement of engineers. However, even with accreditation there is still tension for those who 'teach' engineering. Are we educating the next generation of engineers or training them for professional practice?

Shulman (2005) summarized this tension as:

> Every profession can be characterized by these inherent tensions (the intellectual, the technical and the moral), which are never fully resolved, but which must be managed and balanced with every action. Responsible professional pedagogy must address these tensions and provide the students with the capabilities to deal with them.
>
> (p. 59)

We will explore what is meant by *responsible professional pedagogy* in both engineering and law education and offer some examples of these pedagogies in practice later on in this chapter.

Signature Pedagogies

Donald (Chapter 3) considers teaching and learning within and beyond the disciplines in engineering, law and English literature using the philosophical criteria of empiricism, pragmatism and morality to structure her discussion. She goes on to describe engineering as being characterized by empiricism and pragmatism in the main and focusing on the question: 'Does it work?'. Law is seen to be characterized by pragmatism as well as morality and focuses on the question 'Does it fit?', whilst English literature is seen to be principally characterized by morality and the question: 'Do you agree?'. These defined characteristics of disciplines appear to imply an underlying worth or 'goodness' about the discipline. For us, morality is an issue for all in education, so is empiricism and pragmatism. This is a point we assume that most people would agree with. As educators in a university we must all be cognizant of the many motivations and possible 'career' routes for graduates and equip all to engage equally with society and not look up or down on other disciplines. The perception of the 'usefulness' of a discipline can often be used to confer some lesser status within the academy.

We will structure our discussion around engineering education as an example of a discipline that is trying to break with its signature pedagogy (i.e., of pragmatism and empiricism). We will also look at an example outside the field of engineering to highlight how another subject, law, has challenged the traditional teaching and learning boundaries.

What Can I Do as a New Lecturer?

One of the hardest things for new and experienced faculty to do is to challenge the way of approaching the teaching and learning of a subject. New faculty programs often introduce academics to a variety of teaching and learning approaches that to many seem idealistic and on occasion pure fantasy. Often the cry of *'That would never work in my discipline'* is heard, or *'How do I do that in a lecture of unmotivated first year students?'*, or *'I can't do the marking for that many students and besides rewards and recognitions focus on my research in the main'*. Given these responses, it is indeed astonishing that we even bother thinking about teaching and learning at all. However, if the university experience is about creating and nurturing a sense of inquiry (as many of us think it should be), we need to start thinking outside the silos of disciplines and departments.

Departments aid the administration of the university not necessarily the education of students (and faculty). Disciplines enable us to retreat into our comfort zones and on occasion pass the responsibility on to others, *'That's not what WE do'*. Just because a subject has always been taught in a certain way does not mean that this way has helped all students to learn. Let us not confuse tradition with providing high quality learning spaces for students and faculty alike. Part of what shapes the traditions by which faculty approach their teaching are their own experiences as a student (*'I teach as I was taught, it worked for me, didn't it?'*). *'We have to tell them first all the facts and "stuff" before they can start asking questions'*, is another often heard comment in response to suggestions to introduce Inquiry-Based Learning into degree programs in the early years. We would argue that we need to challenge not just the characteristics of the discipline but also what constitutes the boundaries of *how* and *what* can be taught as part of that discipline.

Hounsell and Anderson (see the next chapter) use the phrase *'ways of thinking and practicing'*, or WTP, to capture what they identify as the characteristics of a particular subject area that students learn. Ways of thinking and practicing range from that which is explicitly taught to the underlying behaviors of people within the discipline. For example, what are the ways of thinking and practicing in psychology? What does it mean to think like a psychologist? Is it more than all the 'facts and figures', is it something else as well? WTP presents an appealing way to consider both the 'what' and the 'how' of teaching in our disciplines.

However, how do we as teachers reflect some of the tangible and not so tangible aspects of our disciplines to our students, and what about attitudes? We could teach all the mathematics in the world to the engineers but to be an engineer is not captured in knowing all the mathematical equations: it is about more than that, thankfully! We would argue that being an engineer is to understand maths as part of a toolkit that constitutes the WTP of an engineer.

Matthew and Hughes (1993) argued that engineering courses needed to rethink the balance in the curriculum between the 'ics' (e.g., mathematics) and the 'ings' (e.g. team working) to ensure that they produced engineers fit for practice in the modern world. Pritchard and Baillie (2006) explored how engineering education can consider extending its remit to include such aspects as participation, politics and policy, and citizenship. These themes are currently rarely raised in engineering curricula. Thus, these authors attempt to challenge what traditionally have been the boundaries of engineering (education) and, potentially, what constitute its WTP. We suggest that although identifying WTP is useful, we should also consider how tradition may be reinforced by a narrow interpretation of WTP. Put differently, we wonder about the extent to which disciplines are encouraged to challenge their identified WTP so as to ensure that they are still appropriate in the modern world.

Examples of Engineering Education that Challenge the Accepted Practices of the Discipline

In engineering the wider needs of society must be taken into account; in fact, it is a legal requirement (CCPE, 2003). For example in civil engineering works an environmental impact assessment is a requirement. This means we must interact with other professions and understand what they tell us. Engineering education has always clearly had an element of technology but increasingly it has a component of people skills (see also Donald). This has had an impact on the pedagogy used within the discipline. Matthew and Hughes (1991) describe the use of a mock Public Inquiry with undergraduate engineers as a means of developing group work, report writing, oral presentation skills as well developing the students' 'people skills'. Here we offer some examples from the world of engineering education to highlight how one might challenge not only the traditional ways of approaching the teaching of a subject but also what are considered the boundaries of a subject. We also include an example from a law course to show that there are many teachers out there challenging the 'signature pedagogies' and WTP of their discipline.

Example 1: Compassion and Peace Practicum – Engineering Design Course, University of Binghamton, USA (Catalano, 2006)

In this course engineers and non-engineers participate in an engineering design project to promote peace and compassion within engineering. The aim is to get engineers to think about these aspects of their work and for non-engineers to think about engineering and the role of engineers. The impetus for this course was the teachers' desire to combine these roles. They asked themselves, "*How does my career as an engineer and educator contribute in any way to the well being of the planet?*" (Catalano, 2006, p. 1). The brief given to the students is: "Do something/anything that promotes social justice and/or peace in the world. The accent in this assignment is on the action. You must use a formal engineering design methodology in the accomplishment of this task" (2006, p. 1). Catalano explains that this brief has been used in engineering courses ranging from heat transfer to senior capstone design modules. Examples of projects undertaken include: designing and building an indoor flower garden for a wheelchair-bound elderly neighbor of a student; building and designing an inner city playground; or fundraising for an informal conflict resolution center on campus for students. The student and staff reactions to these courses are initially hostile and the cry of 'What has this got to do with engineering?' is frequently heard. It is exactly this preconceived notion of what a particular discipline *is* or *does* that we are challenging. Of particular interest to our discussion is that by the end of the course the students are positive about the entire experience. Evidence suggests that the course was the highlight not only of that one year but, in some cases, of their whole degree program. Where did it become written in stone that such humane considerations as peace and compassion are nothing to do with engineering? The non-engineers complain they have to use an engineering design methodology. What culture of enquiry are we supporting when our students reject anything that does not fit with a fixed view of what it means to be a student of a certain discipline? Where do they get these messages from? We could be in danger of putting blinkers on students and ourselves. Instead of enhancing inter-disciplinarity and supporting them for life beyond and during university, we may be forcing them down narrower pathways.

Example 2: Thermodynamics and Feminist and Critical Pedagogies (Riley, 2003)

Riley (2003) uses liberative pedagogies, for example those of Paolo Freire (1970), in the engineering thermodynamics course she teaches to classes of women at Smith College, USA. Riley asserts that the features of liberative pedagogies include being highly student-centered with a view to empowering students to take responsibility for their own learning and to challenge authority and oppressive forces in their lives. It is Riley's hope that by engaging in such alternative approaches to what is a renowned *difficult* topic in engineering she can challenge the accepted ways of viewing engineering, engineers and those who study it and facilitate the students' learning in that subject. In addition Riley wants to open engineering up to non-traditional students (a major mission of Smith College – a female-only establishment). Her goal is not only to prepare students for the engineering profession by engendering in them a more critical awareness of their role, but also to consider what the role of the engineer *could be* if it were to consider more strongly social justice issues at its core.

Example 3: Teaching Human Rights to Law Undergraduates (Murdoch, 2007)

Final year law undergraduates at the University of Glasgow can sign up for an optional course on European Human Rights. The course is entirely self-taught and self-managed by the students. The students are presented with a 'cutting-edge' legal issue in the European Court of Human Rights (ECHR) and they make a submission to that Court using the due process: submission of an application, an admissibility hearing, a chamber hearing and a Grand Chamber in front of the ECHR in Strasbourg. The assessment of the course is based on the professional skills and ethical behaviors developed. The students self- and peer-assess each other through a three-day post-'Grand Chamber' hearing group assessment activity. This is clearly a course in which law students are exposed to 'cutting-edge' legal thinking and at the same time develop the professional skills they will need in their careers. This is not taught in the traditional classroom setting – it challenges where we teach as well as how.

Hard and Soft – A Useful Way of Thinking about Disciplines?

Whilst we accept the view that disciplines have different characteristics we return again to our notion that labels such as 'hard' and 'soft' place a certain, though implicit, value on the disciplines within the academy. We suggest that the labels of 'hard' versus 'soft' are not helpful in promoting new thinking about the 'what and how' of teaching and learning within particular disciplines. What we should strive to avoid are positions where a discipline could look 'down' upon another for reasons varying from being 'useful' or 'not useful' to being a subject that is not 'degree-worthy' (for example, the surfing degree!). Instead the academy should join forces and share responsibility for enabling student learning and focus more on questions like 'How can we all together support and improve the student learning experiences? And how can we, across the disciplines, support students and enable learning spaces that are authentic of 'the real world' (i.e. deal with subjects that are not confined to a single discipline, such as climate change and poverty reduction)?' (see also Kreber in Chapter 1).

In engineering there is a large moral imperative to what we do. The *messing with the world* is not just *messing* for the sake of it, or is it? This bestows a large moral imperative on the engineer, and also the consumer, to consider how demands affect the role of engineers and engineering in society. This means that, as a profession, we are continually open to scrutiny and critique, we continually critique ourselves and what we do. We are continually responding to changes in professional standards to ensure that the engineers of tomorrow are 'fit for purpose'. However, it is timely for us to consider one thing about engineering education, in particular: if we [engineers] are messing with the world just for the sake of it, is society really ready for engineers who have a dominant moral imperative so that the next car or MP3 player may not be built? Is there room in our social consciousness for the moral engineer? Where and what would we do if we were not 'improving our lot' and ensuring 'progress'? How do our teaching and learning spaces in higher education enable students to transcend the current traditions of disciplines and think outside the disciplinary boxes?

This is not an easy discussion and, let us face it, what does it have to do with teaching and learning? For us, everything, as it impels us to revisit the question of what it means to get a university education? As Kirp (2003, p. 53) has stated:

> Universities represent something as ineffable as the common good – more specifically, that higher education contributes to the development of knowledgeable and responsible citizens, encourages social inclusion, promotes and spreads knowledge, increases social mobility and stimulates the economy.

The Role of Inquiry and the Disciplines

McMaster University in Canada (Centre for Leadership in Education, 2001) has been involved in teaching Inquiry for over twenty years in its elite programs and professional schools. Now, Inquiry is being offered at McMaster to all first year students with a growing number of follow-up courses offered in subsequent years. In 2001, over 670 students in year one chose an Inquiry course. Inquiry is about developing the ability to ask questions, developing ways to find answers or at least understand what lies behind the question. It is also about student-centered learning which has at heart the acquisition of skills that are transferable into the workplace. To us it seems that one university has managed to find a pedagogy that allows both education and training to take place simultaneously.

Donald (2002) suggests that the disciplines vary considerably in regard to the arts of intellectualizing the subject matter most salient to their particular agenda. Thus the problem-solving styles in use within the discipline are likely to be different. This means that the problems faced by an engineering professor and a humanities professor are different. What is important is that those who teach are typically experts in the discipline. This implies that they have learned to take for granted the ways of thinking (and practicing) in their particular discipline. Students on the other hand are novices to this particular discipline. When supporting students in their learning it is important to recognize this and make the WTP explicit so that they eventually become intuitive also for the student (Dreyfus, 2004). It is at this stage that students begin to have, as Graff (2003) puts it, a meaningful engagement with the discipline's most basic orientations to subject matter, method and the world. As they progress, hopefully both students and teachers will engage in a critique of WTP within the discipline.

For us this structure of the discipline is all-pervasive, deeply entrenched and tacit – academics learn it through complete immersion. Although the intent of many programs for new faculty is to encourage them, by meeting colleagues from other disciplines, to think about 'how they teach' and consider alternative approaches, few faculty, if any, change their approaches as the culture of the discipline is very strong and smothers the enthusiasm of new entrants (Matthew, 2008).

Hirst (1974) argued that the epistemological structure of academic disciplines determines how they should be taught, thereby, in essence, arguing for signature pedagogies. Specifically Hirst suggested that different disciplines have a 'grammar' of key terms and concepts and a logical order with respect to how the concepts relate to one another and are organized. Thus there are different forms of knowledge that give rise to the discipline (e.g. engineering, law or the humanities). The teaching of these disciplines, therefore, has to convey to the students their epistemological structure and to concern itself much more rigorously with the detailed analysis of the logical features inherent in different forms of knowledge. Thus, by default, there are pedagogies that are appropriate to the teaching (and learning) of disciplines that are not transferable to others. In law education the use of the 'moot' is clearly a signature pedagogy that is unique to law education.

Middendorf and Pace (2004) observed that "we have only begun to understand what thinking goes on in different disciplines, nor do we know the similarities and differences across the disciplines" (p. 2). We therefore suggest that it is how disciplines see themselves that lead to there being signature pedagogies. After all disciplines are trying to produce very different types of learning in students. However, given the need for graduates with common transferable skills and abilities (i.e. a set of generic graduate attributes), we continue to speculate on whether there should not also be some commonalities in the pedagogies used. Robertson and Bond (2005) make a plea "not for unity, but for dialogue that enables the productive co-existence of different way of being" (p. 91).

Responsible Educators

As long as we shy away from these 'harder' debates of how we might actually develop responsible citizens, we do no better than the students who want to know whether what you are teaching will be on the exam or not. As university educators, we are in danger of taking a surface approach to our teaching and just getting the job done. An attitude we do not appreciate in our students. But as with our students, we can encourage each other and them to adopt a deeper more thoughtful approach to education. We can adopt a deep approach to our thinking about pedagogical matters by not limiting our conversations simply to the technical aspects of the education process (i.e. how can I get all this content over in just ten lectures?). Too quickly we get absorbed or focused on how to teach systems design (or the Spanish Civil War) so that we forget to consider how the content fits into a wider remit for education.

More specifically, we need to think about how we might stimulate enquiry in our students (and ourselves) as well as promote responsible citizenship, no matter whether our students are engineers, lawyers or literary critics. When all is said and done, university education and the debates between the different disciplines will go on until we decide what kind of society we (globally) want to live in. We need an education that is, without a doubt, moral for all because after all, morality is not just what we know, but what we do with what we know.

Barnett (1997) considers critique of a discipline as part of its ongoing inherent character needed to ensure its longevity: "In a universe of endemic cognitive and social change, no academic sub-culture can stand still. Critique, therefore, plays more than an identifying – sustaining function. The economic and social capital of each discipline is maintained through critique" (p. 15). How many disciplines within the university are undergoing such critique through continual scrutiny and reflection?

A Final Thought

The university is a collection of many disciplines each with its own ways of thinking and teaching, but all with a common purpose, the creation of a graduate who is 'fit for purpose'. We may have different viewpoints on what that purpose is but let us not shy away from having discussions about the 'purposes of higher education' as such discussions can inform how we approach our teaching and the learning we are trying to encourage in students and peers. We do not need to see disciplines as 'hard' or 'soft', but instead as disciplines that have different knowledge bases and different signature pedagogies. Hopefully, along the way, we can celebrate differences, trade and share ideas about pedagogy and learn from one another.

Let us return to the original idea of a university as some kind of '*commons*'. We would love to see the engineers, the lawyers and the humanities sheep all grazing peacefully together.

References

ABET Inc. (2007). *The basics – accreditation assures quality*, January 1, 2007. Retrieved October 19, 2007, from http://www.abet. org/thebasics.shtml.

Barnett, R. (1997). *Higher Education: A critical business*. Buckingham: Open University Press.

Barrie, S. (2007). A conceptual framework for the teaching and learning of generic graduate attributes. *Studies in Higher Education*, 32(4), 439–458.

BBC News (2007). University non-courses attacked, August 21, 2007. Retrieved August 22, 2007, from http://news.bbc.co.uk/ 1/hi/education/6955701.stm.

Biglan, A. (1973). The characteristics of subject matter in different academic areas. *Journal of Applied Psychology*, 57(3), 195–203.

Catalano, G.D. (2006). *Making Gentle the Life of the World*, Frontiers in Education Conference, 36th Annual Conference, October 27–31, San Diego, pp. 1–4.

CCPE, Canadian Council of Professional Engineers (2003). *Accreditation and Criteria Procedures*, October 12, 2003. Retrieved August 27, 2007, from http://www.ccpe.ca.

Centre for Leadership in Education (2001). *Resources and information*, June 1, 2001. Retrieved August 27, 2007, from http://www.mcmaster.ca/cll/.

Donald, J.G. (2002). *Learning to Think: Disciplinary Perspectives*. San Francisco: Jossey-Bass.

Dreyfus, S.E. (2004). The Five-Stage Model of Adult Skill Acquisition. *Bulletin of Science, Technology and Society*, 24(3), 177–181.

Engineering Council (2004). UK-SPEC is the standard, March 1, 2004. Retrieved October 19, 2007 from http://www.engc. org.uk/ukspec/default.aspx.

Freire, P. (1970). *Pedagogy of the Oppressed*. London: Penguin Books.

Graff, G. (2003). *Clueless in Academe: How Schooling Obscures the Life of the Mind*. New Haven, CT: Yale University Press.

HEQC (Higher Education Quality Council) (1995). *The Graduate Standards Programme: Interim Report*. London: HEQC.

Hirst, P. (1974). *Knowledge and the Curriculum*. London: Routledge, Kegan Paul.

Kirp, D.L. (2003). *Shakespeare, Einstein, and the Bottom Line: The Marketing of Higher Education*. Cambridge, MA: Harvard University Press.

Knight, P., & Yorke, M. (2004). *Learning, Curriculum and Employability in Higher Education*. London: Routledge Falmer.

Kuhn, T. (1962). *The Structure of Scientific Revolutions*. Chicago: University of Chicago Press.

Matthew, R.G.S. (2008). Educational Development Units and Quality Enhancement. In B. Tompkinson (Ed.), *Leading Educational Development* (in press). London: Staff and Educational Development Association.

Matthew, R.G.S., & Hughes, D.C. (1991). What's t'do with Sewage?. *Simulation and Games for Learning*, 21(2), 131–140.

Matthew, R.G.S., & Hughes, D.C. (1993). Civil Engineering education – Time for a rethink? In F.R. Montgomery (Ed.), *Innovation and Change in Civil Engineering Education* (pp. 1–12). Belfast: Queen's University Press.

Meyer, J.H.F., & Land, R. (2006). Threshold Concepts and Troublesome Knowledge – Issues of Liminality. In J.H.F. Meyer & R. Land (Eds.), *Threshold Concepts and Troublesome Knowledge* (pp. 19–32). Oxon: Routledge.

Middendorf, J., & Pace, D. (2004). Decoding the Disciplines: A Model for Helping Students Learn Disciplinary Ways of Thinking. *New Directions for Teaching and Learning*, 98, 1–2.

Murdoch, J. (2007). Personal Communication.

Pritchard, J., & Baillie, C. (2006). How can engineering education contribute to a sustainable future? *European Journal of Engineering Education*, 31, 555–565.

Robertson, J., & Bond, C. (2005). Being in the University. In R. Barnett (Ed.), *Reshaping the University – New Relationships between Research, Scholarship and Teaching* (pp. 79–91). Maidenhead: Open University Press.

Riley, D. (2003). *Pedagogies of Liberation in an Engineering Thermodynamics Class*, ASEE Annual Conference, June 22–25, Nashville, Tennessee, USA.

Shulman, L.S. (2005). If not now, when? The Timeliness of Scholarship of the Education of Engineers. *Journal of Engineering Education*, 94(1), 11–12.

III
Ways of Thinking and Practicing

6

Ways of Thinking and Practicing in Biology and History
Disciplinary Aspects of Teaching and Learning Environments

Dai Hounsell and Charles Anderson

University of Edinburgh

Introduction

A question can be asked of every sector or level of education which seems both straightforward yet fundamental: what is it that the students learn as a result of their experiences? And in higher education, where participation is optional rather than compulsory and where there is not *a* set curriculum but a superabundance of subject areas and course combinations that transmute in countless ways from one university to another, the question becomes a particularly salient one. A common form of response to it has been to stay clear of the tricky waters of subject and course differences, making much broader reference to the role of higher education in instilling distinctive 'habits of mind', 'modes of thought', skill in reasoning and questioning, or perhaps most commonly of all, in the development of students' capacity for 'critical thinking' (see for example Barnett, 1997; Hagedorn et al., 1999; Olson & Torrance, 1996; Trow, 1998). Yet as Middendorf and Pace have recently observed, attempting to base efforts to enhance students' learning on such waymarkers are likely to be frustrated because of an inherent mismatch between the kinds of thinking which are actually called for in specific course and disciplinary settings and "generic formulas for encouraging higher-order thinking" (Middendorf & Pace, 2004, p. 1).

Viewed from that standpoint, an exception might need to be made for the 'conceptual genotypes' which have emerged from research into undergraduate student learning that has been grounded in students' everyday experiences of their academic studies. Two prominent examples of such constructs would be Perry's seminal analysis of undergraduate intellectual development as the gestation of "contextual relativistic reasoning" (Perry, 1970, 1988), and even more influentially, in the depiction of a 'deep approach' to learning and studying in higher education as one that seeks actively to understand, to interrelate, and to weigh arguments against evidence (see for example, Entwistle & Ramsden, 1983; Marton & Säljö, 1976, 1997). Yet while it seems appropriate to argue, as does Ramsden (2003), that a concept such as deep approach should be seen relationally, i.e. it takes on different guises in different disciplinary settings – and a similar case could be made for critical thinking – there are considerable limitations as well as advantages in seeking to capture high-quality undergraduate learning in a single, overarching concept, however elastic it may be. Chief among these is the prospect of diminishing returns in analytical sharpness: the further the students progress in their undergraduate studies, the less the complexity and challenge of what they are learning is likely to be precisely and searchingly delineated.

Our aim in this chapter is to discuss how we tried to traverse this potential drawback, by depicting what students learned, as they grew in their grasp of a body of subject-matter, in a form that could transcend the boundaries of a given discipline or subject area while at the same time capturing some distinctive features of that discipline at or close to graduate-level mastery. Drawing on data from course settings in history and biology, we suggest that the students learnt *ways of thinking and practicing* characteristic of, and particular to, each of these subject areas. These ways of thinking and practicing were not confined to knowledge and understanding, but could also take in subject-specific skills and know-how, an evolving familiarity with the values and conventions governing scholarly communication within the relevant disciplinary and professional community, and even a nascent meta-understanding of how new knowledge within the field was generated. The concept of ways of thinking and practicing in a subject therefore shares the many-sided but interwoven character of learning for the professions, which Lee Shulman has recently depicted as a synthesis of three apprenticeships:

> A cognitive apprenticeship wherein one learns to think like a professional, a practical apprenticeship where one learns to perform like a professional, and a moral apprenticeship where one learns to think and act in a responsible and ethical manner that integrates across all three domains.
>
> (Shulman, 2005, p. 3)

The research from which ways of thinking and practicing sprang was undertaken as part of a project, funded by the Teaching and Learning Research Program of the UK Economic and Social Research Council which aimed both to understand and to enhance the effectiveness of undergraduate courses as "teaching-learning environments" (Hounsell et al., 2005). The predominant concern was with such environments as experienced and perceived not only by students, as has been characteristic of research into student learning (see for example Entwistle, 2003; Ramsden, 1997, 2003), but also by academics who taught these courses. The study also shared with much student learning research a concern with outcome as well as with process and context, and thus with what high-quality learning seemed to entail in the subject areas and settings surveyed, as well as how that was fostered and supported.

The project worked with fifteen departments in a cross-section of subject areas that included economics and electrical engineering as well as history and biology. The focus was generally on a first- and a final-year course unit in each of the departments, which were surveyed using a combination of student questionnaires and interviews with groups of students and with key members of course teams (Entwistle et al., 2003). The analysis of data collected in the initial or 'baseline' year formed the basis for a joint review by the researchers and course coordinators of the effectiveness of the course unit, which could in turn lead into the introduction of agreed changes to the unit in a subsequent year. The impact of these changes was then investigated using the same blend of questionnaires and interviews. The present analysis of ways of thinking and practicing in the two subject areas is based chiefly on the interview evidence. In biology, this comprised 42 interviews with 117 students, and 32 interviews with 32 faculty and others with responsibility for teaching and supporting learning. In history, there were 47 interviews with 168 students, and several rounds of interviews, both formal and informal, with those teaching the modules. The analysis begins with the bioscience findings, focusing first on the final-year and then on the first-year students.

Ways of Thinking and Practicing in the Biosciences

Course Settings in Final-year Biosciences

The development of ways of thinking and practicing in the biosciences could be most strikingly seen in the three final-year course units surveyed, and with respect to two prominent areas of activity: the students' interactions with the primary literature in the discipline and with experimental data, and their efforts to communicate within the subject what they had learned (McCune & Hounsell, 2005). These two areas of activity were prevalent in all three course units, despite quite striking differences in how the three groups of students were taught and assessed. Opportunities within these units to engage with experimental data could arise in formal lectures, in group problem-solving of data-sets generated by guest lecturers active in research, or in the individual reading and private study associated with coursework assignments. And it was in the latter assignments, not surprisingly, that the greatest scope was to be found for the students to gain expertise in communicating what they had come to know and understand, and by what means. Such assignments could take the form of essays (in two of the units) or paired seminar presentations (in a third), and typically called for retrieval and review of relevant published material from the primary (usually journal) literature in the field. Moreover, a substantial number of the students had been on six-month or one-year placements in industrial or academic bioscience research institutes, where they had gained additional practice in gathering and interpreting data, and in presenting the emerging fruits of their work to peers.

Interacting with the Primary Literature and Research Data

In their interactions with the primary literature and with experimental data in the subject, the students were expected to be able to locate appropriate and up-to-date sources of information, to select what was relevant from within those sources, and to demonstrate what they had gleaned in their assigned work:

> "If you're gonna become a scientist, you need to quote papers, you need to have proper up-to-date references. That's one thing they're really pushing you to do this year, they're trying to turn you into real scientists. So if you write essays, you're not gonna get a good mark – even in exams – if you don't use references."

However, it was much more than a matter of following well-established scientific and academic conventions in the subject, important though that was. The students were also learning how to evaluate and come to a considered view on the weight of evidence for a given interpretation. They were doing so, moreover, in areas within the subject where knowledge did not have the cut-and-dried character it could appear to have in textbooks, but was in some instances fragile and contingent, and where there was contestation amongst experts that was as yet unresolved. The following interview extracts are illustrative of these observations:

> "[The guest lecturers are] putting up their experiments [in the class]. Before they can actually give you the results and say 'What does this mean?', they'll go through 'This is the sort of the experiment you would do to find out this sort of result, this is how you would do it, this is what the results would mean for different sorts of situations'. So they actually go through a series of experiments and tell you how they did it, what sort of things are involved, and then they'll give you the results and you'll have to work out the same sort of things that they did."

> "You have to find various papers and understand them by reading them and then you have to summarize what they're saying, obviously whether you agreed with that or not. And [. . .] there's

lots of disagreement, you know they're not all saying the same thing or coming from the same line of thought. So they have different opinions."

"Yeah. So long as you've got evidence to back up your ideas with. As I say, it's not what it is just because it is, you've got to give evidence."

—

"Nothing is ever clear-cut. So I think that's one of the main things we've learned as well, that nothing really proves anything. Well, not one experiment . . . you have to back everything up with several experiments."

"[The placement] makes you think for yourself. 'Cos basically you're studying something that hardly anyone knows as much about as you do."

"It has definitely taught me to think more like a scientist and it has also given me a lot more confidence working in the labs on experiments and the interpretation of results."

Learning to Communicate What had been Learned

As the bioscience students progressed in their studies, so also did their burgeoning grasp of modes and ground-rules for communicating within the subject and the challenges which these posed – what Monroe (2002) calls "the discursive frames, conventions, and constraints that shape the writing fields [. . .] each discipline necessarily cultivates" (p. 5). One such challenge was in coming to terms with different communicative genres (oral presentations, experimental reports, analytical essays) as well as with the forms of language expected in formal and informal modes of communication:

"And for me, okay, the hardest part is going to be we cannot use any lab slang. So, we cannot say, 'Well, we put to the proteins to centrifuge', we have to say, like 'we pelleted the protein', but I mean for everything. [. . .] So, it's really technical, and it's really a good command of the language."

An equally significant challenge came in having to communicate what they had learned and understood not only to their lecturers and tutors, but to their student peers and, when on placement, to a much wider pool of colleagues and fellow-research workers. In consequence, the students developed expertise in meeting the needs of a range of audiences, as indicated in the following two illustrative comments:

"You expect the people reading [what you've written] are going to have that basic understanding so you don't need to explain the basics [. . .] I suppose not to be too afraid of being overly scientific about it, because, if it's going to be read by peers, they'll be able to critically assess it that way and understand it easier too."

"For the group meetings [that we had when I was on placement], we would just be sitting around the table having a chat, it wouldn't be a formal presentation or 'polished' results. You would just say, 'This is the preliminary result I got from such and such an experiment, what do you think of this, is there something I could improve in my experiment?'. Just a general chat. Whereas if you move up to sort of department meetings it would be 'polished' data that you're presenting in a formal manner, so you would have to sort of be able to say, 'These are the experiments that were done and these are my results. I had a chat with people in my group, they suggested that I should do this, so that's what I did and here are my 'polished' results'. [. . .] You would have to give them a lot more background information than necessarily you would with people who work on the same thing as you."

In the interviews with faculty, their concerns to foster in their students various key facets of bioscience ways of thinking and practicing were equally evident:

"Well I guess it's the critical appreciation which ideally I would most like them to have, and that is to develop the skills of not merely accepting what the abstract of a paper tells you. It's being able to look at the data in a paper and then to say or to make your own conclusions as to whether that, whether those conclusions are consistent with the data presented or are they the only conclusions, etc."

"There's nothing [in the module] which would be key knowledge for someone who wants to be a molecular and cellular biologist, because there are various options. What we're trying to do is make them get to grips with a specific topic and analyze the problems associated with that topic, and be able to have a grasp of what's going on, what the research problems are, how you approach finding out more about that topic. [. . .] I just think it's a way of learning to think in particular ways, I suppose, developing their own skills in analysis in that area."

The second comment above reflects a view expressed by several of the teachers, namely that what students learned through tackling a particular body of subject-matter could be considered less important than the wider expertise they were acquiring as potential bioscientists-in-the-making. Some interviewees went further and saw a wider vocational relevance:

"These seminar units reflect the interests of staff [faculty] members at supposedly the highest level of non-experimental work that is available to undergraduates. The encouragement is to go out and look at the original literature. And so it leads an undergraduate into the type of scholarship that they will have to do if they go into science as a career. Certainly if they go into it for a higher degree, which most of our students do. But even if they go into it in industry or even in a related subject like patent law, this is one of the experiences that we hope will be useful to them. The necessity, the absolute necessity to consult the scientific literature outside of mainstream textbooks. The second but just as important is the ability to present these results to their peers."

Course Settings in First-year Biosciences

The learning goals of those with overall teaching responsibility for first-year biosciences course units were somewhat more modest. This does not however seem surprising. Firstly, unlike their final-year counterparts, first-year students have not yet committed themselves to biosciences as a major or main subject, and many will either not pursue it beyond the first year or will take it as a minor or subsidiary subject. Secondly, incoming first-year students are typically much more varied in their prior knowledge of biology, and a core aim of such first-year units is to ensure that the students acquire an appropriately secure grasp of the foundations of the subject and an initial acquaintance with the breadth of sub-areas and interests represented within it. And thirdly, in course units with relatively large and diverse enrolments (in the case of these three units, ranging from a little under one hundred to over six hundred), teaching-learning activities tend to follow the well-established pattern of a combination of lectures, laboratory-based practical work and small-group activities.

Within such constraints, however, it was nonetheless possible for teachers to begin sowing seeds for the development of ways of thinking and practicing:

"I think the concept that nobody knows what's right in everything is definitely what we're trying to put across. The idea that we don't have all the solutions yet, to challenge things, to question things, 'Can both these people be right?'. I think that's very important at an early stage, a good healthy dose of cynicism I think will make you a better scientist [. . .] In the end of the day it's you and your data, and you make up your mind what you think, keep your mind very open in case new data comes in [. . .] Not that we're training them all to be research scientists, but I think that's good training for being a human being."

And despite large class sizes, opportunities to nudge students in this direction could be found in lectures or, as in the following example, in practicals and other group-based activities:

"I guess, in the 'Animal Behavior' lab, the maggots don't always behave in the way that you would want them to. So I guess that's a kind of biological thing, you know, the students predict what's going to happen, and the maggots will either do it or not do it. And you say, 'Well, try to think why they do it, you know, do you always do what you're expected to do? . . . No'. That kind of thing, the unpredictability of biology, maybe comes out in the Animal Behavior lab."

——

"They realize that there quite often aren't answers, direct answers."

——

"We give them information, they have a relatively short period of time in which to assimilate the relevant facts, and somebody in that group has to present it to a larger group . . . And I think it combines skills of combining information, something that they're not familiar with, they probably haven't seen before, and discussing various aspects of an issue – something like cloning a sheep. They looked at it from the scientific side, how it was actually done, [and] from the ethical side, the problems associated with it."

However, there were also many indications in the student interviews that this was not merely an aspiration on the part of their teachers. As the following comments make manifest, the students saw themselves as beginning to adopt a more questioning and active approach to their learning of the subject:

"They do quite often remind you that, you know, you are a biologist or you are a scientist, you are researching this, you are looking into this. So they are always reminding you of that fact which, you do get into that frame of mind, and when you're sitting doing these experiments or investigations, it is quite good. You do think of yourself as researching it or doing it scientifically as opposed to just sitting there doing it as schoolwork or classwork."

——

"Well the lab we had today, we were kind of expecting certain results. We were expecting to go a certain way, but towards the end the [lab supervisor] explained that it may not necessarily have been because of what we were perceiving it to be. Which makes you think, 'well, if that's the case everything could be a bit like that – there could be more than one answer for everything.' [. . .] So yeah, I think they're trying to make us think more about what we're doing, and I think that's probably the most important thing that they're trying to get us to do, is to make us investigate, think for ourselves, don't take things at face value."

——

"[My tutor] seems very interested in getting us to think a certain way, so the assignments that he sets are more about researching and learning how to read scientific papers, things that really are quite useful skills."

Ways of Thinking and Practicing in History Courses

The Diversity of Historical Knowledge

Ways of thinking and practicing in history need to be viewed against the enormous range and diversity of concerns of history as a discipline. Not only does it range over different periods and geographical regions, but it also addresses very different aspects of the human past: political, social, economic, intellectual, cultural, gender-relations, imperial, etc. As writers such as Jordonova (2000) have observed history also does not possess a single agreed, foundational theoretical framework. One consequence for the design of undergraduate curricula of this diversity in focus and concerns is that there is no *specific* body of foundational knowledge that all history students can, or should be, expected to acquire. This broad disciplinary ambit is reflected in the lack of a standard university history curriculum or degree structure; surveying the UK scene as a whole, one is struck by the presence at all stages of a degree program of very different kinds of history, structured in different ways.

Another aspect of the diversity of historical knowledge is that within particular domains of historical study there typically are competing narratives and explanations. In engaging with these competing accounts, students need to be alert to authorial stance and the way in which this stance may be related to the historian's political, social and cultural positioning. The fact that historical knowledge is marked by quite high levels of controversy would seem to have important implications for undergraduate learning and teaching, given that there may be more scope for students to exercise personal interpretation and judgment than may be the case in disciplines where the undergraduate curriculum contains much settled territory.

Central Ways of Thinking and Practicing in History

In addition to the diversity of historical content and distinct differences in curricular structure and organization that have been highlighted in the preceding paragraphs, one needs to be alert to differences between historians in epistemological and ontological stance and the influence of particular traditions of scholarship. At the same time it is important that this alertness to variety does not obscure important commonalities in historical practice. Our interviews, probing historians' aspirations for students, were conducted with lecturers who had a spread of specialist subject interests and were located in contrasting settings. A very strong commonality emerged in these lecturers' accounts of how they wished students to conceptualize historical work and the habits of mind that they wished students to develop. Feedback from a series of presentations we have given to different groups of historians, numerous informal discussions with historian colleagues and a close reading of the literature have allowed us to have some confidence that the ways of thinking and practicing identified in our interviews with historians have wider currency within the profession as a key 'common denominator' in history. These ways of thinking and practicing were viewed as both intrinsic to the discipline and as valued outcomes of historical study. Such habits of mind shaped the aspirations that academics had for their students and can be seen to underpin the various means by which they sought to develop undergraduates' historical capabilities and understanding. To achieve a high quality of engagement with historical topics, students were seen as needing to develop their conceptions of the nature of historical knowledge and evidence and their capacity to interact with that knowledge along the dimensions summarized in Table 6.1.

It is not claimed that the listing above is a definitive statement of the historical purposes and practices pursued in undergraduate courses; and individual historians or departments may place

Table 6.1 Ways of thinking and practicing in history

- appreciation of history as socially constructed and contested
- skilled interpretation / synthesis / evaluation of historical evidence, topics
- placing particular events / topics within broader contexts
- alertness to interconnections among phenomena
- sensitivity to the 'strangeness of the past'
- ability to view events and issues from different perspectives
- readiness to separate out one's own preconceptions
- communicating representations of subject matter in appropriate forms of expression and argument.

greater emphasis on some elements than others. The listing, however, does give a clear sense of what lies at the heart of history's distinctiveness. These ways of thinking and practicing appear to *constitute* the terms in which the enterprise of reading, researching and writing history is framed.

As we will illustrate, the ways of thinking and practicing listed above centrally guided teaching efforts and students' engagement with history within the courses examined in our study. However, it is important not to view the operation of these ways of thinking and practicing in terms of straightforward transmission and reproduction. In discussing how disciplinary practices inform students' experience and understanding, Anderson and Day (2005) have noted that it is important not to reify these practices or to treat them as 'free-standing' elements, independent of the agents who deploy them in specific situations. They are mediated by a lecturer's personal interpretation of these practices, teaching approach (Prosser & Trigwell, 1999) and craft knowledge concerning how a subject should be taught (van Driel et al., 1997). In turn students will appropriate ways of thinking and practicing, in different ways and to different degrees, through processes of individual interpretation and participation. Students' engagement with the ways of thinking and practicing of a discipline, whether it be history, biosciences or any other domain, will be shaped by their background, circumstances, existing knowledge and experience and orientations towards university study. Their involvement with a subject's purposes and activities will also be enabled or constrained by the organizational and curricular structure, level of resourcing and ethos of a specific university context.

Thus ways of thinking and practicing are not viewed as static objects to be passed on to students. The focus rather is on the *performance* of ways of thinking and practicing – a performance that involves dynamic processes of interpretation and construction by lecturers and students within the affordances and constraints of a particular academic environment.

Guiding Students' Participation in Ways of Thinking and Practicing in History Tailoring to Students and Contexts

The ways of thinking and practicing in history identified in the preceding section strongly informed teaching efforts in the courses we studied, very often in ways that were congruent (McCune & Hounsell, 2005) with students' own backgrounds, concerns and experiences. Even within the limited number of history courses examined, differing means were being used in different modules to engage students in ways of thinking and practicing in history. The interaction of institutional-level and module-level factors had a strong bearing on what teaching strategies and activities made sense within a given context. In addition conditions were rarely settled, and there were examples of the need to accommodate to changing circumstances, sometimes at short notice. (Among the adjustments made were those required in response to institutional re-organization, semesterization, staffing changes, etc.) Thus it can be argued from these experiences that rather than seeking to identify an ideal type set of teaching actions that can be applied across all university history departments, development activities are best directed at considering how teaching activities can be carefully crafted to pursue disciplinary practices in ways that are well-tailored to the situation of specific groups of students and what can be achieved in a local setting.

Modeling and Scaffolding of Historical Reasoning

At the same time certain of the general features of course design and teaching approach that were evident in these modules are likely to foster historical ways of thinking and practicing across all history settings. One of these general features was a theme which ran through the design initiatives we pursued with departmental partners of explicitly communicating expectations concerning the pursuit of historical study. One thrust of the explicit communication of expectations involved giving clear guidance, tailored to a course's participants, on how to think about as well as how to go about required historical tasks. Students whom we interviewed also pointed up how helpful it was when their teachers directly modeled historical reasoning. This included in one setting the clear and repeated demonstration in lectures of the interrelations of evidence and argument:

> ". . . It's purely the structure of the lectures. And they emphasize, both aspects that are important are continually – so at the end of it, I mean, if you are going to pick up on the evidence then an argument will be presented: and then a piece of evidence and another argument and a piece of evidence. And it's just reinforcing that which obviously they deem as important."

Appropriate scaffolding of students' own historical reasoning was also provided, for example, by the support given within one course to students' analysis within seminars of the features of contrasting historiographical approaches. These processes of clear communication, modeling and scaffolding also acted to give students a language within which to talk about history and thus provided the means by which dialogue between academics and students, and between students themselves concerning historical topics could proceed.

Aligning Course Activities with Ways of Thinking and Practicing in History

Students' engagement with history was also advanced when the design of teaching, learning and assessment activities was carefully and coherently crafted to draw them into participating in historical ways of thinking and acting. On this theme, some of the interview participants from one first-year module appreciated that the course as a whole had been designed in an integrated fashion:

> "Yeah, I mean I think the lectures are very focused and interact really well with the seminars, so there's definitely a sense that there's design to it, or rather than some modules which you think, you know, what's going on here?"

An important focus of our development activities in the history settings involved departmental partners working to strengthen the alignment of general historical practices and specific course objectives with the nature and sequence of teaching, learning activities and assignments. This entailed actions such as refocusing written assignments to encourage students to reflect more on their own learning and history as a discipline. In addition it was productive to make the rationales underlying the particular design features of a course more explicit and accessible. Understanding the reasoning behind the structuring of content, organization of activities and assessment of a module had benefits for students, particularly if explanations were explicitly related to key features of historical study. Gaining a stronger sense of overall module purposes in relation to fostering ways of thinking and practicing in history and the function of particular activities in taking ahead these purposes also increased the effectiveness of course teams.

Encouraging Students' Active Participation in Ways of Thinking and Practicing in History

The teachers of these courses not only 'took out' to students a clear representation of historical purposes and practices, but also acted to draw students into participating in historical debates and displaying historical ways of thinking. For example, in one first-year module, explicit communication of disciplinary practices was accompanied by a very dialogic introduction to the course's content and concerns that, in the words of one student, provided "the space to handle these different interpretations". Another student on this course observed that:

> ". . . most historians want to, they want to try and find, try and make the picture clearer, try and delve deeper and I think we wouldn't be doing this if we weren't curious and . . . because of the way he is and the nature of the module is sort of quite an open delivering to you. It does make you want to go there and try and work it out for yourself."

Thus on this and other modules students were given scope and encouragement to display their own agency in interpretation. This agency in formulating their own historical arguments and positions was assisted by a sense of academics' approachability and the creation of learning climates where students felt free to ask questions of one another and of historical materials. The following quotation from a first-year interview participant exemplifies how small-group discussion that featured active interpretation of historical questions and evidence could lead students into the ways of thinking and acting of history:

> "When you sort of discuss things in seminars regarding that kind of evidence, you become aware of other people will, may raise ideas that would question it. So ultimately you begin to start asking those sort of questions yourself."

Students also observed that their own effective engagement with history was energized when teachers actively displayed passion for the subject:

> "This one is really lively which is really helpful because the subject has potential to have boring areas. So it is really helpful that he makes it lively . . . Someone who is really enthusiastic and interested in it really makes you think, well it must be quite interesting."

First-year Students' Engagement with Ways of Thinking and Practicing in History

The preceding paragraphs have highlighted the general features of teaching approach and curriculum design that provided the history students with a guided route into the discipline (Northedge, 2003) *and* fostered their active participation in its practices. Encouragingly even in the first-year interviews across the various sites, most student groups were able to give a fairly fluent account of historical purposes and practices. There was a minority of first-year students who showed some resistance to engaging with the expectations associated with historical study (see Anderson & Day, 2005) but the students whom we interviewed predominantly accepted the need to follow the discipline's (sometimes challenging) ways of thinking and acting.

They recognized the need to take an analytical approach to historical study, accepted responsibility for active interpretation and emphasized the importance of an openness to considering different perspectives/interpretations. In the words of one student, they saw the need for "an enquiring mind and an ability to analyze different points of view". Allied to this concern with personal interpretation was a recognition of the importance of adopting a questioning, analytical approach to evidence, which could require not only independent thought but also quite wide research:

> "Reading widely, definitely because of the nature of the interpretation of evidence, you really can't take one person's word for it because you find such differing views and interpretations so you really have to read as widely as possible."

Fulfilling the responsibility of coming up with your own interpretation of historical topics was seen to involve looking at connections between events and themes. Aside from establishing personal connections, some students talked of how their first-year experiences in undergraduate history had enabled them to develop more of a felt sense of the interconnectedness of historical phenomena, as the following quotation indicates:

> ". . . it was the fitting together of things that I found the most interesting part of the whole, of the module, is, is suddenly to realize, although this is a self-evident point, that, that everything has an effect on everything else so that when you're studying the EEC [European Economic Union] you might also be learning stuff which is relevant to, you know, the economy but defense or alignments outside of Europe. So that, you know, 'cause once I understand these kinds of things, studying becomes easier."

Related to this developing sense of the interconnectedness of historical events, some students displayed an implicit grasp of the need to contextualize their approach to a specific topic by framing their understanding of that topic within a wider context and/or time-frame of events. One interview participant, for example, talked of how in constructing a thematic understanding of a topic:

"To understand what's really happening you have to understand what the antecedents there are [*chorus of agreement from other students*] what the past is."

Conclusions

In this chapter, we have explored findings which have resulted from a perspective on undergraduate learning that is rooted *within* particular subject areas and starts from within specific course and institutional settings. From that eye-view, a fundamental feature of what these students seemed to learn from their undergraduate studies could be summarized as characteristic ways of thinking and practicing in the subject, and we have drawn on interviews with the students and teachers concerned to explore what forms these ways of thinking and practicing took in the history and bioscience settings studied. However, it should be emphasized that ways of thinking and practicing in a subject should be viewed just as they are learned, i.e. as integral wholes rather than as disaggregated parts.

Some disclaimers and caveats are also necessary. First, we are not suggesting that every student necessarily masters every aspect of these ways of thinking and practicing, or to the same extent. Our focus has been on what the students collectively learned, rather than to pinpoint individual differences. Second, while the metaphor of apprenticeship clearly has some resonance in relation to the learning of ways of thinking and practicing, it would be misleading to see these students as fully fledged initiates with a common and binding vocation. They were learning to think *like* bioscientists, or *like* historians, and to go about the subject *like* established practitioners within it, but had no need for any formal commitment to the subject beyond graduation. Third, our aim has been to pick out salient features of ways of thinking and practicing in the two subjects which emerged from the course settings surveyed. We would not claim to have identified all or most of the quintessential attributes of each subject; that would be a very much larger, and probably more elusive undertaking. And fourthly, we are not suggesting that our 'from-within', grounded research approach should have dominion in the study of the disciplinary dimensions to learning, but rather that it has an important complementary role to play alongside panoptic, typology-focused approaches of the kind most influentially represented in the work of Janet Donald (2002) (see also Chapter 3 in this volume). As Shulman (2002) observes in advocating a similar twin-track strategy for examining disciplinary distinctiveness in the scholarship of learning and teaching, the challenge lies in interaction and engagement between generalized and particularized approaches.

Indeed, our own attempt to build particularized 'neighborhoods of understanding' (to use Shulman's apt phrase) about the development of ways of thinking and practicing in history and biology has implications not only for research, but also for teaching and assessment in higher education. In the biosciences, where teaching-learning and assessment strategies could take very different forms, the development of ways of thinking and practicing was most clearly evident in situations in which students were pursuing active rather than passive learning tasks – for example, in undertaking experimental work on placements, participating in problem-solving discussions, and presenting orally and in writing (McCune & Hounsell, 2005). In history, it could be fostered through explicit communication of expectations, and support for students through modeling and scaffolding, allied to encouragement of students' own interpretive voice. In both subjects, there seemed further scope for dialogue between students and their teachers about disciplinary purposes and conventions.

But happily, this is territory which others have already begun to map. The notion of 'academic discourse' (Hounsell, 1988) has been reinvigorated by new developments which give emphasis to learning not simply as acquisition but also as participation (Sfard, 1998) in a specialist discourse community of the kind represented by a discipline. One perspective, drawing on sociolinguistic insights, focuses on the need to develop students' grasp of the academic literacies associated with different subject areas (Lea & Street, 2000; Lillis, 2001). Another, as articulated by Northedge (see also Chapter 9 in this volume) rests on the central position of the teacher "as a speaker of the discourse and member of the knowledge community" (Northedge, 2003, p. 172). Three teaching roles are highlighted by Northedge: assisting students in framing specialist meaning, guiding students into less familiar discursive terrain, and coaching students in writing and speaking appropriately within the discourse conventions of the subject.

A different but equally promising line of approach draws on the 'wisdom of practice' and the work of subject teachers. One notable example is van Heerden's account (2005) of how her interactions with students had led her to try to surface ways in which a subject expert like herself had learned how to "think like a chemist", and she goes on to describe how she has sought to develop these capacities in her students through carefully designed teaching-learning and assessment activities (van Heerden, 2005). Finally, and even more ambitiously, there is Pace and Middendorf's attempt (2004) to articulate and exemplify strategies for 'decoding the disciplines' (see also Chapter 8 in this volume). This presents a seven-step model which can help teachers in "introducing students to the culture of thinking in a specific discipline" (Middendorf & Pace, 2004), while also bringing together reports of how the model has underpinned undergraduate teaching initiatives across a broad span of subject areas. In other words, pursuing the twin tracks of generalization and particularization seems to hold promise in teaching about, as well as in researching into, disciplinary distinctiveness.

Acknowledgements

The work reported in this chapter draws on interviews which were conducted and analyzed not only by ourselves but by our colleagues Kate Day, Jenny Hounsell, Judith Litjens, Velda McCune, Jennifer Nisbet and Nicola Reimann. Their invaluable contribution to this work is therefore warmly acknowledged.

References

Anderson, C. & Day, K. (2005). Purposive environments: Engaging students in the values and practices of history. *Higher Education*, 49, 319–343.

Barnett, R. (1997). *Higher education: A critical business.* Buckingham: SRHE & Open UP.

Donald, J. (2002). *Learning to think.* San Francisco: Jossey-Bass.

Entwistle, N. (2003). *Concepts and conceptual frameworks underpinning the ETL Project.* (Occasional Reports, 3) Edinburgh: University of Edinburgh, Department of Higher and Community Education, Enhancing Teaching-Learning Environments in Undergraduate Courses Project. Retrieved 24 October 2007: http://www.tla.ed.ac.uk/centre/etl/publications.html

Entwistle, N. & Ramsden, P. (1983). *Understanding student learning.* London: Croom Helm.

Entwistle, N., McCune, V. & Hounsell, J. (2003). Investigating ways of enhancing university teaching-learning environments: measuring students' approaches to studying and perceptions of teaching. In E. De Corte, L. Verschaffel, N. Entwistle & J. van Merriënboer (Eds.), *Powerful learning environments: Unravelling basic components and dimensions* (pp. 89–107). Oxford: Elsevier Science Ltd.

Hagedorn, L.S. et al. (1999). Institutional context and the development of critical thinking: a research note. *Review of Higher Education*, 22 (3), 265–285.

Hounsell, D. (1988). Towards an anatomy of academic discourse: Meaning and context in the undergraduate essay. In R. Saljo (Ed.), *The written world: Studies in literate thought and action* (pp. 161–177). Berlin: Springer-Verlag.

Hounsell, D. et al. (2005). *Enhancing teaching-learning environments in undergraduate courses. Final report to the Economic and Social Research Council on TLRP Project L139251099.* Edinburgh: University of Edinburgh, Department of Higher & Community Education, ETL Project. Retrieved 24 October 2007: http://www.tla.ed.ac.uk/centre/etl/publications.html

Jordanova, L. (2000). *History in practice.* London: Arnold & OUP.

Lea, M.R. & Street, B.V. (2000). Student writing and staff feedback in higher education: An academic literacies approach. In M.R. Lea & B. Stierer (Eds.), *Student writing in higher education: New contexts* (pp. 47–65). Buckingham: SRHE & Open UP.

Lillis, T.M. (2001). *Student writing: Access, regulation and desire.* London: Routledge.

McCune, V. & Hounsell, D. (2005). The development of students' ways of thinking and practicing in three final-year biology courses. *Higher Education,* 49, 255–289.

Marton, F. & Säljö, R. (1976). On qualitative differences in learning: 1 – outcome and process. *British Journal of Educational Psychology,* 46, 4–11.

Marton, F. & Säljö, R. (1997). Approaches to learning. In F. Marton, D. J. Hounsell & N. J. Entwistle (Eds.), *The Experience of Learning* (pp. 39–58). 2nd Edn. Edinburgh: Scottish Academic Press.

Middendorf, J. & Pace, D. (2004). Decoding the disciplines: A model for helping students learn disciplinary ways of thinking. In D. Pace & J. Middendorf (Eds.), *Decoding the disciplines: Helping students learn disciplinary ways of thinking* (pp. 1–12). (*New Directions for Teaching and Learning, 98*). San Francisco: Jossey-Bass.

Monroe, J. (2002). Introduction: The shapes of fields. In J. Monroe (Ed.), *Writing and revising the disciplines* (pp. 1–12). Ithaca, NY: Cornell UP.

Northedge, A. (2003). Enabling participation in academic discourse. *Teaching in Higher Education,* 8(2), 169–180.

Olson, D.R. & Torrance, N. (Eds.) (1996). *Modes of thought: Explorations in culture and cognition.* New York: Cambridge UP.

Pace, D. & Middendorf, J. (Eds.) (2004). *Decoding the disciplines: Helping students learn disciplinary ways of thinking.* (*New Directions for Teaching and Learning, 98*). San Francisco: Jossey-Bass.

Perry, W.G. (1970). *Forms of intellectual and ethical development in the college years.* New York: Holt, Rinehart & Winston.

Perry, W.G. (1988). Different worlds in the same classroom. In P. Ramsden (Ed.), *Improving learning: New perspectives.* London: Kogan Page.

Prosser, M., & Trigwell, K. (1999). *Understanding learning and teaching: The Experience in Higher Education.* Buckingham: SRHE & OUP.

Ramsden, P. (1997). The context of learning in academic departments. In F. Marton, D. J. Hounsell & N. J. Entwistle (Eds.), *The experience of learning* (pp. 198–216). 2nd edn. Edinburgh: Scottish Academic Press.

Ramsden, P. (2003). *Learning to Teach in Higher Education.* 2nd edn. London: RoutledgeFalmer.

Sfard, A. (1998). On two metaphors for learning and on the dangers of choosing just one. *Educational Researcher,* 27(2), 4–13

Shulman, L. (2002). Foreword. In M. T. Huber & S. P. Morreale, *Disciplinary styles in the scholarship of learning and teaching: Exploring common ground* (pp. v–ix). Washington, DC: American Association of Higher Education & Carnegie Foundation for the Advancement of Teaching.

Shulman, L. (2005). The signature pedagogies of the professions of law, medicine, engineering and the clergy: potential lessons for the education of teachers. Paper presented to the Math Science Partnership (MSP) Workshop, "Teacher Education for Effective Teaching and Learning", National Research Council's Center for Education, Irvine, California, 6–8 February 2005. Retrieved 25 October 2007: http://hub.mspnet.org/index.cfm/11172

Trow, K.B. (1998). *Habits of mind: The Experimental College Program at Berkeley.* Berkeley: University of California, Berkeley, Institute of Government Studies Press.

Van Driel, J.H., Verloop, N., Van Werven, H.I., & Dekkers, H. (1997). Teachers' craft knowledge and curriculum innovation in higher engineering education. *Higher Education,* 34, 105–122.

van Heerden, A. (2005). Articulating the processes at the heart of Chemistry. In T. Riordan & J. Roth (Eds.), *Disciplines as frameworks for learning: Teaching the practice of the disciplines* (pp. 95–120). Sterling, VA: Stylus.

7

Exploring Disciplinarity in Academic Development
Do "Ways of Thinking and Practicing" Help Faculty to Think about Learning and Teaching?

Nicola Reimann

Northumbria University

Introduction

The concept *Ways of Thinking and Practicing* (WTP) in a subject area originated in a large research project which investigated undergraduate first- and final-year teaching-learning environments in a number of disciplines across different UK universities. An important aim of the project was to develop concepts and conceptual frameworks which would help academics to think about learning and teaching and to design and review teaching-learning environments. WTP is one of several concepts which the project generated. It:

> describe(s) the richness, depth and breadth of what students might learn through engagement with a given subject area in a specific context. This might include, for example, coming to terms with particular understandings, forms of discourse, values or ways of acting which are regarded as central to graduate-level mastery of a discipline or subject area. (...) WTP can potentially encompass anything that students learn which helps them to develop a sense of what it might mean to be part of a particular disciplinary community.

> (McCune & Hounsell, 2005, p. 257)

The data from which the concept arose has been discussed in several publications (e.g. Anderson & Day, 2005; Hounsell & McCune, 2002; McCune & Hounsell, 2005; Hounsell & Anderson, this volume; Hounsell & Anderson, 2007). An in-depth discussion of WTP in biosciences and history can be found in the previous chapter.

In my role as academic developer who supports faculty[1] in taking a scholarly approach to the development of their learning and teaching practice, I have become increasingly interested in the ways in which they engage with educational research, how meaningful it is to them and whether it

---

1 Throughout this chapter the word 'faculty' is used to include academics who teach as well as staff whose role is to support student learning in non-teaching roles, e.g. by providing study skills advice or supporting work-based learning in higher education.

helps them to understand and improve their own practice. Having been a member of the research team which coined the phrase *Ways of Thinking and Practicing*, I am also interested in the applicability of our findings and concepts to learning and teaching in higher education and in finding out whether they are in fact of practical use to faculty. Within this chapter I therefore examine the concept WTP as a tool for academic development by considering the views of faculty, explore what they make of the concept of WTP and whether reflecting upon the disciplinary dimension of teaching and learning has the potential to stimulate their thinking about student learning and the enhancement of teaching-learning environments. By focusing on faculty's own views, my intent is to help connect research on learning and teaching (within and beyond the disciplines) with educational practice (e.g. see Thomas, 2004) and, through this, make a small contribution towards bridging the "ideas-action gap" (Perkins & Wilson, 1999).

With these questions and purposes in mind, I carried out a small piece of exploratory follow-on research which combined data collection with academic development events. I conducted four learning and teaching workshops/seminars at three different universities during which twenty-two participants were invited to think about and discuss the disciplinary dimension of their teaching. As a core part of these workshops the notion of *Ways of Thinking and Practicing* (WTP) was introduced. Following the workshops I took reflective notes and obtained additional feedback on WTP either by asking for written comments and/or by conducting one-to-one interviews with volunteers. I also conducted interviews with colleagues who read Hounsell and Anderson's chapter, but were unable to attend a workshop. Twelve interviews were obtained as data for this study. In addition, the views of academic developers were captured through interviews with five colleagues who work with and teach new academic staff on Postgraduate Certificate programs on learning and teaching in higher education, now offered at many universities in the UK. The insights gained from these events and interviews coupled with my own reflections form the basis of the discussion presented in this chapter.

The Disciplinary Dimension in Initial Learning and Teaching in Higher Education Programs

Where and when do faculty get an opportunity to engage with the scholarship of teaching and learning of their subject and the type of concepts and research explored in this book? In the UK the Higher Education Academy (HEA) Subject Centres (see links at http://www.heacademy.ac.uk) follow an intra-disciplinary approach by providing subject-specific events, resources and discussion spaces for specialists of the same discipline or subject group. Discipline-specific issues and questions are also, albeit to a much lesser extent, addressed in Postgraduate Certificate programs in learning and teaching in higher education which new staff in the UK are increasingly required to take. These programs tend to be characterized by a predominantly generic curriculum – usually by necessity as they bring together staff from a large variety of subjects – while the participants often perceive their learning needs to arise from the 'situatedness' of their practice: situated in their disciplines, departments and workgroups. This has the potential to create tensions and dissatisfaction. A recent formative evaluation of programs accredited by the HEA highlights the issues arising from an approach whose default perspective is generic rather than discipline-specific:

> The relationship between the generic aspects of teaching and learning and the more discipline-specific aspects is problematic. Whether participants have trouble seeing how the generic aspects can be applied in their disciplines and departments, or whether there are disciplinary differences not brought out in the programs, is not clear.
>
> (Prosser et al., 2006, p. 4)

The questionnaire used for the formative evaluation asked participants whether the program provided them "with the appropriate balance of generic knowledge and discipline specific support for teaching and support of learning" (Prosser et al., 2006, p. 16). According to the report, the programs were not always regarded as relevant to the disciplines. One example quoted was the lack of attention devoted to subject-specific delivery formats. On the other hand, the fact that the programs succeeded in getting people from different disciplines to talk and even collaborate with each other was valued by some participants and heads of department.

The evaluation report refers to attempts made by program teams to address the disciplinary dimension of learning and teaching in higher education within these programs. This is also confirmed by the interviews I conducted for this study. Staff designing and delivering such programs noted the need to embed a disciplinary perspective more explicitly into courses. However, the academic developers also argued that it was important to justify the generic approach and get participants to value the interdisciplinary collaboration with colleagues from across a wide spectrum of subjects.

The Benefits of Thinking about and Discussing WTP in Academic Development Events

When I started this investigation, I set out very specifically to obtain feedback on the usefulness of the concept of *Ways of Thinking and Practicing* (WTP). What I ended up with was an over-arching sense of the usefulness of engaging staff in discussions with colleagues about disciplinarity *per se*. The experience of the workshops highlighted the value faculty attribute to opportunities that allow them to talk about, reflect upon, share, compare and contrast their own discipline-based practice with that of others. The notion of WTP served as a trigger for such discussions, but in all likelihood many of the other concepts discussed in this book would have produced equally valid and important conversations and insights. The conversations with colleagues from other disciplines and the resulting inter-disciplinary nature of the workshops provided the added dimension of having to make the 'taken for granted' explicit (perhaps in a similar way in which this needs to be done with students).

While the workshops were intended to provide participants with an opportunity to construct their understanding of WTP, I was also developing as well as questioning *my own* understanding of WTP during the process of the research. To each workshop I brought a somewhat changed conceptualization, which was influenced by prior workshops, colleagues' interpretations voiced in interviews and a more fine-grained reading and re-reading of Hounsell and Anderson's chapter. I also started to wonder whether my representation of WTP was 'accurate' and in line with the original data and the way in which Hounsell and Anderson would have represented it. As a consequence I changed some details in the way in which I presented WTP and initiated the discussion in the workshops. Doubtlessly my own interpretation and presentation of WTP had an impact on participants' understanding of and engagement with the concept. In addition, some participants had accessed Hounsell and Anderson's work directly, while others depended on my understanding of their work.

Describing and Discussing WTP

I started the workshops off by asking participants to think of themselves as members of a particular disciplinary/vocational community and to characterize the core ways of thinking and practicing of that community. It was notable that this task evoked a way of thinking about learning and teaching which resonated with a student-centered conception of teaching (Prosser & Trigwell, 1999). Prosser and Trigwell distinguish between a conception which regards teaching as information transmission (teacher-centered conception), and a contrasting conception which regards teaching as bringing about conceptual change (student-centered conception). Their research has demonstrated that higher education teachers who hold a student-centered conception of teaching are more likely to teach and design teaching-learning environments in ways which prompt students to take a deep approach to learning, i.e. an approach which focuses on understanding and has been linked to higher level learning outcomes. It is therefore significant that being introduced to the notion of WTP and thinking about students as '-ists' (e.g. biologists, physiotherapists) in the making moved lecturers away from focusing on the delivery of information and facts. This means that using WTP in academic development has the potential of instigating conceptual change in higher education teachers. The following two quotes illustrate the way in which thinking about WTP moved faculty away from conceptualizing teaching as delivery of 'material' and 'facts'.

Business:
"To try and think on a different level rather than just delivering academic material. (. . .) They were coming at different subjects from a slightly different approach. On both occasions the thing that was holding them together was wider employment skills and personal development skills rather than just the subject material. That was my understanding. So how to think as a bio-scientist, how to think as a historian, rather than actually saying: 'here is a load of things that happened at this date, learn them and you'll pass'."

Medicine:
"In my teaching I am now more likely to [. . .] teach them about these things [WTP] – not facts, but approaches, assumptions and expectations."

The levels of sophistication in the verbalizations of WTP varied considerably among participants. Some struggled to provide any detailed descriptions of WTP, as for instance, a PhD student and teaching assistant who initially described the WTP of English literature simply as 'studying books' and found it difficult to explain what exactly this implied. At the other end of the spectrum were members of staff who expressed the WTP of their discipline in a very developed and explicit manner. The way in which they talked about WTP may be the result of their disciplinary communities having debated extensively what the discipline is about. It may also reflect an individual awareness of WTP shaped by long-standing involvement in the disciplinary community and considerable teaching experience.

Ample descriptions of the WTP of various disciplines were given in the workshops and the interviews. Some participants tried to capture a broad range of aspects and components, while others focused on particular fine-grained elements which they regarded as core to a discipline.

Academic developer:
"I spent quite a lot of time thinking when I first started teaching chemistry about the use of diagrams to represent reaction mechanisms. (. . .) You are trying to represent 3-dimensional molecules doing 3-dimensional reactions, (. . .) on a flat piece of paper (. . .) I did actually with colleagues list out the skills that you needed to be able to represent a simple mechanism and we found at least fourteen separate skills (. . .) Is this a way of thinking and practicing in chemistry? And it would seem probably that it was. But there is an issue of scale. Some of these are very micro-scale things which are really important, but which are perhaps best regarded as something to be too small scale. (. . .) Tacit in that practice is a whole series of (. . .) the basic physical skills of being able to draw hexagons with particular bond angles and represent them reliably on a piece of paper. If you can't do it, you can't actually understand the reaction or communicate it in an exam."

A much broader approach was taken by another interviewee who delineated WTP in theology as

Theology:
". . . how to be critical, engage in theological studies and relate it to change in the world and how to be sensitive to the problems we face and how we can contribute to making the world a better place."

When participants were asked to describe the WTP of their disciplines, the generic and trans-disciplinary nature of many descriptions was striking. In fact, it was surprising that a workshop which asked participants to focus on what was special about their disciplines seemed to result in the identification of more commonalities than differences! For instance, problem solving, decision making and reflective practice were mentioned repeatedly. However, these generic descriptions were then substantiated by discipline-specific explanations and examples, particularly when participants moved more deeply into the fine-grained particularities of their WTP. So decision-making in management, for instance, was described very differently to decision-making in medicine.

One of the assets of WTP as a concept seemed to be that it enabled higher education practitioners to conceptualize transdisciplinary aspects without detaching them from their 'embeddedness' in the discipline. Using the language of WTP allowed them to talk about commonalities between subjects without relinquishing their respective disciplinary distinctiveness as the term WTP suggests something intrinsically different from labels such as 'transferable skills' or 'graduate attributes'.

Commonalities, Contestation and Control within a Discipline

Several participants expressed concern that their WTP might not be the same as someone else's, even if they were members of the same disciplinary community. Among people with the same disciplinary background there was evidence of consensus and commonality as well as contestation and disagreement. Some interviewees emphasized the existence of distinct tribes and sub-disciplines and their perception that these tribes would describe WTP very differently, while others focused more on commonalities.

Information professional/librarianship:
"I was thinking: what is a librarian? There is a huge continuum between a hard edge information professional person and then a person who is in a public library helping people to read."

Academic developer:
"My own experience of this is that there tends to be a lot more commonality than contestation, but there are certainly many incidences where people do not agree in a sense of not so much on whether or not it is or it is not an aspect of disciplinary thinking, but it is a matter of fore-grounding."

Since a considerable proportion of workshop participants came from vocational disciplines, professional bodies frequently featured in the discussions. Within the framework of WTP the role of these bodies can be conceptualized as making the WTP of a particular professional community explicit and engaging their members in an active debate about them. A large component of the work of professional bodies focuses on the development of explicit and agreed statements of WTP which are readily available to their members in the form of professional standards and codes of practice. There seemed to be a relatively high level of awareness of WTP among those practitioners, for instance nurses, whose profession is governed by a professional body. This meant that they had a language at their disposal which allowed them to engage in accounts and discussions of WTP, perhaps more so than other faculty. However, statements of WTP made by a professional body are not necessarily understood and fully endorsed by each individual, nor by the community as a whole.

This raises issues of structure and agency, power, control and ownership. Some participants seemed to accept the standards and guidelines provided by the relevant professional body as the framework within which their practice is situated, while others perceived them as something with which they reluctantly complied, which constrained them or which they actively contested. An individual's stance is likely to be influenced by the role which the respective professional body plays, i.e. whether it governs and regulates the profession or merely serves as an interest group, and by the nature of the community which it aspires to represent.

Arising from these discussions was a sense that what matters most might not be whether a group of faculty are able to reach a consensus on the precise nature of their discipline's WTP, but that they have an opportunity to verbalize, discuss and debate them in the first place. In some disciplines and communities this may take place within the context of a professional body, in others it will not. McCune and Hounsell (2005) emphasize that WTP are not meant to be interpreted as a tool to comprehensively and normatively describe *all* aspects of high quality learning in a given discipline. They stress that the concept is "a means of including (. . .) important themes which might otherwise be overlooked" (McCune & Hounsell, 2005, pp. 257–258) and aims to help us understand "high quality learning *as understood and experienced by staff and students in particular contexts*" [my emphasis, NR] (McCune & Hounsell, 2005, p. 258).

The Notion of Community

WTP is not unique in regarding learning and teaching as situated within the socio-cultural practices of a (disciplinary) community. However, asking faculty directly to conceptualize their own practice as *members of a disciplinary community* and teaching as supporting students in becoming members of this community (see also Northedge & McArthur, Chapter 9) appeared to genuinely open up ways of thinking which may not have been possible had the notion of community not been foregrounded. For instance, aspects such as values and attitudes were included in descriptions of *Ways of Thinking and Practicing* (WTP) that otherwise may not have featured, and some participants' attention was drawn to issues such as student identity. Within this context some 'darker' elements of WTP which are less likely to be explicitly taught were also mentioned. One participant talked about the way in which the medical community deals with the tensions between "being a scientist and a sympathetic human being", which can result in negative attitudes to patients, not showing emotions and using humor to cope with stressful experiences such as patients' deaths.

One question which participants repeatedly raised was whether the students actually wanted to belong to their respective disciplinary communities or whether other (student) communities may be more important to them. Some participants criticized the notion of community as too vague and ill-defined, while others pointed out that it was not easy to determine exactly which community their students should and would be socialized into. In their definition of WTP McCune and Hounsell (2005) do not attribute any importance to "whether or not they [the students] intend to join a given community in the future, for example, by pursuing a particular profession" (McCune & Hounsell, 2005, p. 257). In contrast, participants pointed out that in order to design teaching-learning environments which engage students with WTP, there needs to be clarity as to whether the community is the professional/vocational community outside the university or the academic community within the university, and whether the focus is on a community which the student is already trying to gain access to or whether membership lies in the future. In addition, participants noted that these communities tend to overlap and cannot be easily distinguished. Some programs of study determine the community students are socialized into much more than others, and if a close link between a program of study and a particular community does not exist, faculty felt that a focus on WTP might be more difficult. This problem arises in particular in so-called 'service' or 'non-specialist' courses and in modular programs which combine modules from disciplines different from the ones students are majoring in. Large first-year modules frequently comprise students from a variety of programs of study and it can be legitimately asked whether such modules should aim to turn students into members of a disciplinary community which is not going to be the one they are majoring in. One interviewee used the example of a service course to illustrate the way in which the notion of WTP could still be usefully applied to this type of setting.

Academic developer:
"I used to have to teach chemistry to chemical engineers. (. . .) In fact chemistry was the only compulsory subject for chemical engineers. Bizarre because they didn't come to university to do chemistry, they were going to do engineering (. . .) Do I want them to think like chemists? Not sure I do. I think I want them to be aware of how chemists think, recognize it, but perhaps not to try and bring them across onto the other side as it were. And of course the quality of communication between chemists and chemical engineers is really, really important when it comes to industry."

Conceptualizing service courses as courses whose purpose it is to make students aware of the ways in which people in an associated discipline think and practice assigns them an important function. It implies that students will neither be forced into becoming members of a community to which they may not wish or need to belong, nor will service courses fall into the trap of being reduced to the delivery of basic information in a less important discipline. This approach might contribute to the type of critical engagement with the conflicting values and priorities of other disciplines which Rowland (2006) sees as fundamental for contestation and critical enquiry within contemporary universities.

The Challenge of 'New' and Interdisciplinary Subjects

Although participants were generally keen to discuss the disciplinary dimension of their practice, several of them queried whether WTP as a concept was relevant and applicable to non-traditional disciplines, interdisciplinary courses and inter-professional contexts. The following interview excerpts refer to relatively new subjects which are characterized by a diversity of perspectives and confront students with a multitude of potentially conflicting WTP. The interviewees saw these subjects as quite distinct from established disciplines with a long-standing history, tradition and identity in higher education and emphasized that their WTP may be less developed and/or explicit.

Business information systems:
"The subject is called business information systems. (. . .) It covers everything from quite technical programming, (. . .) right to (. . .) the social effects of the computer age. (. . .). It's a new area, we are saying new compared to something like history or English."

Academic developer:
"There is so much interdisciplinary or non-disciplinary undergraduate teaching going on now. (. . .) I know from my own experience of working in Tourism or Environmental Studies or whatever: what students were getting exposed to were various people from various disciplinary backgrounds doing things in slightly different ways. And both of them are quite new subjects, (. . .) there wasn't a coherent way of thinking and practicing. In fact, the challenge for students was that they went down to the Business School and did Marketing and then they came and did some Geography and then they did something else. And actually it might have been confusing for them and it probably would have been helpful if they had had a more coherent experience perhaps. (. . .) Perhaps there is an issue here that it takes time to develop a way of thinking and

practicing within a discipline. And there may be some interdisciplinary areas that are in fact (. . .) proto-subjects which have not yet consolidated a sort of proper identity, i.e. the people teaching that aren't people who studied it, that's one of the key things."

Academic developer:
"Some subjects, and teacher education is one of them, haven't got a very developed consensus of ways of thinking and practicing. (. . .) It's not very explicit. (. . .) However, the good thing about it is that it means at least it is up for grabs."

Although faculty who came from these less traditional contexts were skeptical about the way in which the notion of WTP may apply to them, it seems that using WTP as a conceptual tool may help to understand some of the underlying dilemmas and issues which these new subjects and courses face. Making WTP explicit through engaging colleagues and students in conversation about WTP, has the potential to highlight possible contradictions and tensions, thus making it easier to understand and address them.

The fact that WTP as a concept is not confined to a narrow definition of discipline and refers relatively loosely to a community also means that it can be used to capture areas of academic practice which do not, and may not even aspire to, have the status of 'discipline' or are straddling the WTP of several disciplines at once. Examples encountered in the workshops were Study Skills, Work-based/work-related Learning and English for Academic Purposes (EAP). WTP might provide a framework which helps to describe the kinds of understandings and skills which staff from these areas want their students to engage with. It may even have the potential of raising their status as it puts them on equal footing with more established disciplines. In work-based/work-related learning, for instance, which has no disciplinary base as such, artifacts such as negotiated learning agreements and portfolios as well as action and learning plans are used to represent student learning and understanding much in the same way in which other disciplines use essays, presentations or lab reports. The challenge of EAP lies in the fact that students taking English language courses come from a large number of disciplines, while its teachers belong to yet another disciplinary community. This raises several questions. Is it possible to detach EAP from either the disciplinary base of the teachers or that of the students? In order to support students effectively, can and must teachers of English language have an understanding of the various disciplines which their students are studying? Do their students need an understanding of the WTP underpinning English language teaching in order to make effective use of the courses which are available to them? It could be argued that the benefit of WTP is that it provides a conceptual framework for the discussion of these types of question and tensions.

Implications of WTP for Teaching

Hounsell and Anderson delineate the ways in which the teaching-learning environments in the biosciences and in history (as encountered in their research) engaged students with the WTP of these disciplines. These modes of engaging students with WTP, such as, for instance, the forms of language, communicative genres and ways of reasoning which are specific to their respective discipline, included aligning a course with WTP, making them explicit, modeling, scaffolding and encouraging active participation in WTP. When the participants in my study were asked about the implications of WTP for teaching, however, not everyone was able to make this connection. In fact, to my surprise there were participants who despite having discussed the WTP of their disciplines in a very detailed fashion, found it difficult to use the concept to think about their teaching.

English Language Teaching:
"I think the idea to engage students [with WTP] is definitely going to be beneficial, but I am not sure how you would do it from the teaching point of view."

It is possible that this observed difficulty was simply due to the workshops not giving sufficient attention to the application of WTP to teaching. On the other hand, it may indicate that there is scope for developing the concept further in a way which brings out its relevance for teaching.

Below I will quote the conclusions which individual workshop participants drew for their teaching. Most importantly perhaps, some participants stated that the notion of WTP had the potential to raise their own and their students' awareness of the 'why' of what is taught and how it is taught.

Management:
"Sometimes you are totally engrossed in delivering the content of the course without actually thinking why you are doing so. (. . .) I felt I must kind of question some of the ways I deliver the course and maybe also have a chance to ask some of my colleagues why we do the things we do on the course."

English Language Teaching:
"Being more explicit about the aims and objectives of each activity. Why are we looking at the text, why have we selected this activity for you to do? Because I am not sure that students are clear about the point of it and we think that the point of it is really obvious, but I am not sure whether they do. (. . .) I don't know when we set out the objective we make it clear *why* we want them to do that and how that is going to benefit their learning in the long term."

Several participants commented that what they took away from the workshop was an increased awareness of the tacit nature of WTP, an intention to make explicit what it means to be part of a disciplinary community and an interest in student identity. There also was a sense of 'we are doing this already': some participants thought that the way in which they taught and organized the curriculum was to a certain extent already aligned with WTP, although they had not been aware of it nor had they made this explicit, neither to themselves nor to their students. When prompted to talk about the way in which their teaching reflected WTP and engaged students with them, the examples mentioned tended to focus on authentic settings, in particular professional practice. This may have been due to the fact that a considerable number of workshop participants came from vocational/professional subjects. When some faculty talked about preparing students for professional practice, there was a tendency to focus on examples illustrating the development of ways of practicing rather than thinking. In these cases the concept WTP had the potential to serve as a reminder not to neglect the development of thinking skills, which are equally required in practice settings. In one workshop the participants (mis-)interpreted WTP as referring to the more familiar theory–practice dichotomy. Many of the teaching examples they provided involved students doing practical tasks or collaborating with professional practitioners outside the university, aspects of professional practice being brought into the university or the simulation of authentic contexts within the university. Somebody even suggested that WTP may ultimately only be acquired in the 'real world' and in professional practice. The following interviewee describes an example of the application of WTP to the teaching of Construction Management:

Construction management:
"They weren't getting any hands-on construction experience. (. . .) This is why (. . .) we have actually taken them away and they have had a whole week of constructing projects. Where they actually have to do the physical work, (. . .) protocol it, fix the stills, erect the building. (. . .) It's real because they do actually build something but it gets knocked down at the end of the day. (. . .) We were lucky that we've got industry to sponsor us and they send a project manager, so a guy from a real construction site, an engineer and some foremen. And we have big diggers and cherry pickers and plant drivers that come down and the students are using all that. (. . .)"

Another example has been taken from architecture where the studio is used as a teaching-learning environment which closely mirrors the working environment of architects.

Architecture:
"The design project is delivered in the studios, which means there is continual iteration, assessment, teaching on a one-to-one basis, or within group formats so that we are part of the community. The separation between the teaching staff and the students is effectively cut down quite considerably. We do sit round the table, they draw, we draw, we participate in the same ways of practice, ways of thinking. We will explain our way of thinking, they'll explain their way of thinking, so it's very much about reflection, it's very much about sharing, and we provide the voice of experience that may influence their ways of thinking and practicing. (. . .) The sort of assessment is almost continuous, from week to week. We speak to the students, we let them make mistakes, we tell them what we think is wrong, possibilities of how to correct them or at the very least simply ways that they should consider."

Finally, constructively aligning (Biggs 1996, 2003) teaching-learning environments with WTP should have considerable implications for assessment. The challenges of WTP for assessment were described by an academic developer:

Academic developer:
"It has enormous implications for assessment because aspects of ontological being, or sense of self, sense of person, these are not things we normally assess and there is in many of these accounts a realization that people who would be otherwise regarded as equal on conventional methods of assessment in fact differ quite markedly in their faculty to think like an economist or whatever."

(. . .)
"I think it [the assessment dimension] is absolutely crucial. (. . .) The problem arises that often in making explicit among themselves [i.e. newly appointed academics] what it is to do or to think like x, there is often disagreement and that creates problems for assessment as well. If they can't agree among themselves, how on earth do they expect those students to choose and (. . .) make the right choice?"

Conclusion

This exploratory study has shown that WTP is a concept which has been and can be productively employed for academic development. It has the potential to engender conceptual change by moving faculty towards a student-centered conception of teaching and, through its focus on disciplinary communities and participation within them, engages them with a socio-cultural view of learning. The fact that WTP is a very open rather than tightly delineated concept has both advantages and disadvantages. Its openness captures faculty's imagination and allows them to apply it to a wide range of contexts and disciplinary practices. On the other hand, additional conceptual clarity would be useful to allow faculty to identify more precisely which WTP (that is, of which community) are referred to in a specific learning and teaching context.

The study has highlighted the usefulness of engaging faculty in reflection and discussion about the disciplinary dimension of their practice. Opportunity for faculty to verbalize their own WTP explicitly and to discuss the concept critically seemed to be particularly effective. The interdisciplinary nature of the workshops contributed to participants' understanding of both the distinctiveness of their own discipline and its commonalities with others. Therefore and somewhat paradoxically, academic development which aims to develop staff's practice *within* their discipline is likely to benefit from going *beyond* their own disciplinary community. Postgraduate Certificate programs in learning and teaching in higher education for new staff are therefore perfect interdisciplinary contexts in which such academic development can take place.

If academic development about "disciplinarity" is useful, we need to ask whether concepts other than WTP should be introduced and would achieve similar levels of engagement. Perhaps introducing faculty to at least one other concept that explores teaching and learning in disciplinary contexts would ensure that complementary perspectives are considered and issues which could otherwise be overlooked are addressed.

Using Baxter Magolda's work (Chapter 12 in this volume) as an example, I will briefly consider the way in which her conceptual framework might usefully complement and extend the notion of WTP. Baxter Magolda focuses on students' development and 'Self-Authorship'. The concept of Self-Authorship arose from a longitudinal study of the development of young adults carried out over twenty years, which started at the time when these adults were undergraduate students. Baxter Magolda's research delineates the nature and development of advanced meaning making which involves cognitive maturity, integrated identity and mature relationships, i.e. epistemological (cognitive), intrapersonal and interpersonal capacities. By using the notion of self-authorship, she draws attention to the gap which frequently exists between students' current meaning-making capacities and the complexity of meaning making expected from them in higher education. Within the Learning Partnership Model she proposes a way to support students in their learning and development. The teacher's role is conceptualized as helping to bridge this gap by stimulating students' development towards self-authorship.

The model provides detailed steps and questions which guide faculty through the process of first identifying gaps and then designing an 'evolutionary bridge' to help students move from one developmental stage to another. It emphasizes the necessity to think about all components of self-authorship, not merely the epistemological (cognitive), but also the intrapersonal and interpersonal dimension, and stresses the importance of providing both support *as well as* challenge in supporting students' academic learning and development. While the approach, the language and the data which generated this conceptual framework are very different to those of WTP, there are nonetheless meaningful synergies between the two concepts. For instance, student identity and participation are core to both models. "Scaffolding" and "modeling" as discussed by Hounsell and Anderson can be said to perform the function of an 'evolutionary bridge'. However, Baxter Magolda's work also raises issues which are less likely to be recognized within the conceptual framework of WTP. The focus on the different stages of meaning making, and the importance of concurrently providing support and challenge, have the potential to invite faculty to look beyond WTP when devising strategies to support students' learning.

The present study has investigated the perspective of faculty and academic developers and their reactions to the concept of *Ways of Thinking and Practicing* (WTP). Further research and development of WTP needs to consider its implications for teaching, assessment and the design of teaching-learning environments and the various ways in which it can be used and applied to enhance student learning. One of the potential advantages of Baxter Magolda's Learning Partnerships Model lies in the fact that it provides concrete guidance to practitioners, similar to, for instance, the "Decoding the Disciplines" model (Pace & Middendorf, 2004; see also Chapter 8). Developing an equivalent model for WTP might help us to recognize more easily where its implications lie with regards to teaching. In addition, a wide range of examples and empirical data might assist practitioners to make the connection between WTP and the development of strategies which engage students with the WTP of their disciplines in their respective contexts.

It has been shown that engaging faculty with the notion of WTP can result in an increased awareness of both the disciplinary and transdisciplinary dimensions of their practice. It has the potential to contribute to a deepened understanding of the distinctive features of the teaching and learning efforts in particular disciplines, students' socialization into the discipline as well as the larger goals of higher education which Kreber calls for in Chapter 1 of this volume. We have thus come full circle: WTP can open up new ways of thinking and practicing to faculty themselves about their roles as educators.

Acknowledgements

I am indebted to the colleagues who participated in the workshops and agreed to being interviewed or provide written comments. This chapter draws on their ideas and could not have been written without them. I am equally grateful to the members of the research team which generated and developed the notion of WTP as well as providing me with helpful comments on this chapter.

References

Anderson, C., & Day, K. (2005). Purposive environments: engaging students in the values and practices of history. *Higher Education*, 49, 319–343.

Biggs, J. (1996). Enhancing teaching through constructive alignment. *Higher Education*, 32, 347–364.

Biggs, J. (2003). *Teaching for Quality Learning at University. What the student does* (2nd ed.). Maidenhead: Society for Research into Higher Education and Open University Press.

Hounsell, D., & Anderson, C. (2007). Knowledge practices: "doing the subject" in undergraduate courses. *Curriculum Journal*, 18(4), 463–478.

Hounsell, D., & McCune, V. (2002). *Teaching-learning environments in undergraduate biology: initial perspectives and findings*. Universities of Edinburgh, Coventry and Durham: Enhancing Teaching-Learning Environments in Undergraduate Courses (ETL) Project, Occasional Report No. 2. Retrieved 25 August, 2007, from http:/www.ed.ac.uk/etl/publications.html.

McCune, V., & Hounsell, D. (2005). The development of students' ways of thinking and practising in three final-year biology courses. *Higher Education*, 49, 255–289.

Pace, D., & Middendorf, J. (eds.) (2004). *Decoding the Disciplines: Helping Students Learn Disciplinary Ways of Thinking*. San Francisco: Jossey-Bass.

Perkins, D., & Wilson, D. (1999). Knowledge into action. *Knowledge Directions: The Journal of the Institute of Knowledge Management*, 1, 65–77.

Prosser, M., Rickinson, M., Bence, V., Hanbury, A., & Kulej, M. (2006). *Formative evaluation of accredited programmes*. Report. York: Higher Education Academy. Retrieved 25 August, 2007 from http://www.heacademy.ac.uk/assets/york/documents/ourwork/research/formative_evaluation_of_accredited_programmes_may_2006.pdf.

Prosser, M., & Trigwell, K. (1999). *Understanding Learning and Teaching. The Experience in Higher Education*. Buckingham and Philadelphia: The Society for Research into Higher Education & Open University Press.

Rowland, S. (2006). *The Enquiring University. Compliance and contestation in higher education*. Maidenhead and New York: Society for Research into Higher Education and Open University Press.

Thomas, G. (2004). Introduction: evidence and practice. In G. Thomas & R. Pring (eds.), *Evidence-based practice in education* (pp.1–18). Maidenhead and New York: Open University Press.

8

Opening History's "Black Boxes"
Decoding the Disciplinary Unconscious of Historians

David Pace

Indiana University

The Role of Disciplines

More than two decades have passed since Lee Shulman called for educational researchers to move beyond generic studies of teaching to create "pedagogical content knowledge" that explores the ways that students learn in particular academic fields (Shulman, 1986). As the present volume amply illustrates, the intervening period has seen at least the beginnings of a sustained and systematic reevaluation of the intersection of the content and the practice of disciplines with student learning. Dai Hounsell and Charles Anderson's work on "Ways of Thinking and Practicing in Biology and History" (Chapter 6) provides an excellent example of the progress that has been made in this area, and it can also serve as the occasion for a consideration of how these insights can be integrated with the actual practice of instructors within the disciplines.

The two "ands" that appear in the first line of Hounsell and Anderson's title capture insights that now seem obvious, but in fact were the result of a great deal of collective work on the part of both faculty and educational researchers. Today, it seems quite natural to juxtapose biology *and* history, thinking *and* practicing. While the authors are open to common experiences of students in the two disciplines, they are quite aware that a generic learning experience cannot be assumed. And they are equally aware that what students are to learn involves concrete practice as well as abstract knowledge. These are crucial starting points for almost any serious attempt to understand or to improve teaching and learning in higher education.

It would, of course, be possible to reify the notion of discipline and to ignore its limitations as a focus for pedagogical exploration. There is clearly a major place for what Hounsell and Anderson call "conceptual genotypes" that transcend disciplinary boundaries (e.g. explanatory concepts, such as the steps in moral and intellectual development presented by Perry, 1970). We must also keep in mind that the disciplines that we know are the result of historical processes that did not cease to operate when the boundaries within the modern university were established. And, as Paul Trowler has argued persuasively elsewhere in this volume (Chapter 15), a host of personal and institutional factors mediate between the patterns of the discipline and their expression in particular situations.

Moreover, references to a discipline may disguise the fact that there are radically different communities of practices within a single department that can generate quite distinct learning experiences. In the case of the research reported by Hounsell and Anderson, for example, it would be interesting to know whether there were significant differences in the testimony of students focused on microbiology and those working within evolutionary biology. And the cross-fertilization of academic fields, such as the increased use of literary analysis in history and of historical analysis in literary studies, may be reflected in the pedagogy of at least some practitioners in these fields.

Yet, the differences in practice represented, at least roughly, by disciplinary boundaries are so great that they remain a very useful basis for pedagogical analysis (Donald, 2002; see also Chapter 3). The very words employed by biologists and historians testify to the radical differences in the experience of academia presented to the students in each discipline. The word "data" lies at the heart of almost any discussion by biologists, but it seldom finds its way into the discourse of historians. The book is generally the "gold standard" of historical research, whereas the article is the more common vehicle in biology. The charts and graphs that convey data and theory in most biological research have no clear visual counterpart in the great majority of historical studies, and poster sessions are a rarity at meetings of historians. The abstract is not a literary convention that most historians feel comfortable with, whereas it is ubiquitous in biology. The life sciences are generally pursued in teams, but the great majority of historians operate as lone wolves.

The importance of such differences are clear from Hounsell and Anderson's interviews. The quotations that they share from students in biology and history suggest that in both fields students are becoming aware of both the need for clear evidence and the fact that arguments must be systematically defended. But the very words of the biology and history students reflect the deep differences in the practices of their disciplines. The emphasis of the biology students on "up-to-date references," their development of a "lab slang," their focus on an audience of specialists, and their awareness of being part of a research group are all, not surprisingly, absent from the testimony of the history students who are operating in a very different disciplinary context. Even a single word, like "interpretation" which appears repeatedly in the conversations with history students, can contain within itself an implicit epistemology that distinguishes this discipline from others. Both groups of students are gaining a sense of the need to consider competing claims for truth and to provide systemic support for positions being argued, but the contexts within which such actions are taken are radically different.

One of the things that makes this line of research so promising and so important for any one seeking to teach within a particular discipline is the realization that instructors do not necessarily have a clear or complete vision of what constitutes their practice and what, therefore, they need to convey to students. Individuals generally go into fields in which they have some natural aptitude, and much of their basic learning may have occurred so rapidly and so painlessly that it never became fully conscious. In any case this early learning is, as a career progresses, increasingly remote in time and ever more deeply buried beneath layers of subsequent knowledge. Moreover, professionals generally live within communities of practice in which shared procedures for problem solving and conceptual frameworks are invisible to those who automatically employ them for higher-level operations.

To use the terminology of sociologist of science Bruno Latour, the basic processes of a discipline become encased in rhetorical "black boxes," resembling the figures placed in engineering diagrams to represent entire complexes of procedures that have been left out of the diagram because they are too basic to need explanation or too complex to fit into the representation. As Latour notes, the natural tendency of members of a community employing such black boxes is to go "downstream," making use of the assumed material to think about larger problems, rather than to move "upstream" by re-examining the validity of basic constructs. To use Latour's example, biologists working on specific problems of heredity are no more likely to reconsider the structure of the double helix of DNA than they are to open up the case of their computers to consider whether the circuits might be more effectively arranged (Latour, 1987, pp. 1–17).

If they are to get work done, all intellectual communities must work in this manner. To continually rethink the basics of a discipline would forgo the possibility of building on previous knowledge. But the efficiency gained by this kind of intellectual shorthand has its cost in the realm of teaching. Practitioners of a discipline may not be consciously aware of elements that are absolutely necessary for success in their field and may even have been socialized to resist the attempt to make these explicit. Living in a social organization that works by swimming downstream from basic practices towards complex intellectual processes, they may feel uneasy about reversing course and spending time opening up the black boxes that must remain closed when they do their professional work.

Educational Research on History as a Discipline

Educational researchers have worked to open some of these black boxes in the field of history, and their research can provide crucial insights into the forms of knowledge and practice required in the discipline. These can be useful both to instructors and educational developers concerned with helping students succeed in history courses and to those in other fields seeking to understand what is unique about operating in their own disciplines. The central figure in this effort in the United States has been Sam Wineburg. In the essays collected in *Historical Thinking and Other Unnatural Acts*, he has not only unearthed hidden elements in the process of doing history, but he has also provided a model that can be easily transferred to the study of learning in other disciplines.

Wineburg began his studies by training professional historians and high school or college students in a simple "think aloud" technique in which they articulated the processes going on in their minds as they did basic tasks in history. In what is perhaps the most frequently cited example, when they were asked to read short passages on the American Revolution, all of the historians, but less than a third of the students, began by moving their eyes to the bottom of the page to consider the nature of the source. In retrospect this difference may seem obvious—historians are better trained to think about the origin of a document and the importance of knowing the identification of the author in establishing its context. But before encountering Wineburg's work, few historians have been aware that it might assist the learning process to explicitly teach this reading process to students (Wineburg, 2001).

Wineburg, however, goes well beyond such relatively straightforward observations. In one study he provided groups of college students and history professors with a series of documents on slavery produced before and during the American Civil War. Faced with Lincoln's complex statements about the subject, students fell into two groups. The first simply reduced Lincoln to the ahistorical category of "racist." The others, seeking some context for his words, interpreted them as the work of a "spin doctor," who was trying to sway public opinion in precisely the manner of late twentieth-century politicians and public relations experts. As Wineburg has argued

> In many readings by college students, Lincoln and Douglas become our contemporaries in top hats, much like characters from a historical novel by James Michener who happen to dress funny but whose behavior and mannerisms are those of our next-door neighbors.

(Wineburg, 2001, p. 18)

The professional historians, by contrast, were involved in a complex process that involved systematically problematizing words and concepts that the students treated as simple and transparent. One historian, for example, when asked to analyze a series of texts by Lincoln used words such as "I don't have enough to go on" or "This makes no sense to me" fourteen times in the process of reading the documents. He constantly returned to documents he had read earlier to help clarify just what Lincoln meant by words such as "God" or "natural rights" to produce a complex and nuanced interpretation of the debates about slavery. As Wineburg puts it, the questions posed by this historian "are the tools of creation, dwelling in the space between his present knowledge and the circumstances of the past" (Wineburg, 2001, p. 21).

At the core of Wineburg's analysis is the realization that the work of historians involves moving from the documents before them to the complex of conventions, values, assumptions, rhetorical forms, power structures, and intentions that summoned forth these particular words at a particular time in the past. To once again quote his description of the work of one of his subjects, "It is not the literal text, or even the inferred text (as that word is commonly used), that this historian comprehends, but the subtext, a text of hidden and latent meanings" (Wineburg, 2001, p. 65). The definition of this subtext involves an effort to reconstruct the rhetorical choices the author made in producing the source. It is necessary to ask whom he or she was trying to convince of what. The historians in Wineburg's study reconstructed such subtexts through complicated processes of analysis such as the construction of mock readers and mock audiences, through whom the potential impact of rhetorical forms were calculated.

These aspects of historical analysis were almost completely lacking in a group of high school seniors Wineburg studied, despite the fact that they were all excellent students whose factual knowledge of the revolutionary period sometimes exceeded some of the historians in the study, who were not specialists in the period. But they were less able to interpret the documents that they were given because their notions of historical analysis provided them with models of reading that were inappropriate for serious historical analysis. This, as Wineburg points out, is in part an understandable response to educational systems that rely upon textbooks that flatten the act of reading and reduce complex analyses to a linear series of factual statements. But, as he eloquently argues, the moral and political consequences of this kind of oversimplification of reality can be severe.

One of Wineburg's crucial insights is that history today is a discipline deeply concerned with rhetoric. As noted above, the word "data" sounds discordant to the historian's ear. It implicitly posits bits of knowledge isolated from one another, whereas the central tasks within the discipline of history involve the weaving of networks of words. This is true at the level of analysis, as the examples just quoted from Wineburg testify, and at that of argumentation, where a position is more often judged as "convincing" or "unconvincing," rather than as true or false.

Wineburg's efforts to analyze the rhetoric of historical argument were complemented in the 1990s by the work of several educational researchers in the United States. While much of this literature focused on students at the secondary level, the insights produced are very relevant to anyone concerned about increasing learning of history among college students. This work is too extensive to be presented in this chapter, but the work of Gaea Leinhardt and her associates on students' encounters with the rhetoric of writing in history classes deserves particular mention. Through exhaustive observations of the process and the environment of writing they have identified three forms of organization that were common in student history papers: 1) the list, in which facts or issues are arranged randomly; 2) the specified list, in which the elements are organized conceptually; and 3) the causal list, in which the order of elements have a direction and motivation. As students move through this sequence of rhetorical forms, they begin to make more effective use of connectors, such as "for example," "first," "because," or "however." And in the process of slowly mastering these forms of organization, they also begin to deal with the use of evidence and the referencing of that evidence in papers (Young and Leinhardt, 1998; Leinhardt, 2000)

The complexity of the reasoning processes and rhetoric conventions revealed in these and other studies can, of course, be thoroughly bewildering to the students in a college history course, just as the students' lack of comprehension can seem incomprehensible to instructors who have inhabited this disciplinary realm for most of their lives. Moreover, college teachers are commonly focused on ways of knowing, whereas in examples such as this, it is complex and often discipline-specific practices that create a bottleneck in student learning. Work such as that of Wineburg or Leinhardt can help us bridge this chasm. It can help us to make explicit the forms of knowing and practicing that are required for success in history classes and to model these for students. But, given the hidden nature of many of these disciplinary ways of thinking and acting, it may be necessary to provide forms of support to faculty trying to teaching them to their students.

The Freshman Learning Project: Observing Disciplinary Differences

In history, as in other disciplines, if we are to maximize our awareness of the impact of disciplinary differences on student learning and to turn these insights into concrete classroom strategies, it will be necessary to complement such work by educational researchers with a serious involvement in the exploration of these questions on the part of actual practitioners in the field. There can be little doubt, for example, that discussions of disciplines will be richer and more reflective of real practice, if faculty working in those fields are taking part. And it is unlikely that these explorations will have much practical impact unless they are championed by professionals in each discipline.

However, precisely what makes this important also makes it difficult. As has been argued above, because of their years of training and immersion in the social world of their disciplines, professionals in a field are often the least conscious of some of the processes required in their courses. Yet, these are the very people who need to be exploring these embedded ways of thinking and practice and modeling them for their students. Without some clear intellectual and institutional support for this process of inquiry and development of new teaching strategies, it is unlikely that very many faculty will be able to successfully complete such disciplinary introspection.

For the last decade the Indiana University Freshman Learning Project (FLP) has been working to create such a framework for engaging faculty in the process of reevaluating the role of disciplines in teaching in higher education. Each year a dozen carefully chosen faculty are led through a process of "decoding the disciplines," i.e. making explicit the kinds of thinking and acting that are required for success in courses in their field. They begin by defining a bottleneck in learning in one of their classes, e.g. a place where significant numbers of students are unable to understand basic material, to master specific skills, or to respond productively to the emotional demands posed by particular historical issues. The FLP fellows then take part in a long interview process, in which they work with the program's staff to define as precisely as possible just what experts do when faced with this potential obstacle to learning. In a two-week summer seminar the fellows work together to develop ways to model for students the specific skills needed to overcome the bottleneck, to give the students an opportunity to practice these skills and receive feedback, and to assess whether learning has occurred (Middendorf, 2004; Middendorf and Pace, 2002 and 2007; Pace and Middendorf, 2004).

The activities of the FLP fellows have revealed differences in thinking and practice across disciplines that have major implications for learning. To take a simple but important example, when visiting classes in disciplines different from their own, for example, fellows noticed that in some fields the class period typically concluded with a clear statement of the established position on the issue being considered, whereas in others a variety of possible perspectives were left on the table. This difference between fields in which classes typically converge on a single explanation and those in which multiple perspectives are treated as equally legitimate can be disastrous for students who bring the wrong assumptions about disciplinary patterns of learning into a particular course.

Differences in sensory modalities have also emerged from FLP interviews and seminars as particularly important. There are disciplines in which visual representation is central and those for which it is of little import. Astronomers in the program have reported that it is the charts and graphs of an article which convey the real information, whereas for most historians illustrations are an afterthought added for primarily aesthetic purposes. Molecular biologists and chemists frequently think in pictures, but instructors in literature seem to rarely depart from the realm of words. Such distinctions are almost certainly of great import for student learning—particularly in the institutional environment of higher education in North America, where students are quite frequently asked to perform in four or five different disciplinary contexts in a single day. But faculty generally have difficulty seeing such differences until they find themselves in an institutional setting that assists them in this process of decoding.

The History Learning Project: Defining Ways of Thinking and Practicing in a Single Discipline

The "Decoding the Disciplines" approach, developed in the Freshman Learning Project, has proven so fruitful that we decided to use it to focus in depth on the implicit requirements for success in a single field—history. The History Learning Project videotaped lengthy interviews in which seventeen faculty members of the university's History Department defined a bottleneck in learning in one of their classes and then worked with a pair of interviewers to make explicit the steps that experts in the field would take to get beyond this obstacle to learning. The results were recorded, transcribed and analyzed, and a chart of basic operations required in history courses was created. The principal investigators of the study then worked with a group of faculty and doctoral students in the department to develop, implement, and assess a series of lessons designed to model a few of these operations in history classes. Finally, pre- and post-tests are being administered to large numbers of students in the department's courses to see the extent to which faculty perceptions correspond to student difficulties (Middendorf, Díaz, Pace, & Shopkow, 2007; Díaz, Middendorf, Pace, & Shopkow, 2008).

By concentrating on bottlenecks in learning, attention was immediately focused on ways in which historians' conceptions of their field and ways of acting within it did not match the ideas or the actions of many of their students. Like a photographic negative, the manner in which students fail to live up to the expectations of their history professors reveals the positive image of the paradigms that shape the work of professionals in the field—paradigms which were often unconscious before being unearthed by our process. For example, one colleague described the ways in which students' knowledge of the Holocaust made it difficult for them to reconstruct the experience of Eastern European Jews between the world wars. This led us to the realization that historians automatically bracket out their knowledge of subsequent events when trying to understand a period—a crucial step that is rarely explicitly taught. Several of the interviewees described bottlenecks that involved students' difficulty in recognizing that artifacts created in past eras were shaped by the values and assumptions of those who created them. This allowed us to make explicit some of the steps that historians automatically go through when faced with a text or visual material from an earlier era.

One large set of bottlenecks involved different understandings of the nature of the historical enterprise itself. From the perspective of the faculty, many students failed to recognize that, while interpretations of the past have to be systematically supported by careful constructions of evidence, this process rarely yields an absolute consensus on the validity of a single position. The historians described their discipline as a slippery terrain in which their conclusions are always somewhat tentative and open to future reconsideration, and in which there is no firm source of authority.

The interviews indicated that this is a major problem, almost a crisis for those concerned about teaching history, as it is practiced today. As the work of Perry and of Baxter Magolda has so cogently demonstrated, the kind of complex juggling of uncertainties that is built into historical practice is an enormous challenge for any student, but particularly for those in the age group of traditional college students. It requires complex cognitive abilities involving viewing issues from multiple perspectives, the construction of arguments according to complex but ill-defined rules of evidence, and a willingness to hold in tension competing interpretations without prematurely collapsing them into a single answer. As Baxter Magolda has argued so eloquently, this requires reservoirs of ego strength that have often not yet been accrued by students during their college years (Perry, 1970; Baxter Magolda, Chapter 12 in this volume; and Baxter Magolda and King, 2004).

To make matters worse, in the last half century historical research has become increasingly complex, as an older emphasis on creating narratives of political and diplomatic events has been replaced by much more complex analyses of a vast range of social phenomena. This involves the practice of seeing elements of everyday life as a crucial part of an evolving history—a practice which is not immediately obvious to many students. Thus, they often treat as irrelevant "filler" parts of a course that the instructor views as central. And these newer historical subjects are often approached in terms of methodologies that are totally mystifying to many students, but so natural to instructors that they are not even defined.

Thus, it is not surprising that our interviews revealed a number of ways in which students' understanding of the tasks required in history courses did not match those of their instructors. For example, faced by an artifact from the past, the first impulse of several of the historians we interviewed—and most likely that of the great majority of contemporary historians—is to problematize its creation. They imagine other forms that the poster, map, or political tract could have assumed. Then by comparing the actual product to these hypothetical creations that might have been produced, they seek to discover what values or concerns were actually present in the minds of its creators. Many students arrive in history classrooms without any mental model for this kind of analysis. They are expected to "see" that a poster, for example, was shaped by particular attitudes towards gender or that the decision to center a map in a particular location reflected attitudes to cultural superiority, but they have no framework within which to conduct such analysis.

Many other ways of thinking and operating that are generally implicit within historical discourse were made explicit in the interviews. Historians have complex but generally undefined protocols for putting themselves in the position of individuals in other times and cultures without imposing the knowledge and values of their own times. They naturally see a great majority of things from the past as potential evidence, at the same time that they recognize that the individuals who produced them were operating from a limited perspective and most likely had their own axes to grind. They operate from the assumption that events, ideas, actions, and artifacts are all subsumed within a larger historical context which shaped them and gave them their significance. But none of these ways of proceeding are built into the human psyche, and they must be taught before large numbers of students can succeed in history courses that require these mental operations.

Beneath these grand schemas for thinking about the past, there are more practical matters that separate historians from their students. Reading strategies that work in many other fields can lead to disastrous results when applied to the lengthy narratives assigned in history classes. Many distinctions that seem innate to historians, such as that between primary and secondary sources, are often vague and ill-defined to students. And recognizing the thesis of an article in history may be far removed from the process of reading the kind of abstract students may encounter in courses in the natural and social sciences (Wineburg, 2001; Pace, 2004).

One of the greatest surprises in conducting the History Learning Project interviews was the frequency with which faculty included emotional issues in their descriptions of the bottlenecks in learning in their classes. This was particularly true in areas, such as African history or Latino history in which students often felt implicated by the actions of individuals or groups in the past with whom they in some way identified. We came to realize that part of the practice of historians is to create certain emotional barriers between themselves and those groups in the past to whom we might be linked by race, ethnicity, or other similarities. Despite the efforts to identify the perspectives of the past, to a certain extent the dictum "That was then, and this is now" is an unexamined given. It is, of course, easy to cite numerous occasions on which, for good or ill, this disjunction between past and present has broken down even for the most detached historian. But, in most situations this way of situating oneself with respect to the past serves to shield historians from identification with the moral failings of groups with which they might be associated.

Students often lack such shields. In their minds there may be no barriers between the actions of particular groups in the past and their own families of origin. They may consciously or unconsciously experience the exploration of the transgressions of such groups as a betrayal of their own family of origin and of the culture that created them. The faculty in our interviews provided ample examples of students who either responded angrily and personally to being asked to explore the actions of particular groups of historical actors or who sullenly withdrew their attention from the course. It is easy for faculty, encased in the protective armor of their disciplines, to be unaware of or totally unsympathetic to the difficulties experienced by students for whom the past and the present bleed together.

Conclusion

The History Learning Project interviews revealed myriad ways in which the practices and ways of thinking that are required in history courses might be potentially of great benefit to students and to the societies that they inhabit. To mention simply the ways of thinking and practicing enumerated above, would it not be desirable to increase students' ability to recognize the ways that individuals' perceptions are shaped by the information provided to them, to better understand how values and assumptions shape perceptions, to reason carefully on the basis of ambiguous evidence, to acknowledge the provisional nature of many judgments, to appreciate the impact of everyday experiences, social situations, and technologies on our understanding of the world and to recognize the power relations built into such experiences, to draw meaning from complex narratives, and to gain critical distance from the groups with which they are associated?

But we are left with the question: is learning history possible? The enumeration of the obstacles to learning provided above might make it seem as if the answer is "no." But we have the evidence that some students have mastered it, even under the tutelage of teachers who were almost entirely unaware of the complexities of the task in which they were engaged. Like practitioners in any other discipline, historians will never be 100% successful in sharing the fruits of their discipline with all of their students. And, in the long run success on a large scale may require serious rethinking of the entire system of higher education. But, as the work of Hounsell and Anderson, Wineburg, and many others has demonstrated, the systematic exploration of ways of thinking and practicing within the discipline can give us tools that we have never possessed before.

Defining these ways of thinking and practicing can help us both to understand why a discipline such as history is difficult for many students and to devise strategies to help students overcome those difficulties. Without this awareness the transition into a discipline may be overseen by faculty who are only dimly aware, if at all, of the difficulty students face in mastering the complex ways of thinking and acting that have become second nature to the professional. The encounter of student and instructor can degenerate into an ugly clash of cultures, in which the demands of the instructor can appear arbitrary and vindictive, and the student's inability to produce adequate results can be viewed as evidence of stupidity or laziness. We can minimize such unfortunate collisions by systematically studying what makes our subjects difficult, and we can learn to more effectively welcome students into our disciplines and to expand our ability to offer more students a place at the banquet of higher education.

Acknowledgements

I want to express my appreciation for the support for this work that I have received from my co-investigators, Arlene Díaz, Joan Middendorf, and Leah Shopkow and from Jeanne Sept and Ray Smith of the Indiana University Dean of Faculties Office and from the Indiana University History Department.

References

Baxter Magolda, M., & King, P. (Eds.) (2004). *Learning partnerships. Theory and models of practice to educate for self-authorship.* Sterling, VA: Stylus.

Díaz, A., Middendorf, J., Pace, D., & Shopkow, L. (2008). The History Learning Project: A department 'decodes' its students. *Journal of American History* (forthcoming).

Donald, J. (2002). *Learning to think: Disciplinary perspectives.* San Francisco: Jossey-Bass.

Indiana University History Learning Project web site. Retrieved November 5, 2007 from http://www.iub.edu/~hlp/

Latour, B. (1987). *Science in action.* Cambridge, MA: Harvard University Press.

Leinhardt, G. (2000). Lessons on teaching and learning in history from Paul's pen. In P. Stearns, P. Seixas, S. Wineburg (Eds.), *Knowing, teaching, and learning history: National and international perspectives* (pp. 223–245). New York: New York University Press.

Leinhardt, G., & Young, K.M. (1996). Two texts, three readers: Distance and expertise in reading history. *Cognition and Instruction* 14 (4), 441–486.

Middendorf, J. (2004). Facilitating a faculty learning community using the decoding the disciplines model. In D. Pace & J. Middendorf (Eds.), *New Directions for Teaching and Learning,* Vol. 98 (pp. 95–108). San Francisco: Wiley/Jossey-Bass.

Middendorf, J., & Pace, D. (2002). Overcoming cultural obstacles to new ways of teaching: The Lilly Freshman Learning Project at Indiana University. *To Improve the Academy,* 20, 208–224.

Middendorf, J. & Pace, D. (2007). Easing entry into the Scholarship of Teaching and Learning through focused assessments: The "Decoding the Disciplines" approach. *To Improve the Academy,* 26, 53–68

Middendorf, J., Díaz, A., Pace, D., & Shopkow, L. (2007) . Making thinking explicit: A History department decodes its discipline. *National Teaching and Learning Forum,* 16 (2), 1–4.

Pace, D. (2004). Decoding the reading of history: An example of the process. In D. Pace & J. Middendorf (Eds.), *Decoding the disciplines: Helping students learn disciplinary ways of thinking. New Directions in Teaching and Learning,* Vol. 98. San Francisco: Wiley/Jossey-Bass.

Pace, D. & Middendorf, J. (Eds.) (2004). *Decoding the disciplines: Helping students learn disciplinary ways of thinking. New Directions in Teaching and Learning,* Vol. 98. San Francisco: Wiley/Jossey-Bass.

Perry, W. (1970). *Forms of intellectual and ethical development in the college years.* New York: Holt, Rinehart, and Winston, Inc.

Shulman, L. (1986). Those who understand: Knowledge growth in teaching. *Educational Researcher,* 15 (2), 4–14.

Wineburg, S. (2001). *Historical thinking and other unnatural acts: Charting the future of teaching the past.* Philadelphia, PA.: Temple University Press.

Young, K.M. & Leinhardt, G. (1998). Writing from primary documents: A way of knowing in history. *Written Communication,* 15 (1), 25–86.

IV

Exploring Disciplinary Teaching and Learning from a Socio-Cultural Perspective

9

Guiding Students into a Discipline
The Significance of the Teacher

Andy Northedge, Open University, UK and
Jan McArthur, Lancaster University, UK

Introduction

This chapter focuses on the higher education teacher's role as representative of their discipline. While other chapters address the nature and meaning of disciplinarity, the character of different disciplines and their various practices in teaching, learning and assessment, this chapter explores the general significance, within the act of teaching, of the teacher's membership of a discipline community.

The role of the higher education teacher has been subject to rapid change, with enlargement and diversification of the student intake and of subject matters, the introduction of mass-production methods, the information technology revolution and far-reaching institutional change. Meanwhile there has been a drive to increase professionalization of teaching (accredited higher education teaching qualifications, probationary systems, schemes for the reward and recognition of teaching), but at the same time an apparent diminution of the teacher's role in the teaching and learning process, with a trend towards emphasizing learning over teaching, and reconceptualizing teachers as facilitators and even as service providers to customers. In an era of apparently limitless electronic access to information, exposition and advice, can we say any longer that higher learning is a process requiring a teacher? When prestigious universities post open-content teaching materials online, what remains of the role of the higher education teacher? Is there still an art of teaching and is a teacher–learner relationship any longer necessary?

In this chapter we argue that the role of the teacher in higher education remains central, that the art of teaching is expanding and that a learner–teacher relationship of some kind always lies at the heart of effective higher education. We explore the implications of a socio-cultural approach to higher learning for understanding the role of faculty. We argue that higher learning remains at root not only a cognitive process but also a socio-cultural one, dependent on meetings of minds and on relationships, however they may be mediated. Students as aspirants to participation in disciplinary communities require the support of established community members. This is the core contribution of teachers within higher education.

To help tease out key elements of the teacher's role as discipline expert, we begin the chapter by comparing the roles attributed to teachers within four types of higher education teaching and learning regime (borrowing Trowler's concept see Chapter 15). We argue that each of the four represents an emphasis on a different facet of the intellectual, social and cultural enterprise of teaching within higher education and that by adopting a socio-cultural perspective all these facets can be addressed together. We then focus specifically on the pivotal role of teachers in supporting students' struggles to make meaning within the context of unfamiliar discourses and show how that draws on the teacher's discipline community membership. Finally, we point to the significance of this socio-cultural line of analysis in addressing new challenges that faculty face.

The analysis presented here arises from over three decades of intensive involvement by the first author in advising and participating in teams of academics as they developed distance courses at the United Kingdom's Open University. This amounted to a form of action research, involving intense debate over pedagogic strategies, followed by extensive, systematic evaluation of outcomes for many thousands of students and subsequent refinement of pedagogic principles. This chapter emerged out of discussion of those principles between the two authors.

Contrasting Models of the Role of the Higher Education Teacher

We begin by reflecting on the roles attributed to teachers by established teaching approaches. In practice, different teaching regimes have made markedly different assumptions. For example, the old-time "Oxbridge" apprentice-scholar model, expected students to "read" subjects for themselves. The teacher recommended texts, set assignments and criticized students' work in tutorials, but direct exposition of discipline knowledge did not necessarily play a major part. Lectures were often regarded as marginal, as we see in this note on the studenthood of William Empson the eminent English scholar: "Empson chose not to attend TS Eliot's 1926 lectures at Cambridge on the metaphysical poets, despite his great interest in both the lecturer and his subject, because it was understood that, as a student, one just didn't attend lectures" (from a review of a biography of Empson by J. Wood in *The Guardian*, 4 June 2005). In this mode of education the roles of the teacher are to point students towards the literature and to be taskmaster, critic and standard setter. The students are assumed to have received enough prior education to be capable of engaging effectively with the discipline for themselves. The teacher's discipline knowledge was more a basis for authority than for feeding directly into the student's learning of the subject.

The lecture-centered model of university education, on the other hand, assumes that students learn through listening to exposition of the subject matter. Thus the teacher must have sound and up-to-date knowledge of the discipline and the communication skills to "transmit" this knowledge to students as a sequence of coherent presentations, each "covering" a topic. A combination of spoken exposition, visual aids and handouts is assumed to be sufficient to achieve the desired "transmission", so that any failures in learning tend to be attributed to poor skill, or application, on the part of the student. With the emphasis on the teacher "delivering content", the elements of the teacher's role are to know, select, synthesize, organize and present discipline knowledge.

By contrast, the "constructivist" approach treats the notion of learning from exposition by the teacher as intrinsically problematic. Learning is viewed as an active, exploratory process, involving each student in developing their own conceptual modeling of the subject matter. Listening to a lecture is seen as too passive to support the key process of constructing knowledge. Instead, the role of the teacher is to create opportunities for students to experience conceptual dilemmas, solve problems, reflect and engage in exploratory dialogue. Thus the teacher's skill lies in being able to identify the key areas of concept construction required for understanding discipline knowledge. The teacher must also develop insight into the kinds of challenge that will trigger concept construction and be creative in designing learning situations to stimulate and support exploratory thinking. The emphasis is on understanding the learning process, the minds of students and the core conceptual challenges presented by the discipline, rather than on being able to present an accurate account of the latest developments in discipline knowledge. Indeed, exposition by the teacher can be seen as counterproductive, in that it undermines students' motivation to construct conceptualizations of their own. By outflanking students' efforts to understand for themselves, exposition is seen as potentially preventing "real" learning. This places teachers in a somewhat contrived relationship with their own discipline knowledge, in that they require subtle understanding of the subject matter in order to design learning situations and to support students' progress in reconceptualizing issues, yet they must forego the satisfactions of actually explaining and telling.

Decoupling of teachers from their discipline knowledge is taken further by radically student-centered models of higher education in which students themselves play a leading role in shaping the curriculum, course content and assessment. Here the teacher's role is to set up structures and contexts for learning and then to facilitate the learning process and be available as a resource. Direct exposition of the teacher's knowledge is marginalized. A teacher who enjoys explaining difficult points and enthusing about recent developments in the field appears self indulgent – not helping students, but contributing to their oppression by reinforcing the hegemony of the academy and the teacher's superior status as its representative. Taken to the extreme, radical student-centeredness raises questions as to whether the teacher really requires discipline knowledge and whether, indeed, the academy is the appropriate setting for education. The teacher becomes a community organizer and facilitator of social change, with education an ancillary component of the mission.

These sketches of contrasting approaches to teaching and learning are not intended to bear rigorous critique, but simply to illustrate very different ways in which the role of the higher education teacher can be characterized. Is the teacher to be a primary source of knowledge, or to hold back to give the students space to learn? Is the teacher's first duty to maintain a detailed up-to-date knowledge of the discipline, or is it more important to develop insight into the minds and lives of their students? Should the teacher focus on setting standards, or on coaxing students to develop their own ways of understanding. On the face of it the approaches sketched appear contradictory and incompatible. Must a choice be made between them? We suggest not. Instead, we view each as having arisen from legitimate concerns and insights and suggest that each draws attention to significant aspects of the complex business of higher learning.

Higher Learning: A Multifaceted Process

The apprentice-scholar model foregrounds the *academic discipline* and the process of guiding the student into competent discipline membership (operating, in effect, as a disciplinary finishing school for already well-educated students). Meanwhile, the lecture-centered model foregrounds the *content* that a course claims to cover, as well as championing the powers of the composed spoken presentation in synthesizing and encapsulating a complex field and in rehearsing challenging ideas. In contrast, the constructivist approach foregrounds the student's *mind* and the conceptual restructuring entailed in making sense of new knowledge. Finally, a radical student-centered approach foregrounds the student's *personal and social being*, from which learning acquires its significance and from which the drive to seek knowledge arises. Rather than privileging just one of the four approaches, an understanding of higher education needs to encompass all the facets of learning to which they draw attention.

This can be achieved by adopting a socio-cultural perspective, which views higher learning as a complex process of becoming immersed in the ways of thinking and knowing of a significant knowledge community. The student thereby acquires the ability to participate in that community's discourses and practices to standards accepted within the community and thus can partake in its trade in knowledge. On this view, learning is not a simple cognitive event – the transfer of an item of information or an idea into the student's mind. Instead, the student's advance in knowledge is represented by the extent to which he or she becomes able to participate more effectively in the discourses of the relevant discipline community. This includes making progress in being able to locate and access discourses on relevant topics, make sense of what is found, make constructive use of it in thought, speech and writing, and have that usage accepted as legitimate by other community members. In other words, higher learning is a psychosocial as well as a cognitive process.

From this perspective higher education can be understood as providing students with interim access to a discipline community, together with support in engaging with its ideas and practices. On the one hand, support is needed for "inner" aspects of learning – the *cognitive development* required in order to be able to make meaning using discipline ideas, and the *realignment of self* involved in engaging with the values and norms of the discipline community. On the other hand, support is needed for "outer" aspects – developing approaches to engaging with the field of knowledge and acquiring skills of participating as a member of the discipline community. If we map this "inner-outer" dimension onto the intellectual and the psycho-social aspects of learning, then we might characterize our four higher education teaching approaches as in Table 9.1.

When we view the four models of teaching in the context of Table 9.1, they appear not contradictory but complementary, focusing attention on different aspects of the support that students need in engaging with higher learning. The key processes of higher learning are not located solely within engagement with disciplinary practices, nor in the accessing of bodies of information and theory, nor in students' cognitive development, nor in their personal growth. From a socio-cultural perspective, teaching and learning cannot be encapsulated within a single arena of development. The teacher has a range of interwoven responsibilities and plays a variety of roles in supporting different aspects of learning.

In this chapter we cannot explore all these aspects, but we will make a start at the bottom righthand corner of Table 9.1, exploring how the cognitive aspects of learning can be understood from a socio-cultural perspective.

A Socio-cultural Perspective on Cognitive Learning

From a socio-cultural perspective, learning is not primarily a matter of an individual mind grappling independently to master new knowledge. Minds function within social milieux. Resnick and associates, for example, posit "reasoning as a fundamentally social activity in which ideas and concepts are literally constituted in interactive discourse" (Resnick, Pontecorvo, & Saljo, 1997, p. 4). Even the activity of reflecting on one's experience of the world, they treat as essentially social. "We are very nearly incapable of learning from experience, except when it is mediated by cultural practices of explanation and initiation into the proper talk of the knowledge community" (Resnick et al., 1997,

Table 9.1 Aspects of the higher education teaching-learning process

	Personal/social learning	Intellectual/cognitive learning
Outer aspects concerning the discipline community, its knowledge, discourses and practices	**Apprentice scholar** approach foregrounds learning how to function as a member of the discipline community, through researching, debating, publishing	**Lecture-centered** approach foregrounds the knowledge produced by the discipline community: how it can be assembled, organized, encapsulated and presented
Inner aspects concerning processes within the mind and social being of the student	**Radical student-centeredness** foregrounds development of self, realignment of values, coping with acquiring an identity as a member of a knowledge community	**Constructivism** foregrounds the processes of cognitive reorganization and development entailed in making sense within an unfamiliar field of knowledge

p. 17). For them a student's "central learning task . . . is to acquire both the organising conceptual theories and the patterns of discourse that are used by particular reasoning communities" (p. 4). But note that theorizing and discoursing are not understood as separable: "discourse *is* cognition *is* discourse . . ." (p. 2). Thus participating in knowledgeable discourse and its associated practices becomes the central learning process. Discoursing is not merely a communication process which *supports* learning. Rather the process of engaging with the minds of others through discourse is the learning process.

And this learning does not consist of a series of purely cognitive events – the transfer of discrete ideas and items of information into the student's mind. Rather, it is a broad advance, on multiple fronts, towards more effective participation in the community's knowledge systems. This maps well onto the enigmatic and perplexing experience of higher learning. Here is a student chat-room message revealing a common theme: "Is any one out there feeling overwhelmed by the reading, or is it just me? . . . wondering if any of it is going in! Feeling bogged down – not sure whether to keep going, or try to recap or what" (quoted in Northedge, 2005, p. 101). Effort invested in learning seldom produces clearcut results. It is generally difficult to point to a moment when the "learning" of a particular concept or theory "happens". Rather, we recognize learning in retrospect – when ideas which once seemed baffling start to emerge in our own thoughts and discourse. In answer to the question "How do you know that you have learned something?" one student wrote, "When you are in lectures, or talking with mates, and some piece of information enters your head, then you know you've learnt it – also when you get interested and start analyzing an idea in your head". Another wrote, "You know something must have begun to sink in when you eventually find the confidence to start thinking about your approach to the next essay". A third wrote, "When you find you can understand new aspects of the subject, then you know you learned what you read before" (Northedge, 2005, p. 79). Learning, then, seems to occur not as a direct outcome of a specific and deliberate activity, but as a generalized consequence of the process of getting on with studying – in other words, of participating in the discourses and practices of the knowledge community.

We suggest it works like this: The student strives (with support) to make sense of texts, lectures and discussions and also to speak and write intelligibly. These activities engage the student in thinking and talking in ways that approximate to the ways members of the community think and talk. In the process, the student's mental organization becomes temporarily accommodated to the task in hand – effectively serving as an extension of the discipline's system of thought. Over time, repeated temporary accommodations produce more substantial shifts, with the effect that the student's mental organization gradually becomes more congruous with the modes of thought and action that characterize the discipline community. Terms gradually become familiar, concepts take shape, facts acquire significance, recognizable themes emerge, arguments flow more comfortably and all begin to cohere as a working system of thought. This piecemeal reconfiguration of mental organization is the essence of the learning students need to achieve through their studies, since it enables them to participate in the discourses through which a community's knowledge is manifested. "The power of . . . concepts, explanations, and forms of reasoning – does not reside in the capacity of single elements to explain phenomena, but in the fact that the different constructs form part of general modes of reasoning" (Resnick et al., 1997, p. 3).

Here, then, is a model of conceptual learning as spontaneous cognitive reorganization, which continues in the background as an unwilled by-product of the processes of striving to make sense of discourse and to contribute intelligible utterances of one's own. It suggests that, contrary to popular metaphors for learning along the lines of storing items of knowledge in a mental data bank, learning is instead more like the invisible shifting of estuary sandbanks as tides carve out new channels. The ebb and flow of thought through the student's mind both shapes and is shaped by the conceptual residue of past engagement in communal thinking. Thus, the learning of specific subject areas is achieved through setting up opportunities for repeated experience of engaging in appropriate flows of ideas and argument. Put more generally, conceptual learning is achieved through regular experience of *meaningful participation* in the discourses and practices of a discipline community.

Of course, as we indicated earlier, much besides conceptual learning is achieved through participating in discipline discourses. The process of participation brings together the inner and the outer aspects of learning. It also brings together the personal and the intellectual. By engaging intellectually and socially with the discourse and the discipline community *out there*, the student develops *internally* the conceptual and cultural wherewithal to participate more effectively. In other words, all four cells of Table 9.1 are brought together in the process of participating in discipline discourse.

However, we return again now to the cognitive aspect, to consider the core challenge of participating in discipline discourses, which is that participation presumes the achievement of shared meaning, whereas the construing of meaning is extremely troublesome when the frame of reference is unfamiliar.

The Challenge of Making Meaning in Unfamiliar Discourse

We begin with an example taken from a distance-taught introductory course in health and social care, published by the United Kingdom's Open University (discussed in Northedge, 2003). Consider the challenge faced by first-year students when they attempt to read the opening sentence of this chapter in a set book: "*The boundary between the medical and the social is a shifting one, constructed in complex ways that reflect both institutional and ideological factors*" (Twigg, 1998). This sentence, which is perfectly transparent to a regular participant in discourses on care policy, is utterly opaque to a newcomer. It is not that the words themselves are particularly unfamiliar, rather that the concepts to which they refer and the relationships posited between the concepts are unfamiliar. The reader first encounters two high-level abstractions, "the medical" and "the social", which appear to be related in some way that involves a boundary. This dividing line is apparently unstable and somehow "constructed". How and by whom? What is the reader to summon to mind? All the student can glean is that there is complexity involved and some connection with two other types of abstract entity – institutional factors and ideological factors. There is nothing here for a newcomer's mind to operate on: no way to begin a thought.

How could one enable students to read this sentence? An eager teacher might provide definitions of the main terms used and perhaps some examples of boundaries between concepts. However, this is a hopeless enterprise, as each definition and example is likely to bring new problems of equivalent magnitude. As Resnick and colleagues report, "analogies offered . . . do not work because students do not yet know the concepts that are used to create the analogies. These concepts are available to teachers because of the discursive community they are part of" (Resnick et al., 1997). In any case, to try to understand a sentence word by word is to render it inert. Its meaning is not deducible as the sum of its words, but has to be understood in the context of debates going on within the discipline. The central problem for students is lack of experience of the kind of debate within which a sentence such as this has resonance. To be able to read the sentence unaided, students need experience of entertaining thoughts of the kind it expresses. In other words, they need experience within milieux where such meaning is traded.

The groundings of meaning are not just cognitive, but also social and cultural. New meanings are apprehended within the social process of communication and they are framed by the social and cultural context within which communication is set. There is no *a priori* base from which new understanding can be built using purely logical manoeuvres. Disciplinary discourse is framed by assumptions which can be apprehended only through engaging in dialogue that invokes them. "*What is being meant by what is said cannot . . . be pursued in terms of . . . 'literal' meanings of expressions*" (Rommetveit, 1979). The route to construing unfamiliar meaning is not through formal logical steps, but through experience of participating in the flow of meaning making within relevant discursive contexts. And these contexts are themselves set within the wider framework of the accumulated culture and ongoing discourses of the discipline. To be able to acquire a facility in using the meaning systems available within a disciplinary discourse, the student needs to accumulate familiarity with the ways of the discipline community – the taken-for-granted purposes, values and methods, the history of key debates, the influence of leading figures – as well with its culture of method, argumentation and communication. These socio-cultural features are not merely "characteristic" of the discipline but *constitutive* of the meanings traded within its discourses.

Acts of Shared Meaning Making

Returning now to our students, struggling with the abstract sentence, what they need is a teacher to supply a discursive context within which the thought the sentence expresses can be encountered as a seemingly obvious strand within a flow of dialogue. Higher learning involves immersion in ways of thinking which are made to seem "natural" in the contexts in which they are encountered. The art of the teacher is to be able to create such contexts and to stimulate appropriate flows of thought. But this cannot be done at arm's length. The teacher has to be able to join the student in a state of intersubjectivity. As Jerome Bruner has pointed out, teaching "rests upon our astonishingly well developed talent for 'intersubjectivity' – the human ability to understand the minds of others" (Bruner, 1996, p. 20). How does the teacher do this? "A state of intersubjectivity . . . is attained at a given stage of dyadic interaction . . . if some aspect of the world . . . is brought into focus by one participant and jointly attended [to] by both" (Rommetveit, 1979). In other words, a teacher needs to be able to focus students' attention on a common object and bring shared framing assumptions into play so that all are attending to the same aspect of the world.

The term intersubjectivity is often used in a general sense to refer to a high degree of common identification and attribution of meanings within a community (as in Trowler's chapter in this volume). However a *state* of intersubjectivity refers to an activity of mutual meaning making between two or more people. On Rommetveit's account, it requires one person (the "speaker") to take the lead in projecting a flow of meaning (generally through language) and at least one other (the "listener") to make a successful attempt to share in that flow of meaning. (In the context of a conversation, the "speaker" role will change hands frequently.) This process of shared meaning making through entering into states of intersubjectivity is embedded in daily life and so commonplace as to seem unremarkable. Yet it is the basis for all communications (and hence for our capacity to accumulate culture across generations). For our purposes here, its significance is that it enables the sharing of meaning between the teacher, who knows how to frame the ideas embedded in the discipline's discourses, and the students who are, as yet, unable to do so independently. But in educational settings, states of intersubjectivity are difficult to achieve and easily disintegrate.

In daily life, states of intersubjectivity are easy to achieve because contexts and activities are rich with shared meanings and customary themes. By contrast, disciplinary discourses offer sparse resources for sharing meaning, so that the teacher's words may fail to generate a shared flow of meaning at the outset – or at a shift of frame of reference, students may "lose the thread", after which continued talk by the teacher is wasted. Some form of initial contextualizing and purpose setting is required, such as an anecdote, a problem, or a picture, to draw students' sense-making powers into the arc of trajectory that the teacher aims to launch. After this, frequent recontextualizing helps to maintain the process of shared meaning making. A key characteristic of a "good teacher" is to be adept at setting up contexts from which states of intersubjectivity can be launched and then to be skilled at maintaining them.

It is important to note here, particularly as academic discourses are strongly text-based, that states of intersubjectivity are not dependent on either speech or contemporaneous participation. Reading, for example, is an act of entering into a state of intersubjectivity with a writer. Similarly, writing involves entering into an imagined state of intersubjectivity with a prospective reader – attempting to invest sequences of words with the potential to stimulate a flow of shared meaning. Thus writing aspires to storing up potential states of intersubjectivity, while reading aspires to a post-hoc state of intersubjectivity with the writer.

Creating States of Intersubjectivity with Students

In the Open University course referred to above, the device used by the teacher to set up a state of intersubjectivity with her students is to tell a story about two drug users (K100 Course Team, 2003). This case study is presented as a series of brief episodes, offering a gradually unfolding narrative which raises significant issues regarding the delivery of care. Eventually, one of the protagonists comes to be discharged from hospital, having had a leg amputated and now requiring long-term support from social services. At this point the significance of transferring from a *medical* care regime to *social* care regime is all too apparent. Now questions can be posed to students in the context of which the Twigg chapter, referred to earlier, offers a helpful analysis (for a fuller account see Northedge, 2003). Thus the student is drawn into a dialogue where the issues with which Twigg is concerned are manifested as life problems for the protagonists and the meanings of the terms she uses emerges from the context. It is not expected that, at this first encounter, students will apprehend much of Twigg's broader theoretical analysis of how policy is shaped by institutional and ideological tussles over definitional boundaries. What is significant is that students have been given an initial exposure to the way such a line of thinking works – the issues it addresses, the purposes it serves, the contexts in which it is potent. At this point, few students will be able to rehearse the arguments independently, but when they next encounter similar debate, they will have a better sense of how to frame such thoughts – where to begin and what trajectory to project.

The aim of the teacher, in designing this teaching text, is to enter into a dialogue with her reader which brings selected issues about access to care resources into the reader's mind – and to do this in such a well contextualized way that she can assume a high degree of intersubjectivity between herself and the reader. Then she gradually shifts the frame of reference, by asking questions, bringing new objects to attention and drawing in new concepts – aiming all the while to keep the reader "with" her, sharing in a carefully constructed flow of thought, which emulates significant features of academic discourse on care. It is the reader who will supply the energy for the act of reading and it is in the reader's mind that intersubjectivity with the author will "happen", but (like any good writer) the teacher has imaginatively enacted her part in this state of intersubjectivity during the process of writing.

The notion of entering into states of intersubjectivity in order to "lend students the capacity to frame meanings" within discipline discourse has been likened to the widely used concept of "scaffolding" new knowledge. However, scaffolding can sound like an "arm's-length" activity, with the teacher setting some supports in place, then standing back while students pursue their enquiries, whereas here we are talking about the teacher jumping in and swimming alongside the students within a flow of shared meaning. It is a communal activity, intended to support students in becoming encultured within the discipline community. What is primary is the teaching/learning relationship and the dialogue. The supportive structuring evolves dynamically within the flow of shared meaning.

It is important to emphasize here the active role the student plays in achieving intersubjectivity with the teacher. Reading and listening are too readily characterized as "passive" modes of learning, whereas making sense in unfamiliar terrain is hard work, however skilled the teacher. Of course, students may scan their eyes over pages, or sit through lectures without achieving intersubjectivity with author or speaker. Words can be registered without meaning being shared. However, where students are given the resources and impetus to enter into a flow of shared meaning, both reading and listening generate very active processes of learning.

When, earlier, we identified "meaningful" participation in discourse as the core process of higher learning, it was this "switched on" form of participation to which we were alluding – where a state of intersubjectivity is achieved. We might have used the term "active participation", but activity in the sense of simply "doing" things does not guarantee "participation". Students often "do" things while remaining firmly rooted in discourses with which they are familiar and consequently learning nothing. What matters is whether something is "done" within a flow of meaning which gives it significance in terms of disciplinary discourse and practice. For us, "participation" in discipline discourse implies a reasonably successfully sustained state of intersubjectivity between student and discourse speaker.

The Significance of the Teacher's Membership of the Discipline

Returning to the main theme of this chapter, we can now see the significance of this teacher's membership of an academic discipline. This is how she knows that "the medical–social divide" is a significant framing device within the discipline discourse and so judges that it will be worth students investing study time in becoming familiar with the ways it is used. By speaking herself (though in writing, in this case), then setting the student activities to work on interspersed with further dialogue from her, she enables the student to experience *in situ* the way this conceptualization is used in discussing care service provision.

However, whereas Twigg engages in mainstream discourse, addressing an audience of discipline peers, the teacher has in effect constructed a temporary forum for debate within which she employs an intermediate level of discourse. This discourse operates by more permissive rules – blurring over into everyday discourse, but gradually tightening the analytical framing as it proceeds. The teacher is able to do this because she is a practised speaker of both everyday discourse and the discipline discourse, so she can draw in elements from the one to help shore up meanings in the other. She is not simply "presenting" a chunk of discipline "knowledge", she is engaging in discoursing with the students – and in a particular way, which allows blurring of the boundaries between discursive arenas and permits approximate usages of ideas and language. As a member of the academic discipline and also a member of society at large, the teacher is able to mediate between the two in a finely judged sequence of manoeuvres.

We should point out here, that our claims that dialogue and teacher-learner relationships lie at the heart of the learning process do not amount to a championing of face to face teaching, or small classes. The case we have been considering is drawn from a distance education context, where many students have no direct contact with teachers or other students and where course populations run to the thousands. Dialogues and relationships can be mediated in many ways, as the growth of internet communities has shown. What is critical is to ensure that the teaching context and process allow states of teacher-student intersubjectivity to be achieved.

In this section we have sketched the processes through which teachers enter into states of intersubjectivity with students in order to support them in construing the meaning of discourse as written or spoken by discipline members. There are other equally important roles for the teacher in supporting students in speaking and writing the discourse for themselves. These too require the teacher to be a member of the discipline and to enter into teacher–learner relationships in order to fine-tune the student's progress towards skilled use of the discourse (see Northedge, 2003). Then there are further roles in connection with the aspects of learning reflected in the other three sectors of Table 9.1, which are beyond the scope of this chapter. However, the general thrust of our argument is that higher learning is not achieved simply through "telling", "informing", "presenting", or "instructing". It arises out of the student participating in dialogues involving members of the discipline community, thereby becoming immersed in multilayered processes of familiarization with the way the discipline's discourses work.

The Four Models Revisited

Having illustrated some aspects of the way our analysis works, we return to the four approaches to teaching set out in Table 9.1 to show how our socio-cultural line of thinking endorses each to an extent, but also presents an alternative angle on it.

Apprentice Scholar Model:
We agree that those students who aspire to become members of the discipline community at some level (perhaps in an associated profession), need practice in something like an apprentice role, where they are treated as novice members of the academic community. However, for this they need to be already quite familiar with the discourse. It is a particularly apt model in the context of PhD studies and is also relevant to project work in later undergraduate stages. It encourages students to practise plying the discipline's trade in knowledge, seeking to develop their own knowledge resources to trade. They can learn how to present their offerings so that other community members accept them as legitimate. It also enables them to develop a workable identity as a member of the community. (Indeed, the whole PhD process might be characterized as enabling the achievement of the transition from a student identity to an identity as a member of the discipline community.) However, the model has little to offer when students are exploring new fields of discourse, where usable resources for meaning are scarce, making unaided meaningful participation in discourse all but impossible.

Lecture-Centered Model:
We fully support the use of lectures in education, but not as the means of "transmission" of knowledge. To the extent that there is need for students to access and internalize up-to-date information, there are much more reliable and effective means, such as texts, handouts and websites. The value of the lecture is as "performance" of the discourse. Provided the lecturer has been trained in the skills of maintaining intersubjectivity with a large audience, the student can participate vicariously in "live" production of coherent, sustained discipline discourse. In contrast with lone struggles to generate intersubjective meaning from texts, the student can be carried along on the momentum established by the lecturer, experiencing the full arc of an argument from its opening problematic, through its use of evidence and logic, to its conclusion. This is by no means a "passive" process for the student, who has to maintain a state of intersubjectivity by striving to follow the meaning – at the same time making connections with what is already known and recording skeleton notes. It is also an imperfect process, with much of the meaning intended by the lecturer not registering with the student. Nevertheless a lecture provides an invaluable source of knowhow about the way the discipline discourse is used to develop meanings within a particular topic area. The teacher as a discipline member can model not only the way the discourse is spoken but also the way discipline identities work – how you position yourself to approach the subject and make sense of it the way members of the discipline do.

Constructivist Model:

As we have made clear, we are committed constructivists to the extent of placing the reorganization and development of the student's concept systems at the heart of learning. However, we view the constructive process as social and cultural. We do not envisage students drawing their own conclusions from experience and each constructing their own idiosyncratic conceptual edifice. Rather, we see the constructive process as one of gradually appropriating conceptual devices from relevant discourses, and doing so largely unconsciously through the experience of using them in the process of participating in discourse (often vicariously). And we would point out that the value of the conceptual apparatus appropriated lies in the extent of its use in discourses in which the student wishes to participate. Students will each achieve their own particular blend of borrowed conceptual structures, and they will continue to extend and modify them (or let them fall into decay) to the extent that they continue to participate in discipline discourses beyond the course of study. But from our perspective, any notion that students follow a personal learning path to arrive at their own knowledge system is essentially misleading, in that it fails to recognize the social nature of knowledge. Certainly there is potential for divergence in personal interpretations and elaborations, but there are also powerful convergent forces which make knowledge tradable within the world. This is a significant issue, in that some of the claims made for various forms of e-learning place great emphasis on the potential for students to pursue their own routes through knowledge resources. From our perspective this is of limited value, because the core processes of learning involve students in carefully framed and guided dialogues. To experience participation in meaning making students will inevitably need to be working alongside a teacher or other students in common discursive terrain.

Student-Centered Models:

Again we see ourselves as enthusiasts for student centeredness, in that we advocate for teachers to pay close attention to the experiences of their students as they struggle with the challenges of learning. But we do not endorse leaving students to set their own agendas, while teachers facilitate at the margins. For us the purpose of teaching is to support the student in learning how to participate in a relevant knowledge community – establishing an unthreatening atmosphere which encourages students to risk "mistakes" as they try out new meanings, but at the same time recognizing that discipline norms will come increasingly into play. Students also need support with the challenging personal process of developing a sense of "belonging" within the discipline community, coping with doubts about new values encountered, and conflicting loyalties to other significant discourse communities. Our model of student-centeredness positions teachers not as neutral "facilitators" but as fully functioning discipline members, drawing on all aspects of their discipline knowhow to support their students' personal development.

Conclusion

In an era of extraordinary change in higher education it is particularly important that we understand the nature of higher learning processes and how they can be enhanced or undermined. Exciting new prospects are offered by the opening up of access to information through the internet and by the potential for transcending boundaries of space and time through electronic communications. But uncertainties lurk as to whether the essence of higher learning will somehow be lost and what the role of the teacher will be as new configurations of higher education emerge.

Our contention is that participation in discourse is fundamental to higher learning, however it may be mediated – and that the involvement of a discipline expert is required if dialogue is not to revert to everyday discourse. Opportunities for states of intersubjectivity between student and teacher are also necessary. Can online discussion replace face to face group work? The question to explore is whether online forums offer the potential for states of genuine group intersubjectivity and hence for participating in mutual meaning making, or whether they simply serve as noticeboards for communal message posting.

Questions of other kinds arise from the expansion of higher education and the growth of occupationally relevant courses, with multiple discipline linkages and no overarching academic community. Which forums then generate the relevant discourses in which students are to become proficient? And what knowledge communities will students be inducted to? Does the teacher become, in effect, a visiting member of a range of relevant knowledge communities, only some of which are academic disciplines?

When so much is in flux there is a danger that change is addressed as presenting essentially technical and administrative challenges – questions of how information will be delivered, or how assessment and quality control will be managed – without recognizing the complexities of the learning processes that need to be supported. It is important that higher education teachers and researchers have convincing models of higher level teaching which encapsulate the subtlety of the roles they play within the teaching–learning process. There can then be the prospect of managing change so that the essential supports for higher learning are preserved.

References

Bruner, J. (1996). *The culture of education.* Cambridge, Massachusetts: Harvard University Press.

K100 Course Team (2003). Unit 10, accessing community services. In K. C. Team (Ed.), *K100 understanding health.* Milton Keynes: Open University.

Northedge, A. (2003). Enabling participation in academic discourse. *Teaching in Higher Education,* 8 (2), 169–180.

Northedge, A. (2005). *The good study guide.* Milton Keynes: The Open University.

Resnick, L. B., Pontecorvo, C., & Saljo, R. (1997). Discourse, tools and reasoning. In L. B. Resnick, R. Saljo, C. Pontecorvo & B. Burge (Eds.), *Discourse tools and reasoning: Essays on situated cognition* (pp. 1–20). Berlin: Springer.

Rommetveit, R. (1979). On the architecture of intersubjectivity. In R. Rommetveit & R. M. Blakar (Eds.), *Studies of language, thought and verbal communication* (pp. 93–107). London: Academic Press.

Twigg, J. (1998). The medical/social boundary. In M. Allott & M. Robb (Eds.), *Understanding health and social care: An introductory reader* (pp. 272–278). London: Sage Publications.

10

Diverse Student Voices within Disciplinary Discourses

Lancaster University, UK

Introduction

In the previous chapter Andy Northedge and I argue that teachers play a critical role supporting the student learning experience in higher education. We outline how learning, from the socio-cultural perspective we espouse, is a "*process of engaging with the minds of others through discourse*" (p. 111). The teacher's role in this process is based upon his or her membership within a disciplinary community. In this chapter I adopt but also build upon this perspective. I discuss how faculty can enable students to simultaneously achieve two things: to develop a capacity to engage in disciplinary discourses, and thereby acquire a *disciplinary "voice"*; but also to retain and develop their own voices. I suggest that it is important that we recognize students as coming to our courses with diverse backgrounds and aspirations, and journeying towards what Baxter Magolda (see Chapter 12 in this volume) calls "self-authorship". This point is addressed in the table included in the previous chapter, where learning is shown to involve both inner and outer aspects as well as social and cognitive elements. Thus the learning process at university is influenced by the relationship between community (i.e., discipline) and individuals (diversity); or between sameness (common meanings) and difference (different views, perspectives, and ideas generated through the process of discourse based on common meanings). The problem we face as teachers is to find the appropriate balance between these forces to effectively support student learning. In other words, our chief challenge is to balance the integrity of our discipline with the authenticity of our students' learning experiences. Such authenticity is achieved when students can be *true to themselves* while learning – expressing and developing their own voices as they participate in the discourses of the disciplinary knowledge community. Below I will offer some suggestions on how to achieve this balance.

This chapter is divided into four parts. I begin by expanding on the concept of different "voices" within disciplinary discourses. Two practical sections follow, highlighting the importance of teachers as full members of disciplinary communities, sharing both their disciplinary authority and their own voice with students. The final section explores the ways in which disciplines are very special spaces in which different voices can be expressed and developed. In these discussions I draw particularly on two concepts from Baxter Magolda's chapter: the journey towards self-authorship and the importance of blending the interdependent authority of teacher and student. Throughout I use a series of vignettes, drawn from the experiences of students and teachers I have encountered during my career as a teacher of politics and economic history, as an educational developer and as a researcher.

Different Voices within Disciplinary Discourses

I use the term "voice" to include a bundle of features that we bring to our discursive relationships with others. These are the features that make each of us distinct individuals, and inform the way in which we interpret the world and relate to others. A disciplinary discourse community is formed by diverse voices engaged in common meaning making. Within your own disciplinary community, where you and your colleagues are experts, you will find shared meaning making relatively easy. Specialized terms, abbreviations, concepts, theories, debates, authors, controversies, and the like, are considered common knowledge. Reference to these will need little or no explanation for meaningful conversation to take place. Shared understanding of meanings, however, does not imply common viewpoints on the theories and debates within your discipline. Indeed an academic environment without disagreement would be both surprising and intolerably dull. Often what excites our passion for our discipline is the batting of different ideas back and forth. At times, we also find great satisfaction in a "meeting of minds", but this rarely means we find someone who thinks exactly as we do. Academic discourse, in any disciplinary community, is an exciting and tumultuous exchange that involves sharing, challenging, changing and debating ideas. We all have our own voices. We all have our own backgrounds, beliefs and interests that shape the context in which we participate in our disciplinary communities. Or as Davidson (2004) describes it, we all have an academic *self,* "the unique learning pathway or intellectual journey by which individual academics come to formulate their identities as medics, historians or engineers" (p. 307).

Just as we have our own voices, so too will our students. As Paul Trowler (in Chapter 15) reminds us, both faculty and students bring their world to the learning situation. But our situation as teachers and as members of our disciplinary knowledge community differs in important ways from that of our students. It is the very fact that we are full members of these communities, and the authority bestowed by that, which makes it easier for us to engage in disciplinary discourse while retaining and developing our own voices. We understand the contestable nature of knowledge. We have experience. We have an internal sense of authority about what we say within this community. Students are students because they lack this. Clearly, to retain, develop and express their own voices within the unfamiliar terrain of a disciplinary community, of which they are not members, is a major challenge for students.

If our aim is to encourage active learning, with students contesting and constructing their own understandings through participation in disciplinary discourses, then it is part of our role to encourage the expression of the students' diverse voices at the same time as we work towards engaging them in common meaning making. We know from the advancement of knowledge in our own disciplines, that novel insights are often generated through the interplay of different ideas and perspectives. The authority we have as members of our disciplinary knowledge communities is not just a matter of us having greater and easier access to disciplinary knowledge. It is also a matter of having developed an awareness of, and tolerance for, the uncertainty that is inherent in the many voices within our disciplinary discourse community – that is, understanding and tolerance for the tentative and contestable. I suggest that it is this understanding and awareness that we need to share with our students so that they too can participate in our disciplinary discourses in their own voices.

Sharing Disciplinary Authority to Enable Meaningful Learning Relationships

In practice learning occurs within the orbit of many contexts, amidst a flurry of influences, some more conducive to learning than others. The relationship between teacher and student (and also between peers) may be influenced by numerous social factors such as prior educational experience and preparedness for university study, socio-economic status, ethnic and cultural background, gender, or previous life experience. Amid these influences the creation and maintenance of a state of intersubjectivity can be troublesome. In the previous chapter we describe this state of intersubjectivity as "*an activity of mutual meaning making between two or more people*" (p. 113). Any of the above factors may build bridges for, or create barriers to, the creation of states of intersubjectivity. They may inspire or distort mutual meaning making. These factors are also all expressions of the diversity within the university community. Our challenge is to celebrate diversity, while minimizing the barriers to states of intersubjectivity.

Faculty and students find themselves in complex relationships defined by authority and power, and influenced by the sort of social factors outlined above. These relationships can influence the learning experience in significant ways. In this section I discuss how as teachers we should aim to share the authority that we have as full members of our disciplinary knowledge community, while also minimizing the potentially distorting effects of the undeniable power relationship between teacher and student.

Students are dependent on the teacher's disciplinary authority and this is perfectly legitimate; it is the essence of being a student, particularly at earlier levels. Students need access to their teacher's disciplinary authority to assist them in engaging with the discourses of the knowledge community rather than passively "receiving" information. Drawing upon their teacher's disciplinary authority students can be empowered to consider, challenge or critique within the discipline's discourses in ways that a "non-member" may otherwise feel unable to do. It is also important that faculty are prepared to recognize and nurture their students' authority, not as disciplinary "experts" or full members of disciplinary knowledge communities, but in the legitimacy of their status as learners, visitors or prospective or intermediate members of disciplinary communities, and journeyers towards self-authorship. In her Learning Partnership Model, Baxter Magolda describes the responsibility of the teacher in this way: "to promote (students') self-authorship while simultaneously supporting learners' current meaning-making" (Chapter 12, pp. 149–150).

Consider the following vignette recalled by a young man called Roddy, studying marine science:

I remember a professor I had once. I respected him because he seemed to be a really brilliant research scientist as well as a professor. I think he genuinely cared about us students. But he could also be pretty fierce. I remember one tutorial when it was my turn to lead the discussion by summarizing the readings about environmental toxicology. I read and read and read. I like facts, so I was determined to get to know all the essential facts. But the professor kept trying to get me to "question the data". I wasn't even sure what that meant. He became pretty provocative and it seemed like he was angry. I could sort of see that I had just amassed this huge quantity of facts. I could also sort of see that there was maybe another step I needed to take. But I couldn't manage it in response to the barrage of questions from him. He was getting so cross and frustrated with me. I was so confused, and the more pressure I felt the more mistakes I made. I started to lose confidence in all those facts that I had. I was so embarrassed. I couldn't question anything, let alone be "critical" of it. I just wanted the tutorial to end and everyone to stop looking at me. . . . If I think back on it, I suppose I did learn from that class that you couldn't just accept what was in the books and had to sort of think about it yourself. But it was still a pretty awful experience for me.

It may be tempting to see this vignette as a tale of being "cruel to be kind". But this teacher has failed to create the basis for a genuine learning relationship where authority can be shared between himself and his student. By adopting an overly aggressive approach, the lecturer is not sharing authority as a member of the disciplinary knowledge community, but rather asserting his power as a teacher within the tutorial over Roddy. Such a demonstration of the uneven power relationship between teacher and student creates a barrier that makes it difficult for Roddy to access and share his teacher's disciplinary authority in order to help him build his own critical interpretation of the readings. The lecturer could have shared his authority by, for example, demonstrating how he would critique the literature, thereby modeling what he wants Roddy to do. This way Roddy and the other students might have experienced a concrete example of the ways in which critical encounters are constructed in this discipline.

There are many reasons why sharing disciplinary authority may not be easy. In the above vignette there may be influences on the lecturer of which we are unaware; the faculty member is himself formed by his background and the environment in which he is now working. For new faculty, sharing their authority with students will be difficult as they are still working to establish it with their peers. In some institutions faculty are also worried that a commitment towards sharing their authority with students, which essentially means to show interest in teaching, is misinterpreted as a lack of commitment to their discipline (McArthur et al., 2004). More experienced teachers may, as Baxter Magolda observes, be "socialized" into not sharing their authority: "They are disconcerted when their familiar ways of teaching are challenged and they fear that sharing authority with students will not produce effective learning" (Chapter 12, p. 155). It is important for new faculty members to resist this, and instead develop an approach to teaching that is built around the sharing of authority. Baxter Magolda refers to the need to *blend* the interdependent authority of student and teacher, as the lecturer in the above scenario could have done by demonstrating to Roddy how one could go about critically examining the disciplinary literature.

Now compare Roddy's experience with that of Claire, studying management:

> *Once as part of a management honors class we had a lecture with a visiting academic. She spoke to us about a very theoretical concept about organization and how change happens. I really liked her. She was quietly spoken, but interesting. But I can't say I really understood much about it. Then at one point she stopped talking, and sort of paused, maybe thinking. Then she said, "I want you to know that this is actually very important. In real life." She then went on to describe a horrible situation in a social work department which was responsible for investigating if children had been abused in their homes. She explained how the social workers and the doctors were all really trying their best to help these children. But it still went all horribly wrong. Then the lecturer described how she had used this concept about organization and change to help the social work department reorganize itself. Then it all started to make sense. Finally I understood that concept a little better And I could also see that the teacher was right. This stuff did matter.*

The teacher has shared her disciplinary knowledge, but importantly she has also placed it in a wider context, accessible to others – to newcomers to the discipline. By doing so she has created a state of intersubjectivity (in a similar way to the health and social care example in the previous chapter). Claire now has a reason to participate, a desire to consider a position, argue against others, and to learn more through participating in further opportunities for discourse. Her interest in the subject, her sense of its value, is the basis upon which she can bring her own voice to these learning opportunities. We can hear Claire's voice in the emotional reaction she had to the lecturer (inner aspects of learning – involving her social being) and in the value she attributes to the knowledge and its potential applications (outer aspects of learning – involving the disciplinary knowledge community and its practices).

It is interesting that the teaching situation in the above vignette is a lecture, far too often considered a passive learning environment. As Northedge and I argue in the previous chapter, a skilled lecturer, such as this management academic, can allow students to actively engage with the disciplinary discourse, even in a large lecture. As Claire is thinking through the implications of what her lecturer is saying, she is bringing her own voice to her construction of meaning. Another common assumption is that tutorials naturally offer greater opportunities for active learning, and thus for students' expression of their own voices. Roddy's experience shows the problems in a tutorial if a teacher exploits the power relationship between student and teacher. Here is a vignette from Alex, studying law, and recalling a different situation, from his second year tutorials:

> I used to absolutely dread the tutorials in one of my second year law classes. The teacher was nice enough and she had actually worked in practice and she knew a lot about the subject. Each week we had two set readings, roughly in line with the lectures. The tutorials were just a series of questions and answers. We had these sort of workbooks with the questions and spaces to write the answers. Every single week the tutorial was full of these long and painful silences. Really awkward and uncomfortable. This would happen every week. She would ask us a question and we would all sit there waiting to fill in the answers. She was nice enough about it. She just kept asking questions, working through the sheet. Oddly enough the subject was quite interesting . . . but I know I didn't want to say anything in case it was wrong.

Questions and answers like this do not allow students to participate in mutual meaning making as the approach implies that the "meaning" has already been made. There is a demarcated space on the workbook for *the right answer*. This provides little opportunity for the teacher to share her authority, thereby enabling it to blend it with the student's own fledgling authority. The teacher is, perhaps unintentionally, placing herself as the sole authority within the tutorial – arbiter of right or wrong answers. In so doing she is not encouraging active learning or critical thinking from her students, despite Alex's opinion that she is kind and interested in them. She has closed the space in which students could express their voices. This situation is possibly more likely to happen with inexperienced faculty. An inexperienced teacher may be attracted to the "comfort" of set answers, particularly in the unpredictable environment of a tutorial. However, creating a situation that allows for all the uncertainty of students' different voices need not be frightening. In fact, it could be immensely rewarding and enjoyable. The lecturer could begin by giving her interpretation of the readings, thus establishing the scope for different views rather than just the elusive "right answer". She could say why she found them interesting, or perhaps highlight points she found confusing herself or disagreed with. Discussion that elicits students' own interpretations or present under-standing, rather than "answers", creates a space in which learning can occur. It provides recognition of the students' developing, albeit interdependent, authority as participants in the disciplinary knowledge community.

Students need to know that it is legitimate for them to say things that are unusual, unexpected, contested, contrary, or even incorrect. They need to know that this is part of the process of making meaning within the disciplinary community. It is a normal part of any educational experience to make mistakes, go down blind alleys, follow red herrings, and get things completely wrong. This happens to the experienced researcher, the professor, the senior lecturer, the PhD student and the first year student. What differs, with experience, is the ability to use one's own sense of authority to work back, remedy a mistake, and then move on.

Sharing our Voices to Enable States of Intersubjectivity

There is a fundamental link between students developing an internal sense of authority and them being able to take part in disciplinary discourses in their own voices. A truly internalized sense of authority can only manifest itself in the individual's own voice. It is therefore important that we share not only our disciplinary authority with students but that we, as teachers, do so in our own voices.

This is critical for two reasons. Firstly, it legitimizes the concept of diverse voices – students can see that their teachers hold different views and express their disciplinary knowledge in diverse ways; thus students can be reassured that the purpose of their learning is to be able to develop an ability to do likewise. Common meaning making (even for the purpose of disagreement) and diverse voices are perfectly consistent. Secondly, using our own voices provides the necessary base for creating states of intersubjectivity and a blend of the teacher and student's interdependent authority.

In the previous chapter Andy Northedge and I explain that we want to go beyond the "arm's length" concept of scaffolding. Rather, the student–teacher relationship should be one of diving into the turbulent waters of the disciplinary discourse community together. How do we manage to be there, by the sides of our students, rather than out in front or standing on the sidelines? I believe that expressing, through your own voice, your enthusiasm for your subject can be a link, and can ensure you are not at arm's length from your students. New faculty, in particular, may feel very aware of their lack of teaching experience, and frequently undervalue the importance of their enthusiasm for their subject in the teaching process. Demonstration of this enthusiasm does not mean a song and dance show, or cracking jokes; it simply means demonstration of the importance of the subject and why you, and your students, would or should want to learn more about it. An example is provided in the way in which Claire's lecturer, in the second vignette, explained the relevance and importance of the highly theoretical discipline-based concepts. Thus going beyond mere enthusiasm for your subject, a teacher must have an *enthusiasm to share* his or her disciplinary knowledge with others who cannot yet fully participate in these disciplinary discourses. While membership of your disciplinary community is your "most powerful teaching asset" (Wenger, 1998, p. 276), it is not sufficient. As Parker (2002) argues, teachers will fail their students if they do not believe in, and are not able to communicate, the importance of their discipline.

Rowland (2005) provides an even richer concept than enthusiasm when he speaks of "intellectual love". In his view, such love "always wants a more intimate acquaintance with the subject matter" and is "strengthened, rather than exhausted, by being expressed" (p. 98). The value you place on the subject you are teaching will help guide students into learning more about it, as in Claire's experience. The key, as I noted already, is voicing your belief in the importance of the subject and your own real and passionate desire to want to know more – *to learn.*

Disciplinary Spaces

The previous two sections have focused on practical elements of teaching and some of the key aspects which faculty need to consider to enable students to participate in disciplinary discourses, while also developing their own voices. In this section, I consider the nature of these disciplinary communities and explain how this chapter rests on a particular understanding of "disciplines"; one which considers them to be special spaces where different voices can be nurtured and expressed. Davidson (2004) describes the boundaries of disciplines as "flexible, culturally determined, interdependent and relative to time" (p. 302). This differs from some more traditional views of disciplines as inflexible or closed places. It accords with Parker's interpretation of a "new disciplinarity" (Parker, 2002), where disciplines are regarded as communities rather than demarcations.

In this section I suggest that it is the very complexity of disciplines, the rigor and richness of the discourses, which enables students to develop their own voices. To achieve the sort of goals outlined by Baxter Magolda requires the complexity, messiness, contestability and creativity of disciplinary communities. It is the drive to simplify and commodify higher education, with attempts to reduce everything to easily accessible subjects and bite-sized modules discouraging efforts towards fuller and more complex engagement with the disciplinary community, that carries the risk of rendering our students mute.

As Kreber has already noted in Chapter 1 of this volume, the terms "subject" and "discipline" are sometimes used interchangeably, and even within this volume the interpretations of different authors vary. Kreber's analysis distinguishes between the subject as what is looked at and the subject as what is looked through or with (i.e., the lens of a particular discipline). While I concur with this, and indeed sometimes use the term in a similar way, there is another common usage of "subject" which signifies something entirely different. This is subject as an administrative unit, a neat piece of learning for students to *obtain*. I draw here on Parker (2002) who distinguishes disciplines and subjects. She describes the latter as something which "can be reduced to common transferable and equivalent subject-specific skills" (p. 375) with an emphasis on "the end product, and skills and competencies" which aggregate over set periods (p. 375). Subjects thus provide little space for students' voices. Subjects are inclusive, Parker argues, in that nearly anyone can take part in studying them, but they are also passive – "they are taught, learned, delivered" (p. 374). In contrast, Parker views a discipline as something that is "practiced and engaged with" (p. 375). Disciplines, therefore, offer spaces for students' independent and active learning.

The Significance of Contesting Knowledge

It is a particular challenge to enable students to work with intermediate forms of the disciplinary discourse, without distorting the essential nature of that discourse. Such intermediate forms operate by the more "permissive rules" outlined in the previous chapter and blur everyday and specialist discourse. In addition, in some disciplines students are likely to come with preconceived views about the nature of the knowledge they wish to acquire, with concepts of *hard facts* or *exact science*. They tend to "implicitly ascribe to science an aseptic kind of infallibility that is a profound distortion of the actual facts" (Arons, 2000, p. 232). Reflecting on Janet Donald's chapter (see Chapter 3) I suggest that the contestable nature of knowledge is common to all disciplines, but the way in which this is manifested and how it is conceptualized, may differ between disciplines. Discussions between full members of a disciplinary knowledge community take place on the basis of an understanding of knowledge as contested and tentative. As Chris Snowdon, in Baxter Magolda's chapter, states: "I want them to understand how information is gained. I want them to appreciate what facts really mean. Tentative facts. That's what all of science is. Subject to change and revision" (this volume, p. 160). But students may have legitimate difficulty trying to deal fully with the contestable nature of the knowledge while they are only able to engage in intermediate forms of the disciplinary discourse. Students may not, particularly at earlier levels, be able to critique or contest the disciplinary knowledge they are acquiring; such inability is, after all, one of the features of the intermediate form of participation. However it is vital, at any level, that they understand that the disciplinary knowledge is contestable, open to critique and examination.

We end up in a real bind, in any discipline, if we try to enable active learning, developing students' own voices, but insist that the knowledge they are acquiring is static, "hard", incontrovertible fact. The latter tends to invite passive learning and demotes the value of students' own voices. The learning experience easily becomes unsatisfying, and learning equated with mimicry, imitations or memorization. Indeed, Rowland (2003) emphasizes the importance of students learning to contest knowledge, at whatever level. Using the example of reading, he argues that readers of a text only have "life" as active participants in the learning process if they are given voice to contest what they are reading. To contest does not mean disagree, but rather to question, consider, debate, anything but passively accept. Rowland argues that this is true of any learning situation, be it lectures, tutorials, online activities or other forums.

Richardson (2004) discusses the case of Pauline, an economics student whose sense of what it means to be a learner of economics becomes gradually changed. Pauline is keen and interested in her chosen subject. She has questions, ideas of her own. She sees a connection between what she is learning in economics and the complex social world around her. Indeed, she starts the course from a perspective that is already moving in the direction of self-authorship. Slowly, however, this changes. She comes to learn, through her assessments, that her own ideas about economics and society are not what is required. As a result, her sense of self as a student changes. She "learns" that she should read and reproduce what is in the textbooks, and "should not hold strong opinions about complex social issues" (p. 517). Pauline then begins to choose examples in her assignments that "fit the assumptions, concepts and theoretical model set out in the course and the textbook" (p. 517). Now, she has tamed "her intellectually engaged, questioning mind, so as to avoid trouble by fitting in to the beliefs and practices of the disciplinary context" (p. 517).

I am not suggesting that Pauline should be trying to disagree with concepts such as "opportunity cost" or "supply and demand"; however, unless she is permitted to engage actively with what she reads it will only ever be a partial learning experience. If we require students to subdue their own voices, to accept knowledge rather than engaging with it, then the entire process is self-defeating. Pauline has been shunted off the journey towards self-authorship and stuck on a siding. She is now poorly equipped to deal with the increasing complexity of the disciplinary discourse should she wish to continue within it. Or, if she does not wish to participate as a full member of this disciplinary knowledge community, there is a permanent distortion in her ability to use what she has learnt by participating in this disciplinary community in other forums.

The Challenges and Importance of Flexible Disciplinary Boundaries

Understanding disciplines as flexible, permeable spaces yet with defined and complex community identities, also helps make sense of some of the practical challenges facing faculty in the modern university. Increasingly, both faculty and students need at some point to work at disciplinary boundaries or cross into unfamiliar discursive terrain. While disciplinary membership is crucial to the act of teaching, many of us teach in increasingly multi- or interdisciplinary contexts. This is the case not only in the newer vocational subjects such as hospitality and tourism or marketing but even in disciplines such as medicine or law. Growing interdisciplinarity demands of students and faculty the ability to participate in discipline communities of which they do not aspire to full membership.

If you are teaching in a subject that crosses disciplinary boundaries it can be particularly difficult to pitch the appropriate level of discursive engagement. As Rowland (2003) observed, there is a danger of ending up with "non-disciplinarity" rather than multi-disciplinarity. In a situation of non-disciplinarity the level of engagement with any of the associated disciplines is so superficial that it is either meaningless or impossible to take part in any of the disciplinary discourses that could inform the disciplinary community. Rowland (2003) also warns that: "Theories derived from one context of knowledge cannot, however, simply be transferred into another. It is a process which, fired by curiosity, should be at once rigorously disciplined, and also imaginatively playful" (p. 24).

The potential pitfalls are evident in the experience of an archaeologist, acting as a specialist lecturer on a forensic science course. His purpose was to explain archaeological techniques and methods for application in forensic science; he therefore had to decontextualize the techniques and methods from archaeology. However, applying such decontextualized knowledge to a discipline they are only learning to participate in is immensely difficult for students. In this case the students found ways of bridging the two disciplines, relying on whatever resources they had at their disposal. To the lecturer's surprise, when he came to mark exams, he found that many students had tried to explain the archaeological techniques using examples from the Romans, not forensic science. Yet, he had never mentioned the Romans. The students appear to have instinctively reverted to what they believed to be the appropriate context, which in this case was an *everyday* (non-specialist) knowledge of the Romans acquired perhaps from secondary school or television. They tried to find their voices given the resources they had to draw on. Thinking back on this, the lecturer decided that he had underplayed the difficulty of crossing between these disciplinary discourses. When the lectures were given again, he took time to explain explicitly that the techniques were being used outside their archaeological origin (decontextualized) and that it was important for the students to consider them from within the domain of forensic science. In Kreber's terms (Chapter 1 of this volume) the lecturer must help the students distinguish between the subject and the disciplinary lens with which they are exploring it; between their focus on forensic science and their approach based upon the disciplinary knowledge community of archaeology.

Engaging with other disciplines, at some level, is also crucial to the maintenance of a disciplinary community as a critical, creative space, rather than an atrophied body of received wisdom. Davidson (2004) argues that teachers need to "look over the hedges surrounding their own disciplines, into the fields of neighbouring disciplines" (p. 305). He describes a state of decentered self, where you do not leave the terrain of your own discipline, but you are able to step back and consider it and challenge it. By looking at different disciplinary worlds you can confirm and challenge your understanding of your own disciplinary "country". Not only does such an approach help to keep a disciplinary community dynamic, on a practical level it provides an essential insight into the varied terrains being navigated by many of your students – experienced through their many voices.

Conclusion

Learning and teaching within higher education is complex. The complexities become less daunting, however, when we connect community and diversity. Participation in disciplinary discourses involves the sameness of common meanings shared by the discourse community members and participants, and the diversity of the many different voices. Community and diversity are not concepts at odds with one another, and with diversity we have the contestability of knowledge. Indeed, it is within the safety of a community that creative conflict, or contestability, can take place (Palmer, 2000). Communities are always formed by both sameness and difference. This is echoed in the four squares in the table included in the previous chapter: the outer aspects are those shared by the disciplinary community, the inner aspects those particular to individual students. Our role as teachers is not to hide all this complexity and difficulty from our students. Our role is to advise on the appropriate level of engagement for them at different stages of the learning relationship, and to help to provide ways of doing this – combining our disciplinary membership and our abilities to create and sustain states of intersubjectivity.

This adds further importance to the teacher's role as there can be no "one size fits all". Like learning itself, the teaching role is fluid, enigmatic, changing and challenging. Acknowledging this complexity is often a useful step for teachers dealing with it in the increasingly demanding world of higher education. Of course, many faculty working within higher education would probably agree with Baxter Magolda who observes that nearly everything in higher education institutions is against making such learning partnerships work! While accommodating the many different voices of your students into the learning relationship may seem an overwhelming task, these relationships are not altogether different from those you have with your disciplinary colleagues. They are just occurring at a different level. We assist our students in constructing meaning within the disciplinary discourses as we share our authority as full members of the knowledge community. But to make this experience authentic, that is for students to undertake it with and through their own voices, there must be space for the differences that we know exist in such communities, as well as the shared meanings and discourses. These disciplinary communities are themselves complex; their boundaries are defined, yet socially constructed and flexible.

Baxter Magolda's image of a journey towards self-authorship reminds us too that the learning relationship changes over time, manifesting itself differently at different levels of student participation in the disciplinary community. Experienced teachers can tell you that there is nothing more rewarding than witnessing your students' voices *change* over time. Such change is expressed as they come to understand themselves as moving towards fuller membership of the desired disciplinary community or come to use their intermediate membership in more confident and autonomous ways. The table included in the previous chapter also documents these changes. At different times the emphasis may move between the four squares, between inner and outer as well as between social and cognitive aspects. Learning always involves a mixture of them all, but the blend and balance of this will change; *as it should* – to reflect changes in the learning relationship and the students' developing voices.

I conclude with a final vignette to show what can be achieved in practice.

A lecturer in Popular German Culture teaches a fourth-year honors class on critical theory (for the lecturer's own discussion, see Phipps, 2001). It is a challenging subject, drawing on the work of German theorists such as Theodor Adorno. The grand finale of the course comes with a cabaret put on by the students. The cabaret serves many functions. It brings together aspects of the culture they have been studying, including the writings of the theorists, the social context in which they worked and the social contexts in which their work has been interpreted and used, including modern Britain. The cabaret further allows the students to participate in the disciplinary discourse in one of the most creative and challenging forms – through satire. The lecturer argues that for students to be able to satirize the material well, they must really understand it. Beyond this, it is a celebration of those students' voices. And for an extra twist, the lecturer encourages the students to also satirize the course itself. In one sense, they are providing feedback, or course evaluations, but it is also so much more than that. Here, at the end of the course, the lecturer is providing the ultimate form of recognition of her students' diverse and developing voices, enabling them to provide feedback on her teaching, not through standardized forms or teacher-prepared formats, but truly in their own voices. The teacher's role in the learning relationship has thus changed too over their time together. She is sharing not only her disciplinary authority with them, but celebrating their authority as students; as peers working together, analyzing, dancing, critiquing, singing, learning. Further, she is sharing her authority as teacher. In recognition of their journey towards self-authorship she acknowledges her students' ability and right to judge and criticize her and the course. Gently she has started to let go of the strands of interdependent authority blended between her and her students. And they too have started to let go, engaging in the disciplinary discourses in their own voices and on the basis of their own authority.

References

Arons, A. (2000). Science: The art of inquiry. In D. DeZure (Ed.), *Learning from change: Landmarks in teaching and learning in higher education from Change magazine 1969–1999* (pp. 232–233). London: Kogan Page.

Davidson, M. (2004). Bones of contention: Using self and story in the quest to professionalize higher education teaching – an interdisciplinary approach. *Teaching in Higher Education*, 9(3), 299–310.

McArthur, J., Land, R., Earl, S., Elvidge, L., Juwah, C., & Ross, D. (2004). *Promote: Alternative ways of fostering educational development*. Edinburgh: Napier University.

Palmer, P. J. (2000). Community, conflict, and ways of knowing: Ways to deepen our educational agenda. In D. DeZure (Ed.), *Learning from change: Landmarks in teaching and learning in higher education from change magazine 1969–1999* (pp. 204–205). London: Kogan Page.

Parker, J. (2002). A new disciplinarity: Communities of knowledge, learning and practice. *Teaching in Higher Education*, 7(4), 373–386.

Phipps, A. (2001). Measuring performance: Some alternative indicators. In M. Walker (Ed.), *Reconstructing professionalism in university teaching* (pp. 129–148). Buckingham: The Society for Research into Higher Education & Open University Press.

Richardson, P. W. (2004). Reading and writing from textbooks in higher education: A case study from economics. *Studies in Higher Education*, 29(4), 505–521.

Rowland, S. (2003). Learning to comply; learning to contest. In J. Satterthwaite, E. Atkinson & K. Gale (Eds.), *Discourse, power and resistance* (pp. 13–26). Stoke on Trent: Trentham Books.

Rowland, S. (2005). Intellectual love and the link between teaching and research. In R. Barnett (Ed.), *Reshaping the university: New relationships between research, scholarship and teaching* (pp. 92–102). Maidenhead: The Society for Research into Higher Education & Open University Press.

Wenger, E. (1998). *Communities of practice: Learning, meaning and identity*. Cambridge: Cambridge University Press.

11
Guiding Students into a Discipline
The Significance of the Student's View

Lewis Elton

University College London and University of Manchester, UK

Introduction

I was asked to comment on Northedge and McArthur's analysis of the teacher's role in guiding students into a discipline (Chapter 9) and, to a lesser extent, to tie Hounsell and Anderson's work on 'ways of thinking and practicing' (Chapter 6) into my discussion. Where does one start in responding to pieces of writing, with which one so largely agrees? My intent here is to offer a few observations on both these chapters. Specifically I will attempt to situate my discussion within the main theme of this book: the relationship between the context or discipline-specific aspects of learning and those that are generic or perhaps, as Kreber puts it in her introduction, 'context-transcendent'. I suggest that there are two chinks in the otherwise excellent armor of both the chapters:

- The chapters are written from the teacher's point of view; yet they include passages which should have been spoken by students.
- The division between what is generic and what is discipline-specific is far from simple.

I will therefore explore, through specific examples, these chinks in order to illustrate the following general matters: First, student perspectives as expressed by the student and their consequences for the teacher, in even the most teaching-centered approaches, i.e. lectures and reading; second, the complex relationship between what is primarily generic and what is primarily discipline-specific; and related to this, much of what appears to be generic is in effect strongly discipline-dependent; and much is indeed generic, but does not appear to be so.

The first point will furthermore allow me to reminisce on my own experience, for which I have gone back to my own school and university days well over sixty years ago (in my last years at school and when I took the Cambridge Mathematical Tripos), even though this was likely to be an exercise doomed to failure, in view of the passage of time. The second point will occupy most of the chapter and will, I hope, demonstrate also the third one, that the division between generic and discipline-specific is far from straightforward. Finally, you will see from the Conclusion that writing the chapter has proved to be a learning experience for me and to some extent I am asking you to join me in that experience.

Student Perspectives as Expressed by the Student and their Consequences for the Teacher

Project Work in the Sixth Form

When I was seventeen and still at school, a new physics teacher appeared who came with two qualifications that caused us sixth formers to stand in some awe – he had industrial experience and he had a PhD, but we soon learned that what he really stood out for was his enthusiasm for physics and his friendliness to us. However, what turned out to be the most important characteristic of 'Doc' Britton, as we called him, was that he introduced us to project work in the laboratory. Until then, laboratory work had been used in the main for carrying out exercises – it would have been quite wrong to signify these with so romantic a title as experiments – the purpose of which was to 'verify physical laws'. Naturally, sometimes they failed to do this and in such instances we were told to 'do it again'. The thought that we might have discovered an until then unknown physical law never entered our heads and would of course have been absurd. Soon we 'cooked' the numbers, so as to get expected answers – a soul-destroying exercise, which I came across again some years later when I was a demonstrator in a first-year laboratory class in physics for budding medical students. But 'Doc' would have none of this; he started us on project work, where the outcomes were unknown and there was no way of verifying the results by looking them up in physical tables. Naturally, the results were not 'important' – I remember measuring thermoelectric effects at metal junctions between two metals, which were not such as to show effects of practical importance – but the results were my own and could not be looked up in a book of physical tables: a thrilling experience at seventeen!

Twenty years later, such project work was introduced into degree courses – always in the final year and often in the final term, because students had first to 'learn their stuff'. Thanks to Doc, I knew better and introduced such work into first-year laboratories with considerable success. Nearly forty years later, I was involved as a curriculum adviser in a first-year electrical engineering course and found to my horror that students were still expected to verify wellknown laws. However, the person in charge was receptive to my ideas and within a year those students were doing genuine laboratory work. Thank you, Doc!

And what happened to Doc? Five pupils from the first five years of his time at the school, which never had more than 250 pupils, became professors of physics – none thereafter. Had he lost his enthusiasm? It did not seem so, when many years later the five professors nominated him successfully to the Institute of Physics as teacher of the year. So this story ends with a conundrum, but one that I learned from too – life is more complicated than physics.

The Cambridge Mathematical Tripos, 1942–2007

To revive my memory, I started by reading what advice undergraduates (Cambridge-speak for students) are given today when they first start on this course (see www.maths.cam.ac.uk/undergrad/) and found that essentially nothing has changed, except that undergraduates are now extensively advised (warned?) of what is in store for them. It all came back – the importance of the lectures and how to profit from them; the role of the supervisions (Cambridge-speak for tutorials) and how to profit from them; all from a strongly didactic teacher's point of view. I of course had one-to-one supervisions, while now they are normally two-to-one; yet there is no suggestion that undergraduates could in any way learn from each other. This explained to me why it had never even occurred to me to discuss any of my work with fellow students, even though one lived on the same staircase as myself! The advice, furthermore, was given in an essentially perfectionist way – follow it and all will be well – which is all right for the 'best' students. Here is an example:

> Mathematics is just a different way of learning and no worse than the wading through of hundreds of often contradictory textbooks that many of your friends will have to suffer. And

there are few more satisfying academic achievements than the successful proof of a tricky mathematical proposition.

So there was nothing to be gained from facing contradictions in this apparently most positivist of disciplines and any idea of the 'Oxbridge' apprentice-scholar model (see Northedge and McArthur) was far from the way that we, as students, were – and still are – treated in that Tripos. Although this may show that even the most apparently generic aspect of teaching and learning can be strongly discipline-dependent, it also appeared to show that teachers in these courses were unable to bridge the gap between an intelligent schoolboy and a mature academic. Furthermore, no warning was given of an issue that is probably particular to mathematics, namely that it is a subject that for any one student is easy up to a certain point and then becomes quite suddenly impossibly difficult. For some, this happens at O-level, for some at A-level or beyond; for me it happened at the beginning of Part II of the Tripos, after I had sailed without difficulty through Part I. Fortunately, I was saved by the war; I was only allowed two years and was awarded an unclassified war-time degree on the basis of an almost failed first year of the Part II! A few years later, I took a London External Degree by correspondence, found that all of it was within my limits and finished top of the year!

Of course, supervisors are now expected to receive some training (see www.maths.cam.ac.uk/undergrad/), or at least "they should attend one of the training sessions; students have the right to expect trained teachers". So, one training session makes a trained teacher in Cambridge.

Enough of indulging in memories. They have, however, had a strong effect on the second of my chosen careers – the improvement of university teaching and learning. I now know how much more there is to good teaching and learning than is dreamed of in the philosophy of Cambridge Dons; so let me return to Northedge and McArthur.

Shared Meaning Making: Familiarizing Students with the Way the Discipline's Discourses Work

I particularly like that the authors eschew an 'either/or' approach, in favor of a 'not only/ but also' one – in some ways similar to the difference between the Aristotelian excluded middle and a Hegelian synthesis. They treat higher learning as a "multifaceted process", and as they concentrate on a constructivist approach, I will concentrate on an apprentice scholar approach (i.e., how to function as a member of the discipline community, from the moment that a student enrolls on a university course). I will start by illustrating my point through an analysis of academic writing in a chosen discipline, an essential tool of the budding academic (Elton, 2008).

Academic Writing
Student writing in an academic discipline is, if taught at all, taught either in an academic writing unit, which rarely if ever can go beyond the generic, or within a disciplinary department, where there is rarely the appropriate expertise in academic writing. It is then not surprising that Husain and Waterfield (2006) suggest that "First-year students feel that the key to success lies not in producing a well-structured and well-written piece but in complying with some mysterious tacit code which they cannot access" (p. 27).

Furthermore, I believe that real success in students learning how to write in their discipline requires a collaboration between disciplinary specialists, writing specialists *and* students, particularly because, as Husain and Waterfield recognize, of the overwhelmingly tacit nature of the knowledge required. The concept of tacit knowledge was originally put forward by Polanyi (1967), and to make tacit knowledge overt is commonly associated with expressing it through words, the basic building blocks of any form of writing and an essential pre-requisite for a discussion of 'acts of shared meaning'. Only, if we first have an understanding of words, can we share meaning. So let me try to analyze the meaning of words, starting with what, arguably, is one of the best known but also most difficult passages in the Bible – John 1: 1 – which is explicitly about 'The Word'. In the Authorized Version it reads: "In the beginning was the Word, and the Word was of God and the Word was God." What is the meaning of the word 'word' here and how does it relate to modern meanings? Furthermore, this is a translation from the Latin which in turn was a translation from the Greek and both of these, when translated literally, end with "and God was the Word" (in Latin: *et Deus erat Verbum*). So we have to add problems that arise from translation to an understanding of the meaning of words. Goethe, in *Faust*, Part I, wrote: "Im Anfang war die Tat"; i.e. "In the Beginning was the ??" I give this first in German, because any translation into English adds an uncertainty. How does one translate *Tat*? My two dictionaries (Langenscheidt and Collins) both give "Deed, Act, Action": which is most faithful to the original? And translation inevitably adds to the uncertainties. Yet is there any other building block that we can use to convey meaning? There may be a clue in the Goethe quotation, if we could only know exactly what it meant (deed, act and action can have very different meanings).

Although there is a plethora of generic work in the United States in connection with what there is usually called rhetoric, the problem of teaching academic writing related to particular disciplines seems first to have been taken up seriously by Nightingale (1986), who very clearly highlighted its difficulties:

1. Writing is an essential tool for learning and should not be used only to demonstrate to teachers what students have already learned;
2. Students require teaching about the particular language demands of different subject areas;
3. Teachers have a responsibility to express their expectations of students' writing explicitly and concretely;
4. Students should be encouraged to act on comments they receive on their writing.

She also recognised the importance of involving students as teachers: "Even students who do not write very well themselves are able to make insightful comments on others' work" (p. 9). An article which Nightingale (1988) wrote two years later addressed:

one of the myths perpetuated by people who wish to encourage improved communication skills, but who seek a relatively straightforward solution to the problem. Not only do they assume that the problem is with basic skills . . . but also they neglect the considerable body of informed opinion which argues that the language which students generate when they speak and write is as important in their learning as the language which they read and hear. . . . Teachers should assign writing and speaking tasks which assist in assessing whether students have learned . . . Students need to acquire new vocabularies and to employ styles as required by varying subjects. No 'writing' teacher (usually in an English department) . . . is able to address all those specialist demands.

(p. 266)

The point was followed up after nearly twenty years by Haggis (2006). Here are a few relevant passages from her deep and dense article which, in contrast to much recent writing in the *Times Higher Education*, does not put the primary blame on students:

What is potentially difficult for some students is that these underlying principles are usually only implicit in course outlines, assessment instructions and assumptions about the structuring of work, and are therefore difficult for those unfamiliar with the discourse to see and understand.

(p. 524)

Embedded, processual complexities of thinking, understanding, and acting in specific disciplinary context need to be explored as an integral part of academic content teaching within the disciplines themselves. . . . It is unlikely that two academics even in the same field would articulate and model such processes in exactly the same way. . . . Such processes are partly hidden even from academics themselves.

(p. 530)

It is the responsibility of the teacher, not the learner, to consider what might need to be changed.

(p. 533)

In the meantime, an enormous amount of relevant work on 'writing in the disciplines' has of course appeared, but nowhere is there any mention of tacit knowledge.

Tacit Knowledge
It may be thought that, for the purposes of the teacher, all that is needed is to make tacit knowledge overt, but is that so? Not, if we follow Polanyi (1967), who argued that making tacit knowledge more overt can distort it, i.e. that "we can know more than we can tell", so that no knowledge is ever wholly impersonal or wholly expressible in words. A similar point is made by Richardson (1976) in his interpretation of Wittgenstein's philosophy of language that "a word's meaning is determined by its application" (p. 47). Both quotations indicate that knowledge can never be made wholly overt through the use of words. This goes beyond the readily accepted fact that a knowledge of, say, a skill cannot be wholly obtained from a description of the skill; it applies even to purely intellectual knowledge. In fact, no knowledge can ever be wholly transmitted by words and therefore other channels of transmission are essential. Goethe, in *Faust*, may have exaggerated in giving primacy to action, as opposed to the word, in its ability to transmit knowledge; let us just concede that both are needed. And this is likely to be even more so for tacit than for overt knowledge.

Can students perhaps learn tacit knowledge from experience without being explicitly taught it? Here I am hypothesizing, because I do not believe that anyone has tried it, but – following Goethe's dictum "In the beginning was action" (or should it be "act" or "deed"?) – students who are experientially acculturated into their disciplines (see Hutchings and O'Rourke, 2002) may well learn also to express themselves in it.

Outcomes of this Analysis
Having started with a general statement about the nature of tacit knowledge, hypothesized how it might be made overt through words and briefly made a detour into the meaning of words, I tentatively concluded that words by themselves are inadequate to make tacit knowledge explicit and this led me to hypothesize that tacit knowledge perhaps could be made overt through a combination of words and actions. This in turn led me to the possibility that enquiry-based learning might be a vehicle for unlocking students' writing skills in a way that didactic teaching has not been able; that is, that enquiry-based learning might allow for a unification of students' academic practice and writing about that practice, in a way that traditional didactic teaching could not.

And at last I have come round to one of the main purposes of my response to Northedge and McArthur: academic writing is an essential aspect of 'acts of shared meaning making' and I believe that it cannot be obtained from the majority of current teachers, who lack a critical understanding of 'academic writing'.

Ways of Thinking and Practicing (WTP)

Furthermore, academic writing is very different in different disciplines, which is well illustrated by Hounsell and Anderson, who analyzed *Ways of Thinking and Practicing* in two disciplines, biology and history – which surely must include explaining to others, and not only within a particular discipline.

Ways of Thinking and Practicing come out of and are closely associated with the processes of learning and teaching, in that teaching – in the most general sense – leads to learning, which in turn is made explicit through "ways of thinking and practicing" and, once one departs from very general principles, it is apparent that *Ways of Thinking and Practicing* are very different indeed in different disciplines.

The discipline which I will choose here is history, but if it is true, as one of Hounsell and Anderson's study participants says, that "maggots don't always behave in the way that you want them to" (in this volume, p. 76), how much more is this likely to be true of history where instead of studying maggots, we study people. Hounsell and Anderson know this of course and demonstrate just how varied central ways of thinking and practicing in History can be; what I want to add is how varied the *reporting* of thinking and practicing in History can be, through a dialogue between two historians, Fogel and Elton (1983) who

> approached history with greatly different backgrounds (one trained as an economist in the age of econometrics and mathematical models; the other trained as a Tudor historian at a time when medievalists who concentrated on studying the details of particular documents were highly influential.
>
> (p. 123)

They did not come to agree, but they grew to respect each other's very different approaches to the writing of History.

How might this conclusion affect the teaching and learning of history, or – to put it in the way of Hounsell and Anderson and going beyond teaching and learning – how can it affect thinking and practicing in history? Should undergraduate students be presented with one particular approach, chosen by their teachers or agreed between teachers and students; should they be presented with several, possibly quite radically different, approaches and choose one, or should they be presented with several, possibly quite radically different, approaches and compare and contrast them? Legitimately different responses can be given to these different questions, but what is clear is that they all fit into Hamlet's conclusion, previously used to argue against the limited teaching philosophy of Cambridge Dons, now to be used regarding a related discipline, that "there are more things in heaven and earth, Horatio, than are dreamed of in your philosophy". Quoting Hansell and Anderson, that there are "ways of thinking and practicing characteristic of, and particular to, each of these subject areas", I hope that I have illustrated through the particular example of history that "ways of thinking and practicing" within even one discipline is contentious. Of course Hounsell and Anderson agree that there are considerable differences between historians in epistemological and ontological stance and the influence of particular traditions of scholarship. To illustrate this point with just one example: the idea that any appreciation of history is socially constructed and contested would almost certainly not have been acceptable to Elton.

I believe that *Ways of Thinking and Practicing* is an important concept that can be viewed in two very different ways. One can think of it in connection with high-level skills and abilities, the achievement of which is often difficult to verify. One can also think of it in connection with tacit knowledge (see above), in which case the word 'difficult' should probably be replaced by 'impossible', because it is of the essence of tacit knowledge that spelling it out distorts it! Perhaps we as academics should accept that there are aspects of a curriculum that are important but the achievement of which cannot be verified. Their achievement then depends on intangible qualities like the enthusiasm of both teachers and students – aspects perhaps that make their relationship joyful, but which we cannot legitimately expect to emerge from either all teachers or all students.

The Complex Relationship Between What is Primarily Generic and What is Primarily Discipline-Specific

Let me return now to the role of the teacher, the focus of Northedge and McArthur's chapter. The different possible roles of a teacher are described by Northedge and McArthur in generic terms, which is normal, but here again each generic role manifests itself very differently in different disciplines. I want to contrast here the very different forms that the roles take in the different disciplines, by contrasting the descriptions of these roles in the soft disciplines, with which Northedge and McArthur are primarily concerned, and the hard ones, with which I am more familiar. In the process I hope to throw further light on my earlier question of how student perspectives are perceived by students but also move to my second question of how students, and their teachers, see the issue of what is generic and what is discipline-specific.

Making Students Think

We have already seen an example of the difference in the apprentice-scholar model. In all the positivist sciences students are not primarily expected to read widely and critically in their discipline and to present their views. Instead, they have to create and solve problems, carry out experiments (except perhaps in mathematics) and interpret their outcomes, and possibly they are asked to read more widely in the philosophy and ethics relevant to their discipline. As the amount of 'stuff' that students have to assimilate tends to be much larger in the hard sciences than in other disciplines, there is in general much more transmission learning, whether through lectures, course materials or even discovery learning. Yet, teachers should always remember that what is important is not what is taught but what is learned, that in general more than half of what is presented is not absorbed and that different students absorb different halves.

Teachers should also search their souls, regarding the importance of all that they expect students to absorb. In lectures, it is possible to promote thinking and students should learn that even in the most positivist of all disciplines – theoretical physics – there are still arguments which should make them think. Here are some examples, taken off my bookshelves, which indicate how I have in the past included in my lectures instances that ought to make teachers and their students think. (A health warning: such examples are inevitably in a specific discipline, in this case physics, and are also idiosyncratic; but I try – *in italics* – in this and the following section to spell out for teachers in any discipline more general lessons in how to promote student thinking.)

- The famous lectures of Feynman included problems designed to get first-year students to think, which the majority seemed unable to do (Feynman, 1963). As these were some of the brightest in the country, do we have to conclude that the majority of students can learn only by rote in their first university year or did he just set his expectations too high? The fallacy here is that while thinking 'within the frame' can and indeed should be expected from students, *do not expect too much; thinking 'outside the frame' – and that is what he expected – may well be beyond the abilities of all but the best of first-year students.*
- Whitrow (1989) presents views of time, from prehistory to the present day, which challenge the all too common belief that there were only two views of time, before and after Einstein. To give an example, the move from thinking in the present to thinking in the past, present and future – a move which is pre-historic – must have been a huge step. *Many students find*

it difficult to appreciate that thinkers in the past were no less intelligent than those of today, i.e. that knowing less and being less intelligent are very different matters.

- Ziman wrote three books which should thrill any intelligent undergraduate. From an eminent physicist's point of view, he showed respectively that "science is by no means as inhuman as it is sometimes painted" (Ziman, 1968, p. 12), that there was a "scientific dimension of society" (Ziman, 1976, p. iii), and that there were good "grounds for belief in science" (Ziman, 1978, pp. 137–141). He further demonstrates that "physics defines itself as the science devoted to discovering, developing and refining those aspects of reality that are amenable to mathematical analysis" (Ziman, 1978, p. 9), that is, it is restricted by definition to be positivist, but that if such a restriction is extended beyond biology to the behavioral and social sciences, it would be devastating: "The most elegantly articulated and computationally complex model of such phenomena is no more reliable or persuasive in representing or getting at 'the truth' than the logic chopping of a medieval scholar" (Ziman, 1978, p. 28). Thus, physics has been made artificially positivist. Could it be that the positivism of physics lies in the philosophy of physicists rather than in the discipline itself? This is a question that all physicists – even first year undergraduates – should ponder. Let the final word on this subject again be Ziman's: "The proper use of statistical methods is to test theoretical hypotheses, not to generate them out of the computer" (Ziman, 1976, p. 289). As long as this is the case, there is a clear distinction between the physical and the social sciences. Could there be a constructivist approach to undergraduate physics? There is plenty of evidence that areas where definite answers are difficult to find (the physics of weather might be a suitable example) are undervalued for that very reason. *The challenging idea here is that a discipline may be, probably unconsciously, limited to what is solvable in it.*
- Finally, let me refer to two joyous books about the sciences, but biased towards physics: Weber's (1973) *A random walk in science* and Mackay's (1977) *The Harvest of a Quiet Eye*. The former is a collection of quotations, relevant to the sciences, but by no means all by scientists, and contains such gems as Faraday's "One day, Sir, you may tax it" in response to Gladstone, Chancellor of the Exchequer, who asked about the practical worth of electricity, and Wordsworth's "the marble index of a mind forever voyaging through strange seas of thought, alone" on a statue of Newton. The latter is a collection of brief articles by scientists, and I will draw attention to only one, "When does jam become marmalade?", by H. B. G. Casimir. It is lighthearted but on a wholly serious issue: the linguistic insularity of the English. *Surely, there are good stories in any discipline; do we as teachers make enough of them?*

Teaching/learning situations along the lines that I have described exist in all disciplines but their nature differs in different disciplines. All I can do is to illustrate their use in one discipline and ask readers to ponder on applying them to theirs. This is just one more example of the issue that matters that in principle can be considered generic, in practice are often seriously disciplinary.

Ethical Aspects in the Physics Curriculum

Neither Northedge and McArthur, nor Hounsell and Anderson, explicitly consider the question of including aspects of ethics as a normal part of any curriculum, although the latter quote Shulman and the Carnegie Foundation concerning its importance. I cannot think of anything more important in inducting a student into the academic community than the principles that ought to govern us in our approach to our discipline. Of course, Hounsell and Anderson make clear that next to knowledge and skills *Ways of Thinking and Practicing* also include an evolving familiarity with the values and conventions governing scholarly communication within the relevant disciplinary and professional community, the latter surely constituting an aspect of ethics. Likewise, Northedge and McArthur, arguing from a socio-cultural perspective, make clear that the student acquires the ability to participate in the community's discourses and practices to standards accepted within the community. Again these standards surely are linked to ethics. However, I would like to stress the importance of ethics a bit more strongly than Hounsell and Anderson and Northedge and McArthur have done, given that the development of ethical judgment and understanding is often considered one of the fundamental goals or purposes of higher education (e.g., Perry, 1970). Likewise, as Kreber points out in Chapter 1, Knight and Yorke (2003) identified ethical sensitivity and the capacity to act morally, as essential aspects of employability.

Teachers in positivist disciplines often shy away from matters of ethics, not because they are irrelevant, which they rarely are, but because they – rightly – think that there may not be definite answers. Indeed, there may not be, but that surely is a reason for inclusion, not exclusion. In other words, introducing ethics into a positivist curriculum *illustrates some of the limitations of positivism (I continue to use the convention of italics to indicate issues of general applicability, but illustrated in only one – physics)*; there is no way of treating the ethics of *any* discipline, except in a constructivist manner, and this is a matter quite separate from the importance of ethics, as such, in *any* curriculum. Incidentally, physics was the first of the sciences which – as a result of the atomic bomb – developed after about 1946 a serious ethical concern, evidenced, for example, in the Pugwash Movement (Rotblat, 1999). Arguably, university curricula should also face the issue of religious fundamentalism; *not in the form of a pseudo-intellectual shouting match, but on the basis of intellectual analysis, as was done for instance for Christianity by Vidler et al. (1963) in a course of open lectures in Cambridge.* Finally, it is worth quoting Kant (1788): "Two things fill the mind with ever increasing wonder and awe, the more often and more seriously reflection concentrates upon them: the starry heaven above me and the moral law within me" (p. 288). He was unable to rationalize these two things, but *should students not learn that there are things that cannot be rationalized and yet are not irrational?*

If I have strayed in the last two sections some way from both the chapters on which I am commenting, it is because I am commenting here not on what they have written, but on what they have not written.

Teachers as Learners

I have tried to put some flesh on the bones of physics teaching and learning, from the points of view of both teachers and learners; let me close with one of my firmest convictions – no teacher should ever stop being a learner. I base this conviction primarily on the work of Humboldt, the founder of the University of Berlin in 1810.

Humboldt's astonishing and astonishingly brief memorandum of nine pages (Humboldt, 1810, English translation: Humboldt, 1970) for the new University of Berlin was profound and amazingly far-sighted. It ought to be remembered that Humboldt's ideas originated in the situation that arose from Prussia's disastrous defeat by Napoleon in 1806, and that they were designed for a university in the service of the State, a concept not unknown in twenty-first century Britain. I firmly believe that it still represents a blueprint – and it happens to be my blueprint – for the best type of university for the twenty-first century. Humboldt was not interested in an otherworldly university and neither would be whoever happens to be our current Minister responsible for universities, but it was Humboldt who realized that a university that had no other objectives than to serve the short-term objectives of the state would fail both the state and as a university.

To understand Humboldt's famous memorandum concerning the relationship between teachers and students requires an understanding of the very German concept of *Wissenschaft* – there can be no perfect translation of this heavily culture-laden concept; from my viewpoint it is arguably best translated (Elton, 1986) as 'scholarship' as a noun, and *wissenschaftlich* as 'scholarly' as an adjective.

The major dichotomy in Humboldt's thinking then turns out to be not between either research and teaching or between teachers and students, but between university and school, and is best represented through the slogan *Bildung durch Wissenschaft* or 'Education based on Scholarship'. Humboldt postulates, and I am certain that he would stand by this to this day, that the university, in contrast to school, treats scholarship always in terms of not yet completely solved problems, whether in research or teaching, while school is concerned essentially with agreed and accepted knowledge. The consequence, as he says in a most thoughtprovoking sentence of his memorandum, is that in universities "*the teacher is then not there for the sake of the student, but both have their justification in the service of scholarship*".

This principle applies to both research and teaching, since both should be concerned with not yet completely solved problems. It is this principle, which, I am sure, is Humboldt's, which has been guiding university research for the past two hundred years, but which has rarely if ever been put into practice in teaching until very recently in the UK.

Indeed, in practice, a general unity of research and teaching is probably impossible and certainly has never yet been established anywhere (Elton, 2001), and it was not until the advent of Problem Based Learning (PBL) in the 1960s that the principle of 'research like learning' (*forschendes lernen*) became possible, at least in applied disciplines, particularly Medicine and Engineering, where there are 'real' problems. This changed when it was extended into Enquiry Based Learning (EBL), for example in English literature through a seminal paper by Hutchings and O'Rourke (2002). The crucial difference between programs, on the one hand, where undergraduates actually conduct research, and PBL and EBL on the other, is that in PBL and EBL they learn in a research mode. While the former therefore should lead to outcomes of interest and value to the research community, PBL and EBL constitute learning processes in a research mode which can be carried out at any level of sophistication, for example, in project work. The concepts of 'learning through research' and 'learning in a research mode' are not mutually exclusive.

Some may suggest that I am being hopelessly idealistic, but I do not think that I am. EBL is an approach to teaching and learning and, while it will certainly take different forms in different disciplines, it is an approach to teaching and learning which in principle is applicable to all disciplines (see also Rowland, 2000). It is in the tradition of 'discovery learning', which until the advent of performance indicators and mistaken forms of quality assurance used to be respectable in schools, and its main but very radical change from university tradition is that it puts the student and not the teacher in the driving seat. In this, it is in a tradition much older than Humboldt, for it was Lao Tzu (1998) who more than 2500 years ago said that 'of the best teachers the students say that "we did it all ourselves"'. It was of course the students who said this, not Lao Tzu, who presumably recognized the continuing importance, although different role, of the teacher; but it is the basis of all student-centered learning.

To summarize, true Humboldtian teachers are learners who learn jointly with their students and they never stop learning.

Conclusion

I started this chapter with perceiving two chinks in the armor of the excellent chapters, on which I was about to comment. The first was that we – as teachers – can never fully represent the views of our students and I hope that I have demonstrated this point adequately. The second was to challenge the belief that there is a firm division between generic and discipline specific matters, and I have concluded that this oversimplifies the issue: there are many areas which require a synthesis between the two and there are many areas which are at a surface level generic and at a deeper level discipline specific. (A good example is 'lecturing'.) I have learned a lot from writing the chapter and I have, through writing it, come to the conclusion that there are few if any areas that do not require such a synthesis, but that such a synthesis, in large part, constitutes a learning experience through which we can enrich our discipline by adapting and including experiences from other disciplines. However, such an adaptation can only work if we, from different disciplines, meet each other halfway, and I have tried to illustrate this point through a number of examples.

I have also tried in some ways to extend the two papers under discussion, in terms of my own experience as both a teacher and a learner, largely but not wholly in the area of physics (this provided me with another synthesis between the general and the specific!) and I have tried to do this from my point of view as both a teacher and a student. Gentle reader, if you read this paragraph carefully, you will see that I have attempted three quite separate syntheses! Only you can tell me the extent to which I may have succeeded.

References

Bazerman, C. (1988). *Shaping Written Knowledge: The Genre and Activity of the Experimental Article in Science.* Madison, WI: University of Wisconsin Press.

Elton, L. (1986). Research and Teaching: symbiosis or conflict, *Higher Education*, 15(3/4), 299–304.

Elton, L. (2001). Research and Teaching: conditions for a positive link. *Teaching in Higher Education*, 6(1), 44–56.

Elton, L. (2008). Academic writing and tacit knowledge. In preparation.

Feynman, R. P. (1963). Preface to the *Feynman Lectures*. New York: Addison Wesley.

Fogel, R. W. & Elton, G. R. (1983). *Which Road to the Past? Two views of History*. New Haven: Yale University Press.

Haggis, T. (2006). Pedagogies for diversity: retaining critical challenge amidst fears of "dumbing down". *Studies in Higher Education*, 31(5), 521–535.

Humboldt, W. von (1810). Ueber die innere und aeussere Organisation der hoeheren wissenschaftlichen Anstalten in Berlin. In A. Leitzmann et al. (Eds.), *Wilhelm von Humboldts Gesammelte Schriften*, volume X, Berlin Preussiche Akademie der Wissenschaften, 1903–35.

Humboldt, W. von (1970). On the spirit and organisational framework of intellectual institutions in Berlin. *Minerva 8*, 242–267.

Husain, S., & Waterfield, R. (2006). The first year of HE. In S. Davies, D. Swinburne, & G. Williams (Eds.), *Writing Matters* (pp. 27–35). London: Royal Literary Fund.

Hutchings, W., & O'Rourke, K. (2002). Introducing enquiry-based teaching methods in literary studies. *Arts and Humanities in Higher Education*, 1, 73–83.

Kant, I. (1788). *Critik der practischen Vernunft*. Riga: J. F. Hartknoch. (The translation is taken from the *Oxford Dictionary of Quotations*, 4th edition.)

Knight, P., & Yorke, M. (2003). *Assessment, Learning and Employability*. Maidenhead: Society for Research in Higher Education and the Open University Press.

Lao-Tzu (1998). *The Way of Life according to Lao-Tzu: An American Version* (Translated: B. Witter). New York: Penguin Putnam.

Mackay, A. (1977). *The Harvest of a Quiet Eye: A Selection of Scientific Quotations*. London: Institute of Physics.

Nightingale, P. (1986). *Improving Student Writing*. Green Guide No 4. Milperra, NSW: Higher Education Research and Development Society of Australasia.

Nightingale, P. (1988). Understanding processes and problems in student writing. *Studies in Higher Education*, 13(3), 263–283.

Perry, W. G. (1970). *Forms of intellectual and ethical development in the college years*. New York: Holt, Rinehart & Winston.

Polanyi, M. (1967). *The tacit dimension*. New York: Anchor Books.

Richardson, J. T. E. (1976). *The grammar of justification*. Eastbourne: Sussex University Press.

Rotblat, J. (1999). Science and Humanity in the Twenty-First Century. Nobel Prize lecture. http://nobelprize.org/nobel_prizes/peace/articles/rotblat/index.html Accessed 30 December, 2007.

Rowland, S. (2000). *The Enquiring Teacher*. Milton Keynes: Society for Research into Higher Education and Open University Press.

Vidler. A. R., MacKinnon, D. M., Williams, H. A., Bezzant, J. S. (Eds.) (1963). *Objections to Christian Belief*. London: Constable.

Weber, R. L. (1973). *A random walk in science: An anthology*. London: Institute of Physics.

Whitrow, G. J. (1989). *Time in History*. Oxford: Oxford University Press.

Ziman, J. (1968). *Public Knowledge* Cambridge: Cambridge University Press.

Ziman, J. (1976). *The Force of Knowledge*. Cambridge: Cambridge University Press.

Ziman, J. (1978). *Reliable Knowledge*. Cambridge: Cambridge University Press.

V
Learning Partnerships
in Disciplinary Learning

12

Educating Students for Self-Authorship
Learning Partnerships to Achieve Complex Outcomes

Marcia B. Baxter Magolda

Miami University

Educators in the United States and the United Kingdom share a common concern – graduates' ability to successfully use their academic knowledge in their post college work and personal lives. Graduates must be able to translate their academic learning to the "capacity and understanding for working with many different sorts of knowledge in order to engage with complex emergent problems for which there may be a range of possible solutions" (Jackson & Ward, 2004, p. 427). UK scholars frame this challenge as learners making the transition from disciplinary to transdisciplinary learning (Gibbons et al. as cited in Jackson & Ward, 2004). Personal Development Planning, the process being used in the UK for helping learners reflect on their learning and achievement and plan for their own educational, academic and career development, aims to develop learners' metacognition and self-regulatory capacities to make this transition. Similarly, US educators are advocating "intentional learning," as the authors of *Greater Expectations: A New Vision for Learning as a Nation Goes to College* wrote:

> In a turbulent and complex world, every college student will need to be purposeful and self-directed in multiple ways. Purpose implies clear goals, an understanding of process, and appropriate action. Further, purpose implies intention in one's actions. Becoming such an intentional learner means developing self-awareness about the reason for study, the learning process itself, and how education is used. Intentional learners are integrative thinkers who can see connections in seemingly disparate information and draw on a wide range of knowledge to make decisions. They adapt the skills learned in one situation to problems encountered in another: in a classroom, the workplace, their communities, or their personal lives. As a result, intentional learners succeed even when instability is the only constant.
>
> (Association of American Colleges & Universities, 2002, pp. 21–22)

The complexities young adults face in transdisciplinary contexts after college, as well as the complexities inherent in disciplinary learning during college, require something beyond skill acquisition and application. They require a transformation from authority dependence to self-authorship, or the capacity to internally define one's beliefs, identity and social relations (Baxter Magolda, 2001; Kegan, 1994). In this chapter I summarize the learning outcomes advocated both in the UK and US, offer a perspective on the developmental capacities these outcomes require, present possibilities about the developmental capacities learners possess and describe how to construct learning partnerships that help learners achieve the capacities required. Guiding learners through the transformation from authority dependence to self-authorship is a primary challenge for twenty-first-century higher education.

Higher Education Learning Outcomes

Recent national reports in both the UK and US paint a similar picture of the desired outcomes of higher education despite using slightly different language to convey these ideas. US reports (e.g., American College Personnel Association, 1994; Association of American Colleges and Universities, 1995, 2002; Keeling, 2004) emphasize higher education's goal as fostering intentional learning and effective citizenship. Becoming informed, active, responsible global citizens is the first of eight key concepts the UK report *Putting the World into World-Class Education* (Department for Education and Skills, 2004) notes as necessary for living in a global society. Integrating numerous reports US national associations have published in recent years yields a model of contemporary US college learning outcomes that overlaps considerably with the key concepts advocated in *Putting the World into World-Class Education.*

Desired college learning outcomes in the US cluster into three distinct categories (Baxter Magolda, 2004b). *Cognitive maturity* includes the ability to discern the value of multiple perspectives through evaluating relevant evidence, problem solving in context, and making wise decisions based on complex analysis. These outcomes are typically in the forefront of disciplinary learning. A second cluster of outcomes, which I refer to as *integrated identity,* is necessary to enable cognitive maturity. Integrated identity includes understanding one's own history, confidence, the ability to act both autonomously and collaboratively, and integrity. A third category – *mature relationships* – is crucial to cognitive maturity and integrated identity. Mature relationships include respect for one's own and others' identities and cultures to enable productive collaboration to integrate multiple perspectives. As I have argued previously:

> Maturity in these three areas combines to enable effective citizenship – coherent, ethical action for the good of both the individual and the larger community. Effective citizenship requires the ability to evaluate possible actions, interpret contexts and consequences, and make wise choices – all characteristics of cognitive maturity. For these choices to be coherent and ethical requires an internal belief system and an internal identity that together guide action. Ethical action for the good of the individual and larger community requires the capacity for mutuality and interdependence characteristic of mature relationships: it requires understanding of and commitment to one's own interests in interaction with understanding and commitment to the interests of others. To act ethically as a citizen requires intercultural maturity, or the ability to use multiple cultural frames, engage in relationships with diverse others grounded in appreciation of difference, and consideration of social identities in a global and national context (King & Baxter Magolda, 2003).
>
> (Baxter Magolda, 2004b, p. 6)

These three categories resonate with Barnett's (2000a) constructs of epistemology (knowing), ontology (self-identity), and praxis (action). Organizing the Department for Education and Skills' (2004) eight concepts accordingly, similarities emerge with the model of US college learning outcomes. Understanding the key concepts of social justice, sustainable development, and human rights resonates with cognitive maturity. The key concept of values and perceptions, defined in the report as "developing a critical evaluation of images of other parts of the world and an appreciation of the effect these have on people's attitudes and values," recognizes the role of identity in effective citizenship. The key concepts of respecting diversity, interdependence, and conflict resolution interconnect with the category of mature relationships. Thus UK and US scholars offer a powerful, shared vision of the core outcomes of higher education. This vision includes what Robert Kegan (2000) calls informational learning (i.e., fund of knowledge and skills) yet extends further to include transformational learning – the remaking of how we make meaning. Both forms are crucial to prepare learners for success in the complex twenty-first-century society they will inhabit and lead.

Developmental Foundations of Learning Outcomes

Achieving these learning outcomes extends beyond informational learning to epistemological (i.e., knowing), intrapersonal (i.e., identity) and interpersonal (i.e., relationships) developmental capacities that support transformational learning. Here again, UK and US scholars concur. The idea that developmental capacities underlie learning outcomes is illustrated in the following exchange, taken from a course observation study (Baxter Magolda, 1999). Interviewed at the outset of his zoology course, Chris Snowden shared these aspirations for his students:

> I want them [students in Winter Biology] to appreciate the breadth of zoology and its connections to other disciplines. How do we put together disparate ideas? I'll use my research as examples of how one approaches problems. I want them to understand how information is gained. I want them to appreciate what facts really mean. Tentative facts. That's what all of science is. Subject to change and revision.
>
> (Baxter Magolda, 1999, p. 3)

Chris included this vision for learning on the course syllabus. Ann, a senior in the course, shared her reaction in an interview conducted at the conclusion of the course:

> I take sociology as my minor. It is all opinions, not hard-core facts where you are wrong [like Winter Biology]. I know he tried to play it off like there is still a lot of research, that it is a really new concept I guess, but still there is some stuff that is [fact] – like freezing cells. I understand what he was trying to do. He was trying to give examples to show what happened. But if he had just said cryoprotectants whatever, just said the point, I would believe him because he is the teacher. I don't need the proof, it's not like I'm going to argue with him about it.
>
> (Baxter Magolda, 1999, p. 3)

Clearly a disconnect exists. Ann seems to have heard Chris's words because she conveys that she knew what Chris was trying to do. As a senior Ann has succeeded thus far in a rigorous curriculum. Chris was very articulate in explaining his expectations and the course content. Yet Ann does not demonstrate an appreciation for how information is gained. How can this be?

The disconnect between Chris and Ann stems from the frameworks each uses to understand learning and knowledge. Ann views the nature of science as "hard core facts." From this vantage point she interpreted Chris's examples as attempts to prove to her what happened, did not understand his portrayal of cryobiology (the study of life at cold temperatures) as an evolving field, and preferred that he just tell her the facts that she is sure exist. Chris, in contrast, views science as tentative facts, subject to revision. Operating from this vantage point, he attempts to get Ann and her peers to appreciate how information is gained, unaware that Ann's views about science versus sociology affect her learning in his course. Ann uses her current understanding about knowledge and how it is acquired to make sense of Chris's portrayal of cryobiology as an evolving field and facts as tentative.

For Ann to really understand knowledge the way Chris does, she needs particular epistemological, intrapersonal and interpersonal meaning-making capacities. She would need to understand that knowledge is uncertain and created by experts in particular contexts using relevant evidence. She would need to be aware that multiple perspectives derive from how particular people construct knowledge claims based on particular evidence. These epistemological capacities would allow her to understand how science could be viewed as subject to revision. In order to apply these epistemological capacities, however, Ann would also need corresponding intrapersonal or identity capacities. She would need to have a sense of herself as a person capable of participating in this knowledge construction process. She would need to be able to reflect on, explore and choose her values to form a coherent sense of herself, or an integrated identity. This integrated identity would then serve as the foundation for her to interpret her experience and act on it. These intrapersonal capacities would enable her to envision joining Chris in knowledge construction rather than her present "don't argue with the teacher" perspective. Finally, Ann would need interpersonal capacities to meet Chris's expectations. She would need to be able to use others' thinking along with her own without being overly influenced by what authorities tell her. Thus she would need to achieve interdependence – the blend of her own integrated identity, openness to other perspectives, and the ability to critically analyze existing knowledge and other perspectives without fear of disapproval. If Ann had all these capacities, she would be capable of self-authorship, or the ability to internally define her beliefs, identity, and relations with others. As a college senior, she did not have these capacities and she is not alone.

Robert Kegan (1994) argues that much of what contemporary society (including education) expects of students and young adults is "over their heads; " that is to say, the expectations require ways of making meaning beyond those students currently hold. This is Ann's situation; it is likely the situation of many college students in both the US and UK. Helping college students acquire more complex ways of making meaning is essential in light of the demands they face as college students and adults. In articulating what he calls the mental demands of modern life, Kegan (1994) highlights the need for adults to be self-initiating, self-correcting, self-evaluating, responsible for their actions, open to diverse perspectives, and able to connect to partners and children while setting appropriate boundaries, to name just a few. He interprets these everyday demands as requiring integrating epistemological, intrapersonal and interpersonal capacities in a complex way of making meaning. Specifically, he describes this as:

> . . . an ideology, an internal identity, a *self-authorship* that can coordinate, integrate, act upon, or invent values, beliefs, convictions, generalizations, ideals, abstractions, interpersonal loyalties, and intrapersonal states. It is no longer *authored by* them, it *authors them* and thereby achieves a personal authority.

(p. 185, italics in original)

Self-authorship offers a foundation upon which to function in what Ronald Barnett (2000b) calls a supercomplex world. Arguing that higher education is responsible for preparing students to survive in and contribute to this supercomplex world, Barnett explains:

> It is a world where nothing can be taken for granted, where no frame of understanding or of action can be entertained with any security. It is a world in which we are conceptually challenged, and continually so. A complex world is one in which we are assailed by more facts, data, evidence, tasks and arguments than we can easily handle within the frameworks in which we have our being. By contrast, a supercomplex world is one in which the very frameworks by which we orient ourselves to the world are themselves contested. Supercomplexity denotes a fragile world but it is a fragility brought on not merely by social and technological change; it is a fragility in the way that we understand the world, in the way in which we understand ourselves and in the ways in which we feel secure about acting in the world.

(2000b, p. 3)

Barnett emphasizes that supercomplexity is "a matter of handling multiple frames of understanding, of action and of self-identity" (2000a, p. 6). Although he does not use the term self-authorship, his three dimensions resonate with the epistemological, intrapersonal and interpersonal dimensions of self-authorship (see also Kreber in Chapter 1).

My longitudinal study of young adult development and learning (Baxter Magolda, 2001), in which I have followed participants from age 18 to 38, provides empirical support for the argument that adult life requires complexity in how we know, how we see ourselves, and how we construct our relations with others. This study, originally designed to explore gender differences based on the work of Perry (1970) and Belenky, Clinchy, Goldberger, and Tarule (1986), began with 101 traditional age students (51 women and 50 men) when they entered college in 1986 at a state institution in the US with a liberal arts focus. Admission is competitive and the 70% of the entering class of which the participants were a part ranked in the top 20% of their high school class. Their majors included all six divisions within the institution (i.e., arts and sciences, education, fine arts, interdisciplinary studies, business, engineering and applied sciences), and cocurricular involvement in college was high.

Of the 70 participants continuing in the post college phase of the study, 21 pursued additional academic preparation after college graduation, including law school, seminary, medical school, and various graduate degrees. Their occupations included business, education, social service, ministry, and government work. Attrition over the last fifteen years resulted in 36 participants by year twenty. The annual interview began with a summary of the focus of the project, which was to continue to explore how participants learn and come to know. The participant was then asked to think about important learning experiences that took place since the previous interview. The participant volunteered those experiences, described them, and described their impact on her or his thinking. I asked questions to pursue why these experiences were important, factors that influenced the experiences, and how the learner was affected. The interview became more informal as the study progressed and addressed what life had been like for participants since we talked last. These conversations included discussion of the dimensions of life they felt were most relevant, the demands of adult life they were experiencing, how they made meaning of these dimensions and demands, their sense of themselves, and how they decided what to believe. Inherent in these dimensions was their sense of themselves in relation to others and their involvement in significant relationships. Interviews were conducted in person during college and by telephone after college; they ranged from 60 to 90 minutes (see Baxter Magolda, 1992; 2001 for more in-depth methodological details).

Most of my participants made little progress toward self-authorship during college, leaving college relying on externally derived formulas for what to believe, how to be and how to relate to others. They found these formulas wanting as they entered the workforce and adult relationships, contexts in which they were asked to define, express and act on internal constructions of their beliefs, identities, and interactions with others. Their stories offer a perspective on how self-authorship evolves and the kind of educational experiences that assist young people in achieving more complex ways of making meaning.

Journeys toward Self-Authorship

I offer one version of the developmental journey toward self-authorship based on my twenty-year longitudinal study. During the college phase of the study participants relied heavily on external sources of authority. In over 500 interviews in the fifteen years since these participants' college graduation I have heard how self-authorship evolved through their professional and personal lives. These stories are consistent with those told by the collective student development research done in the US.[1] Yet the stories shared here tell only one version of how assumptions evolve from external

---

1 For a summary of this research, see Hofer, B. K., & Pintrich, P. R. (2002). *Personal epistemology: the psychology of beliefs about knowledge and knowing.* Mahwah, NJ: Lawrence Erlbaum Associates.

sources of definition to internal ones. As you read, consider these stories carefully to determine if this version resonates with your students in your educational context and how these stories inform the transitions your students are trying to navigate.

Following External Formulas

Ann's reaction to her zoology course reflects the early part of the developmental journey in which students rely on external formulas for what to believe, how to define their identities, and how to relate to others. Most of my longitudinal participants used this perspective when they entered college and maintained it through their early twenties. Mark's account of how he approached law school reveals the essence of this way of making meaning:

> I came here and I tried to figure out what the legal culture figures is success. I knew [that] a Supreme Court clerkship was, so one of my goals was to aim towards that. So I got here to law school and I figured out, "Okay, well, to be a success here you have to get to know some professors who are influential with judges to get a good clerkship, to get in the pipeline, get in the star system here. Also get on *Law Review*. Write a paper here that you can publish." I thought, "Okay, this is kind of the plan then, step by step." The ultimate plan for success in the legal culture, I mean, go to [this] Law School and do these things, then you've got it made. . . . I would be in the *ultimate* position to do whatever I want to do because I will have done *everything* possible, and then I'd be in a position to make a choice that reflected exactly who I was, or at least more clearly.
>
> (Baxter Magolda, 2001, p. 41, italics in original)

Mark was still following external formulas when he started law school despite a successful college career. As a college senior he understood knowledge as contextual and articulated the process of weighing evidence to decide what to believe. However, he had not yet developed an internal sense of self to bring to this decision-making process. He still assumed that doing all the right things would yield a choice that matched his identity. Like many of his peers, he discovered that to be a faulty assumption.

Crossroads

At various points in their mid-twenties most of my participants encountered the shortcomings of external formulas. The formulas often did not serve them well in complex work roles where they were asked to construct new knowledge and be flexible in light of changing information and ambiguity. Participants' own emerging interests and values often conflicted with the formula. They realized the need to extract themselves from dependence on the external and to develop their own visions, beliefs and identities. Doing so, however, was a challenge as Kurt so clearly describes:

> I'm the kind of person who is motivated by being wanted, I think. I've gone to a couple of workshops and, either fortunately or unfortunately, I'm the kind of person who gets my self-worth [through] whether or not other people accept me for what I do or other people appreciate what I'm doing. . . . I'm coming from a position where I get my worth and my value from other people, which is, I think, wrong for me to do. But that's where I am right now. I feel like whether or not I choose to be happy is dependent upon me and only me. If I say, "You made me mad," or the converse, "You made me happy," then I'm giving all of the power that I have to you. The power of choice is mine, I have a choice of how I want to perceive each and every situation in my life. . . . Obviously I'm not to that point yet because I choose to make myself happy and make myself sad on what other people are thinking. But I think I'd like to someday get to a point where I can say, "Okay, that's your perception. I am not dependent on

you for my happiness or my sadness." And I think that would be a very strong, very spiritual place to be.

(Baxter Magolda, 2001, pp. 98–9)

Kurt shared this perspective in his mid-twenties and later reported, "I spent the entire decade of my twenties getting in touch with who I was and what is important to me" (Baxter Magolda, 2004b, p. 24). His story underscores the struggle to develop an internal sense of self upon which to ground one's identity and relationships. This internal sense of self is also needed to define one's beliefs internally. Like Kurt, most of my participants devoted a considerable part of their twenties to working through the crossroads.

Becoming the Author of One's Life

Successfully navigating the crossroads yielded an internal self-definition that transformed all three developmental dimensions. Dawn described this transformation as resulting from the self-discovery she experienced in theatre. She explained:

The more you discover about yourself, the more you can become secure with it. And that obviously leads to greater self-confidence because you become comfortable with who you really are. My confidence level is so much better than it ever has been. I'm more willing to express my ideas and take chances expressing my ideas. "Who cares what people think?" sort of thing. When you're not as self-confident, you're afraid that people are going to laugh at what you think or you're afraid that they're going to think you're stupid – it's all those petty, little things that inhibit us. Whereas when you're confident, you are more willing to say, "This is my opinion; this is why I hold this opinion. You may agree with it or not, but this is what – with my mind – I have formulated this opinion and that's how I think and feel." I'm not as afraid to be willing to say that because of what I am this is how I feel. I try not to step on people's toes with my opinions, be offensive about it, but if someone asks me for my opinion or advice or how I think and feel about something, I will definitely tell them. And I think self-awareness too, because you realize that it doesn't really matter if other people agree with you or not. You can think and formulate ideas for yourself and ultimately that's what's important. You have a mind and you can use it. That's probably the most important thing, regardless of the content of what your thoughts and opinions are. I suppose it's very idealistic to think that everybody can see that. It's the fact that you can form an opinion that's more important than the opinion itself. But I don't think that happens. So it's kind of a self-confidence and self-awareness thing.

(Baxter Magolda, 2001, pp. 152–3)

You can hear in Dawn's story how her internal self came into being, how it in turn changed her perception and fear of others' appraisals of her, which in turn allowed her to express her own thinking. Thus the epistemological insight that she has a mind and can use it to develop her own opinions was made possible by advances in the intrapersonal and interpersonal dimensions of her development. I turn next to the characteristics of contexts in which participants' journeys toward self-authorship occurred.

Learning Partnerships Model

Listening to my longitudinal participants' experiences in multiple settings (e.g., college, employment, graduate and professional school, community involvement, personal life) revealed many characteristics that promote learning and self-authorship. From those stories I developed the Learning Partnerships Model (Baxter Magolda, 2004a) to promote self-authorship while simultaneously supporting learners' current meaning-making. Kegan emphasized the necessity of providing support when our expectations extend beyond students' current meaning making. He advocates creating:

> a holding environment that provides both welcoming acknowledgement to exactly who the person is right now as he or she is, and fosters the person's psychological evolution. As such, a holding environment is a tricky, transitional culture, an evolutionary bridge, a context for crossing over.
>
> (1994, p. 43)

The Learning Partnerships Model (LPM) creates an evolutionary bridge by merging three supportive components with three challenges in the learning environment.

Support is offered through *three principles*: validating learners' ability to know, situating learning in learners' experience, and defining learning as mutually constructing meaning. Participants reported greater willingness to take responsibility for constructing knowledge and their own beliefs when educators validated their potential to do so. Using their experience offered a foundation for learning and provided support in this challenging process. Having learning defined as mutual construction made it acceptable to participate in the process. These supports assist learners in engaging in the *three challenges* of learning environments that promote self-authorship: knowledge is complex and socially constructed, self is central to knowledge construction, and authority and expertise are shared among knowledgeable peers. Explicit portrayal of knowledge as complex and socially constructed challenged learners to move toward epistemological complexity. Emphasis on

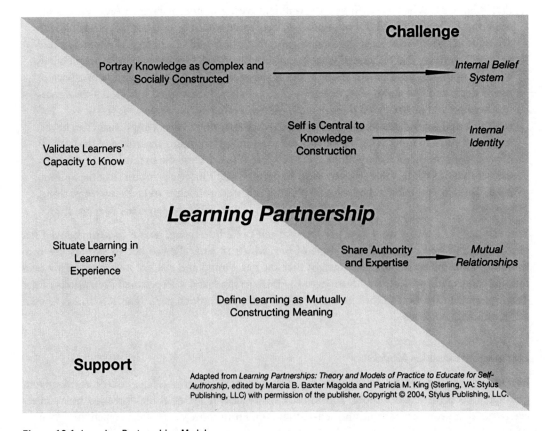

Figure 12.1 Learning Partnerships Model

the role of the self in knowledge construction challenged them to bring their identity into learning thus moving them toward construction of an internal identity. Sharing of expertise and authority in the learning process engaged learners in mutually constructing knowledge and helped them develop more mature relationships. These six components connect to all phases of the journey because the educator is mutually constructing the educational process with the learner. The partnership adjusts as the learner adopts more complex ways of making meaning.

Exemplars

The three supportive principles of the LPM emerged first from my longitudinal participants' college narratives. The three challenges emerged more clearly in the post-college interviews. All six components were visible in an observation study in which I observed three semester-length courses: Chris Snowden's zoology course (mentioned earlier in this chapter), a mathematics course, and a large education course (Baxter Magolda, 1999). Student interviews at the end of the zoology course illustrate how Chris Snowden modeled the LPM in his teaching. Rich explained:

> The whole focus of most of my classes in college have been just regurgitating the facts, with the exceptions of a few like Winter Biology where the base facts were given to you on the ground level and where the actual learning was coming in above and beyond that. The learning was coming in where he would ask what do you think about this, and you couldn't just look on your notes, you couldn't just remember what he said. It is not just blatant memorization; learning comes into it when you are utilizing the ideas towards something new that hasn't been done. That kind of set-up seems to stimulate me more than just being like a computer and storing this information to really do nothing with. This class gave more interest into the applications, what is going on right now, ideas of it, theories on what they don't know. The other classes it was "here is what we know and you have to know it too." There wasn't any fairly mutual exchange between the instructor and the class, no formulations of ideas beyond.
>
> (Baxter Magolda, 1999, p. 122)

The challenge to create new formulations to extend existing knowledge put knowledge as complex in the foreground of learning. Rich appreciated being invited into the learning process with the question "what do you think about this?" Although Rich does not describe the mutual exchange between instructor and class, I observed it regularly. Chris routinely invited students to share their thinking, engaged the class in processing their ideas, and helped them work through the validity of various knowledge claims. Erica offered a perspective on how Chris supported students in facing these challenges:

> He takes the approach that he wants you to do it on your own. He will help you plot through your ideas and he will help you sort out what you are thinking and help direct you and he still encourages you to work independently. He just makes his office setting very comfortable. He'll ask "what are you confused about?" and he will ask your opinion on the matter rather than telling you what you should do. He will ask you exactly what is happening and what you need help with and try to direct you from there rather than presenting himself in a way that is kind of intimidating. . . . I think the way I see it is that he wants you to feel that you are at the same level as him, not in as far as the same knowledge, he wants the atmosphere to be such that you feel comfortable asking him or talking to him in any way.
>
> (Baxter Magolda, 1999, pp. 133–134)

Erica's description of her interactions with Chris reveals that he validated her ability to think and work independently. By asking her to direct the discussion and offer her opinion, he situated learning in her experience. He helped her plot through her ideas, simultaneously directing her and encouraging her to work independently, thus demonstrating mutual knowledge construction. By using the components of the LPM Chris helped his students learn both the content and the thinking processes of the discipline. In doing so he also promoted their development toward the complex ways of making meaning required to view science as "tentative facts, subject to change and revision."

Longitudinal participants' stories reinforce the notion that graduates must be able to translate their disciplinary learning into supercomplex, transdisciplinary contexts. This was most evident in employment contexts in which the three challenges took the foreground. Andrew's description of his work environment conveys these challenges:

> I'm trying to think how to word it, but I guess the true responsibility they give you, I mean, the freedom of work. Sometimes you may just have a manager who hands you stuff and then you do it. Or you're given a responsibility and then you can define your job from there. You take more initiative, rather than it being dictated to you. They kind of give you the ball and then tell you to go play with it rather than tell you how to shoot hoops. We joke at work, we call it the "dump and run," because sometimes it seems like they don't have a very formal training procedure. But by the same token I think it's good because it allows you to find your niche and do your thing. They take the approach if somebody comes in new, looks at the thing, they may find a better way to do it. So they don't like to say, "This is the way it should be done always." They're not afraid to let people reinvent the wheel, especially if it means they come out with a better wheel.
>
> (Baxter Magolda, 2001, p. 253)

Clearly Andrew's management team conveyed that there were multiple ways to approach work, that Andrew could bring his own approach to it, and management and employees shared authority. The opportunity to take initiative to define his work validated Andrew's ability to know. Doing his own thing situated learning in his experience. He did clarify that he and his colleagues were not without direction:

> When push comes to shove they give us the direction we need. But for the most part I completely do not feel like I have management looking over me. I feel that I'm making more of an effort to let my management know what I'm doing so they're kept abreast rather than them coming to me and saying, "Well, what are you doing?" And I think that makes just a big difference in the way you feel. Management never really checks up on you; you're given complete trust. Now if you don't perform, I'm sure things would be said.
>
> (Baxter Magolda, 2001, p. 253)

Direction provided when needed conveys that mutual construction took place when management or employees felt the need for it but otherwise employees were trusted to perform effectively until they proved otherwise. This balance of challenge and support helped Andrew develop more complex ways of approaching his work.

Another longitudinal participant explained more specifically how sharing expertise and authority in a learning partnership works. Gavin described how his boss helped him learn to think for himself in the insurance business:

> It's really nice to know that I can just say, "Mr. Smith, I'm having trouble with – I don't understand this." He doesn't always give me the answer. A lot of times he'll throw back questions like, "Well, what do you think about it?" He always tries to get you to answer it yourself. And if he feels differently, he'll tell you. . . . His method of getting people to learn is he always thinks that if you're a bright enough person you really do know the answer or it's easy enough for you to find out. If we disagree, then he says, "Well, if that's the way you see it,

do it your way and if it works out let me know." . . . It gives me the impression that if my mindset is that I'm going to do it my way, I can do it that way. If it doesn't work, I'll tell him. And a lot of times he'll say, "Well, you'll feel a lot better with yourself because you tried it." So it's a very, very relaxed atmosphere with very, very professional people. They just know how to – it's like they're being a mentor. It's neat.

(Baxter Magolda, 2001, p. 265)

Mr. Smith encouraged Gavin to reflect on his own ideas and expertise to think through his work. When Gavin needed help, his boss provided it without making Gavin feel incompetent. He supported Gavin trying things his way, even if he disagreed. Mr. Smith encouraged Gavin to try out his own thinking in order "to feel better about himself" even when it led to mistakes. This model of supervision balanced the risk associated with employees learning how to work effectively with the long-term benefit of their professional and personal growth.

The Learning Partnerships Model has been intentionally used in multiple settings to design educational practice to promote learning and self-authorship. For example, it is the foundation of the four-year writing curriculum in the Miami University School of Interdisciplinary Studies (SIS). To build an evolutionary bridge from external formulas to self-authorship, the academic staff "created a plan where students would progress from engagement with expressive modes to an increasingly critical awareness of and proficiency in disciplinary forms to the development of interdisciplinary scholarly inquiry" (Haynes, 2004, pp. 67, 70). The SIS academic staff organized this progression into seven increasingly complex stages spread out over the four years of the curriculum. Similarly, the LPM is the basis for a four-semester Earth Sustainability Project in which content is structured around developmental goals to promote increased cognitive complexity and the ability to use disciplinary knowledge beyond disciplinary boundaries (Bekken & Marie, 2007). The LPM is also the pedagogical foundation of Miami's College Student Personnel Master of Science program that prepares graduate students for professional roles in college and university administration (Rogers, Magolda, Baxter Magolda, & Knight-Abowitz, 2004). Systematic attention to the challenges and supports of the LPM help students self-author their professional and personal identity to become effective citizens in the complex world of higher education.

The LPM is a central feature of two experiential learning programs. The Casa de Solidaridad offers students a semester of study and cultural immersion in El Salvador. The Casa, co-sponsored by Santa Clara University and the University of Central America, is open to students from all over the US; the participants are primarily from Jesuit institutions. The LPM guides the pedagogy of the coursework, supervision of work in the Salvadorian community, and the community living component of the Casa to meet the Casa objectives of education for transformation, global citizenship, self-authorship, and institutional solidarity (Yonkers-Talz, 2004). The Urban Leadership Internship Program uses the LPM to supervise ten-week summer internships in urban contexts. Program coordinators note that, "With the support of the Learning Partnerships Model, students can be guided to self-authorship through the challenges of experiential learning – challenges that promote the transformation of other-directed students to self-directed citizens who are engaged in their communities" (Egart and Healy, 2004, p. 149). Detailed discussions of these and other uses of the LPM can be found in *Learning Partnerships* (Baxter Magolda & King, 2004) and *Self-Authorship: Advancing Students' Intellectual Growth* (Meszaros, 2007).

Designing Learning Partnerships

The LPM's use in the US offers hope that educators can design learning environments that simultaneously promote disciplinary and transdisciplinary learning. Table 12.1 provides an overview of the process for designing learning partnerships.

Table 12.1 Designing Learning Partnerships

Phase One – Assessing Learning Goals and Learners' Capacities for Self-Authorship

Step 1	Select a context in which to develop a learning partnership.
Step 2	Identify the learning goals for this context – what should learners know and be able to do as a result of this educational experience?
Step 3	Identify the developmental capacities the learning goals require – what ways of understanding knowledge, oneself, and relationships are required to achieve these learning goals?
Step 4	Identify the developmental capacities the learners in this context currently possess – what ways of understanding knowledge, oneself, and relationships do learners exhibit?
Step 5	Identify consistencies and discrepancies between learning goals and learner capacities; craft developmental goals that will help bridge the distance between current and required capacities.

Phase Two – Designing the "Evolutionary Bridge"

Step 6	Outline the developmental "curriculum" – how can the learning and developmental goals be translated into cumulative steps over time?
Step 7	Address the three LPM challenging assumptions – to what extent are they currently in place and in what ways could they be more explicit in this context?
Step 8	Address the three LPM supportive principles – to what extent are they currently in place and in what ways could they be more explicit in this context?
Step 9	Review the consistencies and discrepancies between learning goals and learner capacities that exist in this newly designed learning partnership.
Step 10	Develop a plan to evaluate the effectiveness of the new learning partnership.

Adapted from *Learning Partnerships: Theory and Models of Practice to Educate for Self-Authorship*, edited by Marcia B. Baxter Magolda and Patricia M. King (Sterling, VA: Stylus Publishing, LLC) with permission of the publisher. Copyright © 2004, Stylus Publishing, LLC.

Designing learning partnerships involves consideration of the developmental capacities that underlie most learning goals. Once learning goals have been established for a particular learning context (step two), it is crucial to identify what those learning goals demand of students, to what degree those demands might be beyond their current meaning making, and how we might organize learning to create a transformational bridge from external formula to self-authorship. Analyzing the ways of constructing knowledge, oneself and relationships that particular learning goals require (step three) gives educators a sense of the epistemological, intrapersonal, and interpersonal capacities needed for achieving those goals. Assessing the degree to which learners possess those developmental capacities (step four) reveals the discrepancies between what is demanded and how learners currently make meaning. This enables educators to identify the developmental goals – the capacities students need to develop to be able to meet the learning goals (step five). The design phase begins with translating the learning and developmental goals into a reasonable "curriculum," or process that welcomes learners' current meaning making and gradually invites them into more complex meaning making (step six). This might take the form of a formal curriculum as in the case of the writing curriculum mentioned earlier or the form of a particular course. The LPM's three challenging assumptions (step seven) and three supportive principles (step eight) help educators intentionally devise pedagogical relations that respect learners' current meaning making yet invite learners to reconstruct their beliefs, values and relationships in the more complex terms required by college learning outcomes.[2]

2 For a detailed discussion of this design process and examples, see King, P. M., & Baxter Magolda, M. B. (2004). Creating learning partnerships in higher education: Modeling the shape, shaping the model. In M. B. Baxter Magolda & P. M. King (Eds.), *Learning partnerships: Theory and models of practice to educate for self-authorship* (pp. 303–332). Sterling, VA: Stylus.

Numerous dilemmas are inherent in designing learning partnerships. Nearly every aspect of the higher education enterprise is designed in opposition to learning partnerships. As Terry Wildman wrote in his analysis of using the LPM in curricular reform at Virginia Tech,

> One of the first things we discover in our attempts to introduce new practices in institutional settings is that the *old designs run deep*. Indeed they are embodied in the classrooms where knowledge is *delivered*, in the curriculum practices where requirements are *checked off*, in the space utilization policies where time is *parsed out* in small manageable chunks, in the textbooks where knowledge is carefully *scripted and de-contextualized*, and even in the organizational structures where disciplines can be *isolated* and protected within their own departments.
>
> (2004, pp. 250–251, italics in original)

These structural barriers, deeply embedded in the fabric of our institutions, work against constructing learning partnerships. Similarly, the recent proficiency testing movement, aimed at ensuring that students possess basic knowledge and skills, often leads to greater rigidity in the curriculum rather than to mutually constructing knowledge with learners. Students' and their parents' expectations for vocational training that leads to successful employment is another source of pressure to tell students what they need to know rather than engage them in learning how to think and function in complex ways.

These pressures are exacerbated by the ways in which both students and educators have been socialized. Students are often socialized in pre-college education to rely on authorities and not take initiative for their own learning. They are disconcerted when these familiar ways of learning are challenged and their learned behavior does not yield success. Educators are often socialized to function as authorities with minimal expectation to share authority with learners. They are disconcerted when their familiar ways of teaching are challenged and they fear that sharing authority with students will not produce effective learning.

These institutional and human dynamics combine to sustain what Wildman called the "old designs" – those that frame learning as the passive acquisition of knowledge. These old designs have not produced the kind of complex meaning making necessary for success in twenty-first-century adult life. Conceptualizing educational practice that promotes the transdisciplinary, intentional learning required for success in contemporary adult life requires transforming learners' and educators' assumptions about the role of learners and educators in knowledge construction. As difficult as this may be, preliminary evidence suggests that it is possible. Wildman (2004) and his colleagues report substantial success with faculty learning communities in which sustained discussion of new frames has enabled implementation of the learning partnerships model. Similarly, Rebecca Mills and Karen Strong (2004) describe reframing their entire Division of Student Life organization to promote self-authorship. Divisions of Student Life in US colleges and universities include functions related to the cocurriculum (e.g., admission, orientation, programming for first-year students, residential life, career services, student activities, leadership, learning assistance, programming for special student populations). These units are staffed by professional educators with advanced degrees and headed by a Vice President. These large-scale efforts show that educators can create new designs for the higher education enterprise that model and engage students in the complex ways of making meaning inherent in self-authorship. To help learners achieve the complex learning outcomes I summarized at the outset of this chapter, educators will need to re-conceptualize the educator-learner relationship. The Learning Partnerships Model offers one vision for engaging students in the ways of making meaning their disciplinary knowledge communities require and simultaneously help them gain the developmental capacity to engage successfully in transdisciplinary communities.

References

American College Personnel Association (1994). *The Student Learning Imperative.* Alexandria, VA: Author.

Association of American Colleges and Universities (1995). *American pluralism and the college curriculum: Higher education in a diverse democracy.* Washington, DC: Author.

Association of American Colleges and Universities (2002). *Greater expectations: A new vision of learning as a nation goes to college.* Washington DC: Author.

Barnett, R. (2000a). *Realizing the University in an age of supercomplexity.* Buckingham: The Society for Research into Higher Education and Open University Press.

Barnett, R. (2000b). Supercomplexity and the curriculum. *Studies in Higher Education,* 25(3), 255–265.

Baxter Magolda, M. B. (1992). *Knowing and reasoning in college: Gender-related patterns in students' intellectual development.* San Francisco, CA: Jossey-Bass.

Baxter Magolda, M. B. (1999). *Creating contexts for learning and self-authorship: constructive-developmental pedagogy.* Nashville, TN: Vanderbilt University Press.

Baxter Magolda, M. B. (2001). *Making their own way: Narratives for transforming higher education to promote self-development.* Sterling, VA: Stylus.

Baxter Magolda, M. B. (2004a). Learning Partnerships Model: A framework for promoting self-authorship. In M. B. Baxter Magolda & P. M. King (Eds.), *Learning partnerships: Theory and models of practice to educate for self-authorship* (pp. 37–62). Sterling, VA: Stylus.

Baxter Magolda, M. B. (2004b). Self-authorship as the common goal of 21st century education. In M. B. Baxter Magolda & P. M. King (Eds.), *Learning partnerships: Theory and models of practice to educate for self-authorship* (pp. 1–35). Sterling, VA: Stylus.

Baxter Magolda, M. B., & King, P. M. (Eds.) (2004). *Learning partnerships: Theory & models of practice to educate for self-authorship.* Sterling, VA: Stylus.

Bekken, B. M., & Marie, J. (2007). Making self-authorship a goal of core curricula: The Earth Sustainability Pilot Project. In P. S. Meszaros (Ed.), *Self-Authorship: Advancing students' intellectual growth, New Directions for Teaching and Learning* (Vol. 109, pp. 53–67). San Francisco, CA: Jossey-Bass.

Belenky, M., Clinchy, B. M., Goldberger, N., & Tarule, J. (1986). *Women's ways of knowing: The development of self, voice, and mind.* New York: Basic Books.

Department of Education & Skills (DfES) (2004). Putting the world into world-class education: An international strategy for education, skills and children's services. Retrieved June 5, 2005, from http//www.planning.ed.ac.uk/Pub/Documents/DfESIntStrat.pdf

Egart, K., & Healy, M. (2004). An Urban Leadership Internship Program: Implementing Learning Partnerships "Unplugged' from Campus Structures. In M. B. Baxter Magolda & P. M. King (Eds.), *Learning partnerships: Theory and models of practice to educate for self-authorship* (pp. 125–149). Sterling, VA: Stylus.

Haynes, C. (2004). Promoting self-authorship through an interdisciplinary writing curriculum. In M. B. Baxter Magolda & P. M. King (Eds.), *Learning partnerships: Theory and models of practice to educate for self-authorship* (pp. 63–90). Sterling, VA: Stylus.

Jackson, N. and Ward, R. (2004). A fresh perspective on progress files – a way of representing complex learning and achievement in higher education. *Assessment & Evaluation in Higher Education,* 29 (4), 423–449.

Kegan, R. (1994). *In over our heads: The mental demands of modern life.* Cambridge, MA: Harvard University Press.

Kegan, R. (2000). What "form" transforms? A constructive-developmental approach to transformative learning. In J. Mezirow (Ed.), *Learning as transformation: Critical perspectives on a theory in progress* (pp. 35–69). San Francisco, CA: Jossey-Bass.

Keeling, R. P. (Ed.) (2004). *Learning reconsidered: A campus-wide focus on the student experience.* Washington DC: National Association of Student Personnel Administrators, American College Personnel Association.

Meszaros, P. S. (Ed.) (2007). *Self-Authorship: Advancing students' intellectual growth, New Directions for Teaching and Learning* (Vol. 109). San Francisco, CA: Jossey-Bass.

Mills, R., & Strong, K. L. (2004). Organizing for learning in a division of student affairs. In M. B. Baxter Magolda & P. M. King (Eds.), *Learning partnerships: Theory and models of practice to educator for self-authorship* (pp. 269–302). Sterling, VA: Stylus.

Perry, W. G. (1970). *Forms of intellectual and ethical development in the college years: A scheme.* Troy, MO: Holt, Rinehart, & Winston.

Rogers, J. L., Magolda, P. M., Baxter Magolda, M. B., & Knight-Abowitz, K. (2004). A community of scholars: Enacting the Learning Partnerships Model in graduate education. In M. B. Baxter Magolda & P. M. King (Eds.), *Learning partnerships: Theory and models of practice to educate for self-authorship* (pp. 213–244). Sterling, VA: Stylus.

Wildman, T. M. (2004). The Learning Partnerships Model: Framing faculty and institutional development. In M. B. Baxter Magolda & P. M. King (Eds.), *Learning partnerships: Theory and models of practice to educate for self-authorship* (pp. 245–268). Sterling, VA: Stylus.

Yonkers-Talz, K. (2004). A learning partnership: U.S. college students and the poor in El Salvador. In M. B. Baxter Magolda & P. M. King (Eds.), *Learning partnerships: Theory and models to educate for self-authorship* (pp. 151–184). Sterling, VA: Stylus.

13

Supporting Student Development In and Beyond the Disciplines
The Role of the Curriculum

Alan Jenkins

Many readers will agree that it is equally important that students learn how knowledge is constructed and evaluated. In addition, some of us will argue that it is also critical that academic teachers understand their role even more broadly than that, not exclusively as assisting students in learning a particular subject, as in helping them to 'think like historians, or physicists, or lawyers', etc. (*although there can be no doubt that teaching the discipline has to be their main role*) . . .

> (Kreber, preface to this volume, pp. xxi–xxii, emphasis added)

The complexities young adults face in transdisciplinary contexts after college, as well as the complexities inherent in disciplinary learning during college, require something beyond skill acquisition and application. They require a transformation from authority dependence to self-authorship, or the capacity to internally define one's beliefs, identity and social relations. . . . Longitudinal participants' stories reinforce the notion that graduates must be able to translate their disciplinary learning into supercomplex, transdisciplinary contexts.

> (Baxter Magolda, Chapter 12, pp. 143 and 152)

The key processes of higher learning are not located solely within engagement with disciplinary practices, nor in the accessing of bodies of information and theory, nor in students' cognitive development, nor in their personal growth. From a sociocultural perspective, teaching and learning cannot be encapsulated within a single arena of development. The teacher has a range of interwoven responsibilities and plays a variety of roles in supporting different aspects of learning.

> (Northedge and McArthur, Chapter 9, p. 110)

Introduction

Issues of intellectual development, academic discipline, student, faculty, and institutional identities resonate through this chapter. It is written with the aim of offering some new perspectives and "practical" suggestions, particularly with respect to curriculum design, which build on the more abstract ideas regarding students' intellectual and discipline-based development considered in this book. In particular, it addresses Baxter Magolda's notion (see previous chapter) of "educating for self-authorship" and also, though to a lesser extent, the work of Northedge and McArthur (see Chapter 9) on "guiding students into a discipline". As a way into this chapter I would like you to consider the three quotations that appear at the beginning. To me they provide contrasting, complementary and in part conflicting perspectives on the role of the student, the academic and the university. To what extent do they match the way you see your role and the function of the university? Do you see your role primarily as teaching a particular discipline or as supporting students' intellectual and civic development? Or is this a false or needless dichotomy?

This chapter is targeted at three broad groups of faculty: first, to those at the beginning of their career, probably taking a course to support them in becoming an effective teacher (of their discipline). With this audience in mind, my intent is to approach this chapter from a practical angle, assuming that those "new faculty" are involved in designing and teaching new courses, trying to move their research forward, and perhaps learning to work with new colleagues (Gibbs, Gold & Jenkins, 1987; Rust, 2000). However, I also hope that I can demonstrate to "new faculty" how the ideas underlying Baxter Magolda's work, and that of Northedge and McArthur, can be useful and helpful for their longer-term development. The second group of readers this chapter is aimed at are experienced faculty who may find that it offers suggestions for reconsidering their own courses but perhaps more significantly for reshaping the overall program(s) their department offers. The third audience includes senior faculty/managers with institution-wide roles, who may feel inspired by this chapter to review how the university at large supports students' (long-term) intellectual development. Here I add that it is both a strength and, perhaps, a limitation of Baxter Magolda's chapter that it offers both a critique and a radical blueprint for a total reform of university/higher education.

A Prologue

I think it is important that readers have some sense of where I am coming from in writing this response to the previous chapter. As you read this prologue, consider how my views match or conflict with your current "position"; that is your own views on the role of the university, the faculty, and students given the specific disciplinary and institutional contexts in which you work. As Trowler argues in Chapter 15, you will bring your own context to the ideas offered in this book; and these contexts will, on the one hand, determine which ideas you find worthwhile and, on the other hand, shape their implementation.

My experience is of some forty years of teaching in higher education. For most of that time I worked outside the research-intensive universities that are the focus of Kreber's second chapter, with their focus on high-level research and developing the next generation of faculty through strong graduate schools. For a long time I taught human geography and contemporary China studies in a then essentially undergraduate teaching-focused institution. At times, the subjects I taught and researched consumed me. However, I was much more interested in issues of teaching and learning and student development. Naturally I was always reminding my colleagues that few of our students would proceed with post-graduate study in geography. Moreover, the content of the courses I was teaching I nearly always saw as a vehicle for students' intellectual and personal growth (this was at first rather implicit, yet as I developed my philosophy of teaching, became more explicit). In contrast, some of my colleagues were more excited by the academic importance of *what* they taught and worked brilliantly at trying to instil in our students similar passions and knowledge. We argued long about these issues and the resultant curricula we taught in the department were a changing kaleidoscope and compromise between our different individual perspectives, varied student responses and changing institutional requirements (Jenkins & Ward, 2001). Even though we were not then familiar with Baxter Magolda's work, we were perhaps unusual in espousing similar perspectives on the need to support students' long-term development. In our case, this was encouraged through an emphasis on active learning, co-operative group projects and making explicit to students that these helped develop 'employability' or 'life-skills' (Jenkins & Pepper, 1988). Also running through all three years of the degree was a 'content' that focused on environmental issues, with an explicit concern for how students might choose to deal with these issues in their future lives (Pepper, 1984). However, all of us had very particular research interests that did not necessarily relate to these 'core' concerns. For some years I was determined to teach a course on western documentary films on Communist China that was for me then a consuming research interest. So eventually we compromised. We created a strong core curriculum to which we all contributed and supported intellectually in our dealings with students. But 'on the side' we each had our own research-based courses into which we tried to attract students. Does any of this resonate with those of you now trying to maintain or develop a research profile as well as teach? And how about those of you in managerial roles trying to support high-level research and support 'effective' teaching?

I then moved to work full time into 'educational development'. As I joined this new tribe of educational developers I had to learn a new language and new practices (Jenkins, 2003). I also, for the first time, encountered very varied views and scholarship on the role of the academic and the university. I met many educational developers who questioned and even resisted (or attacked) what they saw as many academics' preoccupation with their discipline. Faculty's evident commitment to their discipline, and related research interests, could provoke my new colleagues into questioning these academics' commitment to teaching and students, for such values can suggest that a concern for the students' intellectual growth is secondary – or even non-existent! I then surprised myself by starting to espouse the importance of faculty's concern for their discipline. For a range of reasons, mainly initially pragmatic, I argued that unless "we" valued faculty's interests in discipline-based research, "they" would be unlikely to listen to "us" (Jenkins, 1996). Through ongoing discussions with colleagues, and much reading and research, I reconsidered my own understanding of the role of the discipline in students' and faculty's intellectual development and identities. Recently my work has centered on helping faculty (including institutional managers) link what can easily feel like two conflicting roles: those of teacher and discipline-based researcher. I have also become intrigued by how *students'* intellectual development can be promoted through their involvement in discipline-based research. Here Baxter Magolda's perspectives (see also Baxter Magolda, Boes, Hollis, & Jamarillo, 1998) have considerably aided my re-thinking and writing (e.g. Jenkins, Breen, Lindsay, & Brew, 2003; Jenkins, Healey, & Zetter, 2007). Her work has the potential to offer valuable perspectives on our teaching philosophies, practices and policies at whatever stage of the academic journey we find ourselves, and in whichever discipline, professional area and institution we work. But I think we have to transform her perspectives to fit our particular contexts. Perhaps she also opens up the future, where many of our students already are – and where we need to follow.

Baxter Magolda's Perspectives

Readers familiar with the UK television documentary series 7 Up (http://en.wikipedia.org/wiki/Seven_Up%21), which has followed the life journey of a group of then seven-year-olds in 1964 (and related documentary series in the USA, Australia, and South Africa), will recognize the parallels to the approach Baxter Magolda took in her research (Chapter 12). Based on periodic interviews with then eighteen-year-old students who entered a university in the USA some twenty years ago, she has investigated how the experience of university and of 'life' afterwards shapes their understandings of themselves, knowledge and the worlds in which they live. For those of us who consider that the role of the university is to foster students' intellectual growth and an informed citizenry, her research suggests key questions of how and what to teach at university to support this kind of lifetime development. I propose that these questions are just as relevant for the more 'mature' students now increasingly entering higher education as they are for traditional undergraduate students.

The essential insight we gain from Baxter Magolda's research is that for many university students 'knowing something' means to have learned some facts. 'Knowing' is not conceptualized as a tentative, provisional way of understanding a world that Barnett (2000) calls "supercomplex", in which "the very frameworks by which we orient ourselves to the world are themselves contested" (p. 3). This dissonance between many students' conceptions of knowledge as facts to learn and a view of knowledge as provisional and exploratory is powerfully demonstrated by Baxter Magolda in her interviews with a biology teacher and a final year undergraduate in one of his courses. The teacher wants students "to understand how information is gained. I want them to appreciate what facts really mean. Tentative facts. That's what all of science is. Subject to change and revision" (p. 145 this volume). Yet the student's reaction to this biology course and her perception of knowledge is:

> I take sociology as my minor. It is all opinions, not hard-core facts where you are wrong [like Winter Biology]. . . . I understand what he was trying to do. But if he had just said . . . I would believe him because he is the teacher. I don't need the proof, it's not like I'm going to argue with him about it.
>
> (Baxter Magolda, p. 145 this volume)

Baxter Magolda draws from her research key messages and insights regarding curriculum design for individual staff, course teams and institutions. These are brought together in the Learning Partnerships Model where "Support is offered through *three principles*: validating learners' ability to know, situating learning in learners' experience, and defining learning as mutually constructing meaning" (p. 150 this volume). To make the last point more concrete, the above sociology and biology student needs to be supported by the university, and the individual teachers within it, to be able to see the complexities, contrasting epistemologies and controversies of the knowledge *within* these two contrasting disciplines. She also needs to be supported in then seeing beyond, or in effect above, these particular discipline-based 'knowledges' towards a transdisciplinary or meta-disciplinary conception of knowledge complexity.

Baxter Magolda briefly discusses the key curriculum features of courses designed to help students develop more complex ways of meaning-making and some of her publications describe such courses in greater detail (e.g. Baxter Magolda, 1999). However, I suspect that her examples are drawn from a small sample of innovative experienced faculty in particularly supportive contexts; and, just as significantly, from faculty who share her conceptions regarding the role of teachers and of the university. This is perhaps unlikely to include faculty at the beginning of their careers who are faced with multiple demands and limited time; or faculty whose central concern is to pursue discipline-based research. More fundamentally, to successfully support students in biology and sociology in drawing together the complexities of knowledge from these two contrasting disciplines would require all or most faculty in the two departments to co-construct or co-relate their curricula. Such an intervention would probably require the whole institution to support such jointly identified curricula goals. Examples of such whole-institution approaches to curriculum development exist at small, often private, US liberal arts institutions, such as Alverno, Evergreen College or Hampshire, but these stand out because they are so unusual. As Baxter Magolda recognizes, "Numerous dilemmas are inherent in designing learning partnerships. Nearly every aspect of the higher education enterprise is designed in opposition to learning partnerships" (in this volume, p. 155). Citing Wildman's (2004, pp. 250–251, italics in original) analysis of using the Learning Partnership Model in curricular reform at Virginia Tech, she writes: "One of the first things we discover in our attempts to introduce new practices in institutional settings is that the *old designs run deep* . . . (including) in the organizational structures where disciplines can be *isolated* and protected within their own departments."

As I read Baxter Magolda's chapter and in particular its discussion of the structural institutional obstacles in establishing learning partnerships, it gave me a sense of a 'mission not accomplished' in my career as a geography teacher. A colleague and I used her perspective to explore the impact of our innovative geography course on students' lives after graduation (Jenkins, Jones & Ward, 2001). Our study showed that students could clearly identify the meta goals of our geography course and its long-term impact on them. However, it also revealed that the overall university curriculum, including the geography curriculum *per se*, had not explicitly supported these students to relate what they were learning in geography to the other discipline they were majoring in, nor to the wider experiences of studying in college and learning from life outside the university. The course teams and the university had in effect constructed two (or more) separate silos for students to learn within. The students may have reached greater understanding within their discipline, but if students actually moved beyond that *"to translate their disciplinary learning into supercomplex, transdisciplinary contexts"* (Baxter Magolda, in this volume, p. 152) they would have largely done that by themselves.

Adopting and Adapting Disciplinary Perspectives

Northedge and McArthur (Chapter 9), with their focus on the role of the teacher in promoting student learning within the disciplines, provide an alternative, but related, perspective to that of Baxter Magolda. For the beginning teacher in higher education, and for many departmental and institutional programs, they offer perhaps a more realistic or readily attainable approach to curriculum design than Baxter Magolda. However, I also see them providing a way towards Baxter Magolda's more radical vision.

Northedge and McArthur's focus is not at the level of transdisciplinary knowledge but on the "teacher's role as representative of their discipline" (in this volume, p. 107). The role of teachers in higher education, as scholars or experts in their discipline and thus as established community members of that discipline, is to support "students as aspirants to participation in disciplinary communities. . . . *This is the core contribution of teachers within higher education*" (in this volume, p. 161, emphasis added). From their "socio-cultural perspective, which views higher learning as a complex process of becoming immersed in the ways of thinking and knowing of a significant knowledge community" (in this volume, p. 107), the student acquires the ability to participate in the community's discourses and practices in accordance with the standards accepted within the community. This same perspective is also represented in a researcher of physics in his description of the role of his textbook:

> *Science is a conversation.* The conversation has been in progress for a long time . . . science resembles the babble at a very large reception. . . . The participants in the conversation have sorted themselves into groups, sub groups and sub groups, each dominated by a few brilliant conversationalists who set the subject and tone. Some scientists wander from group to group, while others remain fixed. Some groups talk about similar things, and occasionally snaps of conversation pass from one group to another. You have arrived in the middle of a party. . . . *My job is to catch you up on the conversation and show you how to find your way to the bar.*
>
> (Kinsman, 1965, p. 9, emphasis added)

Northedge and McArthur's approach is a challenging one for it requires faculty to see students as co-enquirers who need support to enter and then participate in that particular discipline-based community of knowledge and practice. While the teacher's knowledge of the discipline *per se* is essential, effective teaching also requires faculty to make fostering *student* understanding of knowledge complexity central to course design, delivery and assessment. Discipline-based knowledge by itself is but a part of what it takes to be an effective teacher. Indeed, at times, Northedge and McArthur's approach comes close to Baxter Magolda's with its emphasis on intellectual and personal development. Specifically, they argue that the teacher's role is that of:

> providing students with interim access to a discipline community, together with support in engaging with its ideas and practices. On the one hand, support is needed for "inner" aspects of learning – the *cognitive development* required in order to be able to make meaning using discipline ideas, and the *realignment of self* involved in engaging with the values and norms of the discipline community. On the other hand, support is needed for "outer" aspects – developing approaches to engaging with the field of knowledge and acquiring skills of participating as a member of the discipline community.
>
> (Northedge and McArthur, in this volume, p. 110)

In addition they point to the limitations of a purely disciplinary approach to teaching and course design. Specifically, they emphasize the role of the faculty in creating a state of *intersubjectivity*, that is a process of mutual meaning-making between faculty and students. They further argue that "disciplinary discourses offer sparse resources for sharing meaning" (in this volume, p. 113) because the teacher's authority, including that of discipline expertise, may in effect not support the learner new to the discipline. "Here we are talking about the teacher jumping in and swimming alongside the students, within a flow of shared meaning. It is a communal activity, intended to support students in becoming encultured within the discipline community" (in this volume, p. 114).

This perspective validates my current interest in adapting the US practice of undergraduate research for selected students to mainstreaming undergraduate research for all students (Healey & Jenkins, 2006; Jenkins & Healey, 2007; Jenkins, 2007). In such courses and programs the focus is on the student constructing meaning out of being involved in disciplinary or transdisciplinary research or inquiry – not in the student receiving discipline-based knowledge from the teacher. In terms of the central themes of this book, the view of the teacher as a co-enquirer with students collapses the arguments as to the value of the discipline-specific and/or generic (or as Kreber puts it, "context-transcendent") approaches to teaching in higher education. Both approaches need to link or fuse into "intersubjectivity" (Healey & Jenkins, 2003).

Implications for Curriculum Design

Northedge and McArthur point to the limitations of a purely discipline-based approach when they argue that "disciplinary discourses offer sparse resources for sharing meaning" (in this volume, p. 113). They also implicitly point to the difficulties of implementing Baxter Magolda's model of Learning Partnerships when they argue that "the teacher has a range of interwoven responsibilities and plays a variety of roles in supporting different aspects of learning" (in this volume, p. 110). Recognizing these interwoven responsibilities opens up possibilities for all faculty – should they choose – to selectively incorporate key perspectives from Baxter Magolda's work into their courses and programs in any disciplinary, department or institutional context.

The formal curriculum is where the worlds of individual faculty and students interact and where the departmental and institutional contexts play key roles in determining what is learnt and how. However, even at the beginning of their careers faculty have the power to (in part) shape the courses they teach. At times, course design is conceptualized as a rational purposive process relatively free of context. Biggs' (2003) model of constructive alignment belongs in that category. The emphasis this model places on the need to design courses around learning outcomes is clearly valuable. However, in my view, models such as this one fail to explicitly recognize that:

- academic staff have conflicting goals (for example, myself espousing the long-term goals of a core curriculum in geography but also being determined to teach particular research interests);
- curricula are forged by academics in a course team and department with differing educational perspectives, and with "interwoven responsibilities"; and
- key aspects of the course are shaped (and even determined or restructured) by the institutions and, in some cases, national systems in which we work.

One way that individuals, departments and institutions can take into consideration these wider contexts and also integrate aspects of Northedge and McArthur's and Baxter Magolda's work, is to understand curriculum design through the analogy of a Ouija board (see Figure 13.1). As such, the curriculum, at any point in time, is portrayed as a product of a range of forces including: support for student learning out of class; aims and objectives; changing external quality requirements; institutional requirements and cultures; available resources (including staff time); linkages between teaching and research; and theories of student learning (for example, those described in Chapters 9 and 12).

Faculty seek to control, shape and prioritize these "forces" in terms of their own and their students' interests (Jenkins et al., 2003, p. 62). Thus with limited preparation and class time, they can include activities and assignments that would meet those aspects of Baxter Magolda and Northedge and McArthur's work that they consider valuable. For example (and this is but a prompt to support your decision as to what is appropriate for your context/discipline, not a firm suggestion to adapt):

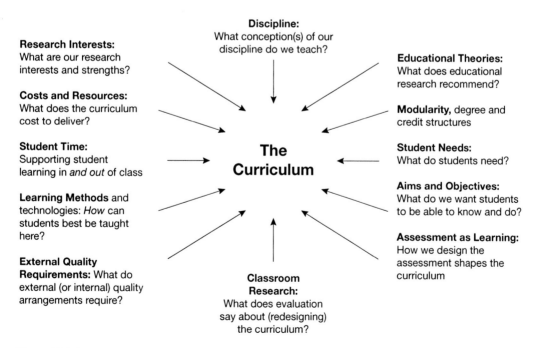

Figure 13.1 Curriculum design – through the analogy of an Ouija board

at the beginning of a course get students in small groups to discuss how they think their knowledge of their discipline helps them to understand a contemporary issue that the course will examine (for example, our understanding of climate change). Then require students to individually write a short essay that sets out their understanding of that issue and what they now find uncertain and/or something they want to explore. Then in a closing class discussion/assignment return to that issue and focus on how the course had moved their understanding forward and the key questions it has raised for their future investigations. This may at least open up issues that you may want to make much more central to the course later as you gain confidence in this approach to course design. Some of you individually may want to make such concerns central to (some of) the courses you teach; however, to realize that aim you will probably have to persuade your colleagues that this is your role in the course team. Those of you in senior positions in the department can work to ensure that the whole program in your discipline/department is restructured to (in part) focus on student long-term intellectual growth.

While it could be argued that Baxter Magolda's call for students to be able "to *translate their disciplinary learning into supercomplex, transdisciplinary contexts*" (in this volume, p. 152) requires implementation over a whole institution, aspects of it can be incorporated into individual courses and certainly by a discipline-based course team or department. For disciplines, in mine and many others' judgments, are not the tightly bounded constructs as which they are sometimes portrayed. As Trowler states in Chapter 15 of this volume:

> the problem with this kind of categorization is that while it seems to make sense when disciplines are viewed through the wrong end of a telescope, from a great distance, the distinctions begin to fall apart in the analytical hand when one looks at disciplines close up. The fractures within them become very apparent when the analyst steps out of the helicopter, as do the similarities between what – from a great height – seemed very different subdisciplinary areas.
>
> (p. 183)

To this I would add the fractures within disciplines and their similarities, and indeed commonalities, when seen across disciplines that also become very apparent whether one focuses on disciplinary content, or on epistemological and research perspectives (Brew, 2001). Arguably this is particularly the case for disciplines such as geography that are not tightly bounded (Healey, Jenkins & Kneale, 2000) and for the growing number of professional areas (for example, media studies, business, or urban planning) that now are central to the curricula of many universities.

If you agree with this analysis then it opens up possibilities for individuals and course teams to support students in moving towards a more 'supercomplex' and 'transdisciplinary' understanding, within a firmly discipline-based (and/or department-based) curriculum. The geography curriculum that my colleagues and I taught considered environmental issues from highly contrasting epistemologies and research methodologies: scientific, humanistic and philosophical perspectives linked and clashed throughout the three-year program. In course essays, debates, or courts of inquiry (Jenkins & Pepper, 1988) students were required to periodically reconsider their understanding of these issues and, to an extent, consider how this might shape their lives after graduation.

Let me now return to the disciplines that the US senior student was studying when interviewed by Baxter Magolda. Biology and sociology (as do all disciplines) offer opportunities to make explicit to students how very different epistemologies or perspectives on knowledge reveal different aspects of knowledge complexity. Biology curricula offer students the opportunity to learn that within the dominant disciplinary positivist paradigm, the outcomes of research rest on an interpretation of data at a particular time and based on then current knowledge of the world. Furthermore, they offer opportunities for students to learn that the "facts" may not be certain and may change in the light of further investigations. One way to help students reach this understanding is to move through the history and development of the knowledge base of the discipline from present day "edge of knowledge" to previous ways of explaining/knowing (Emptage, 2007). Furthermore, biology curricula that bring out how biology is used in society (for example, the application of knowledge gained through the human genome project) opens up profound ethical and political issues as well as the opportunity for biology curricula to support students' understanding of transdisciplinary research (McCune & Hounsell, 2005; J. Potter, Personal communication, 2007; H. Sears, Personal communication, 2007). Sociology curricula offer students the chance to explore aspects of the social world they inhabit and will inhabit after graduation and to study those aspects through many contrasting perspectives or dichotomies: global/local; structure/agency; culture/nature; gender/sex; qualitative/quantitative (Jenks, 1998). Clearly, course teams have to structure the overall curriculum to make these contrasting perspectives explicit and teach the course in ways that support the students in continually reshaping their understanding of this complexity. The ways in which course teams might choose to do this are varied. The case study of a final year synoptic course in English (as illustrated in Figure 13.2) is offered as but one alternative "model" – not as *the* route to follow.

Thus a course team (or an institution) could build into a final year dissertation (or research assignment) a requirement that such individual study is set in the context of the epistemological perspectives encountered through the course and how that understanding may shape their lives after college. Alternatively, . . . *that is for you to decide!* The central point is that disciplinary courses can and, I would add, should support students in moving towards supercomplex, transdisciplinary understanding. Indeed, from this perspective, I in part disagree with Northedge and McArthur's argument that "disciplinary discourses offer sparse resources for sharing meaning" (in this volume, p. 113). Instead, I argue that the value of becoming immersed in a discipline is, or can be, that what seemed so clear in one's initial exposure becomes fractured and reshaped as one's understanding of the discipline progresses. It is precisely through specialization within and across a discipline or professional area, and at times by stretching beyond that discipline, that our understanding can

- This final-year capstone course for English Studies at Oxford Brookes University is compulsory for students taking a degree solely in English and strongly recommended for those studying English and another discipline. (Brookes operates a US style credit or modular course where many students specialize in two disciplines.)
- The overall focus of the English course is to help students develop critical understanding of the ways in which texts come into being and can be analysed using a range of epistemologies: "formalism", "cultural materialism", Marxism, feminism, post-colonialism, etc.
- Over the three years students follow selected specialist historical period based core courses (e.g., Victorian literature, Renaissance literature) and one honours level module based around individual staff members' research expertise.
- The capstone course brings all students together to analyse common issues in contemporary literature. Assessment by exam and course work require students to take a critical and individual overview of their whole English programme: to consider what pathways they have followed during it and, crucially, where they are at the close of the degree and where they are taking both the subject and themselves (e.g., whether into work or into postgraduate study).

    (Oxford Brookes University, 2007; R. Pope, Personal communication, 2007)

Figure 13.2 Synoptic Module in Contemporary Literature

become 'supercomplex'. This is where department and institutional leaders can intervene in important ways. For example, institutional leaders can shape and determine institutional curricula requirements so that these support students in bringing together their understandings from the range of courses they have studied during their degree. Institutional and department leaders can build into the regular annual review of courses questions and procedures that require or support faculty in considering how their programs are supporting students' longterm intellectual growth. Furthermore, pragmatically, many universities, and certainly those with research aspirations, will want to organize staff around disciplines, or related research groupings, to strengthen their research potential. Thus the programs offered to students are likely to be organized by disciplines/departments. In most institutional contexts, therefore, it is within disciplines that Baxter Magolda's ideas may be most practically realized.

In Conclusion: Groping Towards the Future

I have argued that a discipline-based approach to course design as suggested by Northedge and McArthur can open up knowledge complexity to students to meet the ambitious goals that Baxter Magolda proposes. In most departments and institutions this is a practical way forward to support students' long-term intellectual growth. In this final section of the chapter I want to return to my earlier cryptic comment that "Baxter Magolda opens up the future where many of our students already are – and we need to follow" (p. 159).

The practical difficulties of adopting her Learning Partnership Model are immense. Thus, I stated earlier that helping the student studying biology and chemistry draw together the complexities of knowledge from two contrasting disciplines would, in effect, require all or most faculty in the two different departments to co-construct or co-relate much of their curricula. Such an intervention would probably require the whole institution to support such curricula goals. Baxter Magolda herself reports on the difficulties involved in implementing her ideas, even with strong high-level central support. Yet, as Kreber argues (Chapter 1), today's students are very different from those college students that Baxter Magolda started to research some twenty years ago. Present-day students may well be mature students who already have a lot of experience that the university needs to value and help them better understand. Many or most of them will now be working part time or may have family responsibilities. These experiences need to be seen by them as linked to their university studies and not as further separate silos. When these students graduate they are going to enter into a workforce and societies that are being continually restructured and in which they need to find some personal meaning. Furthermore, since the late 1970s UK university curricula have moved from the then dominant single subject degree towards the 'US model' of a student taking two or more disciplines. In addition many students now take professional courses that are not tightly discipline-based. Surely then it is the university's, course team's and individual academic's role to help them draw together and understand that supercomplexity. To express that differently, I am arguing that new faculty, and certainly an established course team and the university overall, need to give greater emphasis to educational theories of student intellectual development, and in particular the research on student long-term intellectual development, than did previous generations of university teachers. The curriculum Ouija board needs to be shifted in that direction.

Ideally, faculty will be supported by institutions and national systems that seek to support all course program teams in achieving those goals. This will clearly be difficult. We have very few established or developing models to consider. From her US-based perspective, Baxter Magolda looks positively on those UK institutions implementing Personal Development Planning (PDP) where students are supported often by central (careers) units to chart their individual progress, particularly with a "skills"/employability focus through college and beyond (Higher Education Academy, 2007).

From my particular UK-based perspective I am skeptical of many such programs. In the institutions with which I am familiar, faculty seldom see these initiatives as being based on academic (disciplinary) values. I do recognize, however, that in institutions with strong centrally determined and employment-focused *teaching and learning regimes* (see Trowler, Chapter 15) such PDP programs may be an effective way of realizing Baxter Magolda's vision. It would appear that we need a range of models to try out and then evaluate in terms of their impact.

I am much more attracted, from afar, by those US institutions that have implemented senior capstone requirements, whether these are discipline-specific or cross disciplinary. For example, at the University of Portland in the senior capstone requirement,

> students bring together the knowledge, skills, and interests developed to this point through all aspects of their education, to work on a community project. Here students from a variety of majors and backgrounds work as a team, pooling resources, and collaborating with faculty and community leaders to understand and find solutions for issues that are important to them as literate and engaged citizens.
>
> (Portland State University, 2007)

Similarly the University of South Carolina (2007) capstone "reviews the accomplishments of the undergraduate experience and prepares students for their transition out of the university into either the workplace or graduate studies".

Perhaps I am seeing these (and related) US institutional initiatives (Berheide, 2007; Fanter, 2006; Henscheid, 2000) through rose-tinted glasses. However, both initiatives described offer frameworks to meet your students' needs and to reflect on your departmental and institutional contexts. This is clearly where those of you with institution- and department-wide responsibilities can play central roles. Regardless of whether you are in such senior roles or a new faculty member seeking to design or teach an individual course, I hope I have persuaded you that the concepts introduced by Baxter Magolda, and by Northedge and McArthur, are not only vital to meet the needs of students and wider society, but also practically realizable.

References

Barnett, R. A. (2000). Supercomplexity and the curriculum. *Studies in Higher Education*, 25(3), 255–265.

Baxter Magolda, M., Boes, L., Hollis, M. L., & Jamarillo, D. L. (1998). *Impact of the undergraduate summer scholar experience in epistemological development*. Internal report. University of Miami, Ohio.

Baxter Magolda, M. B. (1999). *Creating contexts for learning and self-authorship: Constructive-developmental pedagogy* (1st ed.). Nashville, TN: Vanderbilt University Press.

Berheide, C. (2007). Doing less work, collecting better data: using capstone courses to assess learning. *Peer Review*, 9(2). Retrieved October 23, 2007 from http://www.aacu.org/peerreview/pr-sp07/pr-sp07_research.cfm,

Biggs, J. (2003). *Teaching for quality learning at university*. Buckingham, UK: Society for Higher Education and Open University Press.

Brew, A. (2001). *The nature of research: inquiry in academic contexts*. London: Routledge.

Emptage, N. (2007). Research-led teaching: the evolution of a tutorial style, *Illuminatio*, Eighth Edition, Oxford University Learning Institute. Retrieved October 23 from http://www.learning.ox.ac.uk/oli.php?page=9.

Fanter, A. (2006). Preparing for post-college life: capstone and keystone courses. Retrieved October 23, 2007 from http://www.worldwidelearn.com/education-articles/capstone-keystone-courses.htm.

Gibbs, G., Gold, J.R. & Jenkins, A. (1987). Fending for yourself: becoming a teacher of geography in higher education. *Journal of Geography in Higher Education*, 11(1), 11–26.

Healey, M. & Jenkins, A. (2003). Educational development through the disciplines. In R. Macdonald and H. Eggins (Eds.) *The scholarship of academic development* (pp. 47–57). Buckingham, UK: Society for Higher Education and Open University Press.

Healey, M. & Jenkins, A. (2006). Strengthening the teaching-research linkage in undergraduate courses and programmes. In C. Kreber (Ed.) *Exploring research-based teaching. New directions for teaching and learning*, No. 107 (pp. 45–55). San Francisco: Jossey-Bass/Wiley.

Healey, M., Jenkins, A. & Kneale, P. (2000). Small worlds on an interconnected planet: Teaching and learning geography in higher education. In V. Rust (Ed.) *Improving student learning through the disciplines* (pp. 125–134). Oxford: Oxford Centre for Staff and Learning Development.

Henscheid, J. M. (2000). Professing the disciplines: An analysis of senior seminars and capstone courses (Monograph No. 30) Columbia, S.C.: University of Southern Carolina, National Resource Centre for the First Year Experience and Students in Transition.

Higher Education Academy (HEA) (2007). Personal development planning (PDP). York: HEA. Retrieved October 23, 2007 from http://www.heacademy.ac.uk/ourwork/learning/pdp.

Jenkins, A. (1996). Discipline-based educational development. *International Journal for Academic Development*, 1(1), 50–62.

Jenkins, A. (2003). Crossing continents. In P. E. Kahn & D. Baume (Eds.) *Making sense of staff and educational development: A directory for educational change* (pp. 215–216). London: Kogan Page.

Jenkins, A. (2007). Adapting US undergraduate research to UK and other international contexts. Retrieved October 23, 2007 from http://www2.warwick.ac.uk/fac/soc/sociology/research/cetl/ugresearch/.

Jenkins, A. & Healey, M. (2007). Critiquing excellence: Undergraduate research for all students. In A. Skelton (Ed.) *International perspectives on teaching excellence in higher education* (pp. 117–132). London: Routledge.

Jenkins, A. & Pepper, D. M. (1988). *Enhancing employability and educational experience: A manual on teaching communication and groupwork skills in higher education*. Birmingham: SCEDSIP. Retrieved October 23, 2007 from http://www2.glos.ac.uk/gdn/pepper/index.htm.

Jenkins, A. & Ward, A. (2001) Moving with the times: An oral history of a geography department. *Journal of Geography in Higher Education*, 25(2), 191–208.

Jenkins, A., Breen, R., Lindsay, R. & Brew, A. (2003). *Re-shaping teaching in higher education: Linking teaching and research*. London: Routledge/Falmer with the Staff and Educational Development Association.

Jenkins, A., Healey, M. & Zetter, R. (2007). Linking teaching and research in disciplines and departments. York: HEA. Retrieved October 23, 2007 from http://www.heacademy.ac.uk/research/LinkingTeachingAndResearch_April07.pdf.

Jenkins, A., Jones, L. & Ward, A. (2001). The long-term effect of a degree on graduate lives. *Studies in Higher Education*, 26(2), 149–163.

Jenks, C. (Ed.) (1998). *Core sociological dichotomies*. London: Sage.

Kinsman, B. (1965). *Wind Waves, their Generation and Propagation across the Ocean Surface*. New York: Prentice Hall.

McCune, V. & Hounsell, D. (2005). The development of ways of thinking and practicing in three final year biology courses. *Higher Education*, 49(3), 255–289.

Oxford Brookes University (2007) English synoptic module. Retrieved October 23, 2007 from https://kmis.brookes.ac.uk/csms/wval_unit.query?code=U67083&format=SYLLABUS&pid=35059245432240342.

Pepper, D. M. (1984). *The Roots of Modern Environmentalism*. London: Croom Helm.

Portland State University (2007) Senior capstone. Retrieved October 23, 2007 from http://www.pdx.edu/unst/capstone.html.

Rust, C. (2000). Do initial training courses have an impact on university teaching? The evidence from two evaluative studies of one course. *Innovations in Education and Training International*, 37(3), 254–262.

University of South Carolina (2007). University 401 – senior capstone experience. Retrieved September 7, 2007 from http://sc.edu/univ101/courses/univ401/index.html.

Wildman, T. M. (2004). The learning partnerships model: Framing faculty and institutional development. In M. B. Baxter Magolda & P. M. King (Eds.) *Learning partnerships: Theory and models of practice to educate for self-authorship* (pp. 245–268). Sterling, VA: Stylus.

14

Constraints to Implementing Learning Partnership Models and Self-Authorship in the Arts and Humanities

Vicky Gunn

University of Glasgow

Introduction

> No responsible scholar believes that humanistic study directly fosters private virtue and responsible citizenship. On the other hand, most scholars do believe that by engaging in humanistic study they are doing something worthwhile in a larger sense; they are simply uncertain how to connect this larger public good with their private scholarly activity.
>
> (Harpham, 2005, p. 25)

In this statement, the Director of the National Humanities Center (USA) Geoffrey Harpham captures a common disconnection between *the study of the humanities* from *the education of those who study the humanities.* He appears to forget the mediating context in which we socially engage with our students and the direct and indirect impact that this has both in and outside of our disciplines. For me, our classrooms are the bridging environment between what we, as academics, individually study and with whom we share that study and its practices socially. As a result we need to beware of failing to address the nature of the educational environment fostered within the Arts and Humanities by its faculty members: How we teach what we have been studying privately is as important as what we teach. How we teach is simultaneously both one of the public aspects of our private scholarly activity as well as an intrinsic part of that activity and this symbiosis is directly linked to the public good. Surely both disciplinary content and its context of generation create a whole greater than the sum of its parts? Harpham's statement is, of course, a reduction of the variety of viewpoints expressed within the Arts and Humanities, but it sums up one reason as to why the Humanities subjects have been tainted with a perception of conservatism in their approaches to different methods of education: We focus on product and forget process. We, the argument goes, have been excellent at challenging traditional modes of thought within our subjects but have uncritically accepted habitual procedures of discipline generation.

The collective membership of Arts and Humanities subjects in higher education, of course, are not change averse. We may well attempt to embody boundaries through such things as subject benchmarks, signature pedagogies, subject centers such as those offered within the remit of the UK's Higher Education Academy, even degree titles, but in reality paradigm shifts in content and context occur all the time. The content of the Arts and Humanities programs is (i) variable dependent on where they are studied, and (ii) does not remain static. Over the last two decades undergraduate courses have been reconfigured to align with these changes (Bassnett, 2002, p. 104). Initial general survey courses have been replaced by thematic ones and then, in some cases, returned to surveys. What used to be mandatory elements of programs have become optional if not extinct and alternative compulsory elements have been developed. New technologies have been employed to act as both efficient repositories of information/resources and locations in which students can debate key topics and generate new ideas and forms of expression. Take up of these changes is also variable, but it is clear from their existence that we are both willing to and capable of reconfiguring our learning environments.

This chapter aims to provide the reader with some reflections on the difficulties of implementing Baxter Magolda's model within the Arts and Humanities. It is designed to be read not as a critique of her work but rather as an attempt to encourage the reader to respond to questions that assist thinking about curriculum redesign and its relationship to the disciplines as represented within universities. It is divided into two sections: an outline of Baxter Magolda's assumptions followed by a discussion of the key constraints to implementing her proposals. The latter section explores the constraints through the themes of personal beliefs, the disciplines, and the institutional perspective.

Outline of Baxter Magolda's Assumptions

Her key assumptions seem to be as follows:

(1) Graduates need to be able to translate what they learn as undergraduates into adequate responses to situations in which they find themselves after their university studies. To do this students need to be able to transform from dependent to autonomous agents. This is where undergraduate programs intersect with the life-long learning agendas.

(2) Academics need to consider how to enable undergraduates to develop not only an intellectual understanding of the provisionality of knowledge (cognitive maturity), but also effective intrapersonal and interpersonal capabilities to enact this complex way of thinking both inside and outside of the classroom (integrated identity and mature relationships). This sees Higher Education as providing an environment for more than just cognitive skills.

To provide the sort of undergraduate education most likely to facilitate appropriate outcomes for these assumptions, Baxter Magolda suggests universities should consider developing Learning Partnership Models that generate the potential for self-authorship. To do this she asks us to design undergraduate programs that integrate three principles of support with three key challenges to how our students might come to understand our subjects. For simplicity these are outlined below:

Key Supportive Components Necessary in the Learning Environment

- Explicit validation of our students' ability to know both our disciplinary knowledge and to develop a broader range of capabilities. (The authentic enactment of respect of and belief in our students.)
- Situating learning in our students' frames of reference and experience. (Exhibiting a real desire to understand where our students are 'coming from' and moderating our methods of instruction and our approaches to the students' potential for learning in the light of this understanding.)
- Defining learning as mutually constructing meaning.

Challenges Provided by Undergraduate Learning Environment

- Explicitly assisting students to recognize that knowledge within our subjects is provisional and subject to revisions to which they can add.
- Developing programs that push the students into gaining the self-confidence to make informed judgments; that enable them to develop ideas in response to disciplinary questions that are not entirely dependent on external influences.
- Enabling students to share authority and expertise with their peers and us.

Baxter Magolda does not prescribe how we should practically achieve this, leaving it up to disciplinary approaches and individual academic staff to translate her ideas into actions.

Key Constraints

Personal Beliefs and Brown Paper Bags

Arguably, the biggest constraint for implementing the learning environment offered by Baxter Magolda is our ability to intellectually critique what she has to say. As academics in the Arts and Humanities we are, by training and desire, called to question her methodology, her evidence, her rhetoric and ultimately her conclusions. In the main, this is the sort of approach to knowledge that we wish to see from our students. Indeed, not engaging in the intellectual debate about the assumptions Baxter Magolda offers would be like placing our heads into a brown paper bag. It certainly would not be modeling our understanding of the provisionality of disciplinary knowledge. From a purely intellectual angle, neither of her key assumptions is without possible criticism. She assumes, for example:

(1) That a supercomplex post-graduate work environment is the predominant context in which our graduates will find themselves and that this is universally best served by autonomous agents. Where's the proof?

(2) That Higher Education can provide an environment in which academics are able to explicitly challenge and develop not only how students think but also their broader individual and group psychological and personality processes. Given the pull of the disciplines to influence Faculty staff how realistic is this? Or are we already doing this but not in a clearly measurable way? Also, what is the ethics of this? Self-authorship is a great aspiration but what happens if it takes a moral high-ground – do those students who can't match its requirements become the inferior body?

Despite these concerns, she is not alone in her assumptions. Indeed, they match closely the assumptions currently focused on with respect to the development of graduate attributes in English-speaking Universities across the globe (Hager & Holland, 2006). For this chapter I am going to suggest that we see the assumptions behind Baxter Magolda's approach to learning and teaching in Higher Education as red herrings that distract us from two more essential questions:

Will what Baxter-Magolda suggests in terms of program design improve the quality and experience of undergraduate learning in our disciplines? And if it does, is this more likely to offer outcomes that correlate with her two central assumptions? If the answer to the first question is 'in many cases, yes', the answer to the second one may well be the same.

If we accept this position for now then we need to consider our personal resistances to Baxter Magolda's views. Put frankly there are two key areas for resistance: (i) she's linked the intellectual with the personal, asking us to be both involved in the development of a broader range of capabilities and provide different types of learning environments to those we might consider as the norm within our disciplines; (ii) she's an educationalist. As was noted in the opening quote, some of us are just not that sure we have the ability to influence the broader personal capabilities of our students, and some of us are not that sure if we trust the educationalists who suggest we should. What is clear from the research on both conceptions of pedagogies and implementing generic attributes in the higher education curriculum is that with respect to discussing learning and teaching, academics in disciplines from outside the educationalist world divide into a variety of observable categories. Broadly speaking we range from the comfortably didactic to the outrageously interactive (Barrie, 2006; Kember, 1997; Zukas & Malcolm, 2000). The trouble is that Baxter Magolda seems to privilege the latter approach over all the others. The support for argument is of course in her data, but for those of us unfamiliar with such data it is hard not to be suspicious of its veracity.

That she comes from the perspective of an educationalist, a discipline in its own right with its own structure of propositions, truth criteria, methodologies and values, is problematic. *Why should we who belong to different disciplines allow another discipline to determine how we might teach?* Though the participants in Baxter Magolda's study came from different disciplines, intellectual suspicion warns us that her interpretations of this data relate to a set of assumptions that underpin the educationalist perspectives privileged in the predominantly English speaking 'developed' world. Her data is mediated through her discipline's interpretative frameworks and for those outside the discipline, this makes it questionable.

However, what if we are actually reproducing educational situations which implicitly privilege other approaches without really being aware that this is what we do? The central question to ask here is *how do we manage complex situations that do not necessarily look like our usual comfort zones of 'traditional teaching'?* Do we fall back onto externally provided formula or do we try to explore the complexities and ambiguities of these different environments? Or do we, perhaps, do a bit of both?

Some would argue that in the so-called non-vocational subjects we have been privileging 'positivist' transmission over holism. In actuality there have been over twenty years of learning and teaching initiatives undertaken within Higher Education in the UK and the Arts and Humanities have been relatively significant players. It is also clear that the Arts and Humanities are becoming less dependent on employing new faculty whose own undergraduate learning experience was limited to just lectures and tutorials. Moreover, most academics in the Arts and Humanities do not see themselves merely as transmitters of knowledge, but have a basic underlying but unspoken assumption that the learning relationship is more than the sum of its teaching parts. Somewhere most of us probably believe that students learn and make disciplinary connections provided by a variety of methods of instruction, non-teaching social contexts, and interpersonal exchanges, and that these: (i) are not all determined by us and (ii) collectively encourage the graduate outcomes required for life-long learning. In this context our focus on subject matter is reasonable. That we then divide up into categories as to how these outcomes are achieved is not surprising. Reducing this larger assumption to a focus on us as transmitters misses this point. The omission of this may be as much a methodological problem in the educational literature as an absence.

Nonetheless, as Faculty members in Arts and Humanities departments we do need to respond to changes in the ways our disciplines are perceived, the students who take them, and the numbers of students taking them. It strikes me that Baxter Magolda offers a useful interpretative framework upon which to make both our *a priori* assumptions explicit and respond to some of these changes.

Academics need to return to some basic questions in this process – what was the learning environment I learned in, why did I like it, and how did other students in my year feel about it? These may seem unsophisticated but perhaps a serious constraint for implementation is any unspoken assumption on our part that all students are either completely like us or not like us at all. The first places students as preferring to learn within the models that suited us, the second that if they're not like us they're probably not up to doing the subject (at least not well). Intellectually, of course, we don't homogenize the student body and can point to this from the grading systems we use. After all we acknowledge our students' cognitive diversity through a series of assessment scales. However, if we are unable to concede that environments can be improved to enhance the learning of more of our students at undergraduate level then we are falling back into over-simplifying their capabilities.

Disciplines and Detours

Once we have overcome our own personal philosophical demons the next hurdle to face is our disciplines, especially as some of the demons were probably developed within the context of our exposure to those disciplines early in our academic careers. It is clear from the other chapters in this book that conceptualizing what a discipline 'is' is, in fact, problematic and contested. This is never more so than for the subjects which make up the Arts and Humanities. Some would be considered (irresponsibly) non-vocational, abstract subjects (for example, Classics, Literature Studies, Philosophy, History, Religious Studies, Film and Media Studies) and some applied ones (such as Theology, Psychology, Geography, Archaeology, Foreign Language Studies). For those of us who work underneath the umbrella of the Arts and Humanities, we are more likely to identify our distinct subjects as our disciplines rather than associate ourselves explicitly with an Arts/Humanities sobriquet. Mary Henkel (2000) has also illustrated that the sense of disciplinary cohesion is not the same for all the disciplines represented here. Historians, apparently, have a stronger sense of being part of a disciplinary community than scholars in English literature, for example.

The problem is not that we identify with our disciplines but that when push comes to shove we try to protect our community with inferred rules that seem rigid: 'teaching should be done this way', 'students should be able to do such and such', 'the content needs to be covered before they can get a handle on the broader questions at stake'. Our, often tacit, collective fantasy of what our disciplines are has the power to influence how we think learning should occur within our subjects. Of course once we get to a point of stating how our subjects *should* be learned it becomes much harder to understand how our diverse student body actually learns. From this position it is not hard to see why Baxter Magolda feels the need to remind us that accessing the students' frame of reference is important in creating a supportive learning environment.

There is another disciplinary constraint to implementing Baxter-Magolda's ideas: the beliefs we identify as notions of authority, power, expertise and position with a disciplinary setting. In proposing we create learning partnership models in higher education settings, Baxter-Magolda suggests that to do so we need to define learning as mutually constructing meaning and enable students to share authority and expertise with their peers and us. The question here is, *are we, as members of disciplines, willing to reframe our role as authorities in order to enable learners to become authorities?* Put simply the answer is, *yes, sometimes.*

Perhaps the most important structure that militates against this is the higher education system itself. Academic acquisition of expertise occurs within exposure to social practices that both value and reinforce the notion that we are specialists. When it comes to challenging our own experience of our authority, these social practices, with their hierarchies of degrees and threshold requirements for academic employment, are arguably as powerful as our identification with our disciplines (though it is difficult to see the two as separable). Undergraduate learning of an Arts discipline is predicated on a power dynamic established between those who have a length of exposure to the discipline, proven relative mastery of the subject matter, and signs of authority (such of degrees, titles, rooms on campus) and those who, relatively, do not. In this there is no getting away from the fact that we do occupy positions of authority. In a way, our authority isn't the issue, it's (i) how we collectively use it to establish structures that cut students off from the subject, and (ii) how, as individuals, we use it with our students. To a certain extent Baxter Magolda is saying this in her focus on the three principles. If we value the students' capabilities, access their frames of reference when redesigning programs and courses, and if we see learning as mutually constructing meaning arguably we will both collectively and individually enact these.

However, there is always the possibility that we hold these beliefs, but *do* something slightly different. *Do the methods of instruction we perhaps claim as disciplinary, genuinely encourage dialogue between ourselves and our students, at the same time as providing spaces in which the students are pushed to become more self-confident?* This question is not to detract from the point I made earlier about our *a priori* understanding of the interconnectedness between the various methods of instruction and the general environment in which our students learn. It is, however, to point out that sometimes we consciously believe learning occurs as a relationship between ourselves and the students at the same time as practicing teaching models that seem in their nature to eschew those beliefs. If this is so, we have taken a detour into accepting that we act as we perceive rather than the direct route of alignment where what we believe is acted out in actual practice.

For example, I have a disciplinary background in History. I perceive lectures and seminars as a relative mainstay for the engagement with the subject at an undergraduate level. Within the design of my sessions, because I also believe in establishing dialogue with my students, I will (i) utilize a variety of approaches so that the lectures are not entirely didactic, (ii) try not to lead the seminars by establishing tasks that remove me from student discussion. I even ask my students about why they like or dislike the subject I teach. I am fairly confident that most students pick up the complexities of historical meaning construction in this and their surrounding university environment. However, I also accept the disciplinary norm of the '*essay which responds to a thorny historical issue*' as appropriate assessment, the situations in which I teach are relatively one-dimensional and, in the main, I control what they look like.

To genuinely give up some authority I would need to negotiate forms of assessment, design of sessions (both in terms of what we do and where we do it) with the students, as well as encouraging student involvement in my research projects where they related to areas the students identified as of interest. Anything else would, for me, be tokenism. The first two are, of course, logistic nightmares and as much to do with the institutional infrastructure as the discipline (though as I suggest below, they are not impossible). The third is doable yet is the one that is most often left out of the equation. And, with respect to Baxter Magolda's suggestions, perhaps it is here, on the crossroads between our teacher and researcher roles, that the real disciplinary tension lies. Arguably, were we to open up the research processes to our undergraduates and expose them to a variety of research and institutional situations through these processes, we would be able to provide the range of 'unknown' individual and social circumstances likely to offer the development of intellectual and interpersonal maturity outlined by Baxter Magolda.

None of this detracts from the idea that our disciplines are significant and in that significance given authority. Our identification with a discipline is not, of course, just about bolstering our own authoritative position within it, but also about managing the sheer amount of knowledge we are required to master. Discipline identification allows for parameter setting in a world of ever expanding information. Even specialization has its limits.

Bile and Bureaucracy: Engaging with University Organizational Structures

In their chapters, both Baxter Magolda (Chapter 12) and Trowler (Chapter 15) touch on the impediments to change provided by our key occupational environments: our departments and our institutions. How do these pressures manifest themselves? I would suggest they break down into at least three themes.

The first can be referred to as daily communication activities. These are the common verbal utterances that express personal feelings but also generate an environment which impacts on how we come to perceive both our institution's and our students' capabilities. Typical examples of these might be, 'that can't be done'; 'we used to be able to expect such and such from the students'. Phrases such as these can be demoralizing and powerful, especially if you are new to a department and only just getting to know the processes for program and course design within the institution. This sort of bile might be quite cathartic in the face of the tensions caused by workplace change-overload, but a surfeit of it will invariably lead to motivation heartburn. Collective beliefs expressed in such daily communication activities simplify and caricature situations of complexity. *What conversational frameworks do you use and does your department privilege when any attempts are made to interpret lack of interest or motivation in the subject on the part of the students?* Of course, student expectations of the department and the peer culture with respect to learning also play their part. Just as we may be liable to caricaturing the situations in which we find ourselves, so are the students (Gregory, 2007). Moreover, introducing new or untried approaches to the learning environment often leads to conservative responses (at least initially) from students.

The second theme is: priorities, workload models, heads of department and bureaucracy. If the departmental culture is predicated on research excellence the level of openness from other colleagues with respect to enhancing the learning environment can be restricted if not downright obstructive. Moreover, you may have your own priorities with respect to research that mean you not only identify with departmental colleagues but also wish to see the culture maintained. Often this sort of culture will be embedded within the workload model being employed by a school or department (if it has one). Indeed, even where the perception exists that promotion occurs through merit in the full range of academic responsibilities (research, teaching, administration or service) the workload model may privilege one area to the detriment of the others. If this is so in your department, it would be unethical to suggest that you reprioritize to increase a teaching role, but there can be no doubt that without the restructuring of priorities and the attendant support that would need to come to assist this, implementing a more holistic approach to the learning environment within a department is tricky.

Consequently heads of department have some (but not universal) power to assist any recon-figuration of the learning relationships. Even a cursory glance at research on group dynamics makes it quite clear that a head of department influences departmental culture. A head of department who is genuinely interested in teaching is going to be far less of a constraint than one whose primary (if not only) focus is on research. Perhaps, the constraint that impacts the most on new members of academic staff attempting to implement Baxter Magolda's model is the professional variability of senior staff with respect to the undergraduate learning environment. This, however, is not specifically a disciplinary issue, but a wider institutional one. (It is clear though that fields such as English literature and History have been less open to engaging with learning and teaching issues as subjects for worthy debate, so there may well be a relative disciplinary impact in terms of how heads of department in these areas relate to attempts to implement changes (Calder, Cutler, & Kelly, 2002; Huber & Hutchings, 2005; Salvatori & Donahue, 2002).)

In the context of this point, resistance to applying Baxter Magolda's model also relates to the links between assessment design, departmental values of particular assessments, and the quality assurance (QA) processes that often reassert these values. What Baxter Magolda suggests is not just about exposure to alternative situations in which learning occurs, it is also about providing chances to reflect on these different situations both formally and informally. It is not enough just to provide experiences which provoke a range of responses to alternative situations. These responses need to be reflected upon at least in part within assessment procedures. The departmental culture of what is appropriate and manageable in terms of assessment from both a disciplinary set of assumptions as well as a general level of self-belief in what we as academics are capable of assessing is critical here. If our concerns are then embodied in a QA process it can become almost impossible for new lecturers to effect change. The most obvious examples of this are the debates that occur within departmental learning and teaching committees about the relative weighting of different types of assessment. Are essays really the mainstay of an Arts and Humanities education, for example? They tend to be weighted as such. Perhaps the uncomfortable question to ask here then is, *do we collude with a departmental culture because it is easier and possibly more sensible in terms of our own career progression, or do we act independently to effect enhancement of the learning environment where we feel it is necessary?*

The third theme relevant to this discussion is: relationships between departments and their institutional setting. Negotiations between Arts and Humanities departments and their institution's management are *not* always fraught with conflicts. Nonetheless, management in the Higher Education sector generally has undergone considerable change and expansion in the last two decades. The associated funding challenges and rhetoric of accountability that have driven the change seem to have led to a less harmonious relationship between those identified as 'academics' and those identified as 'managers' (Deem, 2006). In actuality, there are so many differences in today's higher education from that of two decades ago that comparisons seem to lead to a mythologizing nostalgia of some golden age (Tierney, 2003). Arguably, the relationships now being negotiated are different, less well known, and based upon diverging expectations than those in place before the expansion of higher education.

Crudely put, there are at least four potential clash points between the two groups and any one of them can obstruct implementing the learning partnership model: ideological opposition, use of buildings, academic development strategies, and money. The first and fourth of these are complex. There is so much variation within these two in terms of individual views and institutional differences (historical, culture, financial) that a single paragraph in one chapter could not do them justice. The second potential area for conflict is more easily accessible and perhaps of more relevance if the reader is reasonably new to an academic post. It strikes me that what Baxter Magolda is actually asking of us is both to reconfigure our authority at the same time as offering a variety of multi-dimensional learning environments. It is here that the greatest constraints lie for individual members of disciplines because this is where disciplinary associations, institutional realities and pedagogical desires cross. Let us take the Arts-type seminar for example. For me, it is within this discursive environment that the students really come to terms with the materials of my subject. Though I may signpost the contradictory arguments of a topic in lectures, I hope that the students will 'own' these arguments in the seminar and debate their relative pros and cons with each other. To enable this I might set up a series of questions that require discussion, or I might get the students to establish the questions as they discuss the topic, or I might just depend on one or two students delivering presentations and then hope a debate ensues. Arguably, these methods could be seen as formalizing progression, with me establishing questions in the first year (a modeling process), the students establishing questions collaboratively in the second year, and then the students individually both establishing and answering their own questions in the Honors years. Instinctively, I like this design. I think it will lead to the students understanding the essentials of the subject at an undergraduate level. Whilst facilitating the seminars I'll try to exhibit the principles of support at the same time as pushing the students towards the unknown aspects of the subject. Fortunately, I have access to teaching rooms that allow me to do this. Some of them even have the equipment to allow students to develop visual presentations. I am dependent on a room booking service, so this is variable, but in the main I can normally ensure somewhere for seminar work.

However, if we take Baxter Magolda seriously, she is pointing out that perhaps it isn't enough to just focus on environments to create meaning in our subject matter, we also need to consider whether the social situations in which learning occur are varied enough to expose students to the need for a range of interpersonal responses dependent on situation. The physical environments in which the learning takes place are therefore important here. The typical seminar room as well as the seminar design is only one such environment, abstract and educational. Effectively we give our students exposure to the same social situation over and over again. If we want to generate simulations of other settings then arguably we need alternative architectural contexts.

Perhaps a useful reflective question here is, *do we use the physical infrastructure as an excuse not to create alternative learning situations?* My own answer to this would probably be, 'it's not quite as simple as that'. It isn't just about the buildings, it also reflects my own limited, discipline-focused, experience of educational social settings. I'm just not that confident that I would know what other settings might look like. As I suggested earlier such an answer is illustrative of how disciplinary associations, institutional realities and pedagogical desires meet. Of course, alternative practices such as disputations, collaborative presentations, re-enactment of key areas of academic debate as court cases, student enactments of applied disciplinary projects, and simulations of other professional environments are all manageable within traditional lecture and seminar rooms, but we probably need to find out how to do them ourselves first.

This then ties us into the third of the headings I listed above, academic development strategies and, more specifically, our engagement with those folk who are interested in how to foster effective learning environments. *To what extent do we seek out academic/faculty developers to discuss how to implement different approaches such as that proposed by Baxter Magolda? Do we allow identification with a discipline to act as a barrier to multi-disciplinary approaches to student learning environments?* Our resistance to seeking advice and dialogue with other academics from outside of our departments and disciplinary background is of importance. However, so are the strategies and approaches taken by academic development units in our institutions. Arguably, the academic development units' members need to model the principles and challenges suggested by Baxter Magolda.

Conclusions: Red Herrings and Ethics

It was noted earlier that some of our criticisms of Magolda Baxter might be red herrings that deflect us from the more central question of how we can enhance our students' learning. Indeed, by seeing our engagement with Baxter Magolda's ideas as an intellectual exercise we end up losing the bigger picture, which suggests to me that we see our environments as 'single situational'. We respond as critical students in a classroom, one approach in one social environment. How do we vary this approach to recognize that different situations may call for different approaches? This after all, is the sort of question we might wish to start with when we come to redesign courses and curriculum using Baxter Magolda's model for programs. Her point surely is that our students leave university with a variety of intellectual attributes but these are often not matched by those dimensions (individual self-awareness and effective relationship interactions) needed to respond to the variety of situations in which our students find themselves. Is this what we in the Arts and Humanities do? Elsewhere Baxter Magolda has noted that in new situations students fall back into borrowing from external sources to generate how they should act rather than constructing new ways of acting relevant to the given situation (Baxter Magolda, 2004, p. 71). *Have we gained so much intellectual and social maturity in our disciplines that we enact the same approaches whatever the situation (even situations that are outside disciplinary requirements)?* This is important because if that is what we mirror in our disciplinary learning and teaching then we need to consider the efficacy of such an approach in terms of student outcomes.

Furthermore, whilst there is some comfort to be gleaned from disciplinary membership, there are also some negative side-effects. Identification with a discipline is powerful for many, even when it is clear that there is no intellectual cohesion agreed by all or even the majority of the members of a discipline. Being part of a self-identified group in which we become expert at certain social and intellectual practices is fun. However, our resistance to look outside our fields for advice may be fuelled by that self-identification. Certainly, the tacit hierarchies of which subjects are more important in the Arts and Humanities than others can be a real barrier to engaging in multi-disciplinary work. This is further magnified when we act out of implicit or even explicit value judgments about fields outside of our Arts and Humanities background. As was pointed out earlier, to implement different learning environments we might need to look elsewhere to learn about alternative ways of generating them. My final question then is thus to do with the ethics of academic inter-professionalism: *What are the professional ethics of not listening to educationalists when we are employed, in part at least, as educators?*

References

Barrie, S. (2006). Academics' Understandings of Generic Graduate Attributes: A Conceptual Basis for Lifelong Learning. In P. Hager & S. Holland (Eds.), *Graduate Attributes, Learning and Employability* (pp. 149–168). Dordrecht, NL: Springer.

Bassnett, S. (2002). Is There Hope for the Humanities in the 21st Century? *Arts and Humanities in Higher Education*, 1(1), 101–110.

Baxter Magolda, M. (2004). *Making their Own Way.* Sterling, VA: Stylus Publishing.

Calder, L., Cutler, W. & Kelly, T. (2002). History Lessons: Historians and the Scholarship of Teaching and Learning. In M. Huber & S. Morreale (Eds.), *Disciplinary Styles in the Scholarship of Teaching and Learning: Exploring the Common Ground* (pp. 45–69). Washington, D.C.: American Association for Higher Education and the Carnegie Foundation for the Advancement of Teaching.

Deem, R. (2006). Changing Research Perspectives on the Management of Higher Education: Can Research Permeate the Activities of Manager-Academics? *Higher Education Quarterly*, 60(3), 203–228.

Gregory, M. (2007). Real Teaching and Real Learning vs Narrative Myths about Education. *Arts and Humanities in Higher Education*, 6(1), 7–27.

Hager, P., & Holland, S. (Eds.) (2006). *Graduate Attributes, Learning and Employability.* Dordrecht: Springer.

Harpham, G. (2005). Beneath and Beyond the "Crisis in the Humanities". *New Literary History*, 36(1), 21–36.

Henkel, M. (2000). *Academic Identities and Policy Change in Higher Education.* Higher Education Policy Series: 46. London: Jessica Kingsley.

Huber, M., & Hutchings, P. (2005). *The Advancement of Learning: Building the Teaching Commons.* The Carnegie Foundation for the Advancement of Teaching. San Francisco: Jossey-Bass.

Kember, D. (1997). A Reconceptualisation of the Research into University Academics' Conceptions of Teaching. *Learning and Instruction*, 7(3), 255–275.

Salvatori, M., & Donahue, P. (2002). English Studies in the Scholarship of Teaching. In M. Huber & S. Morreale (Eds.), *Disciplinary Styles in the Scholarship of Teaching and Learning: Exploring the Common Ground* (pp. 69–87). Washington, D.C.: American Association for Higher Education and the Carnegie Foundation for the Advancement of Teaching.

Tierney, W. (2003). Cultural Disintegration and the Decline of the Engaged Intellectual: the transformation of academic work. *Discourse*, 24(3), 371–383.

Zukas, M. & Malcolm, J. (2000). Pedagogies for Lifelong Learning: Building Bridges or Building Walls. Accessed May 5, 2008 at http://www.open.ac.uk/lifelong-learning/papers/.

VI
Disciplines and Their Interactions with Teaching and Learning Regimes

15

Beyond Epistemological Essentialism
Academic Tribes in the Twenty-First Century[1]

Paul Trowler

Lancaster University, UK

Introduction

This chapter concentrates on change in higher education, in particular the enhancement of teaching and learning there. The approach adopted is rooted in policy sociology, whose interests lie in looking at policy formation and policy "implementation"[2] and in exploring the relationship between them and any gaps between expectations and outcomes. Underneath the specific discussion of the chapter lies one of the classic issues of sociology: the interplay between structural and agentic factors in social reality and social change. On the structural side lies the power of disciplines to condition the behavior of academics, their practices, values and attitudes. On the agentic side lie questions of narrativity, identity construction and power plays. Social worlds are both constructed and enacted, both agentic and structural in character. Janet Donald notes in Chapter 3 that students bring their world to the lecture theatre. This chapter emphasizes that faculty also bring their worlds to teaching contexts. It is true that the epistemological differences between disciplines are important: disciplines have different ways of thinking and practicing (see in particular Chapters 6, 7 and 8 in this volume), different tribes inhabiting the different disciplinary territories, and in this sense the structural power of discipline is important. But so are other structural factors such as educational ideologies and the influences of early socialization. As well as structure though, agency is important and for this reason we should be wary of making generalizations about the inhabitants of disciplinary territories: agency means that the regularities imposed by social structures are always provisional. This is especially true when we attempt to generalize about practices and attitudes less closely tied to the knowledge characteristics of disciplines such as some of those associated with teaching, learning and assessment.

---

1 A version of this paper has been published as Trowler, P. (2006) Academic Tribes: their significance in enhancement processes. *Proceedings of Utvecklingskonferensen 2005 in Karlstad.* Lund: University of Lund, pages 15–24.

2 The scare quotes here indicate that one should beware of seeing the implementation process as separate from the formulation process because policy is formed in the implementation of it.

Empirical Background to this Chapter

The ideas in this chapter are based on a number of previous studies of mine, details of which can be found on my website, referenced in the bibliography (Trowler, 2005). Here though I am drawing particularly on the initial results of research conducted in South Africa in the early part of 2005. This was a study of a single university which had recently been created as a result of the merger of four smaller institutions. These had been very different in size, resources, student body and historical background. Two of the larger sites contrasted particularly starkly. One had historically been a disadvantaged and predominantly black university, the other historically a white very advantaged university. Two smaller, more specialized campuses were also included in the merger, each with a very distinctive identity. The interest for me in conducting interviews and focus group studies across these campuses was in the new "common curriculum". The senior management team of the merged university had instructed now-merged (but previously separate) subject departments teaching on different campuses to adopt a common subject content. How would lawyers on one campus negotiate a common curriculum with lawyers on another when both had been teaching somewhat different subjects in sometimes quite different ways in very different contexts? Where would the differences lie? What factors other than the knowledge structures of the disciplines would affect the movement towards a common curriculum? To what extent would a common curriculum be achieved? And how far was the agency of people within the universities significant in all of this process compared to structural factors?

As a research site I reasoned that this higher education environment – quite different and in a sense more "exaggerated" than that of the UK – would allow me to see more vividly phenomena that exist elsewhere but take a more muted form. As an outsider too I would be able to see things a little more clearly than would be the case in an environment which had become naturalized for me, the UK higher education scene. The site is not a "typical" one of course, but is highly illuminative of change processes.

The Nature of Epistemological Essentialism

Epistemological essentialism suggests that knowledge characteristics represent a key driving force of social life with other factors being epiphenomenal. Thus, for example, the influence of academics' backgrounds is seen as insignificant compared to their socialization into the knowledge characteristics of their discipline, their epistemological features: "Characteristics imported into the academic profession by individual members from their personal background and prior experiences . . . [are] . . . the least important components of academic culture" (Clark, 1987, p. 107)

In the study of higher education there is considerable literature based on this essentialist thinking (Clark, 1987; Davidson, 1994; Gregg, 1996; Lodahl & Gordon, 1972; Ruscio, 1987; Shinn, 1982). Perhaps the most famous is Tony Becher's 1989 study *Academic Tribes and Territories*. Here knowledge structures, the epistemological core, are fully explained. The argument is that they have a cognitive dimension (elaborated by Kolb, 1981 and Biglan, 1973) and a social dimension (developed by Becher himself).

The *cognitive* dimension divides disciplines into hard and soft, pure and applied, to give a four-cell matrix. Hard disciplines have well-developed theory, universal laws, causal propositions, they are cumulative and have generalizable findings. Soft disciplines by contrast have unclear boundaries, relatively unspecified theoretical structure, are subject to fashions and have loosely defined problems. Pure disciplines are self-regulating and not directly applied to the professions or problems in the outside world, while applied disciplines are regulated by external influence to some extent (for example the Law Society) and are more applied within the professions and to problems.

The *social* dimension again offers a four-cell matrix. This time the axes run between convergent and divergent on the one hand and urban and rural on the other. Convergent disciplines have uniform standards and a relatively stable elite. Divergent disciplines sustain more intellectual and deviance and frequently experience attempts to shift standards. Urban disciplines are characterized by intense interaction and a high people-to-problem ratio. Rural ones have bigger territories, less interaction and a lower people-to-problem ratio.

Combining these epistemic features it appears possible to say that physics for example is hard, pure, convergent and urban. Sociology is soft, pure, divergent and rural. Engineering is hard, applied, convergent and urban. Economics is hard, applied, convergent and rural.

Or not. The problem with this kind of categorization is that while it seems to make sense when disciplines are viewed through the wrong end of a telescope, from a great distance, the distinctions begin to fall apart in the analytical hand when one looks at disciplines close up. The fractures within them become very apparent when the analyst steps out of the helicopter, as do the similarities between what – from a great height – seemed very different subdisciplinary areas. However, this is not the place for a critique of the validity or heuristic power of the Kolb/Biglan and Becher depiction of epistemological structure.

Knowledge and Culture

Assuming for current purposes that this description characterizes the epistemological core – the Territories of Becher's book – then what of the cultural epiphenomena, the Tribes? Becher talks about the hierarchies found within the different disciplines, the gatekeeping practices, the nature of innovations within them, communication patterns, career trajectories and life patterns of faculty in different disciplines. He and other authors even talk about issues such as office decoration differences and the kind of sports and other leisure pastimes preferred by the different tribes:

> Although it was not part of my purpose to enquire into the private, as against the professional, lives of those I met, it was . . . apparent from the incidental remarks they made that the physicists were inclined towards an interest in the theatre, art and music, whereas the engineers' typical leisure activities included aviation, deep-sea diving and 'messing about in boats'. The biologists, along with the historians, tended to the view that theirs was 'a discipline for loners'.
>
> (Becher, 1989, p. 106)

Becher argues that the ways in which particular groups of faculty organize their professional lives are related in important ways to the intellectual tasks on which they are engaged. But sometimes he and other authors go beyond professional lives, or move into areas of professional life that have only tangential connection to those intellectual tasks. One author, for example, argues that there is a link between disciplinary epistemological structure and conceptions of quality: "All in all there seems to be a certain basic difference in conceptions of quality especially between the soft, rural and divergent disciplinary areas and the hard, urban and convergent disciplinary fields" (Kekäle, 2002, p. 73). One could even argue that approaches to leadership are similarly conditioned:

> Soft, pure, divergent and rural disciplines [like sociology] . . . dislike efficient, hard result-oriented management at least partly because it provides inequality or seems to be against democracy and equal opportunities in decision-making. . . .
>
> [In hard, pure, convergent and urban disciplines] . . . the exact methods and the hard convergent nature of the disciplinary knowledge seem to provide clearer guidelines for management and academic work. The approach to leadership seems not be critical, but pragmatic and straight-forward, sometimes even technical.
>
> (Kekäle, 1999, pp. 232–3)

Prima facie it seems more reasonable, though, to suggest that there are important differences in what students learn, including the kinds of discourse they learn to use, ways of acting, and even sets of attitudes, ways of thinking and practicing (WTP) as Entwistle (2005) and McCune and Hounsell (2005) and others put it: "coming to terms with particular understandings, forms of discourse, values or ways of acting which are regarded as central to graduate-level mastery of a discipline or subject area" (McCune & Hounsell, 2005).

It is unclear in these kinds of accounts, though, where the boundaries of epistemological influence might lie. Ylijoki goes much further than McCune and Hounsell when she talks about the disciplinary 'moral order', perhaps too far:

> Besides the common cognitive basis, disciplines have their own social and cultural characteristics: norms, values, modes of interaction, lifestyle, pedagogical and ethical codes. . . . The socialisation of students basically involves a successful commitment to the moral order of the disciplinary culture of the study field . . . The moral order constitutes . . . what is considered to be good, right, desirable and valued as opposed to what is regarded as bad, wrong, avoidable and despised.
>
> (Ylijoki, 2000, pp. 339 and 341)

For the purposes of this chapter my interest is in the linkages between disciplines and learning, teaching and assessment practices. I argue below that one goes too far in suggesting that teaching, learning and assessment practices are uniformly and reliably closely tied to epistemological structure. Looking at the literature on this – which is diverse and frustratingly unstructured – one can see claims about linkages in the following areas among others:

- Teachers' interactions with students
- Teaching methods employed
- Goals of education
- Theories of teaching and learning
- Orientations to students
- Conceptions of quality in TLA
- Moral orders of studying
- Faculty's approaches to assessment instruments
- Place of student opinion in TLA
- Students' appreciation of lectures/formal tuition

Quite what the mechanism of linkage is and how strong the link is often only vaguely elaborated, if at all. Some of the terms used to describe their linkage and what is linked illustrate this: they range from relatively "soft" terms such as "preferences", "styles", "rituals", "tendencies", "conceptions" to harder ones such as "approaches" or "practices".

The epistemological essentialist argument in relation to teaching, learning and assessment is made perhaps most strongly by Ruth Neumann and others (Neumann 2001; Neumann et al., 2002; Neumann, 2003): "academics in soft applied disciplines are open to collaborative teaching; and as in hard applied fields . . . [have] a concern for comprehensive coverage of theory and the acquisition of practical skills . . ." (Neumann et al., 2002, p. 411); "In general teaching methods in soft pure disciplines are in smaller groups . . ." (Neumann, 2003, p. 233). The following table summarizes some of the claimed differences between the disciplines in teaching, learning and assessment in Neumann's work:

There are many problems with these kinds of generalizations, and they center around the power of structures other than discipline as well as the agentic role of individuals and groups to chart their own course in teaching and learning practices.

Table 15.1 Linking epistemological characteristics and learning, teaching, assessment and curriculum

Teaching, learning and assessment differences	Hard, Pure, Convergent, Urban	Soft, Applied, Divergent, Rural
Common assessment instruments:	Multiple-choice, closely focused exam	Open exam, coursework, continuous assessment
Marking practices:	Guides to assessment criteria	Intuitive marking
Student's skills development:	Skills and logical reasoning	Critical ability, fluency, creativity
Teaching approaches:	Presentational techniques	Face-to-face settings
Use of ICT:	ICT applications extensive	Limited ICT applications
Curricular structure:	Linear progression in curriculum	Spiral curriculum
Student group work:	Small groups work on predetermined problems	Small groups work discursively

Why Does It Matter?

Determining the limits of the power of knowledge structures is important for reasons beyond simple academic interest. How significant one considers disciplinary differences to be conditions policy and practice in a number of areas in higher education. These revolve around the question of genericism versus disciplinarity. In the UK for example, attempts to enhance teaching and learning have taken both the generic and the disciplinary approaches, articulated in quite separate organizational structures. The Learning and Teaching Support Network included 24 subject centers based in universities each designed to enhance teaching and learning in their subject area, a clear disciplinary approach. The Institute for Learning and Teaching in Higher Education, by contrast, took a generic approach – looking for ways of enhancing teaching and learning across the system as a whole. These organizations were merged into the Higher Education Academy, but this was not an easy process. Genericism versus disciplinarity became a highly contentious and political topic.

At an institutional level, educational development courses for new faculty and others may similarly adopt a generic or a disciplinary-specific approach. The textbooks they draw on have in fact been criticized for not distinguishing enough between the disciplines in terms of the recommendations made or examples used (McGuinness, 1997).

Furthermore different disciplines have different capacities, for example in grant-getting, student recruitment and so on. Being able to make such distinctions is important for institutional management, particularly at a time when managerialist approaches are predominant. A more subtle "market gardening" rather than an homogenized "agribusiness" approach to the management of different disciplines and their institutional realization in departments is important. So for each of these purposes and others, being clear about the nature and limits of disciplinary differences and their effects is very significant.

Re-conceptualizing the Significance of Disciplines

An alternative way of seeing disciplines is as significant, but as only one structural factor amongst several and as mediated by agency. From this perspective disciplinary cultures are conceptualized as open, natural systems which are influenced multi-causally. Seeing disciplines as having a structural character but also being constructed by the narratives of those within them is important too: the stories faculty tell each other about disciplines and subdisciplines are very significant and help create a kind of reality themselves.

Because narratives about and identification with disciplines are such significant factors in higher education, the evaluation of the national Learning and Teaching Support Network confirmed the wisdom of taking a disciplinary approach to the enhancement of teaching and learning in higher education. But the evaluators were clear that this was not because disciplines themselves are intrinsically important, rather because faculty *consider them* to be important:

> The policy of trying to enhance quality through using subject networks, which was tried in various ways before the inception of the LTSN, seems to us to be working. Importantly, it has 'buy-in' from teachers who are skeptical of other approaches to quality enhancement . . . Our first annual report . . . identified the most commonly deployed argument in favor of a subject-based approach as essentially a social or cultural one, emphasizing the importance of disciplinary networks and peer groups. . . .
>
> These arguments suggested that academics seeking guidance about teaching will tend to give most credibility to peers from their discipline and are skeptical of what they may see as platitudinous generic educational advice. This view, held widely by Subject Centre staff, does not appear to rest on a belief that teaching and learning issues are fundamentally different in each subject area. We suggested that the arguments we heard for a subject-centred approach were fundamentally about *method* (specifically, the desirability of naturalistic interactions with teaching colleagues) and not about *content* (what one might talk about in these interactions).
>
> (LTSN, 2002)

Teaching and Learning Regimes in Higher Education

My argument, then, is that context is very significant in conditioning how disciplinary differences are articulated: context is the territory in which disciplines are performed. This is alluded to in the chapter by Hounsell and Anderson in which they discuss how disciplinary practices are mediated by lecturers, interpreted by students and enabled or constrained by specific contexts. One very significant aspect of context is *culture*. Here culture is seen not as a product of discipline but as dialectically related to it, and to other structural factors. However the problem with that concept is that it usually has jelly-like characteristics: it is very hard to pin down. Also it applies to the whole range of practices, values, attitudes and taken-for-granted assumptions, not just those to do with teaching, learning and assessment. To address these twin problems of the analytically diaphanous and all-encompassing nature of the concept of culture I prefer to use the much more specific notion of teaching and learning regimes.

This notion is rooted in the theoretical turn towards socio-cultural theory, particularly communities of practice and activity systems. Unlike them, though, teaching and learning regimes are focused on only one area of activity and there is no assumption of shared sets of values and attitudes: power, conflict and diversity are almost always found within teaching and learning regimes. Another difference is that teaching and learning regimes are predominantly analytical rather than substantive in nature: a form of "ideal type" in Weber's sense. Looking at teaching and learning regimes represents the choice – choosing a "figure" on which to focus and thus at the same time setting what becomes defined as "ground" into the background. This is 'only analytical' for two reasons – doing this separates out what are in practice intimately connected phenomena, and the focus on teaching and learning regimes represents only one choice of focus out of multiple possibilities. The purpose of doing this though is to deconstruct relevant aspects of culture at the local (departmental or workgroup) level in order to illuminate relevant aspects of context and so understand the likely prospects of change there and how the enhancement of practice may be achieved more effectively.

I suggest that one can identify eight "moments" in teaching and learning regimes, dynamic and interrelated dimensions which together give to a particular context a unique configuration which is significant when innovation is attempted. These are: tacit assumptions; implicit theories (of teaching learning and assessment); recurrent practices; conventions of appropriateness; codes of signification; discursive repertoires; subjectivities in interaction; and power relations. They are listed separately in this way for heuristic purposes. The disadvantage of doing this is to lose the essential inter-connectedness that binds them together.

If teaching and learning regimes are the figure that we choose for analytical purposes, then what of the "ground"? In relation to contextual characteristics of significance in the enhancement of teaching and learning, significant dimensions of context behind teaching and learning regimes include: leadership characteristics locally and institutionally; competing agendas that are current in relation to teaching and learning; Great Culture (wide cultural characteristics of the environment); institutional characteristics, including corporate culture; and of course disciplinary characteristics and narratives about them. It is important to note that both figure and ground instantiate not only structural but agentic factors, that is, they exhibit features which are both enacted *and* constructed.

Let me make a few further points about teaching and learning regimes before I go on to illustrate the eight moments using examples from the South African study I referred to earlier. First they are not necessarily cohesive, and in fact rarely are so. One respondent told me that in his department there were "more factions than people", yet the notion of a teaching and learning regime is still applicable because the context he refers to displays a unique and dynamic configuration which could be described in terms of the eight moments.

But, secondly, it is important to see that sometimes even where there are many factions there are also some shared assumptions and practices underneath, though these are sometimes "smaller", harder to see. One anthropologist has referred to conflicts within cultures as being only "ethno-graphic dazzle" – obvious characteristics which hit the observer in the face but which hide the "real" situation of consensus underneath (Fox, 1980). To prioritize consensus over diversity in that way is an error. Both exist and both need to be accorded equal analytic weight. So, for example, in a teaching and learning regime there may be divisions over the relative priority that should be given to teaching versus research, while in the same context there is a taken-for-granted acceptance about the kinds of students that should be admitted or about assessment instruments that are most appropriate.

In terms of the boundaries of teaching and learning regimes, one cannot in practice determine where they lie: teaching and learning regimes, like the characteristics of culture generally, are vertically nested, and horizontally multiple. They are open, not bounded, although they are often bounded perceptually: identity at both the individual and group level comes from identifying what we *are not* as well as what we are, in drawing largely imaginary boundaries around ourselves (Woodward, 1997). And in relation to that, teaching and learning regimes themselves are subject to narrativity which influences their character in important ways: "back-stories" which participants tell each other about their history have significant influences on current practices as those under-the-stage talk, where close colleagues share gossip and scandal. Finally, it follows from what I have said above that teaching and learning regimes are in a state of provisional stability – any description of them is true only for now.

Let me now illustrate each of the eight moments using examples from the South African study.

Tacit Assumptions

One of the characteristics of teaching and learning regimes in particular and culture in general is that they categorize reality in particular ways: they "sort things out" (Bowker and Star, 1999). One respondent noted that in his context faculty believe they just "know" what "proper" academics are, and what they are not. Thus someone with a student academic development function, tasked to improve students' academic literacy, is simply not considered a "proper academic". This categorization has a number of implications for their position and power in university.

Similarly there are sets of assumptions about the nature of 'our' discipline and the relationship it should have with the outside world. One head of department noted that faculty in the department unquestioningly assumed that contact with industry would "pollute" their students with uncritical and task-focused approaches, and so should be avoided:

> "One of the things, one of the other things that departments like ours in this country can get split about is do we work with industry or not? . . . My sense is that we need to be a lot more like law or medicine where the profession has a positive link with us, not this view that advertisers are evil. You know, there's a wonderful Auden poem:
>
> > *Thou shalt not be on friendly terms*
> > *with guys in advertising firms**
>
> But my contact in advertising, John, is wonderfully critical, and also wonderfully generous with ideas, and I think academics can get so possessive and anal about ideas. But when I go to John we talk openly, and he gives me five good ideas and maybe I give him five good ideas."

A third example comes from law. On one campus of the newly merged institution a "pure" approach was taken to legal education: students got the diet of law, and law only. On another campus students were exposed to courses on philosophy, literature, etc. Neither questioned what they did until exposed to the other. At that point faculty from the latter campus criticized the former for producing "legal barbarians", but at the same time began to reflect on their own assumptions.

Implicit Theories of Teaching and Learning

There was a clear division among my South African respondents between those who believed in innate student ability which was more or less immutable, and those who believed that student performance was heavily conditioned by their background and was malleable. Clearly, in South Africa there are still huge divisions between advantaged and disadvantaged students. These two implicit theories about the nature of student ability each have very contrasting implications for practice: should students be left to essentially sink or swim in the higher education context? (those with natural ability will, after all, survive, those without would fail anyway, from one of these points of view); should there be very strong provision of student support to counteract disadvantage?; or should there be much more radical changes to the higher education curriculum and practices to make it a more hospitable environment for disadvantaged students who come with different types of cultural capital?

One of my respondents gave a specific illustration of how practices changed when implicit theories about these issues were challenged:

> "We had a member of staff, a theoretician, who, when he came here said – 'Standards are the key thing – we should select our students and leave them to sink or swim. I'm the only person around here who's maintaining standards and I shall maintain standards.' He came from an American situation and had to have the difficulties of certain groups of students in South Africa pointed out to him. Once he realised this he changed his position. . . . We looked through our materials, our workbooks. We found examples about the . . . walls of an igloo. Many of our black students didn't know what an igloo was! We even got to the point of talking about the processes in a photographic plate in a camera. We eradicated these culturally based examples – has there been a transformation in teaching our discipline. Decidedly, yes."

---

*Reproduced courtesy of Cambridge University Press

Recurrent Practices

Recurrent practices are those which are performed habitually and in an unconsidered way, it is simply taken for granted that "this is what we do around here". One example is the use of lectures to transmit material to students. In some disciplines in some contexts this is a recurrent practice, stereotypically in maths and physics. Yet one physicist I interviewed challenged these practices while at the same time lamenting their widespread use in his department. He was very keen to introduce much more individual interaction among students, much more one-to-one support by lecturers, the use of workbooks and problem-based learning. He wanted students to meet problems and get stuck, and then – with support – to find a way through. He wanted students to construct knowledge about physics within their own frame of reference by fully engaging with physics problems. Here was a head-on challenge by a "Lone Ranger" in this physics department. He expressed the hope that his colleagues would come round to his way of thinking, but it was clear that the sets of practices being challenged were very firmly entrenched and despite his senior position in the Department it was clear he would have a hard time moving out of his teaching and learning ghetto.

> "Under-prepared African students were now entering higher education in bigger classes. And the challenge was to transform our discipline to take care of that. . . . Even 10 years since democracy the entry level of students is not that great. . . . There were two options: to create a foundation year or to be a bit more radical and to transform the teaching of the discipline to meet the challenges [of much larger classes and under-prepared students]. We changed the teaching environment from one where the lecturer delivers the material to one which the environment where students get a chance to work through the material with a chance for group discussions afterwards. . . . As academics in this discipline there are certain processes that go through your mind and we wanted to give students exposure to that: the thought processes in interacting with these difficult concepts.
>
> There is nothing to lose with students getting things wrong or being stuck – engaging with the material helps them to get a handle on where the problem is, where they are stuck. Anyway we found that pass rates went up. . . . But other modules did not teach in this way unfortunately and other academics in our discipline looked at you and said 'why aren't you doing your work as a lecturer?'"

This example shows how educational ideology, in this case a progressivist one (Trowler, 1998) mediates disciplinary factors, either "real" or constructed, and contributes to the mix of the local teaching and learning regime. In this case an alternative structural factor, ideology, uniquely realized by my interviewee added to the particular configuration of this context.

Conventions of Appropriateness

One striking example of the unconsidered adoption of standards of appropriateness and inappropriateness in terms of practices, decisions and choices in a particular context related to the use of graduate teaching assistants (GTAs). Some respondents said that GTAs were only ever used in year one of the degree ("of course!"). Tutorials were highly structured and GTAs were given a clear script and set of tasks for students to do. Others, however, said that GTAs were only used in the second and third years ("of course!"). Faculty delivered the lectures and GTAs led fairly unstructured discussions about them in seminars with students. Here were completely contrasting sets of conventions about what was appropriate and inappropriate use of GTAs, conventions themselves founded on a set of tacit assumptions.

> "At first year on this campus we believe very strongly in the tutorial which they don't on the other campuses. It was the one thing we were not prepared to compromise on – If the tutorial

in the first year was done away with by the common curriculum it would really compromise us. . . . A tutorial is a first-year session run by a postgraduate and they discuss work students prepare the week beforehand. It's the only time they are getting, not quite one to one but fairly individual attention. We can spot weaknesses and so on. They don't have an equivalent on the other campuses: they did away with tutorials as having only a nuisance value, being a luxury. They don't use postgraduates in that way, supporting the teaching of first-years."

Codes of Signification

Codes of signification refer to the responses that are evoked by particular "signs" in specific contexts; what are sometimes referred to as connotative codes. These responses are often emotional, involve stereotypes and of course are related to tacit assumptions. Advertisers encourage audiences to develop and mobilize carefully built codes of signification in relation to products. In teaching and learning regimes, by contrast, codes of signification grow in more serendipitous ways. In the South African study it was clear that different campuses mobilized codes of signification about each other which were wrapped up with evaluations of quality, race issues, assumptions about their students and practices and so on. In a sense the extent to which these codes match the "reality" is not particularly significant, such subjective responses have real effects even though they may be based on stereotypical views, even upon racist assumptions in some cases. This is illustrated by the following quote:

> "As we merged . . . the first thing that became apparent was that UniY didn't have the same academic standards and the same regard for teaching as we did. . . . The idea was that we would form one big school of [our discipline] across all the campuses. The heads of [that discipline] met together to discuss the merger – but it quickly became apparent that no-one understood what the others were doing. So even between UniX and College Z there was a cultural difference. . . . And then we had the UniY scenario where they were MILES behind us. And the biggest problem we had was – how do you tell somebody that they are not very good? . . . When you have different institutions with different academic cultures it's very hard for people to believe that they are not doing the best job. . . . We have a strong culture of teaching and learning but University Y to tell you the truth had no culture at all. However, they have now adopted most of our courses, but that was hard work. So now we've got a common curriculum in [our discipline] which is very very learner-based. . . . One of the best things we've done is the optional Saturday morning tutorials. We go along with some PhD and MA students and give extra help to the kids working through the workbooks. The staff in UniY said 'if we did that our students wouldn't come because our students are different from your students.' And that's been the big thing with the merger – everybody thinks they and their students are different."

Discursive Repertoires

Socio-cultural theory emphasizes the development of discourse communities characterized by intersubjectivity, by mutually understood ways of interpreting and producing text. There is an element of structural functionalism in this way of thinking, the assumption that consensus is privileged over difference, and that diversity is somehow "normal" while conflict is just "dazzle". While rejecting that consensual approach it is clear that as workgroups engage together over long periods of time on common projects they do develop distinctive ways of talking, writing and interpreting text. These are not the only discursive resources available to them, but they represent a broadening of the options available for discursive production. Meanwhile disciplines have their own particular discourses, and within them contextually specific sub-discourses (Winberg, 2003). Again, a mix of structural factors shaped by agentic realizations in local contexts shape in turn the discursive repertoires in use there.

In the South African context I found that the back-stories, the narratives that groups shared about their history and the broader context, were extremely important discursively. There was a cast of characters about whom views were shared and disputed, a series of events which were thought to be of significance for the present day, and a set of issues which were wrangled over and which impinged on current discussions in significant ways. This back-story mediated and made contextually specific the discursive characteristics associated with the discipline, although these remained strong.

One focus group revealed a common set of discursive resources which was shared in a very distinctive way. Built up over a period of years, and to some extent self-selecting, the members of this group were all steeped in constructivist educational theory. They had read many of the key texts, discussed the ideas and attempted to apply them in the science degree foundation course they designed and delivered. Their production of text in the focus group interview was littered with metaphors, references and vocabulary derived from this literature and way of thinking about education. This had little, if anything, to do with the scientific disciplines in which the members of this group were socialized, but rather was a product of the group itself. A very clear discursive community was in place here.

But this commonality, this level of consensus in terms of discourse was unusual. More frequently there are alternative, sometimes competing discourses in operation. So for example this head of department draws on managerialist discourse, probably in unhelpful ways, in dealing with the common curriculum issue:

"In my opinion there was a very poor academic standard [on campus X]. The people who were running this were competent in teaching and nothing very much else. When we came to take over . . . the first thing I did was to try and streamline undergraduate studies. Coming together with campus X gave us the opportunity to re-write and regularize what they were doing. . . . We had to increase the number of credits for each course because the administration had been hugely out of proportion to the learning outcomes [on small credit courses] . . . It was a nightmare.

We left the most difficult characters out of the negotiations: We decided early on that this really wasn't an ideological battle and I didn't have the time or patience or energy to take those people with me.

Now that we are actually doing it we are finding that it's not easy. On paper it was a lot easier. What we're finding now is that that high-point of co-operation is something really of the past. One of the people who was involved is now out of the equation – she was a fantastically good planner and clear strategic thinker. So even though she didn't know too much about the area, some areas, she had very good structural vision. . . . And the people that we are left with are a lot more . . . prepared to argue over everything. What we are concerned with now is the lack of communication. . . . They don't answer our letters. . . . In our planning document we have common outcomes but we don't have a common grading system and have to try to agree on one."

Subjectivities in Interaction

Personal and professional identity, or – in postmodernist discourse – "subjectivities" are intimately related to the interactional context of individuals. The process of "hammering" against each other means that subjectivities are shaped, defended, reconstructed and negotiated in interaction with others. From an individual perspective this history of subjectivity development results in a life story about the self. In the South African context "personalities" are very significant in change processes:

the new black Vice-Chancellor and his very particular approach to management; key political figures, their personal predilections and sets of issues; the individuals who are capable but didn't get the job because they were male, white and middle-class. Subjectivities are very significant elements in the back-story, and are very much shaped by the history and context of South Africa, particularly the history of struggle against the apartheid regime and one's role (or narratives about one's role) in that. Context and subjectivity interact, each shaping the other, and the character of the multiple subjectivities that dynamically coexist in a teaching and learning regime has important implications for practices, issues and agendas as well as upon the shape of and divisions within a teaching and learning regime.

Particular individuals can be powerful or not in different contexts and this is partly to do with interaction of subjectivities:

> "In any merger situation you have the philosophical issues and you have the personalities. We had a lulu of a personality! I don't think I'm exaggerating when I say he was a little Hitler. He was in charge of disciplines X and Y. . . . But he was so obstructionist and political that the academics in discipline Y couldn't get on with him – several of them left.
>
> We found out in our first few meetings with him that he was the arch-commonality man – We must have common tests, common curriculum, common everything. And anyone who didn't believe in this philosophy, didn't agree with him, had to be reported. He was so authoritarian with his staff it meant that they couldn't discuss the common curriculum freely with us. I said 'do you know what this [attempt to standardize] means logistically, and do you know what it means to people's autonomy to teach what they want?' So when we came to working out the common curriculum in discipline X it wasn't academically based, with a careful analysis of our country's needs, the trends, students' needs and the nature of the discipline. It was personality based, the cut and thrust of personality."

Power: Its Microphysics

Power is manifested in numerous forms (Lukes, 2005). It may involve the simple application of brute force: "do this or there will be serious consequences for you". It may involve the ability to set the agenda, and to exclude certain issues from the agenda. Or it may involve a more subtle, "reality-shaping" power, the ability to shape the hegemonic discourse.

The application of power was very evident in the newly merged institution I studied. One of three departments in the same discipline quickly mobilized available resources to make sure that their approach to the curriculum and its delivery was the one to be adopted and that that discipline became centered on *their* campus.

> "We were desperate to stay here – if we could swing it we would try to. I think we had an advantage in that they [law on campus X] had very little resources, very limited library facilities in particular, and we had all the access to databases and online stuff. . . .
>
> When I think back to how we came to persuade them, it was about people: persuasive personalities taking the initiative. In truth we had sway of numbers. So when we said 'look we got the great course of first year level' (and we did our homework in advance) it was very hard for campus X to argue against it. . . . There were a number of strong personalities in our department who really pushed their particular teaching interest and research interest.
>
> You had your people who clearly saw it as their territory trying to persuade everybody else. It was power plays, horse trading, "we will give you this if you give us that". Usually one dominant player took the lead. There are individual personalities, powerful personalities, strong players, who feel they own their specialisms and tend to dominate. They are going to

squeeze out specialists who are less able to make their case. Coming from a position of authority they came in and laid it down – 'we've always done it like this' – and they intimidated people."

Implications of This Discussion

I began this paper by emphasizing that the discussion was not a purely academic one but was intended to bring out the implications of moving beyond an epistemologically essentialist position in undertaking change processes oriented to enhancing teaching and learning in higher education. The corollary of the foregoing set of arguments is a series of propositions about change and change management. These are as follows:

- Any attempt to introduce innovations to enhance teaching-learning should focus on the potential interactions between the innovation and the relevant characteristics of local cultures, their teaching and learning regimes.
- In order to do this fully it is important to develop an anthropological awareness of context as well as a good understanding of disciplinary narratives.
- This is best done by managers, leaders and change agents who are relatively close to the action, such as heads of department. At this level it is possible to see the unique character of the moments of a particular teaching and learning regime, and their possible consequences for change.
- Innovators should expect the interaction between innovations and local cultures to involve "domestication", in other words the adaptation of innovations to local contexts so that they are used in different ways than elsewhere. Meanings are partly developed locally, and contextually contingent meanings emerge with social practice.
- Rational-purposive approaches to change which adopt an homogenized, totalizing approach are unlikely to result in the kinds of outcomes that may be expected by their protagonists. Outcomes will be different in different places, and simple "transfer" of innovations from one context to another will in practice not take place.
- In thinking about context it is important also to think about history and process: how context came to be what it is, what the back-stories are, and where the local context is situated more broadly. It is important to think about the dance as well as the dancer.

As well as making such high-level generalizations about change generally this chapter suggests a way of depicting workgroups by offering the analytical lens of the teaching and learning regime. Again, the depiction of workgroups involved in teaching, learning, assessment and curricular change through the lens of teaching and learning regimes is not just of academic interest. David Dill (1999) suggests that organizations with a "learning architecture" tend to look elsewhere for examples of good practice. So should reflexive departments and workgroups – doing so helps them see themselves better as well as seeing others.

Departments and workgroups also need to look inwards at themselves, uncovering tacit understandings and recurrent practices that sometimes have deleterious consequences for their students. The processes of looking *out* and looking *in* go hand-in-hand. Many respondents in the South African study, while abhorring the process of merger and the imposition of a common curriculum, noted that the process of dialogue with other departments and other campuses had helped them to see their own practices in a new light: to reflect on practices and attitudes that they had not considered in an evaluative way for many years.

But in becoming reflexive they need to go beyond looking at simple practices (for example how problem-based learning is used at another university) and to see those practices in the context in which they are situated: to see both the dance and the dancer. Deconstructing the relevant elements of context around teaching and learning in higher education through the framework of the teaching and learning regime concept is a way of helping them to do this, it is a way of conceptualizing the territories in which practices are realized.

Concluding Comments

This chapter has offered a way of unpicking the local articulation of disciplinary differences, and of emphasizing the significance of context and history in understanding social practices. It has shown the significance of the sociocultural dimension of higher education practices, including the consequences of the operation of power and the development of subjectivities within particular cultural contexts.

The chapter has highlighted the implications for changes aimed at the enhancement of teaching and learning, emphasizing the issue of congruence or "fit" between context and innovation. It has offered health warnings about structural functionalist, essentialist and determinist/reductionist understandings of disciplines and their power.

And finally the chapter has tried to emphasize the significance of the meso-level of analysis as well as the higher level of analysis at which discussions of disciplinary differences are often framed. Issues of meaning and affect in particular come to the fore at this level of analysis: teaching and learning regimes are, in effect, webs of meaning and of feeling, localized worlds created within a nexus of social structures by agents acting together in the world.

References

Becher, T. (1989). *Academic Tribes and Territories*. Buckingham: The Society for Research into Higher Education and Open University Press.

Biglan, A. (1973). The characteristics of subject matter in different scientific areas. *Journal of Applied Psychology*, 57 (3), 195–203.

Bowker, G., & Star, S. L. (1999). *Sorting things out: classification and its consequences*. Cambridge, Mass.: MIT Press.

Clark, B. (1987). *The Academic Life: small worlds, different worlds*. Princeton: The Carnegie Foundation for the Advancement of Teaching.

Davidson, G. (1994). *Credit Accumulation and Transfer in the British Universities 1990–1993*. Canterbury: University of Kent.

Dill, D. (1999). Academic Accountability and University Adaptation: The Architecture of an Academic Learning Organization. *Higher Education*, 38 (2), 127–154.

Entwistle, N. (2005). Learning Outcomes and Ways of Thinking Across Contrasting Disciplines and Settings in Higher Education. *The Curriculum Journal*, 16 (1), 67–82.

Fox, R. (1980). *The Red Lamp of Incest*. New York: Penguin.

Gregg, P. (1996). *Modularisation: what academics think*. In Higher Education Quality Council, *In Focus: Modular Higher Education in the UK*. London: HEQC.

Kekäle, J. (1999). 'Preferred' Patterns of Academic Leadership in Different Disciplinary (Sub)cultures. *Higher Education*, 37, 217–238.

Kekäle, J. (2002). Conceptions of Quality in Four Different Disciplines. *Tertiary Education and Management*, 8, 65–80.

Kolb, D. A. (1981). *Learning styles and disciplinary differences*. In A. Chickering (Ed.), *The Modern American College* (pp. 232–255). San Francisco: Jossey Bass.

Lodahl, J. B., & Gordon, G. (1972). The structure of scientific fields and the functioning of university graduate departments. *American Sociological Review*, 37, 57–72.

LTSN. (2002). *Final Evaluation Report*. York: LTSN.

Lukes, S. (2005). *Power: a radical view*. Basingstoke: Palgrave Macmillan.

McCune, V., & Hounsell, D. (2005). The Development of Students' Ways of Thinking and Practising in Three Final-Year Biology Courses. *Higher Education*, 49, 255–289.

McGuinness, C. (1997). What constitutes good learning and teaching in higher education? Views from staff development handbooks. *Psychology Teaching Review*, 6 (1), 14–22.

Neumann, R. (2001). Disciplinary Differences and University Teaching. *Studies in Higher Education*, 26 (2), 135–146.

Neumann, R. (2003). A Disciplinary Perspective on University Teaching and Learning. In M. Tight (Ed.) *Access and Exclusion* (pp. 217–245). Oxford: Elsevier.

Neumann, R., Parry, S., & Becher, T. (2002). Teaching and Learning in their Disciplinary Contexts: a conceptual analysis. *Studies in Higher Education*, 27 (4), 405–417.

Ruscio, K. P. (1987). *Many sectors, many professions.* In Clark, B. R. (Ed.), *The Academic Profession* (pp. 331–368). Berkeley: University of California Press.

Shinn, T. (1982). *Scientific disciplines and organizational specificity.* In N. Elias, H. Martins, & R. D. Whitley (Eds.), *Scientific Establishments and Hierarchies* (pp. 239–264). Dordrecht, Reidel.

Trowler, P. (1998). *Academics Responding to Change: new higher education frameworks and academic cultures.* Buckingham: Open University Press/SRHE.

Trowler, P. (2005). http://www.lancs.ac.uk/staff/trowler/cv.htm (accessed 19.8.05).

Winberg, C. (2003). *Language, Content and Context in the Education of Architects.* In R. Wilkinson (Ed.), *Integrating Content and Language: meeting the challenge of multilingual higher education* (pp. 320–332). Maastricht: University of Maastricht Press.

Woodward, K. (Ed.) (1997). *Identity and Difference.* London: Sage.

Ylijoki, O-H. (2000). Disciplinary Cultures and the Moral Order of Studying. *Higher Education,* 39, 339–362.

16

Exploring Teaching and Learning Regimes in Higher Education Settings

Joëlle Fanghanel

City University, London

Introduction

In this chapter, I discuss some of the implications for practices in higher education of the theoretical framework of *Teaching and Learning Regimes* (TLRs) outlined in Chapter 15. I first highlight its distinctive theoretical significance for understanding disciplinary groups in higher education. Focusing on the experience of academics in practice, I illustrate how TLRs operate through the use of a vignette, and I sketch out some practical implications of TLRs theory, considering specifically: 1) what implications there are for apprehensions of the discipline; 2) what lessons might be in it for faculty development; and 3) what strategies this might imply for managing academics. In the concluding section of the chapter, I highlight some specific challenges inherent in this theoretical framework for researchers and academics.

Understanding Disciplinary Contexts through TLRs

The most recent successful attempts at explaining how learning (and therefore change) occurs in practice have relied on theoretical models that examine the dynamics within communities of practice (Lave & Wenger, 1991) or more broadly within activity systems (Engeström, 1999 for example). In a Community of Practice framework, learning is examined as occurring through progressive 'legitimate participation' into the activities of a group. This model for learning is akin to a cognitive apprenticeship model where novice learners observe, question, and listen to experienced colleagues to acquire knowledge of a field. Activity systems theory also envisages learning as a social activity, but the emphasis is on the systems within which a community operates. In activity system theory, learning and change cannot be dissociated from the structural dynamics of the operational context. It is not possible to understand a learning community outside of the structures and context within which it operates. Trowler's framework of *Teaching and Learning Regimes* (TLRs) builds on this body of literature, with a specific focus on academic teams and departments. He shows how structural and 'agentic' forces (broadly the way individuals construct and respond to what they experience as reality) come into play to fashion disciplinary groups. Whilst his framework has heuristic power in explaining the dynamics at this level of practice, the implications are more analytical than practical. This theory provides a better explanation of how a disciplinary group works, and therefore points to appraising in a new way how learning and change occur within a group.

Trowler's chapter offers for example a reconceptualization of the notion of discipline. It proposes that conceptualizing disciplines solely with reference to knowledge characteristics yields a partial and relatively abstract account of them. Such approaches are essentialist; they suggest that disciplines are relatively stable units, with relatively stable sets of intellectual and social conventions. They occult the sociological dimension. Seeking to uncover the social reality of disciplinary groups (focusing therefore on the discipline in practice) brings to the fore its complex make-up. It complements approaches that deconstruct disciplines with reference to knowledge structures and properties (see for example Donald in Chapter 3), and those which acknowledge the 'situated' dimension of disciplines (see Hounsell and Anderson in Chapter 6). It enables a broader reading of the disciplinary map.

By focusing on disciplinary groups in order to understand how a discipline is conceptualized and 'lived', Trowler brings to the fore the subtle and often unrecorded elements that make up a disciplinary group and account for conceptions and enactment of the discipline within that group. It brings into the equation three ingredients that are absent from epistemological accounts (Donald, 1995, 2002 for example). First, it poses the question of the role of power within disciplinary groups, and across disciplines, and of the roles that tensions, compliance, and coalition might play in disciplinary groups; second, it emphasizes the contingency of disciplinary conceptions, and the transience of what might look like disciplinary traits or essences; and finally it brings to the centre of the debate on disciplines the issue of how individuals and structures interrelate to produce phenomena, activities, or events. The latter is crucial; focusing on this sociological conundrum indeed highlights the tensions between individuals and structures. By adopting a stance on structures informed by Giddens – whereby a dialectical relation exists between individuals and structures (both impacting on each other) – Trowler depicts the social reality of university departmental regimes, teaching and learning regimes as he calls them, as turbulent spaces where disciplinary identities are both enacted and constructed. Rather than presenting disciplines simply as instantiations of an epistemic order, he sees them as living, situated and context-grounded objects. From this standpoint, Trowler envisages disciplinary knowledge as being in part the expression of a power position – a positioning. He doesn't deny of course that disciplines also have cognitive/epistemic content.

Broadly, *Teaching and Learning Regimes* (TLRs) describe local cultures at the meso-level of practice (departmental or teaching group) in universities. Trowler has identified eight 'moments' constitutive of these regimes: recurrent practices; tacit assumptions; implicit theories of teaching and learning; discursive repertoires; conventions of appropriateness; power relations; subjectivities in interaction; and codes of signification. These moments combine and interact to construct the teaching and learning environments in which academics operate within their disciplinary group, in practice. They come together in complex and subterranean ways to frame the practices and beliefs of a given group, accounting for the way that group (and the individuals within it) construct their reality, and how they enact these constructions in practice. Whilst these moments operate at the meso (intermediary) level of practice, they can emerge from other levels. At the macro-level for example, elements such as national agendas on widening participations, national quality frameworks for the delivery of programs, the body of research on teaching and learning, etc., can permeate local regimes. In the same way individual characteristics, biographies, beliefs and behaviors (pertaining to the micro-level of an activity) also operate at the meso-level. TLRs therefore designate a web of flows which interact with each other to account for a local culture and its *modus operandi*.

Identifying Components of a TLR

In his chapter, Trowler stresses the elusiveness of TLRs, and indicates that using extreme cases can help highlight their make-up – hence his examples collected from South African universities; in the same way, TLRs are particularly perceptible by newcomers to a regime. I therefore illustrate what a TLR might look like through the eyes of a faculty member new to teaching in higher education in the UK, using a vignette which relates his perceptions as he joins his new Mathematics department. This vignette is based on actual data collected for work investigating teaching constructs in higher education faculty (Fanghanel, 2007a), from which the quotes are extracted, but practical details and circumstances are fictitious.

> *Dave is a full-time Lecturer in Applied Mathematics at a UK university. He is 40 years of age and was educated in Spain. He has taught in higher education for five years, including in the United States, before accepting his first post in a well-established UK university. His department is located in a School that brings together all mathematical activities and includes cognate disciplines (astronomy, engineering, etc.). There is a strong research agenda at the university. It is of medium size for the UK – just over 10 000 students – and attracts students from different countries and backgrounds, with a significant majority of local ethnically diverse students. His department includes mostly male staff, many of whom are employed as Full Professors.*
>
> *As a newcomer of foreign origin to this site of practice, Dave is in a good position to note practices that differ from other places where he has worked, and his description of the milieu in which he is teaching highlights the different moments of the TLR specific to his department.*
>
> *He reports on some of the* **implicit theories of teaching and learning** *in this new environment. His department tends to recruit students with average or low mathematical profiles. It is understood in the department that students come here because they couldn't get into the Business School, where stricter admissions criteria are applied. Applied Mathematics is not considered as prestigious as other disciplines (Astronomy or Pure Maths) in the School. Colleagues in the department accept that students who enroll here do so because they want to prove to future employers they have a good degree; hardly any will continue towards a higher degree. Teaching methods and approaches used in the department condone this state of affairs (see 'recurrent practices').*
>
> *One of the* **tacit assumptions** *of this group of academics is that as a result of this, students will not be motivated by the subject itself, but rather by the outcome. They come in intent on completing their degree successfully. As a newcomer to this place, Dave perceives that colleagues in the department have devised a curricular approach that instantiate this tacit assumption – practices which differ from the ones he was accustomed to in his previous employment in the States or in Europe where a 'sink or swim' approach tended to prevail. Group tutorials, assessment methods, and approaches to feedback address these tacit assumptions (see below).*
>
> **Recurrent practices** *in the department seem almost paradoxical to Dave at first. It is accepted that while the standard offer for entry is B-C-C, it is common practice to accept students who have obtained a D in their A-levels (one of the qualifying examinations for entry into higher education in the UK). Dave comments:*
>
>> Now it is beyond me why they [colleagues] would choose that but that's their choice and we have to deal with it. We have to draw in numbers, there is money depending on that. So be it . . . It really challenges you to get them interested in these things. . . . There have been one or two people who have had quite a culture shock with that . . . interesting discussions!
>
> *To shore up the department's chances of success, the teaching and learning methods include specific approaches to support students to 'see them through':*

I like helping students but for some reason there seems to be also a certain passive knowledge by the weak students that no matter what they do here we will pull them through. Maybe – I have never thought of that before – that's the explanation for why they don't have more drive.

Dave contrasts these recurrent practices with others he has experienced before:

In the States, five years ago, I basically designed my own course. I was told 'teach mathematical methods for physicists, here we have a very diverse student body, some people have a hard time with it, some people have come here with a strong knowledge in theoretical physics, make sure you get them all on the same level, and make sure they have also covered and understood a set of mathematics'. And I did that pretty much on my own.

In a university system where nobody cared about people dropping out, thinking they were just not cut out for university studies, people learn differently. You offer them a course with different things. . . . Here this is far too complicated because we are too worried – we . . . some people here are too worried – that if they [students] don't come to the lectures, they will fail.

This department's TLR is of course to be put in the broader context of the UK higher education landscape, where participation and diversity are encouraged, where retention has serious economic implications for universities, where curricula are increasingly 'applied' in focus, and where the relation to the economy is assumed by the funding bodies. In the same way, TLRs include normalized behaviors emerging from regulatory frameworks or disciplinary conventions, what Trowler calls **conventions of appropriateness***:*

Nothing is common sense you know. A typical example – at some point, I returned the mid-term tests to the students, and one of my older colleagues saw that and looked aghast and said you let the students know about their mid-term tests? I said 'what is the problem, I actually went to a lot of trouble marking them, I want them to look at my comments, they have to learn something', and he said 'no, no, no, this is 10% of their final mark, you have to hold on to these grades'. You know it is one of these things, I thought common sense was mid-term tests are meant to give students feedback and this person said 'oh no we can't do this'.

The teaching of Mathematics in this department comes with its own **codes of signification.** *In talking about how the word 'tutorial' is used in his department, Dave illustrates that this 'signifier' has specific connotative meanings ('the signified') in the university in which he teaches.*

This is all new to me actually. What I was more used to was tutorials where students have a tutor assigned to them, where students actually come after they have done their coursework, then present their coursework to the persons in the exercise class. Here it is very different. It is based on questions from students. I thought first 'what a great idea' and then you notice how students take this and you realize a number of them have got as far as raising their arm, reading out the question to you and looking up with big glazed eyes. They expect everything to be done for them. They expect things but they are not . . . they are not ready to put in that much effort. You know if somebody comes to me and asks for help, and I can see that this person has struggled for maybe even twenty minutes with the problem and got sort of stuck, I love to help them, it's fun, it's fun teaching. But here we are worried about retention rates, we are very consciously or subconsciously shaping the teaching and exams in such a way that you give those weak students that they can just pass. They might fail and we can't have that.

Dave identifies that the 'tutorial' in his department means something very different from what it meant in his previous post. It is not a place to discuss amongst peers, guided by the tutor, but a place to remedy students' weaknesses or laziness and to allay staff fears of student failure. This example shows how intimately this moment is related to **discursive repertoires.** *In his department, the 'tutorial' has become a euphemism for 'not failing students'.*

Power relations *are an important component of TLRs. It is clearly established in Dave's department that newcomers inherit programs on which they have little say. Whilst he might like to teach on graduate programs, there is not always the option of doing that. Full Professors tend to occupy these positions.*

A crucial issue in TLRs is that of the individual, and his/her relation to the group – the **subjectivities** *of academics within a group. As a newcomer in this department, Dave acknowledges the idiosyncrasies of some of his views in a community that is, on the face of it, relatively coherent about its mission (attracting as many students as possible, seeing them through successfully) and its collective approach (teaching strategies, an applied curriculum). He explains how he contains his own personal views on how to teach Mathematics, and accepts the boundaries set by the group:*

> I do have strong opinions on some things. But first of all I have to learn about how the system works before I start playing around with it, so the way for example you have to teach a course a few years in a row usually which means – you first find out what they need and then you start making adjustments, and the liberty for that I have. So that's why I said you know there are lots of rules that are terribly burdensome at the beginning but it sort of . . . they don't actually affect the content very much or the delivery as much . . . it sets the boundaries.

Whilst he feels that, as a foreign newcomer to this community, his subjectivity cannot find full expression in respect of teaching and learning, Dave finds ways of asserting it through his research:

> The thing is I am not really fussed about whether I teach mathematics or physics or I don't know, I mean I could teach chemistry for all I care, though I might have a harder time teaching it myself but. . . . It is not really what makes me an academic, what makes me an academic is my research – there I am very fussed.

This vignette illustrates what a TLR might look like in a specific Mathematics department. A current of contestation, restraint, and tensions underpins much of what Dave highlights when describing practices within his department, confirming the turbulence of TLRs. Structures, colleagues, and ways of doing things in the department collide to make the teaching of Mathematics what it is in that department, and to frame Dave's practice. He indicates that within that, he has scope to act as he chooses in some areas of practice, particularly in his research (see above) but also in some aspects of teaching:

> Everybody does it this way, it works, that's the way the system is, you just go along with it. But then on the other hand it slowly dawns on you that these things are mostly external and don't really touch the way you teach. The syllabus is utterly fixed, I have not much liberty in changing the content. But how I deliver, that is really up to me. So there is a certain freedom.

Implications of TLRs for Engaging with Disciplinary Groups

As indicated earlier on in this chapter, TLRs theory has implications for analyzing the way local culture and disciplinary groups function. It broadens the notion of academic territories and environments to include for example questions of power, control, agency and subjectivity.

Apprehensions of the discipline within a given TLR will vary and are better conceptualized as 'positioning' than as unmediated translation of epistemological beliefs (beliefs about knowledge). Whilst TLRs is mainly an explanatory framework, implications for action can be inferred, particularly in the context of promoting and supporting change initiatives. I now turn to these.

Agentic Conceptions of Disciplines

The socio-cultural focus of TLRs enables a grounded approach to examining disciplines and yields a non-normative vision of what a discipline is. Whilst it is accepted that structural and ideological disciplinary schools of thought (e.g. humanist, critical theoretical, or post-modern approaches to Literature) create their own communities within departments (Evans, 1988), there exist more subtle nuances generated by individual or collective conceptions of the discipline, which a TLR lens can bring to the surface. This doesn't invalidate approaches to change that focus on discipline-based understandings of practice (many recent quality enhancement initiatives in the UK do) but it does moderate the duality taken for granted between generic (informed by ideological or other beliefs) and disciplinary characteristics in faculty's teaching approaches.

In a separate study investigating pedagogical constructs (Fanghanel, 2007a), I was able to identify the specific agentic ways in which faculty conceptualized their disciplines. Table 16.1 documents the discipline characterizations that emerged from the study, based on interviews with faculty. These characterizations stress the agentic dimension in the way faculty conceptualize their disciplines, a point also underlined by Hounsell and Anderson (see Chapter 6 in this volume). They are used here to illustrate the variability of discipline apprehensions.

It is clear from the above that the way academics characterize their discipline varies according to what I have called elsewhere their 'pedagogical focuses', i.e. their curricular intention. Conceptions can be composite, and include several dimensions. Some dimensions reflect the content, the heritage of the disciplines, some focus on knowledge structures and methodologies, whilst others are much more political (in a broad sense) and reflect ideologies and critiques of the world. Such varied conceptions can co-exist within a departmental team and are inherent in the dynamics of TLRs.

Socializing into Disciplinary Groups

The social dimension of the discipline is well documented, beyond the work considered in this book (Becher & Trowler, 2001; Henkel, 2000 for example). The way newcomers to a disciplinary group engage with their new community of practice has not been the subject of much research, although Trowler and Knight (2000) have dedicated an important study to those new entrants and have outlined innovative ways in which new academics can be socialized into a disciplinary group. TLRs theory can provide some insight on the main issues facing a newcomer, with specific reference to the discordance that might be felt not just between his/her own beliefs and approaches, and that of the department, but also between that and the programs of study aimed at introducing new faculty to teaching in higher education. Instances of such dissonances have been identified in my own work (Fanghanel, 2004), which broadly referred to: the difficulty of transferring practices and ideas to a different teaching environment; the collision of competing beliefs about knowledge and learning; the limited influence a junior position in an academic department affords, when it comes to trying to change practices; and the congruence (or lack of) with beliefs and practices inherent in the department new faculty are joining.

Faculty new to a disciplinary group (or a department) need to gain informed awareness of the environment in which they will operate. Whilst they bring to it their own identity, this identity will be further formed and transformed through interacting with that group. The following practical advice based on acknowledging TLRs within a teaching group is relevant for newcomers into a

Table 16.1 Dimensions in academics' conceptions of their discipline in a socio-cultural framework

Dimensions in conceptions of the discipline	Discipline	Respondent emphasizes the following characteristics
The discipline as epistemology	Psychology	A methodology-driven discipline, all-encompassing, cumulative, chronologically grounded, includes within it divergent epistemologies
	Sport Science	Discipline as a science. Scientific knowledge at the center which gives the discipline historical legitimacy
	Nurse Education	Allegiance to two disciplines, and congruent epistemologies (education–nursing) backgrounding of content
	Mathematics	Emphasis on abstraction, beauty, and harmony of the discipline
	Econometrics	The discipline as a methodology
	Chemistry	Emphasis on beauty, harmony, and universality of chemical principles
The discipline as application	Languages	Self-referential (language is about communication) discipline, with backgrounding of content; also bringing into relation with the "whole culture"
	Human Resources Management	A discipline to directly inform and ameliorate professional practices, backgrounding of content
	Mental Health (in medical syllabus)	A sidelined undervalued disciplinary input detached from main syllabus, to provide GPs with 'bedside manners' and effective ways of relating to their patients
	Civil Engineering	Close link to industry with a slightly critical agenda
The discipline as ideology or critique	Geography	A radical/political discipline that opens new perspectives on social issues, includes divergent epistemologies
	Multimedia	The emphasis is on developing creativity, includes divergent epistemologies, allegiance to two disciplines – technical aspect is underplayed
	Digital Arts	The emphasis is on developing creativity (artistic dimension), includes divergent epistemologies, allegiance to two disciplines – technical aspect is underplayed
	Medical Psychology	A sidelined almost 'provocative' disciplinary input detached from main syllabus to raise awareness of future GPs
	Classics	A radical discipline, discursive, and tentative, with universal ramifications, accommodates divergent epistemologies
	Chemistry	A critical and political discipline, universality of chemical principles
A functional utilitarian dimension to the discipline (as status-enhancing)	Nursing	No specific disciplinary content in university contact, learning takes place in practice – emphasis on raising profile of professionals, credentializing function of the syllabus
	Information Science	Scientific and political dimensions in the discipline – emphasis on raising profile of professionals + historically grounded, includes complex/contested epistemologies

disciplinary group. Much of this advice is based on adopting a dialogic approach to understanding practice – through two-way conversations, observation and networking:

- It is necessary to develop an awareness that TLRs operating at the level of the department 'glue' entities within it together and account for the dynamics within the department.
- The stances generated from within a given TLR may clash with experiences in the educational programs for new lecturers and with experiences of colleagues in other departments. There is much to be learnt from those dissonances, both in terms of understanding one's own environment, but also of challenging it where appropriate.
- Seeking the support of mentors who can articulate elements of the context is crucial. Transmission of knowledge about practices (of learning how to do things) ought to be complemented by discussions on local characteristics – aspects of TLR moments.
- Bearing in mind that discussions with newcomers can be as useful as discussions with experienced colleagues, it is advisable to seek opportunities for informal discussions on the following broader issues:
  - conceptions of teaching
  - what is being sought to be achieved
  - best ways of promoting learning
  - effectively communicating with students
  - managing research, teaching and administrative duties
  - opportunities for exchanging ideas
  - opportunities for professional development
  - opportunities for collaboration within and outside of the department
  - getting feedback on one's teaching
- It is useful to approach probation and career review procedures as developmental events, and to use those as tools for understanding local practices, the linkage to institutional requirements, and as opportunities for developing one's career.
- Developing networks and social space both within and outside of the department (including through the channel of institutional educational programs) will enhance understanding of context.

Faculty Development

Implications of TLRs for faculty development are significant. While it is impossible to generalize about approaches to faculty development, the link of this function to quality management and performativity (Skelton, 2005), and an emphasis on the utilitarian features of a university education (Fanghanel, 2004; Malcolm & Zukas, 2001; Manathunga, 2006) are inscribed in its foundations. This is particularly true in the UK where it has been directly linked to the Dearing (NCIHE, 1997) agendas of remediation, rebalancing teaching and research functions, and linking higher education and economic needs. This has generated an emphasis on management of practice, and genericist approaches to convey that. Faculty development practices have tended to favor generalist approaches, and in some instances "a phobia about disciplinary content" (Manathunga, 2006, p. 24).

The need to focus on subject specific aspects of teaching and learning is clear in Hounsell and Anderson's chapter (Chapter 6); it interrogates faculty development practices. Their invitation to consider how teaching activities can be tailored to specific groups of students in situated contexts pertains to the same emphasis on the discipline, at the expense of more generic educational aims. Whilst there has been a clear recent movement towards developing more discipline sensitive approaches to educational development (Healey & Jenkins, 2003), some reservations have also been voiced about 'going totally native'. D'Andrea and Gosling (2005) in particular have warned about the dangers of losing the benefits of generic educational research findings through "low-level reinvention of the wheel within closed disciplinary communities that are unwilling to look beyond their own boundaries" (p. 63). TLRs theory with its emphasis on the socio-cultural dimension of practice goes some way to supporting this assertion and would suggest an approach to faculty development that takes account of disciplinary specificities but also of local regimes, also providing routes for change that allow for agentic appropriation (elbow room) within specific TLRs.

At the same time, heeding Trowler's health warning that TLRs represent local phenomena within a wider 'ground', inter-TLRs interactions should be encouraged. Educational programs that bring together academics from different departments provide a space for academics to meet the Other. This gives them the opportunity to attribute, through these encounters, new meanings to their own practice and understandings of teaching and learning. Narratives about learning taking place across TLRs are many in the repertoire of faculty developers, and examples of "extreme collaborations" (Holtham et al., 2006) across disciplines are also emerging.

I have shown earlier how disciplines can be 'constructed', suggesting that the emphasis typically given by academics to subject content, epistemological dimension or ideological beliefs inflect their conceptions of the discipline. Educational programs that explore those constructions are likely to help clarify and explain conceptions and beliefs, with mutual benefits to both developers and academics. It is indeed important that faculty developers are also exposed to perspectives that might challenge their own beliefs, so that their understanding of disciplinary differences is refined, as they sometimes underestimate discipline specificity, confining themselves to the generic teachings of educational theory.

Further recommendations for faculty development input might include:

- consultancy within departments that enable teams to locate their own identities and priorities within the institutional framework
- looking at developing teams as well as individuals (at present most faculty development programs focus on individuals)
- a role in generating meanings about the way the department relates to individuals and to institutional policies and structures
- an educational role in articulating to managers implications of specific pedagogies expounded on the programs (benefits, threats, and costs).

In respect of 'developing the developers', TLRs theory can help raise awareness amongst faculty developers of:

- the need to expand their intellectual repertoire beyond the cognitive dimension, taking account of the realities of social practice, and of individuals and subjectivities within it
- the need to listen and take account of local cultures in responding to teaching and learning issues
- the crucial role they have in surfacing and explaining the complexity of teaching practice, particularly in their interactions with higher education leaders
- the need to adopt a principle of dialogic education (or "knowledge as conversation" (Barnett, 1994)) to emulate open and critical analyses and reciprocal understandings of practices.

Managing Disciplinary Groups

As suggested by Trowler, TLRs theory has implications for leaders and managers in higher education. An awareness of the complexity of the cultural make-up of disciplinary groups might usefully serve to problematize the managerialist approaches to change that prevail in higher education. Managerialist change initiatives tend to adopt relatively linear strategies: deploying policies through the setting out of objectives and targets, providing guidelines for their implementation, and measuring performance through a set of objective criteria. In reality, this leads to compliance rather than reflective adoption of change. Further, the impact on practice is rarely what the policy-maker intended (Reynolds & Saunders, 1987), and it is naïve to assume direct congruence between a policy statement and its interpretation and application in practice (Fanghanel, 2007b). Understanding that policy is mediated through TLRs in which translation to practice occurs, brings in a salutary insight into how a policy statement might be mediated on the ground. Trowler's suggestion that space be allowed for 'domestication' of innovation and change might imply, for example:

- using generic policy requirements reflecting institutional needs which require local adaptative responses
- promoting self-regulation at local level
- focusing on appropriation of change/innovation rather than surface compliance
- promoting a 'learning' culture where R&D approaches are possible
- evaluation of practices at local level that are complex, reflexive, and focus on educational value – leading to genuine improvement of practice, not simply 'box-ticking'.

The role of the team leader or head of department at the liminal space between the macro- and the meso-levels of practice is therefore pivotal as representing the articulation between the political, disciplinary, and community-related realities of practice, and institutional requirements and needs. This position enables him/her to have a leading role in helping to translate policy requirements in ways that are relevant and meaningful for his/her disciplinary group.

This has implications for the way the head of department operates – preserving local ideas and values of the disciplinary group in his/her dealings at institutional level whilst fostering 'downwards' a culture of collaboration to harness some of the tensions within TLRs.

The challenges of TLRs Theory

TLRs theory is a useful analytical tool in theorizing the relationship between macro and local contexts, and the dynamics within academic teams. I have shown how this framework can usefully inform understandings of the make-up of a discipline, and reflections on socializing in disciplinary groups, developing faculty, and managing departmental teams. I now turn to examining some of the limitations of this framework in informing practice, and conclude by offering further reflections on Trowler's chapter.

Applicability to Practice

While TLRs theory addresses and broadens the debate on 'structure vs. agency' by bringing to the fore the many components that characterize a teaching and learning environment – the cognitive, affective, discursive, semiotic and practical aspects that make up the culture of a given academic group – it doesn't specifically analyze the way individuals interact with structures. Individuals' agency within TLR is conceptualized at a relatively abstract level of analysis and this dimension remains understated – as it does in Engeström's activity system theory, briefly explored at the beginning of this chapter. As a result, the issue of 'power' whilst it is acknowledged (and very easy to identify in the South African context) remains almost academic. This is an important point as there are many marginalized identities in higher education, globally. For example, universities increasingly employ contract researchers, fixed-term teaching staff who come and go unnoticed, unheard, often untrained and marginalized (Reay, 2000). Gender issues also remain understated. Focusing on 'teams' serves to emphasize coherence or conflict, leaving aside those less visible, and less powerful voices – some of which are so tangential that it is unclear whether their influence can be felt in TLRs.

From the perspective of managing higher education teams, an awareness of TLRs theory can be invaluable for managers seeking to introduce change within a culture. It draws their attention to a web of factors that need to be taken into account for sensitive and effective change management. This framework emphasizes the conflictual dynamics of a disciplinary community. Some of these conflicts are related to the very individualistic and competitive ways of working in academia – where individual rather than collective performance tends to be the measure of success. TLRs theory doesn't fully account for this relationship to the macro-level, nor does it provide an explanation of how consensus is reached within an academic group – or of whether it is reached. I have suggested earlier that dialogic management of teams was an effective way of dealing with this. A more systematic framework of "deliberative democracy" (Kandlbinder, 2007, p. 57), and enabling teams to "work through deliberation" (ibid.) might be a way forward.

Boundaries and Historicist Residue in TLRs

To conclude this reactive chapter, I will focus on two issues which address the question of boundaries within and across TLRs, and the historicist residue in TLRs.

Trowler clearly indicates that the moments identified in TLRs are in fact interconnected, and their deconstruction only serves analytical purposes. As one reflects on these moments however, the question emerges of how they relate to each other, whether some play a more crucial role than others, and whether there might be some hierarchies (causal or in their ontological status) between them. For example, there might be a relationship of antecedence between 'discursive repertoires' and 'conventions of appropriateness', and 'tacit assumptions' or 'recurrent practices'. None of these moments emerges *ex nihilo* (see section below on the historicist dimension). Further research investigating these relationships might provide useful pointers for transfer to practice.

The issue of boundaries across TLRs is not considered in Trowler's chapter, nor is it clear how boundaries of a given TLR are being erected. Where does a TLR begin and where does it stop? For example, in large university departments that harbor a considerable array of sub-disciplines, can one detect several TLRs? Is there a meta-TLR that drives the dynamics of the large group and marks it as exogenous to other disciplinary groupings? In this respect, the relation to the discipline is important for two reasons it seems. First there is an increasing tendency towards 'genericism' in the higher education curriculum (learning to learn, employability skills, reflective skills, critical thinking). This leads to developing 'post-modern' curricula where the moral or pragmatic connection to the real world is emphasized beyond the disciplinary components (e.g. ethical issues in a biochemistry curriculum). Second, curricula are increasingly interdisciplinary and teams therefore heterogeneous (including non-academics and disciplinary aliens). As academic identities become more hybrid, might TLRs become hazier? Or, as institutional identities become more contrasted in the face of increased differentiation of mission, might TLRs become more corporate? The issue of the boundaries of TLRs and their permeability to contiguous contexts is certainly worth considering.

Finally, there is a strong historicist dimension in any theoretical stance informed by a socio-cultural take on reality. In such a perspective for example, discipline epistemologies are representative of dominant beliefs about knowledge which are anchored in historicity. This kind of pervasion of the broad historicist context is significant. Whilst it may engender relatively coherent (though conflictual and turbulent) local departmental cultures in a context like Europe or the States where we are dealing with a social system that is more diverse than polar, in South Africa where the disjuncture between home and dominant culture can be acute, it is hard to see how it is actually enacted at the departmental/team level without strong power games. The South African examples in Trowler's study for example bring with them the history of a specific intellectual heritage in which problematic supremacy, violence and oppression, access to culture (a very high degree of illiteracy), the status of the written word amongst groups which have long privileged an oral tradition, and a relatively new agenda of 'transformation' and 'reconciliation' transpire. Complex identities and strong ideological positions (the post-apartheid official agenda is one of 'reconciliation': how does this translate into the curriculum and who dictates the terms?) are present within that. This 'extreme' example might provide fertile ground for further analyzing the historicist dimension of TLRs, thus further exploring the link between macro- and meso-levels of practice.

Conclusion

This chapter has outlined the distinctiveness of TLRs theory in accounting for the dynamics of local cultures in academic departments. Recognizing that TLRs are difficult to capture in practice in their entirety, it has illustrated the different moments of a TLR through a vignette presenting TLRs in the eyes of a newcomer to the UK higher education system. Whilst recognizing in the first place the heuristic value of this theoretical framework, this chapter has also indicated some areas of practice where knowledge of TLRs might have significant implications for action. It was shown that useful lessons could be drawn for different categories of academics within higher education.

Reacting to an innovative way of conceptualizing practice is in itself challenging and many of the suggestions made in this chapter are as yet untested. At the same time, some significant aspects of TLRs theory relate to elements that are elusive to capture – meanings, subjectivities, and affect. This, alongside the relatively uncharted relation between those 'localized worlds' and the broader historicist context, make it all the more tentative. It may however be appropriate to open up tentative avenues for practical implications of a theoretical framework which foregrounds the provisional and tenuous nature of the regimes under scrutiny. Whilst it is possible to illustrate how TLRs might operate in practice, and give a broad-brush notion of what the implications might be for the academic community, it would be unwise to prescribe recipes and seek to normalize what remains a contingency-bound constellation of turbulent encounters.

References

Barnett, R. (1994). *The Limits of Competence: Knowledge, Higher Education and Society.* London: Open University Press/SRHE.

Becher, T., & Trowler, P. (2001). *Academic Tribes and Territories: Intellectual Enquiry and the Culture of Disciplines* (2nd ed.). London: Society for Research in Higher Education and Open University Press.

D'Andrea, V., & Gosling, D. (2005). *Improving Teaching and Learning in Higher Education: A whole institution approach.* Maidenhead: Society for Research in Higher Education and Open University Press.

Donald, J. G. (1995). Disciplinary differences in knowledge validation. In N. Hativa & M. Marincovich (Eds.), *Disciplinary differences in teaching and learning: Implications for practice* (pp. 7–17). San Francisco: Jossey-Bass.

Donald, J. G. (2002). *Learning to think: disciplinary perspectives.* San Francisco: Jossey-Bass.

Engeström, Y. (1999). Activity theory and individual and social transformation. In Y. Engeström, R. Miettinen & R.-L. Punamäki (Eds.), *Perspectives on activity theory* (pp. 87–106). Cambridge: Cambridge University Press.

Evans, C. (1988). *English People: the experience of teaching and learning modern languages in British Universities.* Buckingham: Open University Press.

Fanghanel, J. (2004). Capturing dissonance in university teacher education environments. *Studies in Higher Education, 29*(5), 575–590.

Fanghanel, J. (2007a). Investigating university lecturers' pedagogical constructs in the working context. *Report on Research Project for the Higher Education Academy,* http://www.heacademy.ac.uk/ourwork/research. Accessed July 2007.

Fanghanel, J. (2007b). Local responses to institutional change: a discursive approach to positioning. *Studies in Higher Education, 32*(2), 187–205.

Healey, M., & Jenkins, A. (2003). Discipline-based Educational Development. In H. Eggins. & R. Macdonald (Eds.), *The Scholarship of Educational Development* (pp. 47–57). Buckingham: Society for Research in Higher Education and Open University Press.

Henkel, M. (2000). *Academic Identities and Policy Change in Higher Education,* London: Jessica Kingsley.

Holtham, C., Courtney, N., & Barratt, M. (2006). Information Architectures for Quality Management, *BMAF Subject Centre Annual Conference,* Oxford, 6–7 April 2006.

Kandlbinder, P. (2007). The Challenge of Deliberation for Academic Development. *International Journal for Academic Development, 12*(1), 55–59.

Lave, J., & Wenger, E. (1991). *Situated Learning: Legitimate Peripheral Participation.* Cambridge: Cambridge University Press.

Malcolm, J., & Zukas, M. (2001). Bridging Pedagogic Gaps: conceptual discontinuities in higher education. *Teaching in Higher Education, 6*(1), 33–42.

Manathunga, C. (2006). Doing Educational Development Ambivalently: Applying post-colonial metaphors to educational development? *International Journal for Academic Development* 11(1), 19–29.

NCIHE (1997). Higher Education in the Learning Society. *Report of the National Committee of Inquiry into Higher Education.* London: HMSO.

Reay, D. (2000). 'Dim Dross': Marginalised women both inside and outside of the Academy. *Women's Studies International Forum*, 23(1), 13–21.

Reynolds, J., & Saunders, M. (1987). Teacher Responses to Curriculum Policy: Beyond the 'Delivery' Metaphor. In J. Calderhead (Ed.), *Exploring Teachers' Thinking* (pp. 195–213). London: Cassell.

Skelton, A. (2005). *Understanding Teaching Excellence in Higher Education: towards a critical approach.* Abingdon, Oxon: Routledge.

Trowler, P., & Knight, P. (2000). Coming to Know in Higher Education: theorising faculty entry to new work contexts. *Higher Education Research and Development*, 19(1), 27–42.

17

Teaching and Learning Regimes from Within
Significant Networks as a Locus for the
Social Construction of Teaching and Learning

Torgny Roxå and Katarina Mårtensson

Lund University, Sweden

Introduction

In Chapter 15, Paul Trowler discusses how traditions about university teaching are formed into local cultures. He describes aspects of these cultures – *Teaching and Learning Regimes* (TLRs) – and notes some of their implications. By portraying aspects of teaching and learning traditions he offers the opportunity for reflecting on, discussing and deconstructing them. In this chapter we will draw on Trowler's model as well as some of our own research and thereby try to tease out some principles that could inspire individual faculty in their efforts to reform teaching in their discipline or department.

In discussions about teaching and learning comments are sometimes made about what is and what is not possible in certain disciplines. One can hear statements such as: "You can do this in organic chemistry but you could never do it in inorganic chemistry." Or, "You have to understand that in history there are so many facts to get across that any method of instruction other than a lecture is surely ineffective." Although these remarks may appear exaggerated – perhaps even satirical – in nature, they illustrate the common notion that the disciplines, by themselves, define what is and what is not possible in teaching. The assumption is that there are correct and incorrect ways, adequate and inadequate ways to teach and to learn a particular subject. This is an essentialist argument, namely that the nature of a discipline, its epistemological structure, methods of inquiry and validation procedures, determine how to teach it.

Whether or not assumptions about the best ways to teach are actually determined by the discipline or whether they are socially constructed and over time formed into traditions are interesting questions but not the primary concern of this chapter. The issue that concerns us is how teaching can be developed in particular disciplines, and how faculty members can develop professionally as teachers. In our view, an ideal situation is when faculty and teaching develop in the same way as researchers and research do – as an ongoing enterprise to explore better ways to understand and perform the practice one is devoted to.

We are not taking sides against or in favor of the essentialist view that the disciplines dictate what is "the best way to teach". Instead we accept the idea that academics trained in the research of a particular discipline for a long period of time naturally use methods and perspectives similar to those that they experienced when pursuing their studies. Nevertheless, we adopt the more relativistic view that assumptions governing arguments on how to teach are also socially constructed and therefore contestable. As such, our main purpose in this chapter is to explore how focusing on socio-cultural issues can support the development of teaching. Our perspective is similar to the one portrayed in *Academic Tribes and Territories* (Becher & Trowler, 2001), where the authors explore the variation in academic lives on a global scale. By using material from a wide range of sources they construct an exposé on how academic life is influenced both by the discipline (*the territory*) to which the individuals belong and by the local culture that the specific group of people (*the tribe*) constructs during its day-to-day activities. The core message is that in order to fully understand what shapes academic life, and the teaching, learning and assessment practices in particular disciplines, one has to look at both the influence of epistemological structure (as well as methods of inquiry and validation) and how traditions, practices and arguments are constructed in the flow of social life.

The Importance of the Social Context

The notion that university teaching is hard to change is probably familiar to many academics (Barr, 1998; Entwistle & Walker, 2000; Ramsden, 2005). Questions that arise are: What constitutes this resilience? Is it because of the structure of the disciplines? Does a discipline actually demand certain methods of teaching? Is a discipline taught uniformly all over the world? If not, what accounts for the variation in teaching traditions within the same discipline?

A study conducted in the UK and Finland (Lindblom-Ylänne, Trigwell, Nevgi & Ashwin, 2006) investigated the relationship between faculty's approaches to teaching and teaching context. Two approaches were distinguished: One is teacher-focused and characterized by an intention to transmit information and the other is student-focused and characterized by an intention to promote conceptual change in students (Prosser & Trigwell, 1999). The disciplines considered in the study were grouped according to Biglan's (1971) soft versus hard dimension. Hard disciplines are those that use well-developed theories, rely on universal laws, and are cumulative (for instance the natural sciences). Soft disciplines, by contrast, work with unclear boundaries, relatively unspecified theories and deal with loosely defined problems (for instance the humanities and social sciences). The results of the study showed a link between teaching approaches and discipline. "Teachers from 'hard' disciplines were more likely to report a more teacher-focused approach to teaching, whereas those teaching 'soft' disciplines were more student-focused" (Lindblom-Ylänne et al., 2006, p. 294). However, of particular interest to us is the finding that an individual faculty member teaching the same subject in different social settings may adopt different ways of teaching depending on where he or she teaches. Or as Lindblom-Ylänne and colleagues put it, "the same teacher in different contexts may adopt a different approach to teaching" (p. 296). The authors conclude that teaching methods and traditions are linked to *both* the discipline and the specific context in which teaching happens.

The variation in teaching approaches and methods even within particular disciplines, as described in the UK/Finland study, points towards a possibility for development of teaching. If teaching is not entirely determined by the discipline, but also influenced by the context in which it takes place, then change in teaching is possible as a result of changes in context. A context can be material in nature, for instance the technology and physical surroundings that are available, but it can also be social in nature, as in the interactions between specific individuals working together within a particular department. In this chapter we focus on the social context of university teaching.

Trowler offers an analytical tool that might assist faculty in understanding the socially constructed features of their teaching and learning context. While he acknowledges that the essentialist view is valid if disciplines are viewed from a distance, he claims that socially constructed traditions and habits become more and more important the closer to the actual practice we get.

Trowler's position is that faculty members are knowledgeable agents consciously constructing their teaching practice, meaning that they could very well teach differently if they believed in the alternative. However, since they are also influenced by colleagues and students, and by the culture in which they teach, there is a tension between their agency and their environment. The reason for choosing one of many alternatives is usually a result of the relationship between the agent's, that is, the faculty's, personal intent and the tradition that has developed in the local teaching and learning culture, as he or she experiences it.

This implies a certain understanding of culture. In this case, culture is not a *product* of an organization or group of people; rather the organization can be seen as if it *is* a culture (Alvesson, 2002). Hence, a culture provides a sense of identity to members of an organization; it facilitates commitment, enhances stability, guides and shapes behavior, and provides motivation for members to do what is considered to be the "right thing to do" (Alvesson, 2002, p. 24). It follows from this that culture has structural properties, and is therefore to be understood as continuously constructed as it becomes visible (Giddens, 2004). According to this perspective, faculty members constantly interact with culture and construct the culture simultaneously. The culture offers support for their actions (e.g. suggesting certain ways of teaching), and provides a starting point for improvisation and innovation.

As a consequence, Trowler describes aspects of local teaching and learning cultures that are more or less visible. However, a specific Teaching and Learning Regime (TLR) is not to be mistaken for a force or a boundary. It does not force individual faculty to do anything but functions as a handrail, something to cling to for stability and security or to use as a starting point for excursions and inventions.

Drawing on data collected in South Africa, where he studied the merger between four higher education institutions, Trowler convincingly and in detail describes eight "moments", or aspects in a constant state of flux, of a TLR. These are:

- tacit assumptions
- implicit theories of teaching and learning
- recurrent practices
- conventions of appropriateness
- codes of signification
- discursive repertoires
- subjectivities in interaction, and
- power: its microphysics

In a specific teaching context, for instance a department, these aspects blend into each other. The result is a certain way of doing things, a traditional way, and a more or less unique and characteristic pattern of teaching behavior, coupled with a related conversational pattern. In order to understand how this can be modified, the main issue to explore is how TLRs are constructed and maintained.

Firstly, a TLR is to be seen as the foreground to an even greater culture, which functions as the background, for instance the ethos of an entire institution. In the foreground faculty reflect and discuss their teaching experiences, using the discursive material that is available to them. In these day-to-day conversations about teaching and learning certain interpretations and explanations appear more often than others. Over time, these conversational patterns result in structures that are perceived as stable. They are then usable for faculty as they try to make sense of what is going on around them. For newcomers these patterns may appear as ready-made and taken for granted, a reality with which one has to cope (see Fanghanel, Chapter 16 in this volume, where she illustrates through authentic examples how each of these moments may be experienced or become visible at the local level). Secondly, a TLR is not a construction of consensus. Instead it can be both contested and fought over. That is also often its history, intense debates about teaching and learning alternatives resulting in a dominant perspective which rests in the consciousness among faculty members for, sometimes, long periods of time. In extreme situations almost no one has to support a TLR any longer, but it can still influence how things are done. A majority of the individual faculty may assume that all the colleagues believe in a certain teaching strategy, even though this does not necessarily have to be true. This focus on faculty's interpretations of their context is an important feature of a TLR. Thirdly, a TLR is related to identity, both individually and collectively. Being part of a TLR for a considerable time means that the individual has, through interaction with colleagues, constructed an identity partly dependent on that very TLR. And since identity, from a socio-cultural perspective, is constructed in the process of interaction between the individual and 'the others', the identity can be constructed both as a positive interpretation of a TLR, but also in opposition to it. Even if an individual were critical towards the tradition, a change in that very tradition would influence his or her identity. Therefore it must be kept in mind that change and development means messing with people's identities. It makes development highly emotional. To use the words of Becher and Trowler (2001): "When people's identities are at stake, passions run deep" (p. 126).

Teaching and Learning Regimes and Faculty Members

It is our experience that faculty members connect easily to the TLR concept, no matter which discipline they represent. In the pedagogical courses we offer for faculty at our university, with approximately one hundred participants each year, Trowler's model is introduced and discussed. They easily identify the different "moments" in their own departmental or disciplinary context.

The faculty members report that they experience their local teaching context as a gradually shaped tradition. They are also aware of the fact that the tradition, here the TLR, in which they are active, has both advantages and disadvantages. The advantage is that it forms a discourse distinguishable from other social contexts. It is a part of the disciplinary discourse into which they attempt to invite the students – in much the same way as Northedge and MacArthur describe in their chapter in this volume. Another advantage is that it secures a certain level of quality; it constitutes a tradition that has worked in the past and probably will work in the future. The disadvantage is that the TLRs appear limited in their capacity to be responsive to changes in the wider context or among the individual faculty members. Attending a pedagogical course often has the effect of participants generating new insights, ideas and perspectives about teaching and learning. In order to adapt these to their discipline faculty have to try these out in conversations with their departmental colleagues. If the ruling TLR does not encourage pedagogical conversations, frustration can emerge and the opportunity for development and enhancement of teaching practice may be held back (Trowler & Cooper, 2002; Fanghanel, 2004).

Using the view of modern social science on structure and agency (Giddens, 2004), TLRs offer possibilities for the active and knowledgeable agent, here the faculty member, to use and construct variations from the structures while planning and practicing teaching. The TLRs also function as rules that have a tendency to, over time, shape teaching into recognizable and resilient traditions.

Traditions can always be transformed into something else. The concept of the TLR, therefore, has the potential to be of use for developmental purposes. It also reveals opportunities for a more subtle discussion among faculty about what should and could be changed and what should and could not. However, Trowler does not elaborate on how this could happen even though he recognizes that TLRs are constructed and maintained during day-to-day conversations. Hence, strategies to influence TLRs should focus on influencing faculty's everyday conversations, as this is where they construct their understanding of the teaching and learning reality.

In the remainder of this chapter we draw on some of our own research. It explores possible paths for development at individual as well as collective levels. In doing so, we highlight some salient characteristics of communication in academia in general and of communication about teaching in particular.

Where do Faculty Members Construct a Teaching and Learning Reality?

As researchers, academics tend to rely on two networks (Becher & Trowler, 2001). One is rather large involving sometimes several hundreds of individuals, drawn upon for referencing and provision of guidance or orientation. It is within this network that researchers decide what to do and how to position themselves and their research. The other network, typically as small as about ten individuals, is used for testing of ideas, provision of feedback on draft papers, and so on. This network is drawn upon for more personal matters than the large one. It is within this smaller network that academics develop new ideas and nurture them until they are mature enough for the larger network.

The purpose of our study was to explore whether when it comes to teaching, academics may also rely on a small number of people with whom they test out ideas or discuss problems. We surveyed 106 faculty members from various disciplines, inviting them to describe situations where they had sincere and honest discussions about problems or ideas in relation to teaching. The number of reported conversational partners per study participant converged at around ten individuals. This parallels the observation in Becher and Trowler (2001) about the typical size of the smaller research networks.

Our data also provide information on where faculty typically find these conversational partners. They are found almost anywhere: sometimes in the same department, or in the same discipline at another institution, sometimes in another discipline, or in spaces without any connection to academia at all. The respondents also seem very clear on whom they want to discuss teaching with. They do not talk to just anyone; they find the particular person suited for the particular issue at hand. Again this parallels what Becher and Trowler (2001) reported in their book *Academic Tribes and Territories*. The authors note the double-edged character of communication in academia. On the one hand, communication drives the development of research, often in the form of peer-review. On the other hand, however, academics tend to be strangely reluctant to engage in discussion and debate. Specifically, Becher and Trowler observe that

> The inclination to play safe – to minimize the risk of making professional enemies by opposing or being critical of colleagues' views – is also reflected in the preference, noted earlier, of many academics to steer clear of direct competition with others.

(p. 127)

The faculty members participating in our study were also asked to indicate the extent to which they find their local teaching context supportive of discussions about teaching and learning. The responses were juxtaposed with the number of conversational partners they have within their own department. The results showed that the more the faculty experience cultural support, the greater the number of conversational partners they have within their context. Having conversations with colleagues that are part of the local teaching culture is important, since the effect on a TLR probably increases if the conversation can address it from within. Another intriguing feature of these conversations about teaching in the smaller networks is that they mainly take place in private, by the coffee machine, in the car, or in someone's office. They rarely occur in formal meetings or in spaces where someone not invited can overhear them. It gives them a backstage nature (Goffman, 2000) where conversations are more unrestricted than when opened to a wider audience. The tendency to keep these conversations private might reveal evidence of a tacit awareness these faculty have of the ruling assumptions in their local TLR.

In their now classic book *The social construction of reality*, Berger and Luckmann (1966) propose that not all other people are equally important for the individual involved in constructing an understanding of reality. Instead there are a few whose responses are more significant. These *significant others* offer responses of extra importance for the individual. Consequently, and based on our survey findings, we suggest that faculty rely on a network of a few significant others as they construct, maintain, or change their understanding of the teaching and learning reality.

We, therefore, decided to call these smaller networks where individual faculty have sincere conversations about teaching and learning *significant networks* (Mårtensson, Olsson & Roxa, 2006; Roxå & Mårtensson, unpublished). It is within these networks that faculty interact with their significant others. It is here that they put their teaching and learning experiences into words and it is here that they genuinely pay attention to the responses they receive.

The others, who are also present in the wider local context, function as a choir or background. They are there but their responses are not as important as those from a significant other. We note that the significant networks are not traditional networks with boundaries around them. Rather, each faculty member has his or her own group of people to talk to. And the significant others in one faculty's network, in turn, have their significant others to talk to. The result is a complex pattern of interactions where experiences of teaching and student learning are interpreted and discussed, as illustrated in Figure 17.1.

The idea of significant networks implies that important conversations about teaching and learning within, let us say, a department are scattered and mostly private. Experiences are interpreted and evaluated as a series of more or less unique conversations, and they take place privately and in small groups. Messages are carried from conversation to conversation while constantly being subjected to individual interpretation. Furthermore, many conversations can continue for a long time without being influenced by other conversations taking place simultaneously. When faculty members meet

Significant networks:

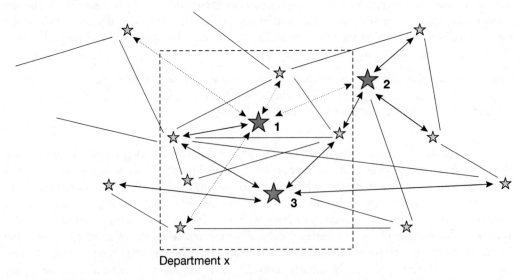

Department x

Figure 17.1 A significant network, where the big stars represent three faculty members. The thicker arrows bind together significant conversational partners. Together all arrows illustrate the web of relations to be found inside and outside a department.

in formal meetings, the character of the conversations is different, more diplomatic, more according to established rules of appropriateness. That is, in these situations faculty members tend to say things more according to what they believe they are expected to say. Therefore the latter conversations may not have the same potential to influence faculty's beliefs about teaching and learning.

Hence, the concept "significant network" can contribute to our understanding of why academic change may be slow and academic cultures may appear resilient to external pressure (Trowler, 1998; Bauer, Askling, Marton & Marton, 1999; Stensaker, 2006). We suggest that the reason is that it takes many conversations, privately and in small groups, to negotiate the meaning of a policy or any other matter that might be important for teaching and learning. And in each and every one of these conversations the individuals construct personal, and in a way unique, interpretations.

Teaching and Learning Regimes and Significant Networks

Teaching and Learning Regimes (TLR) say something about aspects of a local teaching and learning culture that is socially constructed. Faculty's decisions and practices are influenced not only by the nature or epistemological structure of the discipline but also by socially constructed tacit assumptions, implicit theories of teaching and learning, recurrent practices, conventions of appropriateness, codes of signification, discursive repertoires, subjectivities in interaction, and issues of power. Taken together they form a local culture that permeates disciplinary or departmental life in relation to teaching and learning. It becomes a structure to lean on while maintaining quality, it is a resource during struggles for power, and it can generate an experience of constraint for individual faculty trying to do things differently.

Significant networks (SN), on the other hand, say something about where individual faculty construct and maintain their personal beliefs about teaching and learning. In conversations with significant others they interpret and explain the reality they experience. These conversations will result in developed private teaching strategies and beliefs, but they will not necessarily be reported and put to a test during open meetings within a department.

Returning to the starting point of this chapter, we connect the ideas just discussed with the frustration some faculty may at times experience when rejoining their department after having participated in a pedagogical course or workshop. New ideas they have formed that they then wish to bring into the open are sometimes met with considerable objections in the form of traditions about how things should and should not be done. It is important, therefore, to create a situation where these traditions, in the form of a ruling TLR, can be challenged and openly contested. The accounts we have of the conversations academics have within their significant networks reveal a good deal of opposition or at least criticism of ruling TLRs. However, our data also suggest that this criticism is held back during conversations of a more official nature, or in situations where criticism in relation to issues of power and status appear a rather risky endeavor.

Critique, however, is exactly what Trowler intends to promote. In Chapter 15 he argues "Departments and workgroups also need to look inwards at themselves, uncovering tacit understandings and recurrent practices that sometimes have deleterious consequences for their students" (p. 193). The problem to be solved then is this: How can the conversations that take place within significant networks influence the TLR within a department? Our survey findings indicate that faculty members are reluctant to extend these conversations from their backstage homeland to the front-stage land of diplomacy and politics. It is imperative, for this reason, to find a way of transforming the informal significant networks into something that could serve a developmental function within a department or discipline. Wenger's notion of a Community of Practice (Wenger, 1999; Wenger, McDermott & Snyder, 2002) provides some guidance for how this might be accomplished.

Empowering the Significant Networks

Communities of practice are "groups of people who share a concern, a set of problems, or a passion about a topic, and who deepen their knowledge and expertise in this area by interacting on an ongoing basis" (Wenger et al., 2002, p. 4). On the surface this seems to be exactly what significant networks are about. But upon further comparison with the theory of communities of practice there appear to be pieces missing. Wenger (1999) argues that a community of practice requires a *shared enterprise*, that is, a sense of direction. Two further critical features are that it involves *negotiation*, sometimes fierce and tough, and *ways of reifying* (in writing or other media) *the results* of these negotiations. Without an enterprise there would be no shared focus, without negotiation and debate there would be no sense of quality or improvement, and without reification there would be no shared memory of these negotiations and therefore no learning possible on a more collective level.

The accounts we collected of the conversations faculty have within their significant networks show that there is negotiation; problems and ideas are discussed with all the intellectual capacity the participants can mobilize. But there is no obvious reification showing the outcomes of these conversations other than in the participants' memories. Moreover, the enterprise often appears to be unclear. According to Wenger's theory, poor reification results in an ad-hoc manner shift in the focus of the conversations from one occasion to another. This, in turn, may lead to rather poor learning. The conversations are characterized by a lot of problem solving, based on what is currently occurring, and there is a lot of mutual emotional support. But, there is not necessarily much quality learning going on. We suggest that quality learning in an academic context is, among other things, supported by some evidence and anchored in theory. And quality learning, and reportable results from this learning, is, we believe, what is needed in order to challenge the ruling TLR and contribute to the development of teaching in a discipline or a department.

Assumptions about how to document discussions about teaching and learning, or what resources to draw on in these discussions, are partly influenced by the ruling TLR. It stands to reason that it would be difficult to use pedagogical literature as support for certain claims in a context where the value of such references traditionally has been held in low regard. To deal with this problem it is critical to acknowledge the larger culture that encapsulates a given TLR. A ruling TLR in a discipline or department is naturally part of a greater, more far-reaching culture, the culture of the institution to which it belongs. Our own work with faculty in an academic development context, including our research on significant networks, is carried out at a very traditional elite research-intensive university. In order to challenge a TLR in a discipline or department we found it helpful to use the existing structures within the institutional culture as resources or vehicles for change. In essence we argue that it is possible to build a cultural alliance between the micro-level (the individual faculty members) and the institutional macro-level (the ethos of the institution) in order to dispute the recurrent practices of the meso-level (disciplines or departments).

One way to describe or identify the institutional ethos in a research-intensive culture is through the lens of scholarship. Boyer's (1990) model distinguished the scholarships of discovery, integration, application and teaching. Although each was seen as distinct they were also seen to inform one another. Scholarship, he argued, could be observed as academics engage in the search for new insights, integrate new aspects into a personal knowledge base of growing complexity, and let this knowledge base influence the practice they engage in. According to Boyer this practice included teaching. Later work on the scholarship of teaching and learning (SoTL) (e.g. Hutchings & Shulman, 1999; Trigwell, Martin, Benjamin & Prosser, 2000; Kreber, 2002) highlight that important features of SoTL include sharing experiences and new knowledge with others and opening up for scrutiny and peer-review. In a research-intensive environment the idea of dissemination and peer review is a familiar way to develop knowledge and secure quality on a collective level. We suggest that this should hold true for teaching as well as for research.

Three features can be seen to lie at the heart of SoTL: to closely observe teaching and student learning before, during and after teaching; to interpret findings in light of relevant pedagogical research literature and the documented wisdom of practice; and to use the resulting insights to improve teaching and learning. But such scholarship is not complete without documentation, both for later use by the author, but also, and most importantly, for others to read and to comment upon (see also Richlin's (2001), distinction between scholarly teaching and the scholarship of teaching).

One possible strategy by which to empower the significant networks in the direction of being able to exert greater influence on the ruling TLR within a department is to encourage individuals within these networks to pursue the scholarship of teaching and learning. By encouraging faculty to approach teaching from a scholarly perspective, they might become capable of formulating arguments strong enough to challenge a local, ruling TLR. It is crucial, therefore, that academic development initiatives are geared towards offering arenas for scholarly conversations, as well as supporting and rewarding scholarly perspectives on teaching and learning.

Conclusion

Teaching and Learning Regimes (TLRs) say something important about the structures that shape teaching within disciplines and departments. They are resources for faculty members to rely on while formulating, conducting, and debating teaching. But they can also be experienced as constraints, obstructing the kind of debate or inward inquiry that Trowler wants to encourage.

To this we add the dimension of faculty members' lives that are formed in their significant network. Here they meet, mostly backstage, and interact in a sincere way which in turn influences their personal beliefs and abilities to interpret their teaching and learning context. However, as a constructive force that might challenge or develop a ruling TLR, they often appear, at least in our data, to be insufficient. Too often the conversations within significant networks seem to focus on particular aspects of teaching and learning in an ad-hoc manner; they do not draw on the pedagogic research literature and recognized wisdom of practice; and the results are rarely documented. If academics within significant networks are introduced to the scholarship of teaching and learning (and we believe that particularly at research-intensive institutions the idea of scholarship is attractive to academics), they might be better positioned to construct an informed understanding of teaching and learning. Adopting a scholarly perspective on teaching, then, may offer them the tools to influence the TLR that rules in their department.

Baxter Magolda (see Chapter 12) advocates *Self-Authorship* as a desired learning outcome for students in colleges and universities. She describes Self-Authorship as an ability to balance knowledge as a *cognitive resource* with an *integrated identity*, as a developed ability to understand one's Self, and as an ability to *function in relationships* with respect for one's own and others' identities and cultures. Additionally, she argues that

> Maturity in these three areas combines to enable effective citizenship – coherent, ethical action for the good of both the individual and the larger community. Effective citizenship requires the ability to evaluate possible actions, interpret contexts and consequences, and make wise choices.

(in this volume, p. 144)

The concept of self-authorship is equally applicable to academics. Challenging a ruling TLR may be threatening to faculty members' professional identity. It will most likely affect their understanding of the professional self. But it will also be a social act, the outcome of which is dependent on individuals' ability to handle relationships with colleagues. If successful, the act can provide not only an improved capacity to support student learning, but also a sense of self-authorship as well as a positive reputation among colleagues. We therefore recommend that academic development initiatives should address not only perspectives on student learning and teaching but also issues concerning academics' professional identity. Academic developers need to realize that the value of what faculty members learn in pedagogical courses or any other academic development initiative, always has to be negotiated in the social context of departmental and disciplinary colleagues.

References

Alvesson, M. (2002). *Understanding organizational culture.* Sage Publications.

Barr, R. B. (1998). Obstacles to implementing the learning paradigm. *About Campus* (September–October), 18–25.

Bauer, M., Askling, B., Marton, S. G., & Marton, F. (1999). *Transforming universities. Changing patterns of governance, structure and learning in Swedish higher education.* London: Jessica Kingsley Publishers.

Becher, T. & Trowler, P. (2001). *Academic tribes and territories.* Buckingham: The Society for Research into Higher Education and Open University Press.

Berger, P. L. and Luckmann, T. (1966). *The Social Construction of Reality: A Treatise in the Sociology of Knowledge.* Garden City, NY: Anchor Books.

Biglan, A. (1973). Characteristics of subject matter in different academic fields. *Journal of Applied Psychology,* 57(3), 195–203.

Boyer, E. L. (1990). *Scholarship reconsidered. Priorities of the professoriate.* New Jersey: The Carnegie Foundation.

Entwistle, N., & Walker, P. (2000). Strategic alertness and expanded awareness within sophisticated conceptions of teaching. *Instructional Science,* 28, 335–361.

Fanghanel, J. (2004). Capturing dissonance in university teacher education environments. *Studies in Higher Education,* 29(5), 575–590.

Giddens, A. (2004). *The constitution of society.* Cambridge: Polity Press.

Goffman, E. (2000). *Jaget och maskerna 'The presentation of self in everyday life 1959'.* Stockholm: Prisma.

Hutchings, P. & Shulman, L. (1999). The scholarship of teaching: New elaborations, new developments. *Change* (September/October), 11–15.

Kreber, C. (2002). Teaching excellence, teaching expertise, and the scholarship of teaching. *Innovative Higher Education,* 27(1), 5–23.

Lindblom-Ylänne, S., Trigwell, K., Nevgi, A., & Ashwin, P. (2006). How approaches to teaching are affected by discipline and teaching context. *Studies in Higher Education,* 31(3), 285–295.

Mårtensson, K., Olsson, T., & Roxå, T. (2006). *Scholarly dialogues and significant networks – the cradle of scholarship of teaching and learning.* Paper presented at the 3rd annual ISSOTL-conference, November 2006, Washington DC, US.

Prosser, M. & Trigwell, K. (1999). *Understanding learning and teaching. The experience in higher education.* Buckingham: The Society for Research into Higher Education & Open University Press.

Ramsden, P. (2005). *Learning to teach in higher education.* Abingdon, Oxon: RoutledgeFalmer.

Richlin, L. (2001). Scholarly teaching and the scholarship of teaching. In C. Kreber (Ed.), *Scholarship revisited: Perspectives on the scholarship of teaching and learning* (pp. 57–68), 86, summer. San Francisco: Jossey-Bass.

Roxå, T. & Mårtensson, K. Significant conversations and significant networks – exploring the backstage of the teaching arena. Unpublished paper. Lund University, Sweden.

Stensaker, B. (2006). Governmental policy, organisational ideals and institutional adaptation in Norwegian higher education. Studies in Higher Education, 31(1), 43–56.

Trigwell, K., Martin, E., Benjamin, J., & Prosser, M. (2000). Scholarship of teaching: a model. *Higher Education Research and Development,* 19(2), 155–168.

Trowler, P. (1998). *Academics responding to change. New higher education frameworks and academic cultures.* Buckingham: The Society for Research into Higher Education & Open University Press.

Trowler, P. and Cooper, A. (2002). Teaching and Learning Regimes: implicit theories and recurrent practices in the enhancement of teaching and learning through educational development programmes. *Higher Education Research and Development,* 21(3), 221–240.

Wenger, E. (1999). *Communities of practice. Learning, meaning, and identity.* Cambridge: Cambridge University Press.

Wenger, E., McDermott, R., & Snyder, W.M. (2002). Cultivating communities of practice. A guide to managing knowledge. Boston: Harvard Business School Press.

VII
General Observations
on Previous Themes

18

Assessment for Career and Citizenship

Mantz Yorke

Lancaster University

Economic and Social Imperatives

Around the world, governments indicate that national economies rely to a large extent on higher education for success. The emphasis on the economic value of higher education has become more loudly asserted in recent years, perhaps as the implications of globalization have become apparent, though it is visible historically – for example – in the establishment of the Land Grant Colleges in the United States during the nineteenth century, and in the recommendations of the Robbins Report (Committee on Higher Education, 1963) that led to the first major expansion of higher education in the UK. The perspective is one that Becker (1975) described in terms of the development of 'human capital', and is seen as particularly apposite to advanced economies since they are decreasingly able to compete in terms of basic production but instead have to concentrate on the advancement and exploitation of 'high end' knowledge.

One of the difficulties with what has come to be termed 'the knowledge society' is that attention is often given disproportionately to innovation and entrepreneurship (see, for example, Reich, 2002). Whilst these are of obvious importance for economic success, less loudly hailed kinds of achievement, such as the provision of a range of professional services and the management of organizations and projects, also have a vital part to play. A successful economy requires high levels of performance in a wide variety of roles. (In parenthesis, one is reminded of Belbin's (1981) 'Apollo Team' composed of creative people which achieved significantly less well than teams with a better balance of qualities and capabilities.) Lists of desirable qualities in graduates emphasize a range of personal qualities such as self-confidence, independence, emotional intelligence, and reflectiveness, as well as disciplinary knowledge[1] and understanding, communication skills, capacity to solve problems, and so on (one amongst many such lists is given in Yorke & Knight, 2006).

Whilst the economic case for higher education is compelling, there is also a more broadly social case for it, based on the notion of democratic engagement. Dewey (1916) made an explicit link

---

1 However, in roughly half of advertisements in the UK press for graduate positions the subject of study is left unspecified, implying that the organizations concerned are more interested in recruiting clever and able people whom they can train in the specifics needed for the post.

between democracy and education which has for a long time been reflected in curricula in the United States (see Colby et al., 2003, who discuss undergraduate education in this respect) and has more recently emerged into educational policy in the UK. The democratic theme featured prominently in a message from the Council of Europe (2005) to the meeting of European ministers at Bergen, which reiterated the key purposes for the European Higher Education Area as:

- preparation for life as active citizens in democratic society;
- preparation for sustainable employability;
- personal development;
- the development and maintenance of a broad, advanced knowledge base.

Capability, Professionalism and Employability

These purposes align quite well with the idea of 'capability' which was promoted by Stephenson (1992), with 'capability' having a frame of reference that was wider than a simplistic concern with the labor market. Capable people, according to Stephenson, have confidence in their ability to:

- take effective and appropriate action;
- explain what they are seeking to achieve;
- live and work effectively with others; and
- continue to learn from their experience.

Capable people not only know about their specialisms, but also have the confidence to apply their knowledge and skills within varied and changing situations and to continue to develop their specialist knowledge and skills. The construct of 'capability' could be seen as reflecting the aim that graduates should become effective operators in the world throughout their lives (i.e. as employers, citizens, family members and so on). Kreber (Chapter 1) observes that this is the kind of broad aim with which most faculty would probably agree. It is readily apparent that 'capability' implies something rather richer than the rallying cry of 'skills' in the political rhetoric of the UK (see Wolf, 2002, for a discussion of the superficiality of politicians' concepts of 'skills').

Graduates from full-time higher education are typically, but not exclusively, beginning professionals (part-time students may already be established in a professional role) who will be expected to:

- operate autonomously (albeit within limits);
- often work collaboratively;
- demonstrate a range of appropriate personal qualities (trustworthiness, empathy with others, determination, and so on);
- draw on, and apply, both academic and practical understandings;
- work integratively, sometimes on non-routine problems;
- use their powers of metacognition (reflection; self-regulation; etc); and
- be committed to new learning.

Such thinking was influential in the development by the Enhancing Student Employability Co-ordination Team [ESECT] of its 'USEM' approach to employability (see Yorke & Knight, 2006) which stressed the inter-relationship between

- Understanding;
- Skilful practices (subject-specific and generic);
- Efficacy beliefs (and personal qualities and attributes more generally);
- Metacognition.

The capabilities related to study in one or more subject disciplines (the 'U' and 'S' of USEM) are relatively uncontentious. Expected learning outcomes related to 'U' and 'S' are stated, with varying amounts of explicitness, in both the statements ('subject benchmark statements') published by the Quality Assurance Agency for Higher Education [QAA][2] to inform stakeholders about the general features of programs and the institutionally validated specifications for programs and modules. The assessment of these outcomes is, however, more problematic than many seem to believe – see Yorke (2008).

The 'self-system' and metacognition (roughly, the 'E' and 'M' of USEM) were shown by Marzano's (1998) meta-analysis to be aspects of education where the size effects of interventions were particularly high.[3] The USEM account stresses their importance for employability (which is seen as being highly correlated with the kinds of educational outcome generally desired from higher education) but they are poorly represented in specifications and the benchmark statements. Neither are readily amenable to the kinds of assessment typical of higher education, where the resources available to undertake summative assessment are limited. Likewise, the integration that contributes to employability is difficult to grade with precision because in many situations the performance is idiosyncratic, such as in final-year projects of varying kinds.

Knight (2007a, p. 2) pointed out that what he termed 'wicked' competences (under which heading he placed 'soft skills', graduate attributes and complex achievements)

> cannot be neatly pre-specified, take time to develop and resist measurement-based approaches to assessment. They are important to *higher* education, since they are widely valued by employers and smooth the path of study and other forms of research.
>
> (Emphasis in the original)

Much the same could be said of the components of 'graduateness' that were identified by Higher Education Quality Council (HEQC, 1997b, Volume 2, p. 86). Knight also acknowledged the argument of Barnett and Coate (2005) that one of the purposes of higher education was the development of identity, which overlaps considerably with the 'E' of USEM.

Programs of study are often based on aggregations of modules which, whilst acknowledging programmatic intentions, tend to be self-contained and internally consistent in that the specification of intended learning outcomes, content, pedagogic method and assessment of student achievement are aligned (Biggs, 2003). At the module level, this is uncontentious and would be widely acknowledged as virtuous pedagogic practice. The disciplinary components of curricula are arranged in such a way as to optimize coherence and progression. Whilst other curricular arrangements might be preferred by some, the general 'flow' of disciplinary development is generally not a matter for heated discussion.

It is when the curricular focus shifts from subject disciplines to the more 'generic' desired outcomes that problems become more obvious. Many – arguably, most – of these outcomes fall into Knight's basket of 'wicked' competences. They are often 'slow-growing crops' which do not come to fruition within the time-span of a single module.

Ripening may need a program's duration and more. This in itself poses a challenge to the way in which assessment is structured (in Chapter 1, Kreber points to the problem of the locus for the assessment of outcomes). Ripeness, in this context, is more likely to be a matter of judgment than of measurement, and it is difficult for an institution to warrant (or certify) some kinds of achievement

---

2 See www.qaa.ac.uk/academicinfrastructure/benchmark/default.asp.
3 The bulk of the studies analyzed by Marzano were from schools, in which contexts experimental control is easier to achieve; however, some evidence was drawn from post-compulsory education.

(see Knight & Yorke, 2003, pp. 55–6). Warranting is particularly difficult when achievements are 'local' (in Knight's, 2006, term) and contingent: institutions (in contrast to assessment centers) typically do not have the resources to conduct assessments on a scale sufficient to ensure reliability.

Where warranting of achievement is not possible, the institution may be able to warrant the educative *process* experienced by the student. Whilst the institution can state the process (a transcript of modules taken does this at a basic level), it then falls to students to make claims in respect of their achievements and to buttress these claims with evidence. The introduction of personal development planning [PDP] into higher education in the UK[4] has given fresh impetus (following earlier initiatives in the late 1980s) to student reflection on learning and achievement, which ties in with the metacognitive (and unmeasurable) 'M' of USEM.

The development of the self and of higher-order learning are features of the 'employability literature' developed in the UK, and are also of significance in the US and Australia where the term 'workforce development' is the preferred term.[5]

Assessment

The summative role of assessment in the warranting of academic and professional achievement is of major significance to this chapter. However, if many valued aspects of achievement resist measurement-based approaches to assessment (Knight, 2007b), higher education faces a considerable challenge if it is to find a way of optimally informing interested parties about achievements. The more the limitations on warranting are appreciated, the greater will be the significance accorded to the role of formative assessment in helping students to develop – and appreciate their possession of – the broader capabilities that are of value throughout a person's life.

Summative assessment in higher education is subject to the pull of two contrasting 'ideal types' of approach – the 'scientific' in which knowledge is discipline-driven, context-free and objective, and the 'interpretivist' in which knowledge is problem-driven, context-related and subject to human construction. Something of this distinction is caught by Gibbons et al. (1994) in their discussion of 'Mode 1' and 'Mode 2' production of knowledge, and in the testing of the efficacy of treatments where there is argument about the relative merits of those using drugs that have been developed through experiments based on randomized control and those which are deliberately responsive to the idiosyncratic characteristics of individuals. Neither ideal type exists in a pure form, but approaches to assessment tend to be biased towards one or the other. The situation is confused when grading implicitly acts as a 'measure', and the 'measurements' are treated as if they possess properties appropriate to statistical manipulation (such as when a grade-point average or 'honours degree classification' (UK) is being determined – see Yorke (2008) for an extended discussion of why such statistical operations are unwarranted).

Some types of achievement can be judged on the basis of something approaching measurement, whereas others resist measurement. To some extent, this distinction can be mapped on to the type of education objective being used. Instructional objectives are typically associated with problems and solutions that are specified in advance. Some closed solutions, such as multiple-choice item responses, can be treated in a quasi-measurement way: for example, the number of correct responses to a multiple-choice test produces a score. Others, such as those of a more discursive character, can

---

4 Details can be found by navigating from www.qaa.ac.uk/academicinfrastructure/progressFiles/guidelines/progfile 2001.asp.
5 'Workforce development' has a narrower connotation in the UK, emphasizing the further development of those who are already in employment.

be scored according to a template but with a lower claim to measurement. When the solution is open, as when students are faced with a problem whose solution is not a single 'right answer' (i.e. the 'problem' was merely a puzzle whose solution had to be worked out, as in the cases of a crossword or sudoku grid), the assessor can only make a judgment regarding the merits of the response – and the point is even stronger when, as in the creative arts (where Eisner (1979) proposed the concept of 'expressive objectives'), the student determines the problem and attempts to solve it.

Knight (2007b) used the revision by Anderson and Krathwohl (2001) of Bloom's (1956) *Taxonomy of educational objectives* as the basis for an argument that challenges made by higher education to students tend to be more constrained than those made to graduates in employment. Problems in higher education tend to be specified and have solutions which, if not exactly predetermined, can be specified in terms of a marking template. The assessments tend to focus on remembering, understanding, applying and analyzing. Problems 'in the wild' are less bounded, and assessment of success in solving them is more a matter of *post hoc* judgment (especially where invention and entrepreneurship are concerned). Such judgments are likely to include considerations of creativity and evaluation to a greater extent than assessments in academe. Knight's argument is oversimplified, probably to stimulate debate, and there are plenty of opportunities for those in the academy to take issue with it (in the creative arts, for example, creativity is a *sine qua non*).

If assessment in higher education is adequately to reflect the development of capability (in Stephenson's sense – see above) or, more narrowly, the development of students as young or mid-career professionals, it has to allow – as Eraut (2004) suggests in the context of medical education, but surely with a wider relevance – for the *integration* of knowledge, skills and personal attributes. Some might wish to argue that a 'capstone' project, a work placement and co-curricular service learning have such integrative potential. However, the first may be limited to achievements in the academic domain (and hence miss out on practical application), whereas the last two may not contribute to a great extent to an overall index of achievement. The assessment of learning outcomes in relatively small and isolated curricular bundles (as can happen particularly in unitized curricula) leaves the level of integration advocated by Eraut to the individual.

Assessors may have an unreasonably sanguine view of the extent to which complex achievements (often 'wicked' competences) can be assessed. Knight (2007a) asked informants in six subject areas (accounting; early years teaching; nursing; secondary teaching; social work and youth work) about assessment in respect of the following:

- developing supportive relationships;
- emotional intelligence;
- group work;
- listening and assimilating;
- oral communication;
- professional subject knowledge;
- relating to clients;

Table 18.1 Categories of educational objectives

Type of objective	Problem	Solution
Instructional	Specified	Specified
Problem-solving	Specified	Open
Expressive	Open	Open

(From Yorke, M. (2008). *Grading student achievement: signals and shortcomings.* Abingdon, Oxon: Routledge, p. 184.)

- self-management (confidence and effectiveness);
- 'taking it onwards' – i.e. acting on diagnoses (in social work).

He was surprised to find that his informants felt that these were not difficult to assess. It is possible that the respondents simply believed that the assessment methods they used were adequate for their purposes, without subjecting them to critical review (if this was the case, perhaps because nothing happened to suggest that existing methods were anything but robust).

Following this study of the assessability of 'wicked' competences, Knight recommended, *inter alia*, that:

> Any interventions to enhance the assessment of 'wicked' competences should begin by helping colleagues to appreciate the inadequacies of current practices that are typically – and wrongly – assumed to be 'good enough'. This is a double challenge for innovators. Not only does assessment practice have to be improved, but colleagues need to be convinced of the need to improve it in the first place.
>
> (Knight, 2007a, p. 3)

Assessment regimes tend to make the assumption that grades can be awarded against a finely divided scale (often a percentage scale) for complex achievements. Even within the academic domain, this is challenging. One has only to imagine the various kinds of performance that might attract a percentage of, say, 55 (in typical UK usage) when the descriptors of performance level are as in Table 18.2.

Table 18.2 Extract from a set of assessment criteria from a university in the UK

Upper Second Class [percentage range 60–69]

Upper second class answers are . . . clearly highly competent and a typical one would possess the following qualities:
- generally accurate and well-informed;
- reasonably comprehensive;
- well organized and structured;
- displaying some evidence of general reading;
- evaluation of material, though these evaluations may be derivative;
- demonstrating good understanding of the material;
- clearly presented.

Lower Second Class [percentage range 50–59]

Such answers show an acceptable level of competence, as indicated by the following qualities:
- generally accurate, but with some omissions and errors;
- an adequate answer to the question, largely based on lecture material and required reading;
- a good answer to a related question, but not the one set;
- clear presentation;
- no real development of arguments.

Third Class [percentage range 40–49]

Such an answer demonstrates some knowledge and understanding of the area, but tends to be weak in the following ways:
- does not answer the question directly;
- misses key points of information;
- contains important inaccuracies;
- coverage of material is sparse, possibly in note form;
- does not support assertions with proper evidence.

Source: HEQC (1997a, p. 27).

It is worth noting the tendency in this example (which is not untypical of higher education in the UK) to grade on the basis of lapses from excellence, rather than on positive qualities. Assessments based on such criteria do not provide the ideal base from which a student might, when submitting an application for a job, assert success.

Once one gets into the arena of professional performance, as one does in teacher education, social work, healthcare, law, engineering and so on, the challenge is more demanding still, since the interplay between performance outcomes and assessment criteria is highly complex. Simply marking components and totting up the marks ('menu marking', in Hornby's (2003) term) is unsatisfactory, as anyone who has done this appreciates. The whole performance is not necessarily the sum of the individual parts: it may be more; it may be less. The parts might need to be weighted to suit the context. For example, a high level of interpersonal skill is important when dealing with stressed people in difficult personal situations and may outweigh academic expertise, whereas academic expertise may be accorded greater weight in circumstances in which the nature of practice is being critically appraised. It might be better to grade on a pass/fail basis (in some circumstances, a 'pass' is mandatory) with an elaboration of significant features of the performance.[6]

Whereas academics who are assessing performance on professionally oriented programs often (but not always) have a base of practical experience on which to draw, and hence can judge a student's practical effectiveness, those whose programs are not overtly professionally oriented may be being required to assess some aspects of 'generic' capability in what is tantamount to a 'second language' – that of professional competence – which may have been acquired only on an *ad hoc* basis.

The multidimensionality of performance is most clearly to be seen in workplace environments, where problems are often non-standard, with the implication that learned problem-solving routines cannot be applied unquestioningly. The resolution of such 'messy' problems often involves a complex mixture of attributes and capabilities coupled with an awareness that assistance from others might be necessary. The contingent, 'local' nature of workplace tasks implies that the assessment of a student's performance cannot be specified to the level of detail normally applied to discipline-specific studies. 'Menu marking' becomes impossible, and professional judgment is needed regarding the standard achieved. There is an obvious tension between the two roles of tutor/guide and assessor, which is exacerbated when a more experienced colleague in the workplace contributes to both guidance and assessment.

Difficulties with the technical robustness of grading (see, e.g. Milton et al., 1986; Yorke, 2008) and with warranting achievement (Knight & Yorke, 2003; Knight, 2006, 2007b) mean that less weight can be placed on grades and 'honours degree classifications' than many currently believe. The resources are not available to institutions to make a step-change improvement in technical robustness. Perhaps the production of assessments that are 'good enough' for their purposes is the most that can realistically be aimed for. What might 'good enough' mean in this context?

It is a term that implies satisficing (see Simon, 1957) rather than precision. It points towards judgment rather than measurement, and hence to an interpretive approach to assessment rather than to an approach based on (quasi-)measurement. It also implies institutions being open about what they can warrant and about what they can intimate, but without warranting, and awareness on the part of users of the information.

Curriculum and Pedagogy

It is widely acknowledged that assessment has a powerful influence on how students allocate their efforts. The implicit instrumentalism on the part of students is understandable, if not optimal for the

---

6 A problem with pass/fail grading is that it is not accommodated in computations of grade-point average.

longer term. The ideal situation would be for students to give learning priority over performance (the latter rather crudely, perhaps, seen in terms of 'getting the grade'): the work of Dweck (1999) points to the value of students adopting 'learning goals' in preference to 'performance goals'.[7] Some students – especially mature students – show very high levels of commitment that are likely to result in success irrespective of pedagogic considerations. For others, the curricular and pedagogic approaches adopted will be significant influences on success.

There is not the space in a chapter focusing on assessment to deal with curricular and pedagogic issues in depth, but assessment cannot be treated in isolation. A brief outline of some key considerations is offered. This is intended as a pointer towards the development of pedagogic practice in an educational context that is sub-optimal, i.e. where student engagement may be weakened if activities are not formally assessed, or are assessed at a low weighting.

Integration

If it is desired that students should develop and, crucially, integrate their personal qualities; understandings; skilfulness in academic and other arenas and metacognitive powers (the components of USEM), then a case can be made that the curriculum should foster integration rather than leave it to chance. Leaving integration until the final year of study (on the implicit principle that 'they won't be ready for it till then') misses an educational opportunity.

Tinto (1997) showed, in a study at Seattle Community College, that having students engage together in a number of modules led to an improvement in outcomes compared to the previous curricular regime in which students had a freer choice of modules and hence were less likely to meet up and to share their developing understandings. The improvement can be seen in terms of a synergy between social engagement and academic engagement. The revised approach at Seattle has much in common with curricula that have main 'pathways' through an institution's unitized offerings, with students exercising some, but not a free, choice. The issue, perhaps, is the extent to which students are encouraged in their learning to exploit the contiguity of the paving slabs of the pathway.

If integration as indicated above is a valued outcome of curricula, then it makes sense to think of curriculum design from an integrationist, rather than a fragmented, perspective. Learning activities that require multidimensional approaches have a greater chance of encouraging integration. They also demand 'active learning' on the part of students. Pascarella and Terenzini (2005) provided a significant challenge to curriculum designers (which is echoed in Chapters 1 and 2 of this volume) when they concluded from their extensive review of the literature:

> The holistic nature of learning suggests a clear need to rethink and restructure highly seg-mented departmental and program configurations and their associated curricular patterns. Curricula and courses that address topics in an interdisciplinary fashion are more likely to provide effective educational experiences than are discrete courses accumulated over a student's college career in order to produce enough credits for a degree.
>
> (Pascarella & Terenzini, 2005, p. 647)

The integrated curriculum has the potential to allow students to take risks with their learning (and perhaps to suffer interim failure) in a way that a strictly unitized curriculum does not, since students will be risk-averse if the consequence of risk is a lowered grade. As Rogers (2002) observes, learning is a risky business, and interim failure can be a valuable learning experience. Formative assessment

---

7 It is not as clear-cut as implied by this condensation. Pintrich (2000) showed that students who strove for high levels of achievement (rather than those who sought to avoid 'looking bad' in comparison to peers) produced broadly similar results to those adopting learning goals.

which supports students' personal growth in all its respects, and their capacity to present their achievements, is vital.

Engagement

The concept of 'student engagement' has grown in importance as the present century has progressed, with the National Survey of Student Engagement attracting increased use in the US. The level of student engagement is enhanced when students find their studies stimulating, as did the following students who had enrolled on the study unit *Animal and Plant Structure and Function* at Queensland University of Technology:

> I *enjoyed* using my initiative. . . .

> I *enjoyed* learning about building an ecosystem and how the environment affects the type of organisms that can grow there.

> (Meyers et al., 2004, p. 6: emphases in the original)

In 2003 the average rating from a cohort of 300 students was 4.5 out of 5 in 2003, which indicates that the above comments were not outliers.

Set against these comments, a survey of first-year students in the US found that only around half of their respondents enjoyed study reading and reported strong study habits (Noel-Levitz, 2007) and more than 40 per cent of respondents to a similar survey of reactions to the first year in college said that they frequently felt bored in class (Hurtado et al., 2007). Perhaps higher education in general should edge its offerings in the direction of 'disciplinary wonder' (Barnett, 2004, p. 255), or even 'multidisciplinary wonder', and away from the technical rationality and instrumentalism implicit in the 'skills agenda'.

A pedagogy for engagement would include most (and perhaps all) of the following:

- active learning;
- group-based activity;
- the use of information and communications technology and other resources;
- interdisciplinary problem-solving;
- formative assessment.

It also has considerable potential to support learning for career and citizenship.

Coda

Stripped to its essentials, the argument of this chapter is as follows. With higher education playing a role in professional development at various levels, assessment practices face the challenge of reconciling a disciplinary focus with a focus on achievements that are not discipline-specific. Many desirable achievements (and especially those that are general rather than discipline-specific) are not susceptible to 'measurement' and hence are not reliably warrantable by institutions. Greater weight needs to be placed on students' claims for achievements, and the supporting of these claims by evidence. A pedagogy that optimizes engagement is a necessary condition for students' success in their studies, in their careers (whatever form these may take) and as citizens in an ever-shrinking world.

References

Anderson, L.W., & Krathwohl, D.R. (2001). *A taxonomy for learning, teaching and assessing.* New York: Addison Wesley Longman.

Barnett, R. (2004). Learning for an uncertain future. *Higher Education Research and Development* 23 (3), 247–260.

Barnett, R., & Coate, K. (2005). *Engaging the curriculum.* Maidenhead: Society for Research in Higher Education and the Open University Press.

Becker, G.S. (1975). *Human capital.* Chicago: Chicago University Press.

Belbin, R.M. (1981). *Management teams: why they succeed or fail.* London: Heinemann.

Biggs, J. (2003). *Teaching for quality learning at university, 2nd ed.* Maidenhead: Society for Research in Higher Education and Open University Press.

Bloom, B.S. (1956). *Taxonomy of Educational Objectives, Handbook 1: Cognitive domain.* London: Longman.

Colby, A., Ehrlich, T., Beaumont, E., & Stephens, J. (2003). *Educating citizens. preparing America's undergraduates for lives of moral and civic responsibility.* San Francisco, CA: Jossey-Bass.

Committee on Higher Education (1963). *Higher education [Report of the Committee appointed by the Prime Minister under the chairmanship of Lord Robbins, 1961–63].* London: Her Majesty's Stationery Office.

Council of Europe (2005). Message from the Council of Europe to the meeting of ministers of the European Higher Education Area, Bergen, 19–20 May. At www.bologna-bergen2005.no/EN/Part_org/Council_of_Europe/050425_CoE.pdf (accessed 26 November 2007).

Dewey, J. (1916). *Democracy and education.* New York: Macmillan.

Dweck, C.S. (1999). *Self-theories: their role in motivation, personality and development.* Philadelphia, PA: Psychology Press.

Eisner, E.W. (1979). *The educational imagination: on the design and evaluation of school programs.* New York: Macmillan.

Eraut, M. (2004). A wider perspective on assessment. *Medical Education,* 38(8), pp.803–4.

Gibbons, M., Limoges, C., Nowotny, H., Schwartzman, S., Scott, P., & Trow, M. (1994). *The new production of knowledge: the dynamics of science and research in contemporary societies.* London: Sage.

HEQC (1997a). *Assessment in higher education and the role of 'graduateness'.* London: Higher Education Quality Council.

HEQC (1997b). *Graduate Standards Program: final report* (2 vols.). London: Higher Education Quality Council.

Hornby, W. (2003). Assessing using grade-related criteria: A single currency for universities? *Assessment and Evaluation in Higher Education,* 28(4), 435–54.

Hurtado, S., Sax, L.J., Saenz, V., Harper, C.E., Oseguera, L., Curley, J., Lopez, L., Wolf, D. & Arellano, L. (2007). *Findings from the 2005 administration of Your First College Year.* Los Angeles, CA: Higher Education Research Institute, University of California, Los Angeles.

Knight, P.T., & Yorke, M. (2003). *Assessment, learning and employability.* Maidenhead: Society for Research in Higher Education and the Open University Press.

Knight, P. (2006). The local practices of assessment. *Assessment and Evaluation in Higher Education,* 31(4), 435–52.

Knight, P. (2007a). Fostering and assessing 'wicked' competences. At www.open.ac.uk/cetl-workspace/cetlcontent/documents/460d1d1481d0f.pdf (accessed 28 November 2007).

Knight, P. (2007b). Grading, classifying and future learning. In D. Boud & N. Falchikov (Eds.), *Rethinking assessment in higher education* (pp. 72–86). Abingdon, Oxon: Routledge.

Marzano, R.J. (1998). *A theory-based meta-analysis of research on instruction.* Aurora, CO: Mid-continent Regional Educational Laboratory.

Meyers, N.M., Whelan, K.A., Nulty, D., & Ryan, Y. (2004). Enhancing the transition of first year science students – a strategic and systematic approach. Paper presented at the 8th Pacific Rim Conference on the First Year in Higher Education, Monash University, 14–16 July.

Milton, O., Pollio, H.R., & Eison, J. (1986). *Making sense of college grades.* San Francisco, CA: Jossey-Bass.

Noel-Levitz (2007). *Second annual national freshman attitudes report.* Iowa City, IA: Noel-Levitz.

Pascarella, E.T., & Terenzini, P.T. (2005). *How college affects students [Vol 2: A third decade of research].* San Francisco, CA: Jossey-Bass.

Pintrich, P.R. (2000). The role of goal orientation in self-regulated learning. In M. Boekaerts, P. Pintrich & M. Zeidner (Eds.), *Handbook of self-regulation* (pp. 451–502). New York: Academic Press.

Reich, R.B. (2002). *The future of success.* London: Vintage.

Rogers, C. (2002). Developing a positive approach to failure. In M. Peelo & T. Wareham (Eds.), *Failing students in higher education* (pp. 113–123). Buckingham: SRHE and the Open University Press.

Simon, H.A. (1957). *Models of man.* New York: Wiley.

Stephenson, J. (1992). Capability and quality in higher education. In J. Stephenson & S. Weil (Eds.), *Quality in learning: a capability approach to higher education* (pp. 1–9). London: Kogan Page.

Tinto, V. (1997). Classroom as communities: exploring the educational character of student persistence. *Journal of Higher Education* 68 (6), 599–623.

Wolf, A. (2002). *Does education matter? Myths about education and economic growth.* London: Penguin.

Yorke, M. (2008). *Grading student achievement: signals and shortcomings.* Abingdon, Oxon: Routledge.

Yorke, M., & Knight, P.T. (2006). *Embedding employability into the curriculum.* York: The Higher Education Academy. Available at www.heacademy.ac.uk/assets/York/documents/ourwork/tla/employability/id460_embedding_employability_into_the_curriculum_338.pdf (accessed 6 January 2008).

19

Teaching Within and Beyond the Disciplines
The Challenge for Faculty

Velda McCune

University of Edinburgh

Introduction

This book represents both a profound challenge and a potential source of great inspiration for university faculty. It respects the distinctive ways of thinking and practicing represented by academic disciplines and what students can achieve through rich engagement with these practices. More context-transcendent outcomes – such as critical thinking or ethical awareness – are seen as developing through deep engagement with the disciplines. In offering an ambitious account of potential graduate outcomes – encompassing civic responsibility, lifelong learning and sophisticated accounts of employability – it sets out a challenging vision of what higher education at its best can have to offer. Students are seen as developing not just knowledge and skills but rich conceptual frameworks and a capacity to reason within and beyond the particular modes of thinking of their disciplines.

The book also speaks to the ways of being which students need to develop in order to be able to act effectively in a world which is not just complex – in the sense of open-ended real-life situations in which any attempt at a solution will have unforeseen effects – but also 'supercomplex' – where the problems faced are fundamentally unresolvable as competing answers spring from incompatible value positions and ideologies (Barnett, 2004). Even in those areas of the sciences where there are large bodies of well established knowledge, students are likely to encounter situations of complexity and supercomplexity in their working lives. This may arise, for example, in relation to ethical debates. Tackling real-world problems, such as responding to climate change, will often require multi-disciplinary teams and will likely involve stakeholders with different value positions and ways of understanding the world. Given these conditions of complexity and supercomplexity, Barnett (2007) argues that a central task of Higher Education must therefore be to support students in developing a more coherent and considered sense of their selfhood which can support the will to learn and the confidence to commit to their own perspective on an issue.

This rich account of what higher education may achieve asks us to make time to reflect deeply on the distinctive and often partly tacit ways of knowing which characterize our disciplines and to make the imaginative leap required to find ways of connecting our students with the discipline. More than that, we are challenged to think beyond the assumptions and practices of our disciplinary or departmental contexts to consider what other disciplines and settings may have to offer as a source of reflection on our own practices. In order to allow our students to develop the capacity to act in conditions of complexity and supercomplexity, we are asked to consider how we can aid them in the transdisciplinary thinking and new ways of being that this will require.

Teaching to Connect Students with the Discipline

One of the central messages of this book is that teaching is fundamentally about connecting students with the discipline. In order to develop a greater understanding of how this might be done, it is important to find ways of characterizing what it is that students might learn through this connection. Having a richer understanding of the nature of our disciplines provides a basis for reflecting on the challenges which students might face in engaging in the study of a given area. One possibility here is the kinds of typologies exemplified by the work of Janet Donald (Chapter 3). Such typologies focus our attention on the typical knowledge structures and processes of our disciplines and how these impact on our teaching and our students' learning.

A complementary perspective is offered by Hounsell and Anderson (Chapter 6) through their discussion of the *Ways of Thinking and Practicing* (WTPs) of academic disciplines (McCune & Hounsell, 2005). WTPs characterize what students might be expected to learn and how they might develop through graduate-level mastery of an academic discipline. This encompasses not only explicit knowledge, discrete skills or conceptual understanding but also a growing capacity to think and act in ways which more closely approximate the disciplinary engagement of a more experienced practitioner, and a greater sense of how knowledge is generated within the field. Pace (Chapter 8) reminds us of the often tacit nature of these WTPs which may be obvious and unspoken for faculty but a source of great confusion for students.

These perspectives on what students may gain from their disciplinary studies help to open up possibilities for supporting more effective learning experiences. Hounsell and Anderson provide a number of illustrations within their chapter of how this might be done. Their examples often focus on students' active engagement in knowledge construction or on efforts to make the tacit practices of the discipline more explicit. One such example was the refocusing of written assignments in a history course to encourage students to reflect on how they were learning and on the nature of history as a discipline.

The chapter by Andy Northedge and Jan McArthur considers in more depth some of the processes by which students might come to have a better grasp of the WTPs of their discipline. Drawing on the work of Bruner (1996), these authors focus particularly on the achievement of "states of inter-subjectivity", where mutual meaning making becomes possible through teachers focusing students' attention on a common object around which shared framing assumptions may be brought into play. Northedge and McArthur argue that a novice in a discipline cannot be brought to understand the discipline simply by giving definitions, providing analogies or making logical arguments. This is because the basis for understanding is the taken-for-granted methods, purposes, values and histories of debate with which the student is not yet familiar. In other words, knowledge is seen as funda-mentally situated within the evolving practices of the disciplinary community. What the teacher therefore has to do is create a context within which students can focus with the teacher on a mutually accessible example, such as a case study, and discuss this using an intermediate discourse which has sufficient connection with students' current understandings for them to be able to share key underlying assumptions with the teacher. Good teachers are seen as frequently recontextualizing the issue in question in order to allow the flow of shared meaning to continue. Northedge and McArthur emphasize that achieving this flow of shared meaning does not require face to face interaction nor do they see small group teaching as a necessary condition.

If we as faculty are to respond to the challenges raised in connecting students with the discipline, we need to take the time to reflect deeply on the tacit underpinnings of our disciplines and the nature of the difficulties students have in grasping these ways of thinking and practicing. We might want to think about common weaknesses or misconceptions that arise in students' work and what these may signify. We may need to ask ourselves how often we achieve a real meeting of minds with students and how we would even know whether this has been achieved. Not a simple task then but an important one.

Teaching to Transcend Disciplinary Boundaries

The chapters by Donald, Hounsell and Anderson, and Northedge and McArthur illustrate how what students are learning is fundamentally framed by the norms, values and assumptions of their disciplines. These chapters and the related reactive chapters help us to understand how to support our students to come to terms with the ways of thinking and practicing of the disciplines they study but they leave us with an important question unresolved. If our students are to draw on their studies in their later lives – where they will often be working beyond their disciplines – how do they transfer the situated knowledge and practices they have acquired into their later lives?

Perhaps the simplest answer to this question is to suggest that many disciplines are immediately relevant to real-world problems, even when the student is not going to be working directly within a particular field. So, for example, Pace (Chapter 8) points out how the study of history can help students to "recognize the ways that individuals' perceptions are shaped by the information provided to them, to better understand how values and assumptions shape perceptions, to reason carefully on the basis of ambiguous evidence . . ." (in this volume, p. 103). Taking things a step further, several of the authors in this volume discuss the importance of providing students with opportunities to reflect more explicitly on how knowledge is developed in their disciplines. Where students develop a critical awareness of the knowledge practices of their disciplines, and ideally of several disciplines, they are better placed for the interdisciplinary problem solving required to approach complex real-life problems. This relates to the recommendation made by Carolin Kreber, in Chapter 1, on the basis of the work of Palmer (1998), that we make explicit for students not just what they are learning but how they are learning it and why it is important.

The question remains, however, of how to meet the challenge identified by Barnett (2004, 2007) of supporting students to develop ways of being which help them to stay engaged with learning in an uncertain supercomplex world, where some of the problems they may encounter are fundamentally unresolvable. Barnett emphasizes the importance of supporting students to develop a more coherent and independent sense of self to provide a stable base from which to evaluate competing claims and make their own decisions about how to act in the world. He does not suggest that it is possible to achieve a completely coherent and stable identity but rather that it is possible to move towards greater coherence. Nor is he arguing that students make their decisions completely independently of input from others and from their academic disciplines. The aim instead is that students reach a point at which they can develop their own creative and reflective perspective on issues, drawing on others' views and the available evidence without being overly influenced by any one source.

West (1996) makes similar points and illustrates how the process of higher education study can be a particularly important source of support for the developing identities of 'non-traditional' students:

> The basic idea of this book is that higher education is potentially a space in which to manage and transcend feelings of marginalization, meaninglessness and inauthenticity in interaction

with others; in which it is possible, given their support and encouragement, to compose a new life, a different story and a more cohesive self.

(West, 1996, p. 10)

How students might be supported to develop such a sense of self is most directly addressed in this volume by Baxter-Magolda in her 'Learning Partnership Model' (Chapter 12, see also Baxter-Magolda and King, 2004). In this model, the emphasis is placed on showing respect for students' current understandings and world views while drawing them into a process of shared construction of meaning. This process helps students to understand how new knowledge is developed and is intended to aid them in reaching a position where they feel able to form their own viewpoints, whilst respecting contrasting viewpoints and being prepared to learn from others.

This model presents several key challenges for faculty. We are asked, firstly, to find ways of understanding and connecting with our students' current perspectives and stages of development. The extent to which learners are able to accept the challenges posed by our learning environments is fundamentally dependent on the development of their sense of self and of the nature of knowledge. If a student still sees the teacher as the provider of authorized truth and sees herself as a passive recipient unable to contribute to the development of knowledge, or to hold a valuable opinion, then she may well feel threatened and distressed in a learning environment which asks more of her (Perry, 1970). Thus Kegan (1994) emphasizes the importance of providing a 'holding environment' such that students feel welcomed and accepted at their current stage of development but in which they are gradually challenged to develop.

The second challenge presented by Baxter-Magolda's model is one of finding ways of sharing authority and expertise in the learning process and therefore of persuading students to take on greater responsibility for their own learning. She suggests that this can be done, for example, by asking students' opinions and helping them work through a process of evaluating knowledge claims for themselves. Vicky Gunn (Chapter 14) takes a stronger line on this issue suggesting that:

To genuinely give up some authority I would need to negotiate forms of assessment, design of sessions (both in terms of what we do and where we do it) with the students, as well as encouraging student involvement in my research projects where they related to areas the students identified as of interest. Anything else would, for me, be tokenism.

(Gunn, in this volume, p. 174)

This then reminds us of the point made by Jan McArthur (Chapter 10) about the "undeniable power relationship" (in this volume, p. 121) between teacher and student, where the teacher is a disciplinary authority who in the end will be grading students' work, typically to criteria over which students will have no control. This asks us as faculty to think carefully about how much power we might be prepared to give up. Is it possible, for example, for us to give students a say in the defining the process and criteria for assessment (Hounsell, 2007; Quality Assurance Agency for Higher Education, UK, 2007)? We may also want to think, as suggested by McArthur, about how we limit the effect of our power over students and how we use our position of authority to empower them. We can, for example, share our expertise with students such that we enable them to critique the existing literature in ways in which they would not yet feel confident to achieve independently.

Related to the previous two challenges, Baxter-Magolda's model asks us to: show students explicitly how knowledge is constructed; give them a role in creating their own understandings; and help them, where relevant, to accept any provisionality and uncertainty of knowledge claims in the topic under study. Here we see how what we do in teaching students to connect with the discipline can aid them in developing a sense of self which can cope with transcending disciplinary boundaries. When we make the processes of knowledge construction more explicit and engage in states of intersubjectivity with our students we are providing them with the ways of thinking that they need to feel able to take an active role in knowledge construction and to recognize how their discipline relates to other disciplines. We may aid this process, for example, by being prepared to be open with students about how our own perspectives have changed and about any doubts we may have about the claims made within our disciplines.

A key question here is how plausible Baxter-Magolda's suggestions are for undergraduate courses, particularly large courses in the early years. It may not be realistic to imagine that the full Learning Partnership Model could be applied in a first-year undergraduate course but there are examples in the data from the ETL project (see Hounsell & Anderson, Chapter 6) which show elements of the model in the first year:

> The idea that we don't have all the solutions yet, to challenge things, to question things, 'Can both these people be right?'. I think that's very important at an early stage, a good healthy dose of cynicism I think will make you a better scientist [. . .] In the end of the day it's you and your data, and you make up your mind what you think, keep your mind very open in case new data comes in [. . .] Not that we're training them all to be research scientists, but I think that's good training for being a human being.
>
> [first year undergraduate biosciences teacher, cited in
> Hounsell and Anderson, this volume, p. 75]

> Well the lab we had today, we were kind of expecting certain results. We were expecting to go a certain way, but towards the end the [lab supervisor] explained that it may not necessarily have been because of what we were perceiving it to be. Which makes you think, well, if that's the case everything could be a bit like that – there could be more than one answer for everything. [. . .] So yeah, I think they're trying to make us think more about what we're doing, and I think that's probably the most important thing that they're trying to get us to do, is to make us investigate, think for ourselves, don't take things at face value.
>
> [first year undergraduate biosciences student, cited
> in Hounsell and Anderson, this volume, p. 76]

It is notable that these examples come from a science subject, as the sciences typically have a large body of well established and relatively uncontested knowledge, which faculty may reasonably see as a necessary basis for students to be able to engage in a more critical approach to unsettled scientific problems later in a program of study. If we feel it is important, however, for students to begin to see themselves as capable of contributing to debate and of challenging existing opinion, then we are asked to consider what opportunities there may be to begin this process, even in the early years. We might, for example, take the time to help students understand the processes by which established scientific knowledge came to be accepted. Alternatively we might include in the curriculum topics such as research ethics, where there is more obviously contested territory.

Contextual Opportunities and Constraints on Teaching

If we are to respond as faculty to the challenges posed in this book, then it is important to consider what might affect our capacity to change our teaching practices. In Chapter 2, Carolin Kreber reminds us to be alert to how tacit disciplinary assumptions about teaching may sometimes constrain our thinking. That said, there will be many instances in which a focus on the learning of a particular discipline inspires the development of "pedagogical content knowledge" (Shulman, 1987) which may greatly enhance our teaching.

In Chapter 15, Paul Trowler usefully reminds us that the structural features of our contexts, such as disciplinary differences, do not straightforwardly define and constrain our teaching practices.

He illustrates how disciplinary influences play out differently in different contexts and how teaching practices can be shaped both by individual action and by other contextual features such as the "teaching-learning regimes" (TLRs) of departments. Trowler's perspective reminds us that there are possibilities for change in teaching practices, even when disciplinary norms may seem to mitigate against the change we hope to achieve. In thinking about how we might develop our teaching practices, Trowler's notion of teaching-learning regimes suggests some pertinent questions that we might ask in considering what change might be valuable and how we might take it forward. For example:

- What assumptions are we making about teaching and learning and do those stand up to critical reflection?
- What aspects of our teaching or assessment practices are we taking forward out of habit, rather than well-considered rationale?
- How do we talk amongst ourselves about students, teaching and learning? What assumptions are implied by the ways we talk about these things?
- Where does the power to change teaching and assessment practices lie? Who has the ability to set the agenda, or to define how we talk about our students' learning?
- What is the history of this department? How did it come to be as it is and how do we talk about this history?

The answers to these kinds of questions help us to understand what changes we might want to make in our teaching practices and what influences we need to consider in trying to enact them. They may well also lead us into further investigation of student learning and possible teaching practices, when we realize that we do not know whether some of our unquestioned practices are likely to be beneficial for our students. In considering our teaching in these ways, Trowler encourages us to look both within and beyond our local contexts in order to see ourselves and our practices more clearly. This ties in well with Carolin Kreber's point in Chapter 2, about the importance of moving outside our departmental and disciplinary contexts to encounter new ideas and novel practices. Fanghanel (Chapter 16) also reminds us that when we are in the position of newcomer in a particular setting we have an important opportunity to really see the dimensions of the local TLR, which might be more tacit and unquestioned for established participants.

Concluding Comments

This book speaks to the potential for higher education to be a forum in which students have profound encounters with academic disciplines which lay the foundations for rich graduate outcomes rooted in a more coherent, confident selfhood. Where we succeed in meeting the challenges raised in this book the potential rewards are great, where we fail we may find that:

> The encounter of student and instructor can degenerate into an ugly clash of cultures, in which the demands of the instructor can appear arbitrary and vindictive, and the student's inability to produce adequate results can be viewed as evidence of stupidity or laziness.
>
> (Pace, in this volume, p. 103)

But this book is not just about students' selfhood, all of the challenges raised speak to our own selfhood as faculty. When we offer students the pedagogical and curriculum space that they need to develop the capacity to move into unknown territory and to cope with uncertainty we also open ourselves up to risk (Barnett, 2007). When we offer students greater autonomy and share any uncertainties we may have about our knowledge, we have to give up some of our own sense of authority and have the confidence to be more open to challenge and negotiation. When we allow students to develop and share their own perspectives, we run the risk of damaging their will to learn if we are not skilful enough when we evaluate their efforts against the ways of thinking and practicing of our disciplines. We thus open ourselves up to a wide range of challenges to our selfhood as teachers. Further, Gary Poole (Chapter 4) draws our attention to the challenges to our academic identities posed by transdisciplinary encounters. When we step outside our disciplines we open ourselves up to greater uncertainty and may have to let go of our natural tendency to clarify our identities by emphasizing and valuing similarities within our disciplines and perhaps exaggerating our differences from other groups.

The perspectives offered in this book ask for a rich and expanded notion of university pedagogy which requires a substantial commitment of our energies and a preparedness to accept genuine risks. The ideas raised in this book cannot be reduced to simple safe hints and tips or to examples of good practice that we can straightforwardly import into our courses. Instead we are asked to consider deeply the nature of our discipline, the key dimensions of our departmental contexts and to form a rich understanding of our students as learners. On this basis, we can then consider how our teaching practices and relationships might support our students to become individuals who can engage with the challenges of supercomplexity. What is proposed here is a lifelong process of reflection, trial and error and constant responsiveness to changing demands.

References

Barnett, R. (2004). Learning for an unknown future. *Higher Education Research & Development*, 23, 247–260.

Barnett, R. (2007). *A will to learn: being a student in an age of uncertainty*. Berkshire: Open University Press and Society for Research into Higher Education.

Baxter-Magolda, M., & King, P. M. (Eds.) (2004). *Learning partnerships: theory and models of practice to educate for self-authorship*. Sterling, VA: Stylus.

Bruner, J. S. (1996). *The culture of education*. Cited in Northedge and McArthur, this volume.

Hounsell, D. (2007). Towards more sustainable feedback to students. In D. Boud & N. Falchicov (Eds.), *Rethinking assessment in higher education. Learning for the longer term* (pp. 101–113). Abingdon, Oxon: Routledge.

Kegan, R. (1994). *In over our heads: the mental demands of modern life*. Cited in Baxter-Magolda, this volume.

McCune, V., & Hounsell, D. (2005). The development of students' ways of thinking and practising in three final-year biology courses. *Higher Education*, 49, 255–289.

Palmer, P. (1998). *The courage to teach. Exploring the inner landscape of a teacher's life*. Cited in Kreber (Chapter 1), this volume.

Perry, W. G. Jr. (1970). *Forms of intellectual and ethical development in the college years: a scheme*. New York: Holt Rinehart.

Quality Assurance Agency for Higher Education UK (2007). *Integrative assessment: balancing assessment of and assessment for learning* (Guide No. 2). Gloucester, UK: Author.

Shulman, L. (1987). *Knowledge and teaching: foundations of the new reform*. Cited in Kreber (Chapter 2), this volume.

West, L. (1996). *Beyond fragments: adult motivation and higher education*. London: Taylor and Francis.

Index

Note: 'n' after a page number refers to a footnote.

Lightning Source UK Ltd.
Milton Keynes UK
UKOW021431110613

212063UK00008B/176/P